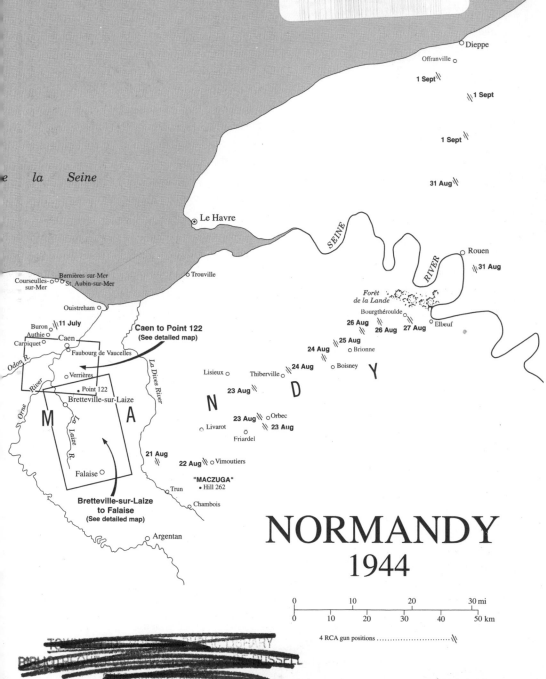

CHANNEL

e la Seine

Dieppe
Offranville
1 Sept \\\
\\\ **1 Sept**

1 Sept \\\

31 Aug \\\

Le Havre

SEINE

RIVER

Rouen
\\\ **31 Aug**

Trouville

Bernières-sur-Mer
Courseulles-sur-Mer O O St. Aubin-sur-Mer

Ouistreham O

Forêt de la Lande
Bourgthéroulde
26 Aug \\\
26 Aug \\\   **27 Aug** \\\
Elbeuf

Buron O   **11 July**
Authie O
Carpiquet O   Caen O
Faubourg de Vaucelles O

Odon R.

Caen to Point 122
(See detailed map)

Verrières O

Lisieux O   Thiberville O   **24 Aug** \\\
24 Aug \\\
25 Aug \\\
Brionne O
Boisney O

Orne River

• Point 122
Bretteville-sur-Laize

La Dives River

M   A

N   D   Y

23 Aug \\\

23 Aug \\\   O Orbec
Livarot O   \\\ **23 Aug**
Friardel O

La Laize R.

21 Aug \\\
Falaise O

22 Aug \\\   O Vimoutiers

"MACZUGA"
• Hill 262

Trun O

Chambois O

Bretteville-sur-Laize to Falaise
(See detailed map)

Argentan O

NORMANDY
1944

0   10   20   30 mi
0   10   20   30   40   50 km

4 RCA gun positions .... \\\

THE GUNS OF NORMANDY

The Guns of Normandy

A Soldier's Eye View, France 1944

GEORGE G. BLACKBURN

Canadian Cataloguing in Publication Data

Blackburn, George G.
    The guns of Normandy : a soldier's eye view, France 1944

Includes bibliographical references and index.
ISBN 0-7710-1500-3

1. Blackburn, George G.   2. World War, 1939-1945 – Personal narratives, Canadian.   3. World War, 1939-1945 – Artillery operation, Canadian.
4. World War, 1939-1945 – Campaigns – Normandy.   5. Canada.
Canadian Army – History – World War, 1939-1945.   I. Title.

D811.B53   1995   940.54'2142   C95-932037-7

Maps by William Constable
Typesetting by M&S, Toronto

The publishers acknowledge the support of the Canada Council and the Ontario Arts Council for their publishing program.

Printed and bound in Canada. The paper used in this book is acid-free.

McClelland & Stewart Inc.
The Canadian Publishers
481 University Avenue
Toronto, Ontario
M5G 2E9

1 2 3 4 5   99 98 97 96 95

Dedicated to all who served in Normandy, and to all who loved them and lived for months on end in dreadful suspense, particularly mothers and wives who, like my dear Grace, never knew when the doorbell rang that there wouldn't be a telegram beginning "We regret to inform you . . . ."

Ubique means that warnin' grunt
The perished linesman knows,
When o'er his strung and sufferin' front
The shrapnel sprays his foes,
And when the firin' dies away
The husky whisper runs
From lips that haven't drunk all day
"The guns, thank God, the guns."

– Rudyard Kipling

CONTENTS

MAPS

INTRODUCTION

--- ✳ ---

THIS WAS TO BE SIMPLY THE STORY OF ONE REGIMENT OF 25-pounders in Normandy engaged in what may have been the most intense clash of arms on any front in World War II, written in such a way as to allow our grandchildren to relive those awful days when the fate of Europe and the course of history, as it concerns the thrust of democracy across this earth, hung in the balance.

However, to make understandable the crucial role of the guns and the awesome concentrations they were called upon to fire day after day, rising to insane levels along Verrières Ridge south of Caen in late July, it has been necessary to describe in some detail the terrible problems confronting the frontline troops and the artillery forward observation officers (FOOs) and crews who shared their lot in every attack and counter-attack.

And since no one can properly appreciate the valour and judge the effectiveness of the frontline soldiers, and the gunners who supported them, who does not fully appreciate the unparalleled severity of the fighting in Normandy, an earnest effort has been made to capture the high tension overlaying every minute of every hour of every day for weeks on end, when massive opposing forces were committed to endless offensive operations designed to overwhelm and destroy each other in a bloodbath that was pursued with unabated fury for almost three months, with neither side allowed any flexibility of manoeuvre – the Allies confined by the perimeters of the bridgehead, and the enemy denied any planned withdrawal by their Führer.

However, locating material describing what it was like at the cutting edge of 1st Canadian Army from the middle of July until the end of August – in effect the fighting from Caen to Falaise that entrapped the German armies in Normandy – was very difficult. No one has succeeded in accurately describing the ferocity of the battles for Verrières Ridge and beyond. And perhaps no one ever will, for few who served with the rifle companies of the infantry battalions, including artillery FOOs and their crews, managed to survive more than a few days.

Some were casualties within hours of joining units, and, of the few who survived to see it through all the way with a rifle company, none seemingly have been able or willing to write of it. During my interviews with them – many of which were conducted right after the war ended, when battle experiences should still have been alive and clear – I discovered that for those who had survived the worst of it, memories of Normandy were blurred and disordered bits and pieces. While retaining vivid impressions, they recalled few details and resorted to generalities when they tried to describe them.

Over and over I heard, "gawdawful . . . terrifying . . . completely demoralizing . . . bloody hell . . . scared shitless," and other combinations of four-letter words favoured by soldiers, but when pressed for details their responses were embarrassingly sparse.

And beyond having no recall of what happened from hour to hour for days on end, some could not even remember having been in an attack where I personally knew they had been. This I found difficult to believe until I tried filling in diary notes of my own memories of later battles in the Rhineland and found myself lost in the same impenetrable fog, unable to account for more than a few hours of the days I had been involved, and what little I could recall had the quality of a nightmare.

Obviously the same combination of exhaustion and terror that makes it difficult to think or see clearly in the shattering confusion and roar of battle (when a man functions only from habit, drill, and discipline), makes it equally difficult to retain coherent, detailed memories, in much the same way the conscious mind is able to recall only a few disconnected details and a general impression of horror on waking up from a nightmare. And so I could only piece together a composite picture, made up of the fragmentary memories of some who survived in humble thankfulness those awful days, and place these back to back with the frightful casualty statistics.

The official record-keepers of those times were of no help; they seem to have been entirely disinterested in recording such matters. Beyond brief references to the weather, there is little recognition of the conditions under which the fighting soldier existed, which, more often than not, were dreadful. While extremely useful in authenticating personal notes and diaries, none of the sparse unit diaries or post-battle intelligence reports make any serious attempt to describe what was entailed in simply staying alive during those terrible days and nights.

This deficiency in the material set down at the time by those responsible for preserving historical records (on which all official and unofficial histories would be based) has led to inaccurate, irresponsible conclusions bordering on outright dishonesty – even in the works of our own official historians – regarding the training and fighting qualities of Canadian officers and men in World War II. And these inaccuracies – insulting to the memory of all those Canadians who died facing the enemy while the official record-keepers sheltered miles to the rear – are being perpetuated by British and American writers and even built upon by some domestic revisionists.

Far from accurately portraying the ferocity of the deadly clashes in battles of attrition reminiscent of World War I, the war historians tend to give the impression that it was some sort of game, played out by cunning generals, with the outcome hinging on the level of "aggressiveness" shown by one side or the other – most particularly on that of the "junior commanders."

It is irritating to the point of enraging to read critical analyses of the shortcomings of men and officers engaged at the spearhead of operations by critics with not a single day of frontline experience. Well-rested, well-fed, safe and secure, writing within the relaxed atmosphere of their homes or offices, with no responsibility for men's lives resting on their decisions, they are sickeningly arrogant. Clearly, when all the sinister mystery is removed from any battlefield as to what the enemy has over there beyond those trees, or among the silent rubble of that village, or in the dead ground just over that ridge, any fool can decide what should have been done and the best way of doing it.

And there is something particularly obscene about the works of historians who conduct coldblooded analyses and write without emotion of the accomplishments of units and the "fighting quali-ties" of men while never giving any indication they recognize and understand the frailty of the human spirit and the resolve of all men, regardless of training or background, when forced to live for days without end in a continuing agony of fear, made manageable only by the numbing effects of extreme fatigue.

I think I would have keeled over in shock had I come across one historian, purporting to describe the battles on the road to Falaise, who once acknowledged that those battles (like those in every major operation extending over several weeks) were not fought by alert, well-rested, well-fed, healthy men, but by men suffering utter exhaustion, from heat and dysentery and the neverending itching induced by lice and sand fleas, from never being allowed to stretch out and get a night's sleep, and from continuously living with grinding tension arising from the irrepressible dread of being blown to pieces or being left mangled and crippled.

Everyone tends to forget just how awful some aspects were. I had to be reminded of my bout with disturbed bowels by an ex-major

of the Royal Regiment of Canada. His recall of one man's dysen-
tery-induced expulsion aroused my own memories of the convulsive cramps and feverish, shuddering ague brought on by that
damnable scourge that struck the Canadian Army around Verrières
before the drive down the Falaise road began, which worsened as
time went on to the point where it came close to putting some
units out of action when supplies of medicine to treat it ran out. Yet
dysentery, if mentioned at all by historians, is touched on only in
passing, as though of no more consequence than some minor irritating inconvenience like lice or mosquitoes.

What a hellish nightmare it must have been for foot-soldiers
with dysentery just to drag themselves over hill and dale, let alone
dash here and there for cover when on the attack, and then dig in
on the objective to meet the inevitable counter-attack. I wondered
then and I wonder still how men found the will to move out from
cover and risk death and crippling wounds day after day until they
were wounded or killed. I saw them do it when they were so
stunned by fatigue they scarcely flinched when an 88-mm whacked
an airburst above them. And I saw them do it shortly after some
opening rounds of a fire plan fell short, causing a few, overwrought
with tension, to cry like babies.

Armchair strategists writing of those days – whether British,
American, or Canadian – have all spent too much time wondering
why they were so slow getting down past Falaise to meet up with
the Americans. They should have spent more time wondering how
men ever summoned up the necessary moral courage and physical
stamina to get there at all.

Those base-wallahs who since the war have dared to criticize the
Canadians for not closing the Falaise Gap sooner – inferring from
what seems to have been slow daily progress a general lack of
aggressiveness – were obviously not around at the time to see and
experience what it was like for the troops at the cutting edge of
the Canadian army. And while lack of first-hand experience in a
writer may be forgiven, no such tolerance can be extended to those

pretending to be historians who purposely ignore the evidence provided by the awful casualty rate among the Canadian divisions, which on the road to Falaise and beyond rose to twice the American rate and two and a half times the British rate (a rate the British considered unsustainable, causing them to set up a new category, "Double Intense," for measuring the intensity of battle).

By mid-August the nine 2nd Cdn Division infantry battalions were 1,900 short of establishment in their fighting strength of 5,040.

As in World War I, some staff officers and field commanders, to escape criticism, blamed the fighting men for failures. Thus we have the ridiculous declaration by Lt-General Charles Foulkes, CO of 2nd Division, that "at Falaise and Caen, we found that when we bumped into battle-experienced German troops, we were no match for them."

"Bumped into"? Foulkes's infantry brigades were never out of contact with the best troops Hitler ever assembled, from when 2nd Division entered battle, south of Caen, to Falaise and beyond. And it was the German elite SS units that were shredded, defeated, and herded to their destruction in the Falaise pocket – not the other way around!

But historians have lent status to such myths, thus guaranteeing their perpetuation by writers following behind, while largely ignoring the fact that the greatest failure in Normandy was the tanks, not the heroes who manned them. Except for a few "Fireflies," created by the British by replacing the 75-mm guns on Sherman tanks with the high-velocity 17-pounders, Allied tanks (American Shermans and British Churchills and Cromwells) were totally outclassed.

Every man in every armoured division, from the Officer Commanding down to the lowliest driver, within hours of arriving in Normandy, was aware that in any confrontation with German tanks, few Allied tanks would live to fight another day. For instance, Panthers could sit back at one and a half kilometres, and Tigers at two and a half kilometres, and knock out Shermans, while the 75-mm gun of the Shermans couldn't penetrate the frontal armour of those German tanks at any range. If this bred caution in armoured units moving up, who could blame them? Yet no high-ranking officer, from Eisenhower down through Montgomery and Bradley to Army and Corps commanders, or back up through the Combined Allied General Staffs, has accepted blame or been held responsible for putting at risk the whole invasion by sending men to their doom in under-gunned, under-armoured tanks. The fact some Shermans were upgraded with 17-pounders before the invasion proves that someone high up realized the extent of the problem, but a conspiracy of silence was imposed at the highest levels of the military and political powers.

It is a matter of record that in 1944 a well-informed civilian − Richard Stokes, a British MP − on many occasions from March to August asked questions in the House of Commons in an attempt to make the government aware of the inferior fire-power of Allied tanks. But all he gained was scornful laughter from incredulous government benches, and outright false statements from Prime Minister Churchill, who, on March 16 and again on July 20, 1944, assured the House: "The next time that the British Army takes the field in country suitable for the use of armour, they will be found to be equipped in a manner at least equal to the forces of any other country in the world."

Incredibly, even as the planners recognized the bridgehead in Normandy might be wiped out before it was properly established, and fully understood the crucial role tanks must play in ensuring its survival, no Allied army commander demanded tanks be upgraded to at least the level of the bastard Sherman "Fireflies," which, though more lightly armoured than German tanks, at least matched them in firepower. As it was, most historians agree the initial landings were saved from devastating attacks by superior German Panzers only by Hitler's interference. The Führer held Rommel's strategic reserves of armour too far from the coast to allow their fast deployment against the landing forces during the hours of darkness, the only time they could safely move up hidden from the deadly Typhoon rocket attacks.

Suppression of the facts may have been justified at the time to prevent demoralization of the Allied armies, but the irrefutable fact that our tankmen were equipped with grossly inferior weapons with which to push through the German Panthers and Tigers on the road to Falaise should not have been ignored by our historians. To have done so is inexcusable.

At any rate, my own awareness of the insulting criticisms of the Canadian soldier in World War II provided the necessary incentive to finish this book, begun back in the summer of 1945 when I was first given the opportunity to research the story of my regiment while stationed in Holland shortly after the war ended. Using personal notes and diaries, official war diaries on deposit at Canadian Army Records at Acton, London, and conducting dozens of interviews, especially with surviving original members of the Regiment who had signed up in September 1939, I wrote the first 132-page core manuscript. And in my attempt to bring to life those far-off days it was always necessary to draw heavily on personal experience, for no one can really describe the experience of another person.

Any reader looking for adventure, must look elsewhere. Even as I made mental notes, and wrote down my thoughts during action for the book I intended to write some day if I survived, I was fully aware that if misery and fear failed to dominate my documentation, it would be in danger of becoming chauvinistic and therefore false. My narrative might stir poignant memories of comradeship and unselfish acts, and sometimes recognize acts of courage – even great courage – but never should it develop in the fashion of an adventure story, for the simple reason that a story that deals honestly with war can never be an adventure story. It may be gripping and even melodramatic in a horrible sort of way, but never, never an adventure story.

In the foreword of his remarkable book *All Quiet on the Western*

Front, about life for the German front-line soldier in World War I, author Erich Maria Remarque said it so well: "Death is not an adventure to those who stand face to face with it." With unique precision and clarity, those few words deny the existence of any romance in the killing ground of a battle front.

The truth of this is known to every man who has survived close shelling or bombing, cowering with painful tightness of breath and panting, waiting for the next instant when he'll be blown to oblivion, or has felt the utter nakedness and vulnerability to those bullets from hidden gun muzzles when at last he is called upon to abandon his safe cover and go forth with trembling legs into the open in the attack.

The regiment of 25-pounders, from whose perspective the struggle for Normandy is viewed in this book, is 4th Field RCA, whose batteries were ordered to mobilize the same day Hitler's legions invaded Poland, on September 1, 1939, two days before Britain and France declared war. And the Regiment was largely up to strength, by voluntary enlistments, when eight days later the Parliament of Canada proclaimed the nation at war with the German Reich.

The Regiment's first year was passed in Canada in makeshift accommodation, including hastily converted stables and pigsties in the exhibition grounds of Ottawa and Toronto. The soldiers were garbed, at least for the first few months, in ill-fitting, shabby, moth-eaten 1914-18 uniforms that were not always complete, forcing some to wear their light civilian shoes on parade and fill out their attire with civilian garments when issued a tunic but no breeches, or breeches but no tunic. Early training, while approached with enthusiasm, was conducted mainly on obsolete equipment such as World War I 18-pounder guns or 4.5-inch howitzers. And sometimes there was no equipment at all, as in the case of troop deployments when trucks could not be rented from local merchants and gunners were forced to walk about among logs set in the ground representing guns, carrying placards representing vehicles (invariably drawing indignant inquiries from civilian passersby curious to know "Why the hell is the Army on strike?").

Canada's embryonic war industries, which at their maturity would turn out a flood of guns, vehicles, ships, planes, and hundreds of other essential items for her own forces and those of her allies – at such a rate that an army division of twenty thousand could be equipped in a week – was, until the summer of 1940, held back by Britain's reluctance to release blueprints and patents of their tools of war for manufacture outside the British Isles. Not until some 224,000 bedraggled British soldiers and 112,000 of their French and Belgian comrades returned to England without guns and vehicles, having abandoned them all at Dunkirk as they made their way to the little boats that had come to rescue them, did Churchill issue his earnest appeal to North America: "Give us the tools and we will finish the job."

On September 5, 1940, the Regiment arrived in Aldershot, England, without weapons or vehicles, expecting to be issued new 25-pounders so they might join in the defence of the realm against the imminent invasion by German hordes fresh from their Blitzkrieg strikes that had brought Western Europe to its knees.

Instead each battery received forty rifles and fifteen cartridges per rifle, mildly consoled by the knowledge they were infinitely better off than nearby units of the Home Guard (the civilian army of men too old or unfit for regular military service), who were equipped with iron-tipped pike poles made by local blacksmiths that would not have been out of place in Oliver Cromwell's army of the seventeenth century.

The first week of October – with the nation standing-to at maximum alertness – the Regiment was equipped with wooden-wheeled French 75-mm guns of 1898 vintage, and seven shells per gun. All of which would have been very funny if the island had not been in such peril, standing alone, with only what help the Commonwealth could then provide, against the combined might of Germany and Italy.

But if Britain's claim that it was prepared to "fight on the beaches . . . on the landing grounds . . . in the fields . . . in the streets . . . and on the hills," was, in the summer and fall of 1940, largely without substance, the threat of invasion by Hitler was real enough. German records would one day reveal that Hitler scheduled "Sealion," as it was known, for September 21, and only postponed it with four days to go when Göring's Luftwaffe failed to knock out the RAF and gain full dominance of the skies over the English Channel, a prerequisite for the success of a cross-Channel seaborne invasion.

On October 12 Hitler rescheduled the invasion for April 1941. But some time over the winter he decided he must first conquer Russia, and on June 22 he turned his armies of three million men and 3,580 tanks eastwards, to the profound relief of all charged with the defence of Britain, including the men of 4th Field, who, having been re-equipped early in 1941 with some less-old British 75-mm guns with pneumatic tires, had become part of "the last line of defence of the City of London" and were awaiting the invasion with some anxiety, even as they took pride in Churchill's statement that "If you Canadians were to leave England, I would not sleep at night."

By September 1941 the Regiment had its full complement of new 25-pounders and the "quads" to tow them about, and from then until the spring of 1944, when not doing garrison duty along the Sussex and Kentish coasts, officers and other ranks underwent intensive training, frequently under the critical eyes and guidance of "the apostles of the gospel according to Larkhill," as British Instructors in Gunnery from the Royal School of Artillery at Larkhill were sometimes known.

During those two and a half years, equipment (particularly radio transmitters) improved remarkably, and modifications to the fire-control system of field guns placed incredible firepower for dealing with "targets of opportunity" in the hands of British Commonwealth forward observation officers or FOOs (captains and the

xxii   THE GUNS OF NORMANDY

subalterns substituting for them). The new firepower was of a speed and mass not available even to the field marshalls and five-star generals of other nations, allowing concentrations of shells of unbearable intensity to be brought down on targets from the twenty-four guns of a regiment within three or four minutes of their being called for by a FOO, and very little longer when the combined fire of all seventy-two guns of the division, or the 216 guns of the corps, was required.

However, until Normandy 1944 – apart from living on the fringes of the German bombing raids on England, including the 1940-41 blitz of London, doing anti-invasion garrison duty along the vulnerable coasts of Sussex and Kent, and contributing to the 1942 Dieppe Raid a small contingent of three officers and twenty other ranks (of whom three were killed and the others taken prisoner, one to escape later back to England) – the war had largely passed the 4th Field Regiment by.

After Dieppe, with 2nd Division infantry battalions having to rebuild, some of them completely (Essex Scottish having only 52 of the 521 who went on the raid return to England, and the Royal Regiment of Canada, with whom the 4th Field lads landed, leaving all but 65 of their 554 officers and men of their assaulting companies dead on the beach or in captivity), other Canadian divisions (1st and 5th) were chosen to join the Allied invasions of Sicily and Italy in the summer of 1943.

And when it came time to select a Canadian division to join two British divisions and three American divisions in assaulting the beaches of Normandy on June 6, 1944, 3rd Division got the nod.

The Regiment, along with the rest of 2nd Division, was left encamped in the fields of Kent among the great masses of men and materials assembled in the southern counties near the Channel ports, waiting their turn to cross over to France and build up the forces in the bridgehead to a level where a breakout might be attempted.

There were rumours that 2nd Division was to go on D plus 7 (seven days after D-Day); then it was D plus 14, and this might have been authentic, but on June 19 (D plus 13) a great gale started to blow in the Channel, wrecking much of the Mulberry artificial harbour installations they'd put together on the beaches, and causing delays in shipping schedules.

Then on D plus 20, the Regiment is placed on six hours' notice. meaning that six hours after the order is received it will move with guns and vehicles to the "marshalling area" from whence it will proceed to the boats.

According to the BBC there is vicious fighting in the area north of Caen . . .

PART ONE: JULY 1-10

Off to War After Years
of Training

I

TO FRANCE VIA LONDON

---------------------------------- ✳ ----------------------------------

IT IS THE NIGHT OF JULY 1, 1944 – TWENTY-FIVE DAYS SINCE
the invasion of Normandy began – and still 4th Field Regiment,
along with the rest of 2nd Canadian Division, is left stewing in restless indolence here in Kent.

You've just come back with a boisterous truckload of gunners
and NCOs off a five-hour pass to Margate . . . or was it Deal? At any
rate, it was a little coastal town near Dover, identifiable by an
unusual pub located below grade in a crypt-like cellar (called The
Crypt, you think), where, for much of those five hours, you helped
somebody celebrate his birthday with many too many gin-and-
lemons. And now you want only to find the officers' marquee tent,
flop down on your bedroll, and flake out for a long and peaceful
night's sleep.

This will be the seventy-third night you have slept on the ground
in this tent you share with the other subalterns and captains of the
Regiment; you should know where it's located. But the night is so
black with the promise of rain, it takes an age to find, and then only
with the help of a considerate NCO. When finally you locate your
bedroll, the desire to lie down fully clothed and drift off among the
dissembling fumes that enshroud your head is irresistible. But even
in your state of vague awareness, in the dim light shed by a heavily

shaded petrol lantern hissing at the far end of the tent, you are conscious of an unusual amount of activity for this hour of the night. This you could easily ignore, but to your utter disgust two of your closest buddies since your earliest days in the Regiment – Lieut. Len Harvey and Lieut. Jack Cameron – inexplicably become insufferable pests, even resorting to kicking the soles of your boots to wake you. And it seems nothing will deter them. Even when you threaten physical assault, they refuse to leave you alone until you accept their advice to get up, shaking your head, and start packing up your bedroll and the rest of your belongings for a trip to the continent.

Once aware they are not joking – that they, along with everybody else in the marquee, really are packing up – the prospect of taking off for France produces a certain sobering effect. But it's only temporary. By the time you have followed the others down to the dark vehicle park and stowed away your gear in your truck, you're more than ready to climb aboard and pass into blessed oblivion for the several hours you expect it will take to get to where you are going – a matter of speculation until you assemble with the rest of the Regiment in a shadowy, dark mass to listen to a distant voice, recognizable as that of the Commanding Officer, Lt.-Colonel C. M. "Bud" Drury, extend a *bon voyage* as he reveals the Regiment is proceeding tonight to London and the East India docks where it will board ships for Normandy.

After referring to the many long years of training, leading up to this day, the CO wishes all ranks well and ends by declaring a general amnesty for those serving sentences for recent transgressions – stating most emphatically that all members of the Regiment are leaving for France with "a clean slate," and a chance to prove they are good soldiers.

As you return to your vehicle, you mull over the profound meaning this last announcement must have for one particular gunner, who, for reasons known only to himself, in recent days absolutely refused to accept that part of his sentence for "field punishment" that involved marching about the detention square for a specified period each day in full marching order, his big pack loaded with sand. While he'd dressed and equipped himself for the task each day, when ordered to march he had simply sat down and refused to budge. However, Sergeant of the Guard "Lefty" George Phillips, one of your Able Troop gun sergeants, refused to be defeated by such mulish behaviour. According to fellow sub-altern Leslie "Hutch" Hutcheon, the duty officer yesterday, Phillips, a husky, athletic man of boundless energy, simply leaned down and, grasping the webbing behind the gunner's neck, proceeded to drag the recalcitrant man round and round the dusty, gritty square on the seat of his pants for the required period of time. Surely the guard must now be as relieved as the guarded that this charade is over.

Calculating it will be dawn before you reach London, travelling at the regular after-dark convoy speed of seven and a half miles an hour, you settle down in your truck for a good long snooze. But this is not to be. Before the convoy moves off, you get a message from your battery commander, Major Gordon Wren, that you are to climb on a motorbike and spend the night riding herd on the convoy.

In your hazy state, this is the last thing on earth you should be doing. Even with all senses sharply alert and fully functioning, it is extremely dangerous riding a motorbike at night on narrow roads and through blacked-out towns and villages crowded in by stone walls and hedges, among shadowy, lurching vehicles and guns – at times barely crawling, while at other times clanking along at break-neck speed, only to be brought up short without warning, to a shuddering, jolting stop. And just to top things off, as the convoy is pulling out of Waldershare Park, it starts to rain.

You decide there is only one way to survive this night, and that's to get in behind one gun and stay there, concentrating on the glow of its white muzzle-cover, faintly lit by the reflected light of its tiny bulb. And that is what you do, though it is not without its hazards as the muzzle continually moves in close to your face and then away again – sometimes so close you have to move your head sideways to escape it, and sometimes so far away you lose sight of it in the foggy drizzle – a nerve-wracking rhythm of speeding up and slowing down, as drivers struggle to accommodate the eternal accordion motion. The regimental diary will record "many minor vehicle casualties" this night. And shortly after 4:00 A.M., during a twenty-minute halt, the shocking news is passed up the column: Gunner G.W. "Doc" Sparling, a most popular 26th Battery dispatch rider, has just been killed by a Regimental Headquarters vehicle trying to regain its position in the column.

By dawn the convoy is passing through a densely built-up area of metropolitan London. During a pause a milkman, dropping off his clinking bottles at a front door near the street, calls out, "Good luck, lads!" and you are reminded that this is not just another convoy on the way to a training exercise.

Later, when the city is waking up and you are passing through the East End, where the worst of the bombing raids of '40 and '41 struck, and which now lies on the centre-line of doodle-bug alley, ladies come out of war-scarred rowhouses whenever the convoy slows down, to pass little cakes and cookies into the back of trucks, or toss them up to sergeants standing with their heads and shoulders up through the roof-hatches of the quads* pulling the guns.

And whenever the convoy stops for more than a moment, they run out with teapots and milk and fill as many of the gunners' cups as they can reach. The speed with which the tea and cookies are produced at the briefest of halts, makes it clear you are not the first convoy of troops to receive such royal treatment passing here on the

---

*   Humpbacked gun tractors, generally known as "quads," short for "quadrupeds," because all four wheels were power-driven.

way to the docks. There's no way they could have known you were coming, but they are prepared for you. This spontaneous generosity on the part of these people of modest means, who lived through the hell of the first blitz and are now living with the flying bombs, is incredible.*

At about 10:15 A.M., the Regiment pulls into an area laid waste by the earlier blitz, within sight of the cranes of the East India Docks. All ranks leave their vehicles and take up residence within the confines of a high wire-fence surrounding a marshalling compound, which reminds some of a recently levelled city dump, complete with acres of rolled brick rubble and cinders, devoid of all vegetation. A lot of green pup tents, floored with straw palliasses, sit in rows, each row carrying a number or letter.

As soon as all the motors are shut off, a voice, with an accent uncannily like the one affected by BBC news announcers, comes forth from Tannoy loudspeakers hanging on posts, instructing you to sort yourselves out: officers to that area, NCOs to this area, and other ranks over that way, where you are to choose a tent in which you can park your personal kit and eventually sleep. The Voice also draws attention to little, narrow, below-grade blast shelters distributed here and there throughout the compound, and offers advice on how to protect yourself against injury from the earth-quaking blast of a flying bomb. You are to assume the prone position, but ensure your chest and stomach are kept up and away from the earth.

The Voice is in the process of pointing out the existence of a couple of large marquee tents, sheltering a great many folding

---

* From June 13 to the end of 1944, flying bombs and rockets killed 7,533 and wounded almost 20,000 London civilians. In 1945, 1,705 more were killed and 3,836 wounded. Outside of London, along the route taken by the bombs, 1,097 were killed and 2,765 were wounded during 1944–45.

tables and a helter-skelter of folding chairs, to be used for messing and other purposes in case of rain, when it breaks into a mechanical drone closely resembling the Speaker of the House of Commons calling for order:

"Take cov-uh . . . Take cov-uh . . . Take cov-uh."

Immediately you are conscious of the unmistakable blabber of the ram-jet engine of a buzz bomb coming up the Thames. While no one questions the experience and advice of The Voice, everyone tries to move casually, not wishing to appear in an unseemly rush to get into a shelter. But when the raucous motor suddenly stops, and the little plane with the stubby wings starts plunging to earth, there is such a scramble for every shelter stairwell that all ranks suffer a legendary number of bruises, minor cuts, and abrasions to all parts of their anatomy. Some shelter openings are so jammed with humanity that dozens are caught outside almost standing upright when the horrendous explosion occurs. Fortunately it is some distance away, and no one is hurt from the blast. But you and many others decide that henceforth you will make for your pup tent and lie prone (face down with chest and stomach above the ground), convinced it is less hazardous than plunging into a throng of flailing hobnailed boots in one of those narrow shelters.

Shortly after this, Major Wren calls an Orders Group in one of the marquee tents to explain the routine. All ranks will be confined to the compound until the marching parties depart for the ships tomorrow afternoon. Vehicle loading will begin at 5:30 A.M.

The voice on the Tannoy speakers again starts droning, "Take cov-uh . . . Take cov-uh . . . Take cov-uh."

The Major continues to read from his notes, studiously ignoring the blabbering, stubby-winged plane, now clearly visible, flying low up the Thames and momentarily bathed in sunlight. But you are not hearing a word he is saying – the raucous sound of that pitiless monster, coming closer and closer with its lethal load, has captured your complete attention. It's flying so low it looks as if it may not clear a humpbacked bridge over a tributary of the Thames (River Lea) that empties into the main waterway close by. The bridge is jammed with noonday traffic crawling slowly over it, including a red double-decker bus moving from right to left. How awful it must be for the people on that bus, watching that thing coming at them. But it clears the bridge and bus with plenty to spare.

Now you realize it is headed straight this way. The Major stops talking, but still nobody moves. Suddenly it turns nose down, and its blabbering ceases. In the ominous silence, some scramble to get down on the ground beneath the flimsy tables, but most sit frozen, watching it plunge into the glittering surface of the water and explode, sending up a violent spume of water and black smoke that drifts slowly up and over the red bus on the bridge, still crawling along in the traffic as the muffled roar reaches you.

Immediately, the Major carries on, outlining the form and procedures that will maintain from now until the Regiment boards the ships for France. But in a few minutes, there's the sound of another buzz bomb coming. It's on a path almost identical to the last one, but when it comes over the bridge, it doesn't plunge into the river.

Obviously it's going to pass over the middle of the compound, and a distinct feeling of uneasiness spreads among all in the marquee. Still no one moves – no one wants to be the first to head for a shelter. Travelling at more than 400 miles an hour, in only a matter of seconds the thing is passing directly over the marquee and is momentarily out of sight. At that instant the guttural roar of the engine stops, and in the eerie silence there's a mad scramble to get down on the ground among a clutter of table legs, chair legs, and human legs.

You land in a spot at the rear of the marquee that provides an unobstructed view of the stubby-winged plane diving straight down among the buildings beyond the bombed-out acres, which means you are among the privileged few to witness a split-second phenomenon in the grey and sultry sky immediately above the spot where the buzz bomb disappeared: a ghostly, shimmering, dark grey concussion ring – not a smoke ring, but the air itself made visible by some freak of refracting light picking up the compressed ring of air, lasting only a brief moment as it expands, quivering, into oblivion, above a huge, roiling black cloud of debris and smoke rising hundreds of feet into the sky, accompanied by a reverberating boom.

And the actions and reactions of this first hour in the compound set the pattern of existence here, as the stuttering doodle bugs continue to come in day and night, some plunging down close by, others far enough away to raise only a dull boom. Some arrive close together, almost following on the tails of the ones before them, and others are up to twenty minutes apart.

Late in the afternoon you are told, by one who has been keeping track, that they are averaging about one every ten minutes. And while the sequence of sounds and action soon becomes familiar, and you learn to take maximum advantage of the peaceful intervals – even as you go about whatever you are doing with one ear always cocked for a faint burbling sound in the southeast sky – you know you'll never be able to say that you got used to them.

Each time you accommodate the instructions of The Voice, droning, "Take cov-uh . . . Take cov-uh . . . Take cov-uh" – meaning, "This one is headed this way and could be dangerous" – the anxiety rises within you, and you're no longer reluctant to hurry to stretch out on your palliasse in the pup tent. Each and every time a buzz bomb is heard coming this way, you experience two or three interminable minutes of painful tension and fear, developing into real chest-tightening terror when the stuttering motor grows louder and louder into a guttural growling directly overhead.

As you run out of things to do, you try to read the pamphlet they've issued you about France, but you can't concentrate on it; you'll read it on board ship. You try to get off some letters home, but you find you have nothing to say; you are not allowed to write about where you are or what's going on here, even if you wanted to. The buzz bombs have not only set the style of life in the compound, but are dominating your thinking as well.

While these hateful robots – significantly called "revenge weapons" by the Germans,* according to the London papers – are not capable of precision bombing, being designed rather to spread terror and destruction wherever they drop in the city, you cannot help admiring the high degree of accuracy so many of them are showing in making it to what must be a prime war target: the docks. Though a certain number are said to be tilting off course and crashing into the Channel or in the Kent countryside on the way to London, those making it here – through what must be the heaviest possible screen of fighter planes, ack-ack guns, and barrage balloons ever assembled – consistently come in over the same bend in the river, following the same narrow flight path, and shut down their motors and dive to earth within what appears to be no more than a square mile, enclosing much of the docking area. Not bad for pilot-less craft after a flight of more than one hundred miles.

In the afternoon the final stages of waterproofing the vehicles is carried out, the oil topped up, and petrol tanks filled. Then "emergency rations" are issued to each man for use on arrival in France.

Once darkness falls it's off to sleep, for there is simply no place that can be blacked-out in the compound. However, this is no

---

* The first of the Germans' two instruments of terror, the flying bomb, was known in Germany as the v-1, for *Vergeltuingswaffen-1*, or "Weapon of Revenge, Number One" (the v-2 rocket would come later). The unmanned aircraft was twenty-five feet long, carrying a ton of explosive in its warhead. It had a range of 155 miles and could outrun fighter planes that weren't already up and waiting, precisely positioned on standing patrol. Of the 8,000 launched against England (5,000 before the end of July 1944), 2,300 reached London, most of them during the first few weeks while defensive techniques were still being developed.

hardship; everyone is so tired, after being up all last night, that sleep comes easily. And though for light sleepers there may be wakeful moments induced by nearby booms, you are not conscious of a single explosion all night.

2

FAREWELL LEICESTER SQUARE

---- ✳ ----

REVEILLE ON JULY 3 IS AT DAWN, AND AT 5:00 A.M. THE DRIVERS start moving the vehicles and guns to the ships. With the daylight, the noise of the city returns, including those creaking sounds of a rusty dock crane on the Thames that became so irritating yesterday as the day wore on. It grates and squeals unceasingly under the weight of guns and heavily laden ammunition trucks being hoisted aboard ships.

For a while you amuse yourself by standing at the fence watching the early-morning traffic of civilian lorries and red double-decker buses crawling over that now-familiar distant bridge, spanning the only visible stretch of river. There is such a sense of unreality about all this, the perspective so bizarre, that you have to keep reminding yourself you actually are in London, wonderful London of so many memories of civilized living in civilized surroundings: of clean streets and Underground stations; of clean bedsheets and pillowcases in fresh-smelling hotel rooms with rugs on the floor and gleaming white-tiled bathrooms with white linen towels draped on steam-heated towel racks; and of white tablecloths in restaurants like Genarro's, where the major-domo, of courtly manners and a distinguished white *mostaccio*, nightly hands out red rosebuds to each lady guest arriving for a matchless, rich minestrone.

You find yourself reliving one particularly memorable leave in London, in November 1942, cosseted in the luxury of the Savoy Hotel, thanks to the generosity of Len Harvey, who insisted on lending you the money to accompany him on "a weekend to end all weekends" when it appeared that 4RCA (4th Field Regiment) was about to be warned for cross-channel action. Stony broke, you'd tried to turn down his offer, protesting that without a pro-longed run of luck at poker it would take months to pay him back. He'd merely scoffed at your protests while making a telling argu-ment: "What the hell. It's only money! Anyway, your bank account will build up fast from now on. You won't be spending any money where you're going!"

Incredible, that more than a year and a half ago all ranks in the Regiment were led to believe a wild rumour that you were about to go into action, simply because it coincided with an order from on high that the Regiment should "arrange for a maximum number to go on leave at once." Thus, wrapped in authenticity, the rumour was accepted as fact, and the feeling that this was your last chance to partake of civilized living enhanced the taste of every glorious hour.

Memories still glow: of Robert Morley in *The Man Who Came to Dinner* at the Savoy Theatre, of the sound of Geraldo's orchestra on the way to dinner after the show, of the swimming-pool-sized sunken bathtub and breakfast in bed in the hall of mirrors that was your bedroom – just the usual crumbly "scrambled" dried egg, soya links, and cold toast, but served with such élan from under silver covers by a waiter in a dinner jacket! Is it possible that life in all those familiar places in the West End is carrying on as usual? It cer-tainly would seem so, if the traffic over that bridge can be taken as evidence. You picture the endless stream of black taxis, with their distinctive, blatting horns, jockeying for position among the chuckling red double-decker buses sailing almost nose-to-tail along Piccadilly, Regent Street, Oxford Street, and the Strand. And people strolling in parks and feeding the pigeons in their beloved Berkley, Leicester, and Trafalgar squares.

You wonder if the theatres are still open. Knowing how Londoners carried on during the first blitz, you feel certain they are – that audiences each night are gasping at the appearance of a swastika on the curtain before the second act of Ivor Novello's musical play *The Dancing Years*, which opened in 1938; that Sid Field, "the funniest man in the world," according to Bob Hope, is still standing each night at centre stage in top hat and tails, weaving and hiccoughing for a taxi, as he sings the song he's made famous, "I'm Gonna Get Lit Up When the Lights Go On in London". . . And the Windmill? Surely that gallant burlesque house with its scantily clad girls is sustaining its unique reputation earned during the first blitz, and proudly displayed in big letters on its marquee, "We Never Closed."

During breakfast, consumed in relative comfort at tables in the marquee, albeit from mess tins, an air-raid siren in the middle distance winds up to its highest pitch and sustains the long, mournful whine of the "all clear" signal, the first heard since coming here.

It might have saved itself the trouble, however, for within a few minutes it is rising and falling in the familiar wailing waves that warn of an impending raid. And soon the first of today's crop of flying bombs is blattering up the Thames and over that traffic-covered bridge.

All day they come in, with only brief pauses in between, seemingly taking turns passing to the right, then to the left, and then directly over the compound, before cutting their engines and crashing out of sight beyond the buildings, but always sending up their towering, black clouds, followed by thunderous roars.

And while you are constantly grateful that they continue to fall elsewhere, you find yourself wincing for the poor souls who may have been living or working near those black clouds, since you became aware yesterday of the appalling consequences of each blasting roar. Through conversations with civilians passing outside the fence, you learned that every flying bomb falling into a residential street destroys half a city block of row-housing.*

No one has any regrets about leaving this grim place when at 3:30 P.M. "marching parties" start departing by bus for the docks to board grey freighters you are told are Liberty Ships. The 181 vehicles and 24 guns of the Regiment, as well as the 36 officers and 673 other ranks (including 59 attached personnel), are divided among three ships.

---

*   Field Marshal Sir Alan Brooke, chief of the general staff, on this very day recorded in his war diary: "Flying bombs becoming more serious danger and likely to encroach on our war effort if we are not careful. . . . The threat is assuming dimensions which will require more drastic action." The next day, July 4, he faced the fact that our "fighter aircraft are not proving fast enough, and the guns are not hitting them." And the following day, his diary entry makes it clear the flying bombs were damaging the war effort: "The Germans fully realize that we are at present devoting nearly 50 per cent of our air effort to trying to stop these beastly bombs, added to which 25 per cent of London's production is lost through the results of these bombs." Not until the end of August, two months later, would the number of bombs reaching London be reduced to a trickle, averaging only twelve a day, with 80 per cent of those making it across the Channel being knocked down over Kent or Sussex. Fighter planes and barrage balloons would account for 32 per cent of them, but the majority (68 per cent) would be shot down by ack-ack gunners, who providentially were equipped with better radar and, most importantly, with shells carrying the new "proximity fuze," a Canadian–American invention of revolutionary design based on a British idea. A tiny radar set in the nose of each shell meant that shells passing close to, but missing, a buzz bomb received a triggering reflection and exploded at the appropriate moment. And as time went on, the Canadian Army would take a direct hand in closing down completely the v-1 attacks on London. While there was no way the men of 4RCA could have anticipated it, the unit was destined to move up the coast of France in September, clearing ports and overrunning the very sites from which these frightful missiles were being launched at the docks in July.

The ship to which your A Troop of 2nd Battery, and at least some part of regimental headquarters, has been assigned was built in less than four days, according to a member of the ship's crew. And this may well be true, since the record, you are told, for welding together prefabricated sections into a completely functioning Liberty Ship is eighty hours and thirty minutes. But when you do a walk-around survey of the ship, you find it hard to believe that anything so large could be put together in such a short time. While she's no *Queen Mary*, she still is 441 feet long (equal in length to almost one and a half football fields) and clearly capable of carrying some three hundred soldiers along with more than sixty assorted vehicles, guns, and limbers, with several trucks loaded with shells.

Big as she is, however, she's still a freighter, with no provision for passengers. Senior officers have cabin accommodation somewhere in the superstructure amidships, but all other passengers below the rank of major are ushered down a ladder-like companionway into a cargo hold, where they're to sleep in hammocks or on the deck beneath them. Since there are no portholes, the hold must be venti-lated by a huge canvas tube, the top end of which is strung up above the open deck to catch the wind created by the movement of the ship, the rest of it snaking down the companionway like a giant, snuffling elephant trunk.

Tonight the ship will lie at anchor, and there will be 305 men in this hold that is rated to accommodate only 250. While there is no grumbling – everyone being very conscious of the fact that the day is not far off when this will appear in retrospect to be the very lap of luxury – you sincerely hope there'll be a good, strong breeze to drive some air down that tube.

Kit stowed, everybody returns to the open deck to watch the vehicle-loading still in progress – cranes lifting and lowering them into the gaping mouth of another hold of the ship. There are many ships at nearby quays, but what attracts speculation are several huge floating structures under construction among a forest of cranes across the way. Formed of concrete, the structures resemble windowless warehouses about four storeys high and the length of a city block. Later you'll learn, on seeing one being towed slowly across the Channel by an ocean-going tug, they are to be sunk off the Normandy beach to form the breakwater for the artificial port "Mulberry."

At supper you have your first experience with self-heating soup, delivered to the cargo hold quarters in cases of cans stencilled "Oxtail Soup."

According to instructions on the can, all you have to do to get hot soup is touch a tiny wick imbedded in a yellow blob of sealing wax on one end of the can with the glowing end of a lighted ciga-rette. But when you do, there is only a slight sputter and then nothing.

This is very disappointing to you and the four or five officers surrounding the test can on the steel floor, studying the holes you'd punched in the top to let out the steam. Everybody is getting a little testy from hunger. To be served nothing but a can of soup for supper is bad enough, but to have to drink it cold is the last straw. After following an improvised drill for a misfire, in good old artillery fashion, someone decides it has irrevocably "gone out," and picks up the can to examine it – only to let it drop in a hurry with suitable exclamatory remarks as he fans his fingers to cool them. The can is boiling, and when you rescue it, using a handker-chief as a potholder, and pour its contents into the waiting cups, you find it is absolutely delicious.

When you take the can apart to examine its innards, you find only a steel tube about the size of your index finger, running down from the top of the can, filled with absorbent cotton stained brown from the excessive heat of the chemical reaction that obviously started when the fuze opened a hole for the air to get in. What an invention! What a blessing this could be for front-line troops not in a position to light a fire or show a light! (That you'll never see another self-heating can in action is not something anyone would want to believe tonight.)

By early evening the ship is loaded, and with the sun still above the horizon, she begins to back up and turn around in the narrow basin. And as she slowly starts downriver, the dock workers who loaded her, and other workers on nearby quays, cheer lustily – some removing their caps to wave goodbye.

You feel so embarrassed you take off your beret and wave back at them, marvelling at their generous, brave hearts. After only two days, you're very glad to be leaving this place – the very bull's-eye of the principal target Hitler has set for his pilotless monsters. Those unsung heroes down on the dock have been there loading ships for days on end, ever since the doodle-bug scourge began three weeks ago, June 13 – carrying on without benefit of uniform or recognition of any kind. And they'll be there tomorrow, and the next day, and the day after that, while every ten minutes or so a mindless angel-of-death hums and blabbers over their heads, and they listen for it to cut out and dive down in nerve-wrenching silence to a towering, black, earth-quaking blast – never far away.

And the image of those men, waving and cheering the departing vessel, is still vivid next morning, when the harbour-master comes out in his plunging craft to where the ship is anchored in the misty Estuary to take off Col. Drury for a shore meeting of the senior officers of 2nd Division. Hailing the bridge with his megaphone, he tells the captain that just after his ship departed downriver last night, the dock where it had been loading all day was struck by a flying bomb and blown to bits.

All of July 4 and 5, the ship lies at anchor far out in the Thames Estuary, somewhere off Southend. When not occupied with "inspections of quarters" by the ranking officer on each vessel, accompanied by the ship's captain, or participating in "life-raft drills," or lining up for meals served off a hatch-cover on the open deck, the men are left to their own devices.

Many have brought along reading material, and card games are popular. Others pass the time writing letters home, which in turn provides work for troop officers who have been designated as censors – a task you find thoroughly distasteful; having to read the intimate thoughts of men written for the eyes of their loved ones, while you look for references to times and places which might be useful to the enemy.

But by far the most popular pastime is a giant crap game on a big hatch-cover, which began shortly after breakfast and seems destined to continue (apart from mealtimes) throughout the hours of daylight all the way to France. On a single roll of the dice, a huge pot, built up by the sheer numbers of gamblers, can be won or lost – not to mention countless side-bets among the onlookers waiting to get a turn with the dice.

Shortly after 7:00 P.M., your ship, along with the others, raises anchor and the convoy gets underway. You are told that the movement is so timed that the ships will be passing out of the Thames Estuary after dark, and through the straits of Dover around midnight. No one but designated subalterns will be allowed on deck after dark. Your shift starts at midnight.

Suddenly you are aware of an atmosphere of tension that wasn't there during the past two days. It's as though everyone now recognizes that 4th Field is finally – after all those years of training and endless rumours of going into action – on its way to war.

3

GATHERING FOR WAR

———————————— ✳ ————————————

IT IS SHORTLY AFTER MIDNIGHT ON JULY 6. THE DARK WATERS
of the Channel, seething leisurely past the side of the blacked-out
ship, are only lightly streaked with luminous froth from the mild
bow-wave the vessel is creating as it slowly and sedately slips west,
past Dover and the white cliffs lying ghostly and vague a few
hundred yards to starboard. It's as though the convoy bound for
Normandy, which pulled out of the Thames Estuary just before
dark last night, is hugging the coast in the hope of tiptoeing past the
giant guns over on the Pas de Calais.

All ranks are confined below decks and won't be allowed up until
0600 hours this morning. The reason given is that the ships may be
shelled as they pass through the Straits, and though the chances of
receiving a direct hit are slight, the hazards from shell splinters are
real enough. You are on deck only because you've been assigned to
stand guard from midnight until dawn at the companionway
leading up from the sleeping hold, to ensure that the order to
"remain below" is obeyed by all ranks. Before coming up on deck,
you were privileged, as one of the designated orderly officers, to
place your bedroll on the floor of the hold, conveniently near the
foot of the open, ladder-like companionway, where you wouldn't
have to stumble through a mass of prostrate forms and kits on the
way out. Thus you were the beneficiary of the freshest air coming

into the hold, being near the lower end of the giant canvas tube carrying air from the open deck. Still, you were relieved when the time came for your tour of duty on deck, and you feel truly sorry for anyone subject to claustrophobia down there.

Waiting your turn to go on duty, you found it impossible to sleep. All you could do was lie there in the inky darkness, on the throbbing steel floor, listening to a cacophony of deep and laboured breathing, snoring, throat-clearings, and periodic coughing spasms – all the while conscious of the irregular gushes of air down that quivering, snuffling fabric tube, dangling a couple of feet above your head. And with each passing hour, that tube became more a source of anxiety than comfort, as you mulled over the dismal thought that that primitive affair was actually the only means of catching the night breezes and ventilating an entire hold and 305 sets of ravenous lungs.

Now standing at the starboard rail of the ship, watching Dover slowly drift by, you speculate how big the splinters could be from 1,300-pound shells looped over by one of the 16-inch "Adolph" guns at Blanc Nez, or the 15-inch guns at Cap Gris-Nez. Only a few days ago you'd sat on the side of that hill rising up behind Dover, there, with fellow 4th Field subaltern Doug MacFarlane, watching shells from one of those cross-Channel guns send up giant geysers amidst a convoy like this, sailing with agonizing slowness past a burning freighter that had been hit and was drifting helplessly, laying down a long trail of black smoke across the sea. There'd been a "shell warning" by way of a siren in the same manner as for an air raid, and a most polite warden had invited you and Doug to make your way to a deep shelter in the hillside designed especially to withstand the frequent bombardments from across the Channel that over the years had reduced poor little Dover to a truly desolate condition. But after the warden had passed on down the road, you'd climbed up near the summit of the hill to the west of the town, feeling secure in the belief that Jerry was only after the ships and would leave Dover alone that day.

With your field-glasses, you'd been able to pick up the tiny flash on the horizon each time the gun fired from the French coast. And after about forty-five seconds, there'd been a fearful wail, rising quickly to an ugly, intimidating howl, just before a water-spout leapt towering out of the sea between the burning ship and the shore, and a monstrous roar rolled up the valley and over the land, echoing and re-echoing down the coast. There had been long waits between each shell, and you'd had to leave to go back to camp without knowing whether any more ships were hit. You calculate that just about now you are passing over the spot where that burning ship lay on D-Day.

Tonight there's much air activity on both sides of the Channel. Waves of bombers have been passing over towards the continent, and the flashing on the horizon and faint grumbling from the direction of Calais probably mean their targets are the launching sites for the V-1s reputed to be there. Now and then a buzz bomb blabbers overhead on its way to London, attracting a gaggle of searchlight beams and a torrent of ack-ack tracers above Kent that releases a myriad of twinkling explosions in the sky, ultimately producing a delayed crackling that comes to you in a spooky, muffled fashion. You imagine you know where those guns are sited, just north of Dover, in Waldershare Park, which from April 19 to July 2 was home under canvas for all 2nd Division artillery, including 4th Field.

It is strange knowing that you are now passing almost within sight of those lovely, green, rolling, parkland fields of the Earl of Guilford, having left there in the middle of the night five days ago to drive all the way up to London to board these ships.

But now, having travelled some 130 miles down the serpentine course of the Thames, out into the Estuary, and around through the North Sea into the mouth of the English Channel, you feel for the first time that you are well and truly launched on your way to France. And this feeling grows deeper as the white cliffs recede into the misty night and you are left alone with your thoughts of what you and all those men down in the hold are about to face in Normandy.

The news from France has maintained a positive bias, underlined by the front-page pictures of visits to the bridgehead by General Eisenhower the day after D-Day, and of Churchill and Smuts only four days later. But while reports have been generally sketchy, so as to provide no comfort or useful intelligence to the enemy, clearly the fighting in the bridgehead has become, if not a bloody stalemate, then the next thing to it: a battle of attrition. Since a week after D-Day, very little ground has been gained by any Allied formation.

You realize huge quantities of men and equipment must be built up before any breakout can be safely attempted, and your own 2nd Division – obviously earmarked months ago to carry out a leading role in such an operation, having been involved in countless training exercises involving "breaking out of a bridgehead" – is only now on its way to the continent. But even allowing for a lengthy build-up period, the inability of the powerful Allied forces already in the bridgehead to expand the perimeter to any remarkable degree after almost a month ashore, surely means that German resistance is formidable.

Undoubtedly there are rough times ahead for the Regiment – just how rough and just how well it will measure up, only time will tell. But of one thing you are certain, no artillery regiment in the history of war has ever entered battle better trained.

Mobilized in the first week of September 1939, it has been in constant training ever since – a matter of fifty-eight months. Regular "permanent force" artillery units might have recorded longer training periods between the wars, but there is a great difference in the intensity and quality of training when there is no war on the horizon and when a conflict is raging and a unit is expecting to be sent into action at any time.

Over the years, gunners, drivers, signallers, and motor mechanics have become so proficient at their jobs, you believe they could almost perform them with their eyes closed. And in the case of the drivers, this is closer to the truth than anyone could possibly imagine who has never ridden in the cab of a truck with one of them on a narrow, twisting, English road in the blackout. How often you marvelled at drivers wheeling recreational trucks full of gunners along winding mountain roads in Wales, through lashing rain and the swirling mists of a pitch-black night on the way back to Senneybridge artillery camp from an evening in Brecon or Merthyr Tydfyl.

How they managed to follow the road, with only the vaguest yellow glow escaping through a tiny nail-hole in each blacked-out headlight, especially on wet, stormy nights (which invariably they were in winter in Wales), you never could fathom. No matter how hard you stared through the windshield, or how intensely you concentrated, only the curling mist or the rain sheeting down immediately in front of the truck was visible to you. Never once during one of those drives could you make out anything of consequence of the road ahead. While the superman in the cab beside you – enlivened for the return trip by several pints of mild or bitter, but armed with some natural form of radar – would be carrying on as though it were daylight, gearing up and gearing down, wheeling around bends you couldn't even see, and all the while rattling off cheerful stories or singing at the top of his lungs along with the gang in the back.

The signallers have become so proficient that reliable communications by land lines or R Talk (radio telephony) – absolutely vital to the operation of artillery, but extremely difficult to come by – are now taken for granted.

Equally accepted as normal is the extraordinary speed with which the regimental surveyors and command-post staffs are able to get all six troops on "regimental grid," with all twenty-four guns parallel and accurately oriented with each other, awaiting the arrival of more accurate survey data from Division that will put the

Regiment on Divisional grid, and in time on "theatre grid" by still more accurate survey information from Corps, tying in the guns of the Regiment with all the other guns in the division, the corps, and the army.*

And of course the men who maintain and fire the guns, the very reason for the Regiment's existence, could hardly be better trained.

As early as the summer of 1942, 4RCA was judged the best artillery regiment in Britain by those gods of gunnery, Larkhill IGs (instructors in gunnery) of the Royal School of Artillery, following a competition in "crash action" on Salisbury Plain within sight of Stonehenge. And the flattering judgement was not without foundation, for crash actions not only have practical application in the rapid fire and movement of modern war, but being the fastest of all

---

* "Grid" refers to the numbered grid lines overprinted on the large-scale military maps by which the position of each troop pivot gun (the right-hand gun of four) can be spelled out in eight-figure coordinates and plotted on the gridded paper of its own troop artillery board, allowing ranges between guns and targets, and switches from a zero line, to be measured and read off by command-post staffs for application to the guns. Getting the guns on "regimental grid" – establishing the position on the face of the planet of each "pivot gun" by using triangulation on distant identifiable aiming points such as church steeples – is carried out by the Regimental Survey Party. At the same time they ensure the guns are parallel on the zero line (a grid bearing, pointing along the axis of advance) by passing a reverse bearing from their director (survey instrument) to each troop director. Divisional Grid arrives later with more accurate survey data to be applied to the guns (in the case of the bearing on which they are laid) and to artillery boards where pivot-gun plots have to be adjusted. Finally the ultimate in survey data accuracy, starting from bronze "benchmarks" imbedded in rock, is brought forward across hill and dale by "chaining" and directors laid and relaid on survey flags. This establishes "theatre grid," ensuring all guns in all regiments, not only in Canadian Army, but throughout 21st Army Group, are accurately oriented with each other, so that any unit can join in a fireplan, or defensive fire, on any front within their range.

deployments, they put to the test all the training and discipline of all ranks. A troop, rolling down the road "on wheels," goes into crash action the moment the Gun Position Officer (GPO) receives over the radio the map reference of an unseen target miles away, with the order "Right ranging . . . Fire!"

To the GPO, who has been assiduously following his map to ensure he knows exactly where he is at any given moment, that message means: Get your guns deployed in the nearest field and put them on line to that target, using your map, your compass, the dial-sight of your pivot gun, and a local aiming point; and then give them the range so your pivot gun can get off a ranging round that will land on or near the target, which your troop commander can see and use to complete the ranging.

Every troop in the Regiment can routinely bring its guns into action and get off the first round within three to five minutes of receiving such a target while travelling along a road. (Three minutes if there is no unusual delay because of the terrain.)

This is no small feat when you consider that before drivers, gun sergeants, and gunners can engage in their teamwork of wheeling the guns onto their platforms and dropping their trails in position to receive the proper line (compass bearing) and elevation (range) from the GPO, he has to locate an open space in which to deploy them, with adequate "crest clearance" (muzzles not pointing at a line of trees or a bluff rising on the immediate front). Then he must find access to this location through the stone wall or hedge that is likely in the way, keeping an eye open for a culvert over the inevitable ditch that is adequate to carry such tonnages as he'll be leading over it. And all the while, he must constantly make sure he keeps himself oriented on the map in relation to the surface of the globe, so he can establish the position of his pivot gun within an accuracy of twenty-five yards.

For the gun crews, putting guns in action and firing has become second nature. And while the official "normal" rate of fire for a 25-pounder is three rounds per minute, and "intense" is five rounds,

4th Field gunners can easily achieve twelve to fifteen rounds per minute.

And then, over and beyond the expertise they've gained in gunnery and other matters military during their four and a half years of concentrated training, the men of the Regiment have developed an extraordinary capacity to take care of themselves in the most primitive and miserable conditions without losing heart.

Having learned first-hand, during your brief time as an enlisted man, the worth of an officer concerned about the welfare of his men, and having had it pounded into you by every instructor during officer's training that the welfare of the men always comes before your own, you had been most conscious of your responsibility when you first joined the Regiment. But concern soon turned to wonder, at the tough, resilient nature of gunners – veterans of endless manoeuvres, exercises, schemes, shoots, and training camps carried out in every kind of filthy weather, on every kind of bleak down, windy mountain, misty moor, and soggy cow-pasture. Even when dumped out into pelting rain in the gathering darkness of a gusty, winter night on Alfriston ranges, to set up guns, haul ammunition, lay signal wire, and bed down among the dripping, prickly gorse to await a dawn shoot, they always managed somehow to maintain their extraordinarily high morale.

And finally there's a reservoir of strength, built up over the years, that could never be expected of a less highly trained unit: the ability of men to carry out jobs different from those for which they originally were trained and to which they are regularly assigned. For instance, many drivers have become signallers, replacing signallers who in turn have become drivers, and so on. This is particularly true of members of the "carrier crews" of troop commanders, who must be able to take over any job at a forward observation post so as to be able to spell each other off during long periods of duty, or in an emergency take over any job left unattended through casualties.

It's hard to imagine any difficulty arising from terrain or weather, or any problem of a technical or mechanical nature connected with guns, vehicles, wireless sets, or other equipment, that hasn't been confronted and overcome on countless occasions during training schemes. In many respects the Regiment could be compared to a reliable, well-oiled machine, that has benefitted from the most up-to-date modifications and been run-in long enough to have all the bugs worked out of it.

It was not always thus. The stories of foul-ups, large and small, reaching back through the years are legion, and all ranks should be grateful they were not committed to battle in those first couple of years of inadequate equipment and training, but allowed to accumulate the superior training and equipment they now possess.

However, this opinion would not be common among the men down in the holds of these darkened ships tonight – at least not among the "originals" who enlisted in the first days of September 1939 and have been waiting ever since to get into action.

4

"COMIN' OUT WITH A NATCH!"

———————————— ❈ ————————————

AFTER BREAKFAST YOU GET A MESSAGE TO REPORT TO THE major on the upper deck that surrounds the central superstructure of the ship. You find him, with a few others of the privileged classes, in what appears to be a rather cramped ward room. At least you assume that's what it is from the used porcelain tea mugs on the tables. For a moment you lapse into fantasy, warmed by the thought that you've been asked up to this relatively civilized spot to share a cup of tea.

But Major Wren promptly puts such wild speculation to rest, making it quite clear you are here on business. First, he requires you to confirm the rumour that you were a newspaperman in Civie Street. Then he parks you at a table in front of a loudspeaker implanted in the cabin wall, hands you a pencil, places a pad of issue message-paper before you, and instructs you to take down the news bulletins from the BBC broadcast about to come on the radio, so that you can type out copies and distribute them among the troops.

When the broadcast comes on, you are relieved to find that it is delivered very slowly and deliberately in short chunks, at longhand dictation speed. This, however, proves most embarrassing to the Major, who assures everyone in the ward room that he never would have gone to all this trouble if he'd known that the announcer was going to talk at such a slow speed.

The way he fidgets about beside you, you can tell he wishes you'd disappear in a puff of smoke. Far from providing an active testimony to his initiative on behalf of the troops, you have turned out to be an embarrassment to him – and in full view of the CO too! While feeling equally foolish, you must persevere to the end, and eventually you type out several copies of the news bulletins containing references to places you'll soon come to know most intimately:

– Canadian troops in the Carpiquet area, west of Caen, yesterday beat back three heavy German armoured counter-attacks within five hours to hold the ground they had gained fighting the day before.

– Very heavy mortar fire was being directed on the Canadians from Carpiquet airfield, where some hangers still are 600 yards ahead of the Canadians, and from high ground further west. One officer described it as the "hottest spot in France."

– In the Canadian sector the Germans have tanks dug in on the high ground behind the airfield and are using them as artillery in support of panzers on the flat surface of the airfield itself.

– British troops on the Canadians' right flank are engaged in heavy fighting.... One report said patrols had established contact on the high ground between Carpiquet and Verson, establishing a solid three-mile knife into the German positions in front of Caen.

– RAF Lancasters and Halifaxes last night followed up their day raid on the "flying bomb" platforms in the Pas de Calais.

– Mosquitoes bombed a synthetic oil plant in the Ruhr.

– More flying bombs were used against Britain Tuesday night and yesterday. Three RAF fighter pilots each shot down three of them while on patrol.

After you've issued several copies for passing around the ship, you have no other duties and are free to enjoy the cruise. It's a lovely, warm, sunny day, and the Channel is remarkably smooth. The ship maintains a westerly course just off the coast of England, and a crew member tells you it will continue until the Isle of Wight, where it will swing south. You find a spot on the starboard side where you can sit and watch the coast go by . . . a wonderful chance to see one of the most interesting bits of coastline in the world. But the long night with very little sleep demands its price; no matter how hard you try, you can't keep your eyes open. And a moment after you've found a flat space on which to flop down, you're asleep.

When you awake, the ship is out of sight of land. The crap game is still in progress, and players and onlookers completely surround the hatch-cover. Late in the afternoon, bits of wood and other debris begin to appear on the waves, and once a body in battledress floats by and is left bobbing face down in the ship's wake.

At about 6:00 P.M. someone calls out, "Hey, there's France!" For a moment everyone around the hatch cover is silent as they stare at the low streak of grey on the horizon, as though sensing it is a historic moment. Then a hoarse voice yells, "Comin' out with a natch!" and they all turn back to the game.

Half an hour later, the ship's engines cease their heavy throbbing and are barely turning over as she edges her way towards an anchorage among the other ships closer to shore.

Slowly she and the rest of the convoy wheel around, in and out past ships at anchor: ships, ships, ships – Liberty ships, battleships, cruisers, destroyers, corvettes, minesweepers, torpedo boats, and landing craft. A few are moving, but most of them lie still, spread out like a great grey herd, covering the whole calm bay from the beaches to the horizon of the open Channel.* Only someone in a

---

* Almost 7,000 ships were involved in Operation Overlord: 200 battleships, monitors, cruisers, and destroyers; 553 sloops, frigates, corvettes, patrol craft, gun boats, anti-submarine trawlers, motor torpedo boats, etc.; and 6,047 landing craft of five varieties, including LCVPs (Landing Craft Vehicle and Personnel) required for the artillery.

plane, like the pilot of the humming Spitfire patrolling above the basin, could ever get a complete overview of the armada suggested by the number of ships visible to you as yours weaves slowly between them, making for an anchorage you suspect is being allotted this very moment by that winking signal-light on a distant ship, to which the shutters on your own ship's lamp are now chattering and clacking in response.

You are still hoping she'll be allowed to drop anchor close enough to shore for you to see something interesting, when she's brought to rest so far out you can barely make out a line of unimpressive buildings, some barrage balloons (the kind used around London) floating over the beaches, and very little else. For those who expected intense activity, there is disappointment. It is all so quiet that the coarse, rusty, clattering chain letting down the anchor seems out of place.

The towering British battleship *Rodney*, whose nine 16-inch guns smashed the *Bismarck* back in 1941, and in the news since D-Day for its role in shelling enemy positions up to twelve miles inland, is sleeping close by. Over on the left, a minesweeper works a section of the sea close to shore. A few landing craft move between the ships, and a couple of motor launches, with miniature barrage balloons riding close-hauled only a few feet above their decks, cross and recross the bay. Barrage balloons of regular size and shape hang over the beach and some vessels are so high and dry they seem to have been purposely beached. With or without binoculars all eyes study the scene, the vast array of ships and the shore, but above all the shore. While the beach at this distance offers no indication of what took place there, let alone what is now going on farther inland, it is still fascinating. It is France!

5

SOMMERVIEU

--- ✳ ---

SLEEP THIS NIGHT IN THE HOLD IS RESTLESS TO SAY THE LEAST. at one point the whole ship rattles from the blasting roar of the great guns of the *Rodney*, bombarding, with methodical deliberation, something far inland. Now and then the deck is splattered with fragments of ack-ack shells sent up against marauding planes attempting to attack the beach and ships. It is a monster barrage, from more guns, you are told, than were assembled to protect London during the Blitz.

Reveille on July 7 is at dawn. Two hours later, shortly after 6:00 A.M., a party of Royal Engineers, after attaching landing craft to each side of the ship, comes on board to take charge of the off-loading of equipment onto these smaller craft providing a shuttle-service between the large ships and the beach. Starting up the rattling winches on the ship's cranes, they remove the hatch covers. Then winchmen, following the hand signals of a director, making motions as though directing a symphony, pluck vehicles out of the hold with steel nets, swinging them high above the deck, before lowering them over the side into the gently heaving smaller craft, officially known as LCVPs, or Landing Craft Vehicles and Personnel. These scow-like, motorized steel boxes are designed to ride in through shallow water until they beach themselves, at which time they drop open their square noses to form ramps over which the vehicles can drive right onto the sand.

One by one, ammunition trucks, guns, limbers, gun tractors, armoured scout cars, van-like HUPs (Heavy Utility Personnel), Jeeps, 15-hundredweight trucks, and Bren gun carriers are raised from the hold as easily as toys from a children's "fish pond." And as each landing craft is loaded to capacity, personnel related to those vehicles climb over the ship's rail and scramble down a rope net, slung down the side of the ship, into the heaving landing-craft.

The sight of the first landing craft pulling away for the distant shore, loaded with recognizable faces and familiar vehicles, each of them displaying your regimental sign – a white "42" superimposed on a red-and-blue background, red on top and blue on the bottom – heightens a sense of anxiety that you realize has been building ever since you pulled out of Waldershare Park.

And it's not too difficult to pin down its origins. While no one knows precisely what lies ahead, all know the hour is close at hand when the guns will be in action, near enough the enemy to shell him, and therefore near enough to be shelled by him.

The question now foremost in everybody's mind is: "How will I stand up under fire?" While every man is entirely convinced he is part of one of the most highly trained artillery outfits in the history of war, having had four and a half years to prepare for this day, no one can tell how he will measure up in action, for no officer or man has ever fired a round in anger. So there is tension, anxiety, and a growing sense of urgency among all ranks.

In great contrast, there is a total lack of urgency among the Engineers. They approach their work as though this is an old routine for them. Obviously they've done many similar off-loadings along this stretch of Normandy coast (and perhaps at more than one bridgehead in the Mediterranean), and under conditions a great deal more trying than exist here on this calm summer day, with nothing flying around the ship but some gulls. But their unhurried, methodical, measured pace is a source of wonderment to all members of 4th Field, and of deep irritation to the more impatient characters on board, particularly those senior officers who feel it necessary to be transparently conscientious and are fidgeting in frustration up on the bridge as they survey the scene from on high. From the look in their eyes, you imagine their frustration comes from being unable to find a way of blaming it all on "the subalterns not taking over." And when, at precisely 10:00 A.M., the winches suddenly go silent, leaving a White Armoured Scout Car dangling high over the deck, Major Wren comes charging down to where you're standing at the open hatchway, inquiring fiercely:

"What the hell's the matter? Why have they stopped?"

You point down in the hold, and he almost falls in as he takes in the scene. The Engineers, grouped around a steaming pot on a hissing Primus stove, are brewing up their mid-morning cuppa. His comment comes straight from the heart:

"My God! Can you believe it!"

However, as with all expert tradesmen who never seem to hurry, but pile up accomplishments in effortless fashion, the Royal Engineers by late afternoon have emptied the ship with only one vehicle casualty, a 14th Battery truck dropped in the ocean when a chain breaks. The loss of a vehicle at this stage is still a matter of serious concern, but it provides Lieut. Ted Adams, an eternally laid-back character (ex-Royal Canadian Horse Artillery troop sergeant-major who'd enlisted as a gunner in 1939) a chance to exercise his sardonic wit while calming down his overwrought battery commander, who saw the vehicle drop and heard the splash. Rushing up to Ted at the rail, he starts spouting a stream of questions in anguished tones:

"Where did it go, Ted? Is it in the drink?"

Still contemplating the rush of bubbles rising from the bed of the ocean just beyond the landing craft, and thoughtfully stroking his reddish-blond "handlebar-hank" moustache, the phlegmatic Ted issues his immortal comment:

"I sure hope she's well waterproofed!"

Guffaws from onlookers relieve the unholy tension, and even Major James Wilson Dodds, the battery commander, breaks into a broad grin as he walks away.

At last your vehicle appears out of the hold, and as it's being lowered into the smaller craft, you climb over the rail and carefully make your way down the rope net. This is a new experience. You weren't on any of the specialized training schemes to which the majority of the officers and men had been exposed, and you become a little anxious watching others scramble down and dangle momentarily over the plunging landing craft. On the way down you have to suppress the image of failing to make the leap into the landing craft now grinding up and down on the side of the ship. But it turns out to be a piece of cake: you step off into the landing craft as she rises on the swell as easily as stepping off an elevator.

When your landing craft grounds onto the beach, the chains holding the ramp are released, and it splashes down directly in front of your vehicle into about a foot or so of water. Your driver, Gunner George Weston, starts his engine, but immediately the captain of the landing craft, who has appeared at the open mouth of the craft to check the depth of the water, gives the signal to cut the engines.

In the stillness that follows, he explains: "Might as well wait – tide's on its way out. In about fifteen or twenty minutes you'll be able to drive off onto dry sand – save a lot of trouble later on, not having to pull the wheels and clean the saltwater out of brake drums and the like."

While you are impatient to get moving and rather resent being held back by this guy, what he says makes sense. You settle down to wait, contemplating the featureless, broad expanse of sand between the outgoing tide and the low bluff, covered with coarse grass, forming the horizon ahead. When you try to establish your position on the map, you realize how difficult it must have been for those landing on D-Day to identify their allotted zones along the beach. Without the aid of the captain of the landing craft, identifying those rather ragged-looking buildings just there on your left front as Courseulles, and just a bit farther left, Bernières and St. Aubin, you wouldn't have a clue where you are landing.

The recent gale, which cluttered some beaches with debris, seems to have swept this one clean. But immediately to the left, no more than twenty-five yards away, lies a big LST (Landing Ship Tank), with so much of her bulk high and dry on the sand, you wonder if she'll ever get a tide high enough to float free.

The captain can't say for sure about this one, but that gale drove a lot of shipping ashore and wrecked much of the Mulberry artificial harbour, over on the right in the distance.

Weston, impatiently watching the line of drying sand, which is creeping towards the ramp as slowly as the second hand of a watch, is inclined to dwell on other things – mainly the endless flaming hours he and the other drivers and mechanics spent waterproofing these flaming vehicles for a flaming wet landing.

The whole thing reminds you of always arriving late at Sunday School picnics or your father's lodge picnics when you were a little boy. No matter how hard you urged your family to hurry, the thing was always in full swing when you arrived. The sound of a big drum, from over where the action was taking place, never failed to induce a sense of breathless excitement. But there was always that last-minute tremor in the knees, a feeling of reluctance to get involved in events already in motion, shaped by others – by those damned early birds. There was a moment when you almost wished you hadn't come. The only cure had been to get involved as fast as possible.

You look down – the tide has almost disappeared back under the lowered ramp. You turn to Weston:

"Okay, let's go."

"Yes, sir!"

In the silence surrounding the beach, the starter-gears grind coarsely round and round, and then there's the furious fanning roar of the engine that sits in the tin box between you. There's the familiar abrupt shifting of gears – this time to bull low, for that wet sand may be soggy, and then the HUP dips down the ramp and bumps off onto the soil of France. Immediately Weston cuts his wheels left, making an obvious detour to splash through a shallow puddle of stranded sea water, growling:

"After all that goddamned waterproofing, she's at least going to get her feet wet!"

After grinding up the sandy embankment, through a gap bull-dozed in the grassy-topped bluff, your vehicle is directed to a track leading inland to a road busy with tanks, Jeeps, dumptrucks, and ambulances. And just a short distance in from the sea, beyond a village called Graye-sur-Mer, you are directed to join other 4RCA trucks in a field where they have been halted to peel away as much waterproofing gunk as possible before proceeding southwest to a concentration area northeast of Bayeux, near the village of Sommervieu. It's about eight miles as the crow flies, but will be a much longer drive by the assigned route.

Everybody is much amused to learn that the first vehicle of the Regiment to touch down on French soil was that of non-combat-ant Curt Embleton, YMCA Auxiliary Services' supervisor. Curt's truck, always the last vehicle in regimental convoys, was the last loaded on the ship in London. Thus it was the first loaded onto the landing craft.

However, many unit vehicles haven't arrived, and at 8:00 P.M. there are some fifty vehicles and two hundred men missing when the Regiment pulls out for Sommervieu. Still, it can't be helped; the timing of all movement along the roads, here, is strictly con-trolled by the beachmasters. (The missing men and vehicles will not catch up until 5:30 A.M., having been held offshore on landing craft for five hours awaiting the tide.)

As the convoy pulls out onto a dirt road, leading south from the sea, everyone's attention is directed to a huge sign warning that no vehicle breakdown must be allowed to block traffic, and that if a breakdown occurs, the vehicle is to be pushed into the ditch and abandoned.

A dust-covered Provost Corps soldier, doing point duty at a crossroads, pumps his arm up and down, vigorously signalling the vehicles to get a move on. And large signs beside the road repeatedly make it clear that this is one of the most important roads in the world and must not be blocked for any reason.

As you pass mountains of petrol tins, ammunition cases, and Compo rations, stacked right out in the open, on both sides of the road, you can see why. It's obviously a principal lifeline for much of the Allied forces in the bridgehead, and will soon be the lifeline of the Regiment.

While evidence of hard fighting is everywhere in the villages along the beach – all badly scarred by D-Day bombardments from air and sea – inland, away from any buildings, the only sign that there was fighting through here is the odd burned-out tank, and here and there along the verges of the road a crude wooden cross stuck in the ground beside a sad mound of dusty earth.

Suddenly the vehicle in front speeds up, and the whole convoy starts moving along at a speed well above anything allowed back in England. As the inevitable accordion motion in the convoy comes into play, keeping up becomes a real problem, and the furious fanning in the tin box begins to sound strained. Weston hunches over the steering wheel, concentrating on holding the bouncing vehicle on the road. Not that much would happen if he failed to do so, there being no ditches of any real consequence and, most surprisingly, no fences of any kind for as far as you can see.

Even over the smell of engine fumes and dust roiling up around the convoy, a pungent odour of crushed grass fills the air as you roar by what, only a few days ago, must have been lush green meadows and pasturelands, but which are now the bleached, sandy colour of dead grass turning to dust.

Several Typhoons and Spitfires are lined up at the edge of a landing strip made of steel-mesh webbing rolled out over the turf like a giant carpet. Their bodies and wings are striped with three white bands (interspersed with black) to distinguish them as Allied aircraft for trigger-happy anti-aircraft gunners during these days of close support by the fighter-bombers. A pilot, wearing dark sunglasses, stands beside the road, watching the convoy go by. It may be his first hour in France too, but to you he appears a dashing figure, a perfect example of "an early bird."

After a few minutes the landscape changes. On both sides are the hedgerows mentioned in that radio newscast the Major had you copy down on board ship: ". . . the difficult *bocage* country . . . the dense hedgerows . . . heavy casualties . . . fanatic counter-attacks . . . Canadians involved in intense fighting around Carpiquet airfield and Caen." You must be quite near those places, for the bridge-head on the map is so tiny that nothing can be far from the front line.

What's it really like to be shelled or mortar-bombed? You look at your driver: he could be dead tomorrow. What's it like to die, or get an arm or leg blown off? That you should turn out to be a coward is beyond consideration. But still, how do you know? You really were quite timid when you were little. Sometimes you've had the feeling that manhood is really only a pose men assume, while remaining boys at heart – particularly those lusty, life-hardened, male animals, who, in the eyes of their peers, are most likely to qualify as "real men."

But you must stop this line of thinking. Now is not the time for self-doubt. There is no turning back. If it really all has been just a pose, then you must continue the pose of being a man and a leader to the very end. Too many will be depending on you making the correct decisions and giving the correct orders – keeping your head when everything is turning into a bloody mess – to do otherwise. That's it, of course: just keep on playing the role of a mature, level-headed, cool man until you buy it, or it's all over, one way or another. Anything less is unthinkable.

Suddenly you are aware your vehicle is turning into an opening in a hedgerow, following the other vehicles as they park around the perimeter of the field. The furious fan is shut off, and there you are, parked for the night in a quiet green cow-pasture, well away from the fighting zones, shut off from the road and the rest of Normandy by a succession of high, thick hedges.

It's remarkably quiet. There's only a faint booming of heavy guns far away on the left, in the direction of Carpiquet or Caen, a sound reminiscent of those bass drums at those childhood picnics.

No sooner are camouflage nets draped across the vehicles from the hedgerows, and personal slit trenches dug, than irrepressible Bombardier Ron Hooper, goal-keeper on the regimental hockey team and fine all-round athlete, produces a softball he has taken pains to bring with him from England, and organizes a long-range game of catch with anybody who wants to join in. The game merely consists of looping towering pitches back and forth across the field in all directions, with Hooper keeping up a steady stream of bantering comments, loud whoops, and joyous laughter. It's really a nothing game, but in these circumstances, the whole thing is very pleasant to watch. You wonder if Hooper realizes what a wonderful job he's doing for morale, not just for those participating in the game, but for the whole Battery and Regiment. Surrounded by all this greenness untouched by war, and all this laughing and shouting, it's as though you are still in Kent.

Just as you dig out your box of "emergency rations" and start to explore its mysteries, which in its sparseness will constitute dinner tonight, a veritable storm of shouting arises around the field. And when you look, it seems all, including Hooper and his pitch-and-catch buddies, are stampeding towards the gateway, where a crowd is gathering around someone who has just arrived in a Jeep.

As you make your way over, you recognize the chubby face and sparkling, mischievous eyes of Padre Ray McCleary, who left the Regiment in the fall of '43 to become chief padre of 3rd Division, and cross the Channel with them on D-Day. What an extraordinary man! Within a couple of hours of 4th Field arriving in France, he manages to become aware of it, has located this obscure concentration area, and is visiting "his boys."

Everybody is crowding and jostling to get close to him, calling out greetings. And he, standing up in his Jeep, his face beaming with a smile from ear to ear, his eyes twinkling and dancing with that well remembered mixture of joy, merriment, and a slight pinch of devilment, is calling out names so rapidly it's as though he's calling the regimental roll. Except he doesn't just call out names — he attaches to most a pungent remark or a sly question showing he hasn't forgotten their scrapes and capers when he was with the outfit.

Unfortunately, he can't hang around; his division is involved in a big attack on Caen in the morning. By the time he has to leave, it seems the entire Regiment, officers and men, is assembled about him, shouting and laughing, reluctant to let him go. And it is obvious he feels the same way, for when he starts off, still standing upright, holding onto the Jeep's windshield reminiscent of Monty, he has his driver circle the field, waving all the time to "his boys," who cheer wildly until he turns out the gateway and disappears.

As the crowd disperses, and the men return to the vicinity of their vehicles and slit trenches, there's a lot of bantering back and forth — perhaps not quite of the "mountain-to-mountain" variety you recall hearing on schemes in Wales, but enough to clearly indicate that Bombardier Hooper's game of catch and the padre's visit have combined to dispel much of the tension that had grown stronger with each passing day, among the buzz bombs in London, on the ship coming over, and then on the drive inland today along roads of intense turmoil, past the refuse and scars of battle, and mountains of ammunition stacked up awaiting the deadly struggles still to come.

Just after 10:00 P.M., in the long, lingering twilight, the air begins to throb with the deep, wavering drone of hundreds of huge, four-engined RAF bombers, coming from England to bomb Caen and its northern outskirts preparatory to a dawn ground attack. The 3rd

British Division will attack on the left, 59th British in the centre, and 3rd Canadian Division on the right after clearing Carpiquet airfield. Wave after wave, in what seems like an endless stream, the Halifaxes and Lancasters roar in from the Channel on their way to laying waste the city.*

It is tremendously impressive. You are a good ten miles from the target area, but the ground shudders from the bombs roaring and flashing on the horizon and heavy ack-ack fire skitters up from enemy guns that appear very close.

Sommervieu lies close to the flight path of planes returning home to their English bases after delivering their bomb load, and the German ack-ack guns continue to try to knock them down as they circle west and north to the Channel. At least one is hit and is on fire as it makes for the Channel.

Among the group left behind this evening in several landing craft "standing off the beach for five hours waiting for the tide," Sgt. Bruce Hunt, 26th Battery Command Post Ack, has a grandstand view of the bombers going and coming, and witnesses the demise of one of them in the sea close by. In his diary, begun just before leaving Waldershare Park, he will write:

> The most impressive demonstration of air power we have seen. The planes pass over us and disappear into enemy territory oblivious of the flak showered skyward to meet them. Their mission completed they emerge a mile or so west of us bound for Britain. For a considerable time the sky is a two-lane highway, with masses of aircraft approaching and returning from the target area. One plane dives into the sea on its homeward journey,

---

* In this first attempt to employ heavy bombers of the strategic air force in a tactical role in Normandy, 2,560 tons of high explosive were dropped by 467 Lancasters and Halifaxes – 16 more and much bigger planes than were employed by the Germans during their infamous raid on Coventry, November 14, 1940.

striking the water with a great burst of flame. The crew, happily, parachutes into the Channel, while air-sea rescue boats travel at high speed to anticipate their arrival.

By the time the last of the planes is droning off in the distance, it is totally dark.

6

COMPO RATIONS

---- ✳ ----

SOON AFTER THE BOMBING ENDS, A MUFFLED ROAR OF GUNS begins in the south and east and goes on all night. At least, each time you awake and sit up in your shallow trench, the sky along the horizon is lit by ragged flashes accompanied by dull rumbling, and you sleep fitfully, for you're mildly afflicted with claustrophobia in your unfamiliar, gravelike abode.

At dawn (about 0420 hours), when the ground attack (Operation Charnwood) is to go in, the bombardment reaches a climax, as hundreds of guns, including those of the cruisers *Belfast* and *Emerald*, the monitor *Roberts*, and the 16-inch monsters of the battleship *Rodney*, open up on a variety of targets not covered by the aerial bombing.

In time you learn that the main part of Caen, lying west of the Orne River, the airfield at Carpiquet, and a series of villages – with names like Verson and Bretteville-sur-Odon, soon to become familiar to 2nd Division – have been taken. But throughout July 8 and 9, the guns of 4th Field remain limbered up in the calm, green pastures of Sommervieu. And when the last vestige of water-proofing gunk is removed from the vehicles, the daylight hours are largely occupied with learning how to deal with "Composite Ration Packs" – boxes of canned rations designed to allow men to mess in small syndicates, each syndicate heating up its own food.

This, evidently, will be the arrangement from now on, and individual boxes have been issued to each gun crew, carrier crew, command-post crew, and so on. But this presents certain problems in logistics. A daily menu, supplied with each box, provides for "breakfast, dinner, tea, and supper" for fourteen men for one day, or seven men for two days, or 3.5 men for four days. Even overlooking the fact there are no half-men in the syndicates, these multiples present puzzles in scheduling and rationing for the mathematically inclined in six-man gun crews, four-man carrier crews, and command posts with more than seven but fewer than fourteen men.

There are various types of Compo boxes, each identified by a letter of the alphabet (from A to E at least) stencilled on the box, each type containing a different variety of tinned food. And deliveries to the troops are not all of one type for one day and another the next, but are a mixture so that there is no telling what you will get next.

COMPOSITE RATION PACK
TYPE E
(14 men for one day)
Contents and Suggested Use

BREAKFAST Tea	*	3 tins (2 tall, 1 flat— Tea, Sugar & Milk Powder)
	†Sausage (1 hr.)	2 tins
	Biscuit *	1 tin
	Margarine *	1 tin
(*Items marked thus are also to provide for other meals)		
DINNER	†Haricot Oxtail (½ hr.)	12 tins
	†Vegetables (½ hr.)	2 tins
	†Pudding (1 hr.)	3 tins (2 large, 1 small)
TEA	Tea	— (*see above)
	Biscuit	— (*see above)
	Margarine	— (*see above)
	Sardines	8 tins
		Please turn over

SUPPER	Cheese	1 tin
	Biscuit	— (*see above)
EXTRAS	Cigarettes	2 tins (1 round, 1 flat— 7 cigarettes per man)
	Sweets	2 tins (1 tall, 1 flat)
	Salt	— ⎧ packed in flat
	Matches	— ⎩ sweet tin
	Chocolate	1 tin (1 slab per man)
	Latrine Paper	
	Soap	1 tablet

DIRECTIONS

Tea, Sugar and Milk Powder.—Use a dry spoon and sprinkle powder on heated water and bring to boil, stirring well. 3 heaped teaspoonfuls to 1 pint of water.

†May be eaten hot or cold. To heat, place unopened tins in boiling water for the minimum period as indicated. Sausage and pudding cut into ½-inch slices, may be fried (using margarine) if preferred.

Please turn over

905. 27042/3744. 190M. 9/43. C.P. Ltd. Gp. 784

The various types of boxes have been shuffled and mixed up at some supply base to ensure variety even within units, and to head off any charges of favouritism that might result from delivery patterns of more popular types of boxes.

The virtues of such rations are easily recognized, particularly for isolated OP (observation post) carrier crews. But still a fourteen-man box means four-man crews eat the same grub for three and a half days, and if, through the luck of the draw, their next box carries the same letter of the alphabet (as it may well do), they'll eat the same thing for seven days. And who's to say they won't get the same box three times in a row, providing no change of menu for ten and a half days.

For a while at least there'll be a certain excitement in receiving a Compo box. Finding you've been given the one with the can of peaches is like winning a lottery.

Since everything is already cooked, the tins have only to be heated up. And though only a few syndicates, such as battery-command posts, have equipped themselves with little petrol Primus stoves, within hours of the need presenting itself, the sand-box stove comes into common use. This consists of a tin box (the bottom half of a hardtack tin) loaded with sand and saturated with petrol. The fumes rising from the sand are set alight, under the other half of the hardtack tin half-filled with water in which the unopened ration tins are set to heat. While very smoky and grossly energy-inefficient, sand-box stoves can't be blown out by wind, and their flickering flames are capable of staying alive through all but the heaviest rain.

A great deal of time is spent reading directions and experimenting with methods of heating the contents of cans of "M & V" (meat and vegetable stew), "Steak and Kidney Pudding" (a can lined with thick dough and filled with a solidified concoction posing as chopped beef and kidney), "Sultana Pudding" (resembling a dried-out fruit cake that can be sliced and eaten cold with slices of canned cheddar), and "Treacle Pudding" (a caramel-coated creation that is especially pleasant when warmed up). One thing you quickly learn is that if the contents of a can requires heating to be really palatable, then it must be heated through and through — something not easily accomplished in the case of the "Steak and Kidney Pudding," due, you suspect, to the efficient insulation provided by the thick mass of dough lining the tin and surrounding the glutinous mess within.

It won't be long before repetition destroys all enjoyment of these rations, but so far Compo meals have been in some ways superior to many past meals developed by the cooks from fresh rations. A notable exception was breakfast the first morning: pre-cooked bacon. Cold, it plopped out of the can in a sickly white, cylindrical blob. Heated, it turned into liquid grease, which when poured off left a pitiful residue of red strings representing the lean meat that had streaked the fused rashers.

In each box there are two tins of "Boiled Sweets" (hard candies that contain no sugar), small slabs of very hard and remarkably taste-less chocolate (one per man per day), and two tins of cigarettes, one flat and one round, allowing seven cigarettes per man per day.

But, unquestionably, the feature of Compo rations destined to be remembered beyond all others is Compo tea: tea made from tea leaves already mixed with powdered milk and powdered sugar. Directions say to "sprinkle powder on heated water and bring to the boil, stirring well, three heaped teaspoons to one pint of water."

Every possible variation in the preparation of this tea is being tried, but so far it always ends up the same way. While still too hot to drink, it is a good-looking cup of strong tea. Even when it becomes just cool enough to be sipped gingerly, it is still a good-tasting cup of tea, if you like your tea strong and sweet. But let it cool enough to be quaffed and enjoyed, and your lips will be coated with a sticky scum that forms across the surface, which if left undisturbed will become a leathery membrane that can be wound around your finger and flipped away like something made of gutta-percha.

The second night, Curt Embleton shows a movie in a nearby field. But much more spectacular than any movie is the nightly show put on by the ack-ack guns in the dark dome of the skies overhead, when Jerry planes come over to bomb the equipment and ammunition dumps scattered among the surrounding fields and the ships unloading at the beaches.

At first everyone is inclined to stand out in the open to watch the spectacular display of fireworks, there being no obvious risk from bombs, since the German planes drop their dazzling flares on drift-ing parachutes miles away over their prime targets. However, when, along with the ripping sounds at high altitudes, fragments of shells begin to shower down, signalled by ominous *thumps* on the ground and sharp *clinks* on the metal roofs of the vehicles, steel helmets come into vogue, and space under vehicles becomes choice real estate.

At least three planes go down in flames.

You were told by the captain of your landing craft that there are more ack-ack guns protecting the Normandy bridgehead than were in action for the protection of London at the height of the Blitz. This you can believe after hearing the fearful racket and watching the show they put on here each night.

And unlike the ack-ack displays you'd watched in England, these seem successful in knocking down many of the raiders or diverting them from their targets, as the general absence of derelict ships lying offshore or on the beaches where you landed would testify.*

---

* In one month after D-Day, 261 Allied vessels were destroyed or damaged by enemy action of all kinds, including air bombing, mines laid along the sea corridors by night raiders, remote-controlled motorboats filled with explosives, and one-man torpedoes. (These torpedoes sank only two minesweepers and one cruiser.) This compares with 606 vessels lost during the period through bad weather and "human error," out of a total of 6,800 vessels involved in Operation Overlord. Besides the 6,047 specially designed landing ships and landing craft in five varieties (more than half provided by the British), there were 200 battleships, monitors, cruisers, and destroyers (of which 143 were Royal Navy or Royal Canadian Navy), and 553 other fighting ships (sloops, frigates, patrol craft, gunboats, anti-sub trawlers, motor torpedo boats, etc.) of which 424 were provided by the Royal Navy and the Royal Canadian Navy, and 129 by the Americans. Not counted as fighting ships were a great number of British and Canadian landing craft, known as "floating artillery," that could have been classed as gunboats. These were landing craft carrying field guns, loaded in such a way as to allow some of them to drench the beach with high explosive shells just ahead of their assaulting infantry debouching from landing craft all around them. The principal landing craft were: LSTs (Landing Ship Tank), LCTs (Landing Craft Tank, smaller and of shallower draught), LCIs (Landing Craft Infantry), LCAs (Landing Craft Assault), and LCVPs (Landing Craft Vehicles and Personnel). These statistics are from Chester Wilmot's *The Struggle For Europe* (London: Collins, 1952), p. 180.

PART TWO: JULY 11-17

Introduction to Battlefield Conditions

7

BURON

--- ✳ ---

AT 0530 HOURS, JULY 10, MINIMUM RECCE PARTIES FROM EACH battery, led by the second-in-command of the Regiment (Major Gordon Savage) and the regimental survey officer (Capt. Len Harvey) are warned to be ready to move in half an hour to locate new gun positions. Three hours later, word comes for the recce parties to rendezvous at Buron, about four kilometres northwest of Caen. At 1900 hours the Colonel returns from a meeting with Brig. R. H. Keefler, CRA (Commander Royal Artillery) at 2nd Division Headquarters, with orders for the Regiment to begin the move forward at 2230 to Buron where the guns will be put in action.

Immediately battery and troop advance parties, each consisting of a subaltern and an ack (a highly trained technical assistant) are sent forward to lay out their allotted positions and plant their gun-marker flags to allow the regimental survey party to carry their survey work right up to the marker of each "pivot gun" (the right-hand gun of each troop of four). The survey party will, first, establish the pivot gun's position on the face of the planet in terms of the numbered "grid" overprinting on the large-scale 1/25,000 map; and, second, will pass to each "director" (survey instrument) set on a tripod in front of each troop position and oriented to an identifiable distant aiming point, a precise "grid bearing," so that when the guns arrive the troop will be ready to pass on to each gun for its "dial-sight" the "zero line" (a grid bearing arbitrarily drawn by Divisional Headquarters through the middle of the enemy front). Thus all guns will be in accurate relationship to each other on "Regimental Grid" and their barrels will be parallel to each other, as a starting point for setting ranges and switches to targets.

The advance parties are advised to take along mine detectors so they may check out their areas as they wait for the guns to arrive.

The regimental convoy gets under way on time, but the narrow roads are so clogged with traffic, it takes three hours to complete the move.

It is a time for mixed feelings. At last the guns are going into action, which is a matter of great satisfaction. But you are told the Regiment could find itself in an anti-tank role in its first position, as a last-ditch reserve against a breakthrough by German tanks.

This sounds a bit far-fetched, considering that Caen is now in our hands.* But the warning has to be taken seriously, and it adds to the anxiety induced by the night move over dark, unknown roads without any lights whatsoever, into forbidding territory from which the sounds of gunfire have been almost continuous for the past three days.

It's not only a black night, but the roads are very dusty, and visibility, always poor, sometimes reduces to zero when you are moving

---

* While the warning about a possible tank breakthrough, like everything else about the Buron gun position, would later be looked upon as nothing more than a way of easing the Regiment into battle conditions before it went into action for real, there were some legitimate grounds for worry. The British 43rd Wessex Division, involved in a right hook meant to carry them to the Orne River, south of Caen, attacking south and east from Carpiquet, through Verson over the Odon River to Eterville and Maltot, ran into some very sticky going from heavy German counter-attacks supported by Panther and Tiger tanks on the night of July 10, that continued well into the next day.

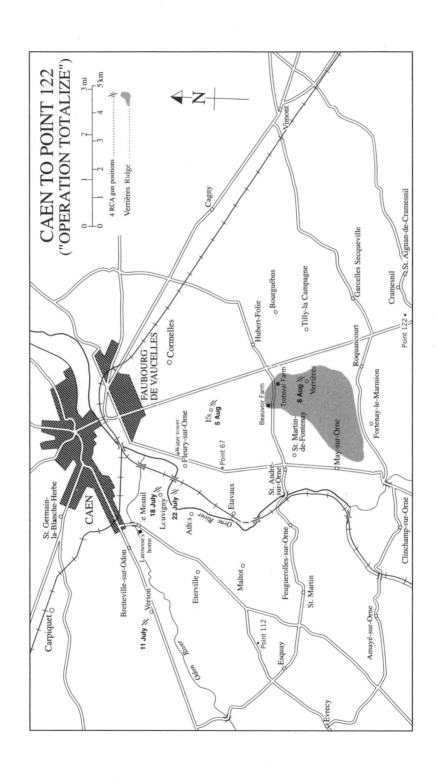

CAEN TO POINT 122
("OPERATION TOTALIZE")

3 mi
5 km

4 RCA gun positions
Verrières Ridge

through the narrow streets of a derelict village. Once, as the convoy is crawling through such a village, it comes to an abrupt halt, and for a time the vehicles sit unmoving with their engines running.

As the dust settles, you can see over on the left, up in the direction of the beaches, that the nightly German air-raid is inspiring the usual fireworks display. Even over the idling truck engines, you can hear the furious pumping sounds of the rapid-firing ack-ack guns – hundreds of muzzles spewing heavenward thousands of white and red tracers, that climb almost leisurely, in endless streams through the wavering searchlight beams, disappearing at great heights where the skies are filled to overflowing with sparkling white bursts.

The reason for the halt becomes apparent as the first, huge, flatbed tank-transporter, carrying a disabled tank, looms up in the gloom and passes between your vehicle and the wall opposite with only inches to spare. For several minutes transports carrying their broken monsters whine and grind by in the dim and dusty night, sometimes scraping the wall of the building opposite. You don't count them as they appear and disappear, but as the minutes pass, and still they go by, you begin to wonder just how many active tanks can be left holding the front up there.

Finally the last one passes and the convoy gets underway again; and while it moves at a crawl most of the time, there are no more long halts until you reach Buron at 1:30 A.M., July 11.

Just beyond the village, the convoy stops on the road until guides from advance parties can lead each troop into its allotted area in the fields. They warn that mines have been turned up around here, and the fields have not been checked out completely. So vehicles are to play follow-the-leader, and the gun sergeants are to dismount and lead their gun tractors in on foot, making sure they follow existing tank tracks. In the dense gloom, with nobody allowed to use lamps-electric, tracks are difficult to see, but somehow all guns are dropped in position with their muzzles pointing south, and all gun tractors get safely back to the main road without blowing up, where they take off back to an area some distance away chosen as their "wagon lines."

After they've left, there is a lot of shouting by the gun position officers of each troop putting their guns on line. Standing with their acks, some fifty yards in front of the guns, working their director with the aid of wavering lamps-electric, they call out to each of their four guns in turn a reverse bearing in degrees and minutes so the gun-layer can set it on his dial sight and traverse his weapon left or right, until his sight is looking directly into the lighted lens of the director and he knows he is laid on the zero line.

But once all the guns in the Regiment have been "put on line" it is suddenly remarkably quiet. The air raid up along the beaches in the north is long since over, and neighbouring artillery tonight seems unusually inactive. Occasionally there are series of explosions in rapid succession, which you ascribe to enemy activity down in the south where fires are flaring on the horizon. But here, only the *clink* of picks and the *snitch-snitch* of shovels digging command posts, gun pits, and personal slit trenches can be heard.

Unquestionably all are conscious that for the first time they are actually within range of the enemy guns. No one seems inclined to talk, and when anyone does say something, he speaks softly, barely above a whisper. And the running patter of derogatory remarks about the army in general, and about the general in particular, that always arose between the gunners engaged in digging during training schemes in England, is totally absent.

Few offer any comment whatsoever. The one notable exception is a man who suddenly starts cursing with great feeling – all the more impressive because he curses quietly, almost under his breath. Questioned by his peers, he explains he was well on his way to completing the digging of his slit trench when he discovered he was uncovering a dead body.

On the way here, you passed through zones of foul odour, readily identifiable as coming from the rotting flesh of unburied dead horses and cows, killed in their stables or fields by shells and mortar bombs. But here, throughout the night, the air is filled with a most peculiarly repulsive odour you have never smelled before. And now and then, when the sultry air stirs, and the ghastly stench assails your nostrils at full strength, you can hardly keep from gagging.

Come daylight you discover the source: decaying bodies of men are everywhere. The sights on all sides are sickening. Obviously the Highlanders of Canadian 3rd Division came up against ferocious resistance from the SS defenders, and not just when they attacked two days ago, but also at some earlier date, for many of these bodies have been here a long time.*

When the battle moved on yesterday, German and Canadian dead were left strewn among the ruins of the village, and in and out of the nearby intricate German trench system that had made this, along with the nearby villages of Gruchy and Authie, a key strong point in the defence of Caen. The heat has done its work, and the indescribable, but unforgettable, stench from the bloated bodies of men surpasses the revolting odours of rotting animals in the nearby fields.

For the first time the men of the Regiment see dead Germans, and the sight induces only mild curiosity, as they study their steel

---

* The Canadians occupied Buron briefly on June 7, the day after D-Day, before being driven back to their startline by the first major enemy counter-attack by a regiment of 12th SS Hitlerjugend Division, under the command of one Kurt Meyer (who, in 1936, as a captain in Hitler's SS Liebstandarte, led the reoccupation of the Rhineland) bent on driving the Canadians back into the sea. Those swaggering, brainwashed young brutes under his command truly believed they could, and when they found they couldn't, they cried tears of frustration in the manner of young boys, which of course many of them were. See page 147 of *Overlord* by Max Hastings (New York: Simon & Schuster, 1984) quoting German Lt. Rudolph Schaaf of 1716th Artillery.

helmets with the two little lightning strokes side by side, signifying that they are SS. But it's another matter to look at the bodies in Canadian battledress, sprawled beside knocked-out vehicles, or huddled behind some bit of ground that had not been cover enough.*

In their diaries on this day, two 26th Battery sergeants make similar observations. Sgt. Bruce Hunt writes: "We see our first German dead. As these represent the ultimate in achievement to which our lives have been dedicated, it's strange the sight produces so little satisfaction; it would be even stranger, I suppose, if it did."

This contrasts with the anguish expressed by Sgt. Charles McEwan on seeing dead Canadians for the first time: "For most of us it was the first dead we had ever seen other than at a funeral, and it ended right then and there all the glory there is in war.

"The sight of dead Germans, no matter in what state of decomposition, does not bother us. But it really does something to you, way down inside, to see good Canadian boys – the pick of our country – lying sprawled across a slit trench or huddled up outside a

---

* At Buron, July 8, Highland Light Infantry had 262 casualties, 62 fatal. Canadian war correspondent Ross Munro, in his postwar book *Gauntlet to Overlord* (Toronto: Macmillan, 1945), would write of the fierce resistance of the Hitlerjugend, at Buron: "The 12th SS, full of young Nazis who had been taught for years to kill and knew little else, had been at grips with 3rd Division since the day after landing . . . Many were youths of seventeen and eighteen, steeped in the Nazi creed and trained through their boyhood for battle. Troops of this division carried out a criminal act on June 7, when they murdered 19 members of the Royal Winnipeg Rifles whom they had taken prisoner. The incident was carefully investigated and later General Crerar officially informed his troops of this murder. But many soldiers knew of this criminal act soon after it happened. The 12th SS was a marked division . . . it was annihilated in the Trun gap (the closing of the Falaise pocket), but it suffered extremely heavily at the hands of the Canadians in this attack on Caen."

burned-out Bren Gun Carrier where they had been shot down after bailing out of the blazing vehicle. It almost makes us sick to our stomachs. . . ."

And in still another diary, begun as a joint enterprise by two Baker Troop sergeants – Johnson and Foley – is found: "German and Allied dead are lying all around in and out of slit trenches. Many of them have been there for some time. They are bloated black and swollen, and the stench of decaying flesh is new and strange and sickening. When daylight breaks, the gruesome job of dragging the dead away from our guns has to be attended to. Quite an initiation. The Glengarians took quite a beating in a sunken road – ambushed."

Burial parties are formed to bury the German bodies in the immediate vicinity. This is allowable, but to bury Canadian bodies, you are advised, the padre must be present, not only to conduct a proper burial service, but also to see that reports are prepared consistent with regulations – and that "dog tags" and map references of the graves get back through the correct channels.

It is afternoon before the burial of the Canadians is undertaken. Over on the right, big guns are rumbling, but here there is only the sound of picks and shovels as the gunners dig shallow holes under the burning July sun to receive the stinking corruptions that once were men. You hear planes, with throttles wide open, high overhead, and a tremendous barrage opens up on ten German fighter planes heading for the ships and the beaches, flying line astern, weaving wildly to escape a profusion of black puffs growing around them. Five are hit and spin down smoking, and five white parachutes drift down in the distance. It's all over in a matter of seconds, but this remarkable display of ack-ack gunnery, the like of which no one has ever seen – not even during the Blitz in 1940 – is cheered lustily by the gunners.

A French civilian, returning to check out the condition of his home in Buron, is offered cans of stew and cigarettes. He in turn comes up with an ancient bottle of a very strong liquor he calls "Calvados."*

He warns that Calvados should be handled with care, and describes, with expressive pantomime, its disastrous effects on the first Canadians who arrived here, alleging that some at least were tipsy when they were hit by an SS counter-attack, with the dire consequences you can now observe about you.

Lieut. Louis Anthony Verdeil, 26th Battery ACPO, who is able to converse with him in French, learns of the deep hatred the people of occupied France have developed for the Boche. The man tells a fearful story of Gestapo savagery on D-Day against Frenchmen suspected of being members of the underground resistance movement.†

You take a break and visit the ruins of the village. Burned-out tanks, Bren carriers, and other vehicles lie here and there throughout the area. And strewn about the trenches is a clutter of German and Canadian equipment, including weapons of all kinds and live ammunition. One of the more curious items you come across lying in the front entry of a broken house is a sizeable case of German rifle ammunition – the brass cartridges as shiny and bright as though manufactured yesterday, but armed with bullets of hardwood, painted red, in place of regular steel-jacketed lead bullets.

----

*   Taking its name from the region, Calvados is distilled from hard apple cider, at an alcoholic strength of seventy degrees, some 55 per cent stronger than the legal strength of forty-five degrees for brandy and Scotch.

†   The Gestapo shot 87 of 88 men of the FFI (Free Forces of the Interior) held in the Caen prison on D-Day. Years after, the author became a friend of the 88th man, Marcellus Barjaud, who survived because he did not respond to the call by the German guard yelling, incorrectly, "Mario Barjaud." He was subsequently transferred with others to the infamous Frennes prison in Paris.

8

INTRODUCTION TO ETERVILLE
AND HILL 112

———————————— ✳ ————————————

AS THE GUNS ARE BEING MOVED INTO POSITION AND READIED for action near Buron on the night of July 10–11, the three infantry battalions of 4th Brigade – the Royal Regiment of Canada (Royals), the Royal Hamilton Light Infantry (Rileys), and the Essex Scottish – which 4th Field will be supporting until the end of the war, are moving into reserve positions four thousand yards south, on the western outskirts of Caen.

From their positions in slit trenches and buildings, taken over from the Regina Rifles in St. Germaine-la-Blanche-Herbe, the Royals can see and hear a tank battle two or three miles to the southwest, which they observe with interest. By midnight, the horizon is grimly lit with the flames of half a dozen or more burning tanks, but they watch with a certain detachment, unaware that the distant battle, raging on throughout the night, is deciding who will possess the fields, the orchards, and a smashed village that within twenty-four hours will be their responsibility.

Desperately, the British are defending their new gains over the Odon against bitter counter-attacks by the SS and their frightful Tiger tanks, bent on wiping out the salient by driving them from Hill 112 and from Eterville, on its northeastern slope, which the Royals will take over tomorrow night.

The British first started fighting for their bridgehead over the

Odon and for domination of Hill 112 two weeks ago, on June 26, with an attack by 60,000 men of VIII Corps and 600 tanks, supported by 700 guns, including battleships anchored off the beaches.

In the opening attack of "Operation Epsom," designed to be the start of an encirclement of Caen through a right hook, they had moved south and east on a four-mile front, west of Carpiquet, towards the wooded ravines of the little Odon river. By the first night they'd gained three miles, but were locked in a struggle of awesome intensity that continued through the 27th and the 28th.

Finally, 11th Armoured Div, in the mud and rain, made it across the bloodstained stream, and on June 29, gained the summit of Hill 112, just in time to repulse a counter-attack by 9th and 10th SS Panzer Divisions of 2nd Panzer Corps.*

The commander of German 7th Army, Colonel-General Dollman, had attached so much importance to wiping out this salient over the Odon, that he'd collapsed and died on the second day of the battle in despair (some say by suicide), believing the British had the all-important heights firmly in their grasp and that he'd let his Führer down. But so tenuous had been the British hold on the hill that, later the same day, Gen. Dempsey, fearing his armour was at risk in the shallow bridgehead, had withdrawn all the tanks of 11th Armoured Division to the north bank of the Odon, allowing the enemy to regain Hill 112. In the four days of Operation Epsom, British 8th Corps lost 4,020 men.

Now, just ten days later, while Canadian 3rd Division and British 3rd Division are consolidating their gains in Caen, battalions of the 43rd Wessex Division are suffering another 2,000 casualties in renewed fighting for Hill 112 as they attempt to extend the Odon salient south and east, down to the Orne by way of Verson, Eterville, and Maltot.

---

* Newly arrived in France from having halted the Russian offensive at Tarnopol, 2nd Panzer Corps carried orders from Hitler to drive the Allies into the sea.

Initially, the dawn attack had gone well, following in behind the huge bombardment, and by 8:00 A.M. the 4th Dorsets had gained Eterville, and other units were well up Hill 112. But the Germans mounted such strong counter-attacks that the British were thrown on the defensive.

Successive battalion attacks by the Somersets and the 5th Duke of Cornwall's Light Infantry failed to gain the summit of 112, and they were forced to dig in on the northern slope of that dominating feature. And two attacks – one of brigade strength supported by M-10s (self-propelled 17-pounders), down the hill from Eterville to low-lying Maltot, about 1,300 metres farther south, had been shattered by the huge Tiger tanks of 2nd SS Panzer Corps and an extraordinarily intense bombardment by guns and mortars massed along the high ground east of the Orne that the Canadians would soon come to know as Verrières Ridge.*

By last light, July 10, the wheat fields between Eterville and Maltot and up the slopes of Hill 112 were dotted with blackened, burned-out Churchills and M-10s.

A vivid description of the severe conditions around Eterville position during the night of July 10 and throughout July 11 was recorded by the historian of the British 43rd Wessex Division:

> . . . Soon after dark the enemy penetrated Eterville, where hand-to-hand fighting with the Cameronians (who'd taken over from the 4th Dorsets) went on all night and continued till 8:00 A.M. when he finally withdrew leaving over a hundred dead. On the front of the 5th Dorset and 7th Somerset Light Infantry, a heavy counter-attack with tanks and infantry developed soon after dawn, only to be beaten back with huge loss, by our artillery, anti-tank and mortar fire.
>
> All day (July 11) Tiger tanks, lying back beyond the crest,

---

* British writers refer to it as Bourguébus Ridge after the village they seized on the left flank during the second day of Operation Goodwood.

probed the forward defences in the open fields. The least move-ment brought down intense automatic fire. The mortaring went on without respite. It must be admitted that the German armour was less vulnerable than our own. If any of our Churchills appeared on the skyline, they were invariably hit and brewed up. The crest of the hill was littered with evidence to this effect. Meanwhile the constant stream of casualties continued to flow. It was only too clear that we had been forced on to the defensive."*

---

* From Second British Army Intelligence Summaries No. 3b, quoted in Report No. 58, Historical Section (G.S.) Canadian Army Headquarters, Dept. of National Defence, p. 45.

9

MOVING UP TO SUPPORT
THE SALIENT OVER ODON

———————————— ✳ ————————————

THE REGIMENT IS NOT CALLED UPON TO FIRE A ROUND ALL DAY, and at 5:00 P.M. it is ordered to move forward to its first real position in action, in support of 4th Brigade infantry moving into the front line tonight. The 2nd Division is taking over from the British about 4,000 yards of the front, running from their positions along the northern slope of Hill 112, northeast to the 3rd Canadian Division, positions centred in Caen.

With the message to limber up and move comes a warning that the convoy may be subjected to some airbursts as it passes beyond Carpiquet on the way to the new positions. This causes concern, especially among the gun sergeants, who are required to stand with their heads and shoulders protruding through the hatch in the roof of their gun tractors when going into action. But nothing descends on the convoy, though Sgt. McEwan's diary will record "a fearful lot of shell-fire" falling to the right of the road on the way forward.

The move is through the smashed village of Carpiquet, past the badly holed and ragged airport, with strips of corrugated iron hanging forlornly from the steel skeletons of hangars. There, advance parties are waiting to lead the Regiment down a steep, chalky trail to an exceedingly dusty sunken road, leading southeast towards Verson and Eterville across a shallow, broad valley of open fields devoid of all buildings, trees, hedges, and even fences. An ideal place for tanks to do battle, you think in your ignorance of the reality of such matters. But nothing seems to have taken place here – at least no derelicts are visible, and until now the lush sugar beet fields have flourished undisturbed except for some widely spaced tank tracks slicing across them.

About a kilometre short of Verson, the Regiment is directed left, into positions in a beet field just off the sunken road.

The two troops of 2nd Battery are positioned unusually close together at the forward end of the positions, directly in front of and less than 100 yards from the muzzles of 14th Battery guns. The 26th is down the slope a little to the left rear. Never before have you seen all twenty-four guns of 4th Field deployed in such a small area, in total contravention of the most basic principle governing the deployment of guns, drilled into every gunner's head during training since Dunkirk: that batteries, troops, and individual guns must be dispersed as widely as practical so as to deny enemy bombers, strafing planes, and artillery the chance to hit a concentrated target.

However, the reason for this jamming up of the three battery positions becomes clear when it is pointed out by Major Gordon Savage, the second-in-command, who is here to watch the deployment, that the whole area allotted to 4th Field is under enemy observation from the distant high ground over the Orne down there on your left front. For this reason he's tried to get as much cover as possible for the troops by crowding them into this one corner of the valley, which bends back behind a bit of a rise with some bushes along the crest. While no troop can be completely hidden from the enemy here, this at least cuts down the amount of enemy high ground overlooking 4th Field.

He doesn't envy 5th and 6th Field, who'll be deploying over on our left, tomorrow, even more plainly in view than 4th Field. The digging is easy, and the guns and ammunition are put below grade with almost leisurely digging. British guns over on the right are rumbling away, but it is so peaceful here, it's as though you are on a training scheme in England. One gunner even remarks that this is just like Exercise Spartan (the largest of all British training schemes) with live ammunition. And as you watch great holes being excavated in the deep, fertile earth – including gun pits eighteen feet in diameter – you can't shake the feeling you are participating in an act of vandalism – an idea that first hit you as you directed the big quads, dragging heavy ammunition limbers and guns behind them, into position over the neat rows of sugar beets, crushing them to pulp.

But then an enemy shell lands with a terrific *crack* on Baker Troop position – just one, as though they are registering a target before it grows too dark. Fortunately it lands far enough away that no one is hurt, for it catches everybody standing upright. But it does make the shovels go faster, and goes a long way to restoring your own perspective of war and its priorities.

The valley opens to the southeast, sloping gently down towards the Orne some six kilometres away, where on the high ground, identifiable on the map as enemy territory just over the river at Fleury-sur-Orne, can be seen one of those peculiarly Norman, concrete water-towers. While directly south, over the road alongside the right of the gun position, the ground climbs gradually to a high point 3,600 metres away, its crest marked on the map by an oval contour 112.

As the Regiment digs gun pits, ammunition pits, command posts, and personal slit trenches, with the reddish glow of a rich sunset casting long, black shadows of guns and men across the beet fields, everyone is more than a bit anxious as to what the future holds for them. But no one has any idea that this will be the worst position the Regiment will ever occupy in action.

It is obvious to officers with maps, and to all who have eyes and can ask questions, that this natural amphitheatre overlooks the enemy-held high ground over the Orne, and that if you can see his position then he must be able to see yours equally well, if not better. Still, no one, no matter how long he stares apprehensively at the unforgettable water-tower standing sinister like a huge mushroom over there across the Orne, can imagine on this quiet, balmy evening what is to come, for no one can bring himself to believe the brass would place in jeopardy all seventy-two guns of the division by deploying them in full view of the enemy.

And even when things turn bad, it will be accepted without beefing, without blaming anybody, as the way war is: hell is to be expected, and the deployment of the guns within sight of the enemy must have been necessary because of the overcrowding in the confined bridgehead.

All six troop commanders are up with 4th Brigade, two with each battalion, but they won't occupy observation posts (OPs) as forward observation officers (FOOs) at the front until the infantry battalions take over from the British some 3,000 yards south of the guns around Eterville, the next village beyond Verson.

The guns aren't firing, though a "hostile mortar list" is received, with no fewer than 112 targets on it.

Just after dark, the field across the road fills with tanks coming back from the direction of Verson. And now and then the valley fills with a deep, reverberating roar of guns somewhere on the left rear. The consensus is that they are mediums (5.5-inch guns) engaged in counter-battery work – delivering 100-pound high explosive shells on suspected enemy gun and mortar positions.

10

ETERVILLE

———————————— ✳ ————————————

SO INTENSE ARE THE GERMAN ASSAULTS ON ETERVILLE AND THE slopes of that infamous Hill 112, rising west of the village, that Gen. Montgomery, Commander-in-Chief of all Allied ground forces in Normandy, in replying this night of July 11 to congratulations from Churchill on the capture of Caen, is impelled to inform the Prime Minister:

"All today 9th and 10th SS Panzer Divisions have been attacking furiously to retake Pt. 112 to the northeast of Evrecy."*

This then is the situation into which the 4th Brigade is moving the night of July 11, when at 11:30 P.M. July 11 the three armoured White Scout Cars of the battery commanders (one for each battalion), and the six carriers of the troop commanders (two for each battalion) who will serve as forward observation officers, join a long line of troops trudging down through Venoix and Bretteville-sur-Odon towards Verson some five kilometres away. Here, they will cross a narrow stone bridge over the Odon and disperse to their allotted positions in and around Eterville in the salient.

After crossing, the Royals will continue straight on into the village of Eterville, a mile southeast of the Odon, to take over

———————
* Winston Churchill, *Triumph and Tragedy* (Bantam Books, 1962), p. 26.

from the Glasgow Highlanders of 15th Scottish Division, who only this day relieved the 9th Cameronians. The Rileys will bear left beyond the Odon, moving forward to the reverse slope of a gentle hill just northeast of Eterville to take over from a battalion of the British Black Watch. On their left flank will be the Fusiliers Mont-Royal, of 6th Brigade, who are taking over from the Régiment de le Chaudière, just short of the road from Caen to Eterville. The Essex Scottish will relieve the Cameronians in their reserve position, just south of the Odon, at Rocrenil, about a mile north of Eterville.

From now on, whenever 4th Brigade is in the line, the CO of 4th Field will move with the infantry brigadier, serving as his "arty rep" (artillery representative), advising and laying on fire plans, involving not only 4th Field and the other two 2nd Division field regiments, but medium and heavy guns as necessary to thicken up support, or concentrate massive fire on enemy counter-attacking forces. Similarly, from now on, each of the three infantry battalion commanders will have one of the 4th Field battery commanders at his side morning, noon, and night.

However, it will be through the eyes of the six troop commanders – the FOOs – keeping the front under constant surveillance from OPs (observation posts) established in close contact with frontline company commanders, that the whole vast network of artillery representatives – leading back through the majors to the colonel, to the Brigadier CRA at Division, to the CCRA (Commander Corps Royal Artillery) at Corps Headquarters – will be kept in the picture. Normally FOOs are attached to specific companies in an operation, and as the battalion moves forward into the line, they move with them. But because it is the first time up for 4th Field FOOs, the FOOs of the British artillery unit supporting the three British battalions being relieved volunteer to guide them into their various positions. This might have worked out to everyone's benefit, except for the innovative method, invoked by the CO of 4th Field, of pairing up FOOs with their guides, resulting in only one troop commander getting to where he is supposed to be. Both 2nd Battery troop commanders, Capt. Stuart "Stu" Laurie, Able Troop, and Capt. Gordon Hunter, Baker Troop, end up with the Rileys instead of the Royals. Capt. "Sammy" Grange, Fox Troop, 26th Battery, who customarily moves with the Essex Scottish, finds himself with the Royals at Eterville, as does Capt. Britton "Brit" Smith, of 14th Battery, who normally would be with the Rileys. And the other 14th Battery troop commander, Capt. Jack Thompson, ends up with the Essex Scottish. Only Capt. Reginald Parker, Easy Troop, connects with a guide that takes him to his correct battalion, the Essex Scottish.

To non-gunners, it might seem of little consequence which troop commander goes with which battalion, since all the guns in the Regiment are available and can be concentrated on targets by any arty rep at any level. Nevertheless – as a matter of tradition, training, and equitable employment of the FOOs – each battery has been paired off with its own battalion for years now: 2nd Battery with the Royals, 14th with the Rileys, and 26th with the Essex Scottish. Thus in this first-ever move up to the front, when FOOs are seemingly shuffled like a deck of cards, and only one of them ends up with the correct battalion, confusion and anxiety are added to an already confusing and anxious night.

Stu Laurie will remember the bewildering turmoil maintaining at the rendezvous point in Bretteville-sur-Odon, where the 4th Field captains are to be met by the guides from the British units they are relieving:

> The rendezvous is on the main street, with a great confusion of troops and vehicles passing through. The place is on fire, and it is being heavily shelled continuously. Finally "Bud" Drury [CO of 4th Field] says, "Find somebody and go with him!"
>
> So we just grab hold of the first Englishman we find who is there to take us where we're supposed to go. As it turns out, he's a guide to where the RHLI are taking over, not to Eterville where

the Royals are headed. Just as we start off, this guy says he knows a shortcut, and as we go along this track we come to a little stone bridge over the river Odon. It's a very narrow bridge, only the width of one vehicle, and there's a great hole blown in the middle of it, so I get out in front of the carrier to try to guide it past the hole. All of a sudden the most god-awful mess of Moaning Minnies comes whirling at us. I dive under the carrier and promptly get run over.

Ryckman [Gunner George Ryckman] lets go of the brakes or something, and it rolls ahead. One track runs over one of my knees. Now, you know the track on a carrier is springy, but it is not that springy! [A universal carrier weighs four tons unloaded.] And I'm screaming bloody murder! So when Ryckman backs it off me and off the bridge, our guide decides we won't go this way; it's a little too tough to get across that bridge.

We go back around and up another way, up a long lane where I notice there are no leaves on the trees – they're all on the ground. The ground is covered with leaves though this is July. And for some reason they've been mounded up in random piles, one here and one there, all along the way. I wonder what the hell is this all about? And when I investigate one of the mounds, I find the body of an English soldier. Suddenly it all becomes clear: all these mounds are unburied dead men covered with leaves that floated down after being blown off the trees by shell-fire. Boy! They really had been plastered on their way in here. And at the moment we aren't doing too badly ourselves.*

Of that night, all FOOs, acks, signallers, and drivers of the six 4th Field carriers, interspersed between companies along the line of march of some two thousand walking troops, moving slowly up that forbidding road during the blackest midnight hours, will

---

* Author interview.

remember above all else the fearful tension. Everyone moving through the sinister gloom past smashed buildings and derelict vehicles, lit only now and then by the flash of a mortar bomb, is subject to it.

At one point the column freezes in the obscene glare of a chandelier flare suspended from a little parachute, dropped by an enemy aircraft droning overhead, and everyone expects the worst. But the thing burns out without anything happening.

This is a new and frightening experience, moving up to the front at night. All are holding their breath, if not physically at least mentally, hoping the changeover can be effected without arousing the Germans and drawing heavy fire before they are settled in trenches.

Brit Smith will remember it as something of a nightmare, with the nervous system strained to the breaking point every now and then, when soldiers shift their packs and the muggy night is filled with an unholy rattling of enamelled tin cups, hanging from a strap on the outside of every small pack, clashing with equally resonant trenching-tools dangling beside them. When whole companies flop down on the road at the sizzle of a mortar bomb or the whine of an incoming shell, Brit is certain the "god-awful clattering is enough to wake every German within ten miles."

Then the racket of vehicles starting and stopping along the last mile to Eterville – when the Royals' column becomes entangled with the British vehicles moving out – is nothing short of horrifying to the ears of men who have been hoping to sneak into the front-line trenches without drawing enemy fire.

Years after, Royals' officers will recall how in the words of one, Robert Suckling, "the quiet of the night is made hideous with the noise of racing motors, clashing gears, and grinding trucks."

However, though there is some mortaring and shelling on the way in, and a lot more after the Royals get into position, the enemy never really takes advantage of the confusion to attack as he had the night before with such ferocity. It would seem the Germans on this front on the night of July 11 are simply too exhausted from all the attacks and counter-attacks in which they have been engaged during the last twenty-four hours in Maltot, on Hill 112, and particularly in Eterville.

II

YOUR FIRST ROUNDS FIRED

IN ANGER

※

BACK AT THE GUNS, DURING THE NIGHT CAN BE HEARD THE
other two 2nd Division regiments (5th and 6th Field) moving their
guns into position down in the valley over on the left. And at dawn,
looking down at them, it is obvious they are even more exposed to
enemy observation than 4th Field. Each freshly dug pit is clearly
visible, and camouflage nets, draped on poles above each gun in
good old Alfriston Practice Ranges' style, in the same way they are
tented over each 4th Field gun, would never confuse any enemy
artillery observer.*

You find it impossible to shake the feeling that there's an irrational "Charge of the Light Brigade" quality about the positioning
of 2nd Division guns. There are awkward questions from your

---

* 6th Field stuck it out for five days in the valley, miraculously losing
only twelve men and one gun. Then, according to their Regimental
History, after firing 250 rounds per gun on a fire plan on behalf of the
British 43rd Division attack over on the right, that began 3:00 A.M. on
July 17, two of their batteries "moved back over the hill behind RHQ,
leaving the old positions rigged as real as our camouflage nets and
wooden pieces could make it. The deception worked, for that morning
Jerry gave it a real plastering which, we saw later, knocked out two 'guns'
and enlarged the old E Troop Command Post considerably."

NCOs, such as "Who was the idiot that picked these positions for 4th Field, Sir?" And the line "Into the valley of death, into the mouth of hell" insists on going round and round in your head.

Still you cling to the belief that Brig. Bruce Matthews, 2nd Canadian Corps CCRA (Corps Commander Royal Artillery), and Brig. R. F. Keefler CRA 2nd Division, are not madmen, that they must have been forced to deploy the guns here because of a shortage of concealed positions within range of possible operations, due to the awesome accumulation of guns in the bridgehead.

Certainly, the sight of the entire division (seventy-two guns) arrayed in such a small area makes you realize the extent of the gigantic buildup that has been going on for a month, and which any day now will be unleashed for the break-out from the bridgehead, an operation for which 2nd Division trained so long in Britain.

Shortly after dawn on July 12, Stu Laurie, up at Eterville, three and a half kilometres southeast of here, reports his OP is being heavily shelled.

At 7:13 A.M. the Regiment fires its first "rounds in anger" on "an enemy infantry area."

At 8:30 A.M. the war diary records the Regiment is "on theatre grid," meaning the positions of your guns are now accurately fixed in relation to all other surveyed-in guns throughout the entire British-Canadian forces in Normandy, allowing all guns to be brought to bear on a single target, if so required, with equal accuracy at any time.

And at about 9:45 A.M. all ranks experience for the first time the nerve-wracking sensation of crouching in holes in the ground as the air is ripped around you and the earth shakes under you. Shells crash in, one after another, until it seems that they'll never stop – the smashes of sound shattering your wits and the shuddering concussions destroying all sense of equilibrium. And when every hole around here must have been hit except this one, it is suddenly quiet – so quiet the buzz of flies is noticeably loud.

Then the damage is assessed. You call over the Tannoy to the guns:

"Number One Gun, you all right?"

A pause, then a faint, "Okay."

"Number Two?

"Okay."

"Number Three?"

"Okay."

"Number Four?"

"Okay."

You can hardly believe it. No one was hit! And no equipment was lost. How utterly miraculous! Obviously slit trenches are the answer, but it is generally agreed that these "are not quite deep enough."

The Regiment's first casualty requiring evacuation is an OP signaller, Gunner Ernst Hodgkinson. Gun Sgt. Nick Ostapyck, of 14th Battery, was wounded slightly yesterday, but he was able to remain on duty. Others wounded today are 26th Battery Signal Sgt. Allan Lawson, Gunner Norman Coughlin, and Gunner Benjamin Parker.

Shelling continues spasmodically, and enemy planes bomb and strafe all positions from Verson up through the valley to Carpiquet aerodrome. Sgt. Bruce Hunt will record in his diary: "Had the distinction of being strafed. A worm's-eye view showed about eight 109s diving on the guns . . . momentarily over the pits, firing all the while. Near misses registered all around us and shelling pretty continuous."

12

FOOS NEED RELIEF AFTER
ONLY TWO DAYS

✳

THE SHELLING THAT SEEMED SO BAD YESTERDAY IS WORSE
today. Right after the Regiment opened up on some counter-
mortar bombards this morning, the Germans retaliated with devastating accuracy, showering the gun positions with shells of all
calibres more or less steadily for two hours, causing eighteen casualties, four of them fatal. Baker Troop suffered especially, losing two
guns through direct hits. The shell that knocked out their Number
Three gun killed Bombardier Ron Hooper and Gunner Mervin
Bond instantly. Three other crew members were evacuated. One of
them, Gunner Adrian Lennon, was wounded so severely he will
not survive.

Miraculously, the crew of Number Two gun, the other gun disabled by a direct hit, escaped without a scratch.

During this hellish period, a heavy shell landed on Easy Troop
Command Post, killing Gunner Norman Lockeyer, and wounding
gunners Ray McLeod and John Weiss. Weiss produced a haunting
image for buddies who set out to catch and restrain him, when he
took off in panic from the wrecked command post, running a
mindless pattern across the shell-torn field with jagged fragments of
shell sticking out of his skull like horns.

Concussion from the same shell rendered the gun position
officer, Lieut. Harold "Ali" Barber, temporarily unconscious, and

burst the eardrums of Signaller Owen Hennessy, who eventually had to be evacuated.

Among the most unforgettable sights during these first days of action, is that of the MO (medical officer), still wearing the three-buckle overshoes he personally adopted as standard footwear on schemes in muddy old England, galloping across the dusty, sun-baked beet field from RHQ on his way to attend the wounded and dying at Baker and Easy troops even before there is any real break in the shelling.

An MO isn't supposed to go to the wounded; they are supposed to be brought to him at his regimental aid post by stretcher-bearers. But Dr. Burt Talmage Dunham is not one to let convention or custom inhibit his actions – as the sound of those ridiculous over-shoes, plop-plopping urgently past your command-post dugout while shells still scream and crash about the position, clearly attests. In the eyes of every man in 4th Field who witnessed his outsized courage and compassion today, he is a special kind of hero. And this is the man who told you one time in England that he was worried he might not show up too well in action – that he was, after all, on his way to becoming a baby specialist when, in a rash moment, he decided to enlist.

Days of the week, having no relevance to life here, have ceased to exist. Dates of the month, being only slightly more useful, threaten to disappear, and certainly will always be the subject of argument, even for those keeping diaries. But some dates will remain imprinted on the brain indelibly, such as July 13, 1944, the first time you are sent up as a FOO.

You only know it's the 13th because late in the day, when the German shelling slackens, you decide it's time you let your wife know you are okay using one of the preprinted cards they issued on the ship coming to France, anticipating conditions might not be conducive to letter-writing. All you have to do is address the card, check off the phrases you think appropriate, (such as "I am well,"

"Writing soon," and sign it, and it can start back to a base post-office through the supply chain, beginning with Sgt.-Maj. Tommy Mann when he brings up the rations tonight. However, dating the card presents a problem. Eventually a consensus of sorts establishes it is the 13th. And just as you launch into a detailed dissertation, pooh-poohing the bad-luck traditions of the date and listing all the good things that have happened to you on the 13th, the field telephone starts buzzing.

"Hutch" takes the message: You are to report to Battery Command Post, prepared to go up to the OP to relieve Capt. Laurie, who has exchanged battalions with Brit Smith. You are to check in with Major Wren at tactical headquarters of the Royal Regiment on the way up. Lieut. Bill Dunning, troop leader (assistant GPO) of Baker Troop, will be going up with you to relieve his troop commander, Capt. Gordon Hunter. You don't have to worry about rations and water; they will be in the carrier now on its way up from the wagon lines. You are to take an ack and a signaller up with you.

Conscious that all members of a carrier crew, other than the FOO, are volunteers (the risks being greater up there) you wonder what will happen now. Who could blame them if they chose not to volunteer for something that could prove even worse than the punishing existence they are enduring here. So when that pungent question, "Who wants to go up to the OP?" is posed, and for several seconds the only sound in the confined dugout is of deep breathing, you worry.

When at last two voices quietly announce they'll go, a wave of gratitude, without parallel, sweeps over you, humbling you as you realize two men have chosen to trust you and share with you the risks up there. Your heart goes out to Gunner Don Kirby, who'll be your signaller, and Gunner John Elder, who'll be your ack, as they fish out their kit from under GA, and extract what they want to take along.

Collecting your helmet and map board, hanging your binoculars around your neck, patting your compass and pistol to make sure they are in their cases on your web belt, and checking your pockets to ensure you've got extra smokes, matches, and lots of "Boiled Sweets," you set off for the battery command post. It's only a short way as the crow flies, just on the right along the sunken road. But not wanting to be caught more than diving distance from a hole when you hear the first whisper of an incoming shell, you lead your crew on a circuitous route, passing behind the gun pits as though on your way to the latrine.

As you stride briskly along, you're suddenly aware that your eyes, with no conscious direction from you, are darting here and there in the manner of an animal – searching, identifying, and measuring the distance to holes or folds in the ground in which you might possibly shelter, should the need arise. How quickly a man adopts techniques for survival once it's necessary. Only yesterday, for the first time in your life, you were forced to dive for shelter from shells and mortars, but already you have learned to tell in a split second – from the slightest whisper, crackle, or whine of mortar bomb or shell – if it's on line, and whether it will land close by or crash harmlessly beyond. Several times today you saw gunners standing bolt upright, watching 5th and 6th Field down in the valley taking their turns being shelled. And at one point, you made note that many kept their heads up to watch shells bursting black and ominous among the gun pits of friends in 26th Battery, less than 400 yards away to left rear.

Just short of the sunken road, you turn right and follow the lip of the field until you reach the dugout excavated in the deep bank next to the shallow ditch and road. Roofed over like your troop command post, with earth-covered corrugated-iron sheets from a hangar at Carpiquet aerodrome, it has been dug, and the earth mounded about in such a way, as to leave the grade-level turf of the lip of the field to serve as a table for the artillery boards. A shallow port, extending the full extent of this earthen table, some six feet long, has been left open for ventilation and light, and this, you note, can be closed off at night by a tarpaulin anchored with stones along the top of the dugout.

To look in, you are forced to kneel on the ground. Working with needle-pointed pencils on the gridded paper pinned to their artillery boards, plotting targets, measuring with arm and arc, and filling in long sheets of paper with neat columns of figures, are two CPO acks (Command Post Officer Assistants), one of them the garrulous Sgt. John Dunsmore. And standing behind them, where he can oversee the work, is Lieut. Gordon Lennox, the CPO.

When Lennox looks up at you wearily, you notice he's covered with dust. All of them are covered with dust – their hands, their faces, even their eyelids – and the wrinkles around their eyes and across their foreheads show up as sweaty, dark lines.

Immediately you realize why, as you follow the course of a truck that has come down off the Carpiquet aerodrome escarpment and is roaring towards the gun positions with a dust cloud billowing up behind it. As it passes within a few feet of where you are kneeling, the dust roils up and enshrouds the dugout and everybody in it. You try holding your breath until it settles, but with no wind it takes an age, and eventually you join the others in coughing and spitting sand.

When finally you can again see into the dugout, Lennox is grinning at you from ear to ear and chuckling in that unique staccato fashion he always manages when things are just too damned ridiculous for sensible comment. Then, as if to say, Look at what we have to work on under these frigging-awful conditions, he hands you up a list of map references under the heading: Hostile Mortar List. There are some forty targets on the list, and when you realize that they are working out the line, range, and angle of sight of all of them for both troops in the battery, you hasten to return it to him.

As he passes it on to the waiting acks, he volunteers: "They'll be sent to the troops on hostile-battery record forms as timed programs for harassing fire tonight. Let's hope some of the guns that have been plastering us are on it."

Dunsmore, who makes it a rule never to miss a chance to comment derisively on each and every situation as it arises, looks up grinning, as he wipes sand from his artillery board with his battledress sleeve. Then, baring his teeth and grinding them as though testing the sand content of his mouth, he starts to sing in a loud and raucous voice, affecting a Cockney accent:

"Ow, Ow, Ow – What a luvully waw! . . ."

However, he immediately loses his audience with the arrival of your carrier with its own dust cloud. You climb in front with the driver, Gunner W. "Buck" Saunders. Lieut. Bill Dunning, who has just arrived from Baker Troop, joins Kirby and Elder in one of the rear compartments on each side of the engine, which, in a Universal carrier, sits amidships dividing the main body-box in two. It must be a tight squeeze. Even when equipment is stowed cunningly by an experienced crew, it always appears to have been loaded helter-skelter, and whoever loaded this carrier was less than experienced.

But somehow they are able to jam themselves in among the clutter of remote-control cables, Compo rations, personal weapons, and a great confusion of small packs, tarpaulins, and extra batteries for the three radio sets: the main 19-set transmitter-receiver, the back-packing 18-set, and the little walkie-talkie 38-set.

As you move off, up the sunken road towards the village of Verson, you marvel at how smoothly a carrier rides. There is only a slight rocking as you pass over the railway crossing. The "bogie wheels," on which the track is suspended, are individually sprung, so that all the lumps and ruts in the worn and shell-pitted road are absorbed by the tracks bulging up and down.

It's been so long since you rode in a carrier it's like a brand-new experience. Although you were taught how to drive one during your officer's training, you seldom have been in one since, even during those big training schemes in England, which raises the whole question of your training for your current assignment with the infantry.

During the years of truly intensive training in England, while you received a solid grounding in the tactical application of artillery in support of the infantry and tanks, you were given no opportunity to work with the infantry as a Forward Observation Officer.

You are confident enough of your ability to handle all the technical work of a FOO – having received excellent training in the basic job of observing fire and correcting the guns onto targets of all kinds, through countless hours of practice on miniature smoke-table ranges, in addition to frequent opportunities to range real guns with live shells onto targets on the Alfriston and Senneybridge ranges. But you have no experience whatsoever working as a FOO with the infantry. On all major training schemes, involving the infantry and other arms of the service – sometimes extending over several days as in the case of the monster exercise Spartan – "Fooing" was always reserved exclusively for the elite troop commanders. Subalterns were kept fully occupied with all the problems of the guns, and seldom had time even to imagine what their captains might be involved in.

And now, only thirty-six hours after the Regiment has gone into action for the first time in direct support of the infantry in the line, you and another subaltern are on your way up to relieve two of these troop commanders.

As you approach the devastation that was once the village of Verson, you find yourself struggling to suppress the tension rising within you. While you think you have an idea what a front-line rifle company position might look like, deduced from seeing that cluster of abandoned infantry slit trenches and bodies lying about at that first gun position back at Buron, you haven't a clue what a battalion headquarters in action should look like. You worry you may not recognize it when you get to it.

Then, one after another, a succession of other silly worries rise up to plague you, until you realize they all spring from one general concern: unless you are careful, you are going to appear stupid in the eyes of the infantry. You tell yourself that all you can do is take things one step at a time, and maybe your inexperience won't show before you have learned the score.

You concentrate on the scene around you.

Verson has been pitifully smashed. As you pass through a tangle of dusty rubble, downed power-lines, and broken walls, you wonder where 4th Brigade Headquarters is located. On all sides are roofless, doorless, windowless, half-standing buildings, smelling of charred wood and the musty dust of ancient stables – overlaid by an all-pervasive acetic odour of souring apple cider leaking from punctured barrels, mixed with whiffs of a distinctive and repulsive odour which, from your Buron experience, you readily identify as rotting human flesh.*

The road you seek leads south from Verson through fields and hedges to Eterville, bearing off to the right, dipping down and passing over a watery ditch, which, according to your map, is the Odon River. The narrow stone bridge spanning this little stream, even in its chipped and scarred state, still exudes a certain charm, and the very fact it is still standing is remarkable. Besides escaping demolition by both sides, it has continued to withstand the passage of 50-ton Churchill tanks going and coming morning and night – to say nothing of 44-ton Panthers and the monster 75-ton Royal Tigers that must have been using it until a few days ago.

----

* Before Verson became a target for German shells and bombs, it was a special target for Allied bombardment as it was the headquarters of the 12th SS Hitlerjugend (Hitler Youth) Panzer Division. And Brigadeführer Fritz Witt, who preceded Kurt Meyer as division commander, was killed here by a British naval shell, June 16.

13

BATTALION TAC HEADQUARTERS
IN NORMANDY

———————————— ✳ ————————————

FOR A SHORT WHILE YOU GRIND ALONG THE NARROW ROAD, lined with trees rising out of a thick hedgerow along its right side, with no sign of troops or equipment of any kind. The fierce sun, which has baked the yellowing wheat fields dry and dusty throughout the whole of this cloudless day, turns blood red on the western horizon, promising another blistering day tomorrow. As it is dropping out of sight beyond the British zone on the right, and the road is about to make a 90-degree turn to the left, having come up against a dense line of trees, you motion to Saunders to swivel the carrier through an opening in the corner of the field on the right, directly into the sun's blinding rays.

Just inside the gateway, you halt the carrier to look around. On your left there are some trenches dug up against a stone wall enclosing some woods. According to the map, the wall, enclosing the heavily treed grounds of a château, marks the northwest corner of the village of Eterville.

Your map reference for Battalion Tactical Headquarters of the Royal Regiment of Canada is this corner of this field, but you see nothing here that in your judgement would be worthy of that resounding title – not that you are qualified to make such a judgement, never having visited an infantry battalion headquarters before in your life.

For a moment your attention is drawn to an opening in the stone wall, where a giant German tank, which you believe is a Panther, points its long-barrelled gun right at you. There being no sign of damage to immobilize the awesome brute, it seems ready to crawl out of there at any moment, and the menace it exudes, even as it lies there dead, gives you the creeps.

You notice Dunning has dismounted and is walking towards someone in the far end of the trenches. When he bends down to talk to him, you recognize Major Wren. Those unprepossessing trenches are battalion tac headquarters after all!

Just as you are climbing out of the carrier, a penetrating voice – high-pitched and strident, but still authoritative in its clipped and rapid delivery – comes from the bush beyond the wall:

"Turn that carrier off . . . bring down mortar fire."

You turn to Saunders and give him a switch-off-engine signal. The rumbling engine dies, but immediately the voice from the bush orders, "Get that carrier out of there . . . bring down mortar fire."

You give Saunders the wind-it-up signal. He pushes the starter and the engine whirrs into life. But while you are looking around to see where you should send the vehicle, the voice from over the wall, like a broken record, orders, "Turn that carrier off . . . bring down mortar fire!"

Saunders looks at you, turns off the engine, and throws up his hands as though to say, "What the hell am I supposed to do?" You really don't know. Obviously the owner of that strident voice is losing, or has lost, touch with reality. But still it is clearly the voice of authority as it again orders, "Get that carrier out of there . . . bring down mortar fire!"

But then another, low-pitched, voice immediately behind you says quietly, "Don't let it worry you, sir. Have your driver park the carrier with those other vehicles down there."

When you turn, a battledress sleeve carrying the royal arms of a battalion sergeant-major is pointing past your ear towards a short line up of trucks about a hundred yards away in the field on the right.

Saunders needs no urging. With obvious satisfaction he winds up the carrier and wheels it away with a rocking flourish to a place of his own choosing. Assuming it won't be long before he'll be pulling out again for an OP, he parks the carrier out of sight on the far side of the tank, even as the voice from the bush is calling, "Turn that carrier off . . . bring down mortar fire!"

As you walk towards the trench-work with the Sergeant-Major, you ask, "Who the hell is that anyway?"

"The commanding officer, sir," he replies, and stalks briskly away from you as though he doesn't want to answer your next question.*

Dunning, who's been down on one knee talking to Major Wren in the trench, stands up when you approach, and informs you that Hunter and Laurie are on their way back to guide you up to your respective OPs.

At this point Wren advises, "You'd better go and find some cover while you're waiting. It can get pretty hot around here – their MO was killed today by a mortar bomb – direct hit on their First Aid Post."

As the meaning of his words "You'd better go and find some cover" sinks in, an unfamiliar wave of nausea surges through you.

Incredulous, Dunning says, "You mean we can't wait down in there with you?"

Fidgeting in some embarrassment, the Major explains, "They wouldn't like it – we're restricted to myself and one signaller. Actually, it can get pretty cramped in here when it's busy . . ."

You feel rage rising out of self-pity, but the conversation is cut off by the deadly swish of an incoming mortar bomb. You dive for the space between the German tank and the stone wall. As you hit the ground beside Dunning, you find you are actually in a shallow trench that someone started but gave up on after hitting a flinty, tightly packed mess of cinders and rock only about six inches

---

* Two days later, July 15, the commanding officer of the Royals was taken back to "B" Echelon, and never resumed command.

down. The way the conglomerate has been scratched and the soft parts torn away, it's as though someone had tried to scrape a hole with only a pocketknife and his bare hands.

The mortaring continues for several minutes. The German weapon is close enough that you can hear the hollow *plunk* each time it sends a missile swishing in over the trees, seemingly from just on the other side of the woods. And they must have this spot well taped, for the bombs are flashing very close, sending hot concussion waves through this narrow alleyway between the tank and the wall.*

Knowing that half your body is above ground is very unpleasant. While the wall behind you offers some protection, the latticework of tank tracks and bogey wheels right beside your head is not as reassuring, and during the bombardment all you can think is: It will all be over if one lands in here between the tank and the wall.

There's a brief lull, then the mortaring begins again. Another lull, and then once more the crashing explosions. Each time, you force your body down as flat as it will go, the rim of your helmet digging into the dirt and your nose touching the same little jagged crevice. You try to concentrate on that crevice, speculating on who scratched it. Whoever it was, you have complete empathy with the poor bugger. You can see him desperately scratching away in his vain attempt to get below grade. Did he manage to survive? Was he one of our boys, or was he a survivor from this tank?

But after a while you only have the wits to wonder one thing: Are you going to live through this? And when the horrendous crashing ceases and you become conscious of a bluebottle buzzing

---

* The very next day, July 14, the Royals discovered a German officer and a signaller hidden in a dugout just to the rear of the battalion area, only a hundred yards from the Verson–Eterville road. They were equipped with a wireless set netted in to their artillery – a "stay-behind party" purposely left there when the Germans retreated before the original British attack that took Eterville.

around you in the stillness of the gathering dusk, the sound is truly wonderful, for it means you are still alive.

During a lull, as the last light fades from the western sky, Hunter arrives back. He squeezes in beside you and Dunning, into what little space remains between the tank and the wall, just in time for another bombardment. When the flashing explosions finally cease, he declares this place is not fit for man or beast – and since Laurie probably won't get back until morning, now that it has grown dark, we should find a better hole for the night.

He reasons there are bound to be trenches dug near that line of vehicles down there in the field, and suggests, "The next time the mortaring stops, let's high-tail it down there and find one."

To you, this makes a lot of sense. You are more than ready to get out of here, for you are beginning to "get the wind up." With the deepening gloom, the flashing of the bombs as they land – lighting up everything for a fraction of a second, including the flinty rocks in front of your nose – seems to magnify their deadly menace and bring their hot breath even closer. So when the mortaring next ends and Hunter yells, "Okay, let's go," you and Dunning scramble to your feet.

Then just as you start running for the distant trucks, you hear a voice from the darkness on the right, sounding like the Royals' sergeant-major, shouting, "Wait! Don't go down there! They've orders to shoot without warning anything moving above ground after dark."

But by the time the significance of his words sinks in, you are completely committed to your desperate dash, pounding full-out after Hunter for those trucks now barely discernible in the dark, and the invisible slit trenches, which you must locate before the next basin of mortar bombs starts crashing down. When only a few yards from the first truck in the lineup, you think you spot a shadowy figure. Instantly there's the unmistakable *click-clack* of a .303 rifle bolt being cocked, as a sharp voice demands, "Halt! Who goes there?"

In that split second, you realize you've no idea what the password is for tonight. And Hunter apparently doesn't know either, for without replying he swerves sharply to the right to put the first big truck between him and the man with the rifle.

And you and Dunning pursue him at full gallop, round the rear of the truck and down the line, now more desperate than ever to find a hole, and wondering what you're going to do if you can't find one.

Suddenly Hunter seems to go down on his hands and knees, and, what is worse, he doesn't try to get up. But when you catch up to him, you see he hasn't fallen, but is standing in a slit trench. With tremendous relief, you jump in too, and a moment later Dunning comes tumbling in between you.

Each of you is desperately out of breath after that fearsome run, but when you hear the stealthy feet of the guards coming this way, you are forced to jam down in a mass of knees and elbows, while suppressing the need to heave and gasp for air, until they've passed out of earshot.

Obviously you have stirred up a hornet's nest among the guards, and confirmed their worst suspicions by running away from their challenge. Fortunately, they didn't follow precisely the drill of shooting anything moving above ground after dark and paused to challenge you – most probably because darkness had just fallen, and they weren't expecting any attempted enemy infiltration for some time. But from now until dawn, you know you are thoroughly and completely trapped in this hole, for these guards, and those who relieve them, will go on believing there are Germans hiding some-where in and around these trucks, and will be alert to every little sound and ready to fire at the slightest sign of movement.

As your breathing returns to normal, Dunning, in a whisper, questions the merits of "the stupid order" to shoot anything that moves after dark.

But Hunter, also whispering, explains that the Royals were warned by the British troops they relieved up here that Jerry patrols make a habit of infiltrating our lines after dark and raising hell in the rear. If our troops were allowed to move freely around above ground, there'd be no way of telling friend from foe in the dark. But this way you can assume that anything above ground is the enemy, and let him have it.

After this, conversation ceases. And soon the pleasure of finding this sanctuary begins to dissipate as you ponder your predicament: the three of you are jammed into a trench that's barely big enough for one. How on earth are you going to endure this the rest of the night?

That you managed to land in such a manner as to allow this bunty, five-foot slit to accommodate (albeit most uncomfortably) each of your six-foot frames, with all heads below ground, is quite incredible. But here you are: Hunter, with his back tight against the far end; you, with your back pressed against this end; and Dunning, squeezed down in the middle facing you – all jammed together in such a way that no man's bottom is in contact with the bottom of the trench, and each man's weight largely, but not entirely, suspended by pressure between a wide variety of parts of the anatomy.

For the most part you find these pressures are bearable, amounting to nothing worse than Dunning's knees jammed into your stomach. But the squatting position, reminiscent of a baseball catcher behind the plate, balancing on the balls of the feet, with bent-back toes eternally forcing your feet upwards towards your shins, induces an increasingly painful paralysis that becomes almost unbearable as the hours go by. And time passes with agonizing slowness. At one point, Dunning can't stand it any more. Declaring he must stretch to get the cramps out of his legs, even if it means getting shot in the process, he stands up, but as he moves he loosens some pebbles and the noise brings the two-man patrol to life. By the sound of their clicking rifle bolts and the clarity of their whispering, they're just on the other side of the nearest truck – no more than twenty or thirty feet away.

"Did you hear that?"

Click-clack.

"Yeh, something just over there!"

Click-clack.

From their agitated tone, you can tell they are very nervous, and their trigger fingers are bound to be equally nervous. So by the time their crunching boots have rounded the truck, Bill is down again, his knees back in your stomach. But in the brief time he was standing up, your position must have shifted slightly, for now you are pressed back against the end of the trench even harder than before, as he squeezes down to get as low as possible while the guards creep by and disappear in the gloom along the line of trucks.

The hours crawl by. Though three men squat together in bizarre intimacy, with their heads no more than eighteen inches apart, throughout an entire night, hours pass without one word being spoken. It's as though the repelling closeness you are forced to bear has made you desperate to place some barrier between you, even if it is no more than the coolness expressed by a refusal to converse.

You try to sleep, but it's next to impossible; you are too uncomfortable for more than fitful catnaps. And whenever you do doze off, it seems that that is the precise moment Jerry chooses to send over one of his heaviest baskets of mortar bombs. Fortunately the hours of darkness are mercifully few at this time of year in Normandy. (From last light about 10:30 P.M. British double-daylight saving time, to first light about 3:45 A.M.)

In the first vague light of dawn, you spot an empty trench not more than twenty feet away. Regardless of the risk, you have to get to it. You stand up as quietly as possible and wait for something approaching normal sensation to return to your tingling legs. Then, when you think your legs are operative, you scramble up and over and down into the empty trench, emulating a giant crab, but faster than any rabbit could have done it.

The trench is cold and clammy from the predawn mists, but it's incredibly roomy – and wonder of wonders, there's a blanket in the bottom. You roll up in it and in seconds are asleep. Almost immediately you are wakened by something sharp jabbing you in the back, and a faraway voice calling, "Stand to! Wake up! Stand to!"

As you squirm away from that painful jabbing and sit up, you realize it's a bayonet on the end of a rifle. But before you can gather your wits and put the blast on this outrageous tormentor, he's gone on to the next trench.

This is the last straw. And by the sounds emanating from the neighbouring trench, they think so too. Gord Hunter has obviously had all he can take. As he rises and starts climbing out of the hole, he roars, "To hell with this!" Spotting you, he calls, "Come on, we'll go back and see if Wren can rustle us up a cuppa tea – I could use one." He strides past you rather unsteadily, on legs that are probably more than half asleep, followed by Bill Dunning on equally rubbery legs. The thought of a nice strong, hot cup of tea makes you drool, and you scramble out to follow them. But then remembering why you were trapped in that hole all night, you call to him, "Wait – those trigger-happy buggers will all be standing to, waiting for us."

Without breaking stride, Hunter wheels left towards the hedgerow separating the field from the sunken road that runs from Verson to Eterville: "We'll go down the road then." And ploughing through a sparse section of the hedgerow, and stumbling down into the sunken road, he goes marching off up the dusty track at 145 paces to the minute, with you and Bill having to really push it to keep up.

Suddenly you feel wonderfully free in the refreshing, cool morning air. And as you reach the gateway at the corner and turn back into the field, you are delighted to see Stu Laurie has come back. He's kneeling down on the rim of the trench near Major Wren, whose head is barely visible above the low mounds of earth marking the trenches of tac headquarters. With everything strangely

quiet – no mortars humming in and crashing about, no crazy, dis-
embodied voices calling from the bushes over the stone wall – you
get a chance to examine these holes in some detail.

U-shaped, the two trenches have been dug side by side, close
against the stone wall. An earthen rectangular pillar, left in the middle of each excavation, serves as a table for map boards, telephones,
radio sets, and clipboards loaded with paper. Each trench is just
deep enough that, with the excavated dirt mounded up around
the perimeter, a man can stand upright to study maps or talk on the
phone with his head below grade. But they are entirely open to the
sky and whatever nature or the enemy may choose to drop on them.

Whatever you imagined a battalion headquarters would look
like, these crude, cramped, open pits surely aren't it. However,
beauty is in the eye of the beholder, and with only Major Wren in
one of the trenches at the moment, it appears quite spacious – out-
rageously spacious to Dunning, it seems. As he stands beside you,
looking down at the Battery Commander talking to Stu, he nods
his head at the trench and in a hoarse whisper, loud enough to be
heard ten yards away, croaks, "Plenty of damned room in there for
all of us last night if we'd been invited!"

Feeling equally mean – your legs still throbbing rheumatically –
you venomously add in even less subdued tones, "Ah, but we were
NOT invited, my friend, subalterns and captains being expendable,
you see."

If the Major hears these pointed remarks, he's too weary to care,
for he shows no reaction. Stu breaks off whatever he's been telling
him and stands up. Smiling at you faintly by way of greeting, he
abruptly turns away, and beckoning you to follow, makes for the
gateway. Leading you out to where the road up from Verson makes
its turn to the left, he points northeast up the track now clearly
visible in the predawn glow and gives you the most extraordinarily
explicit directions on how to get to A Company.

14

THE ORCHARD IN ETERVILLE

———————————— ❊ ————————————

"IT'S VERY SIMPLE. JUST GO DOWN THAT LANE THERE UNTIL you come to a knocked-out 17-pounder with some dead soldiers lying around it. It's right beside a gate at the corner of a field full of dead cows. Turn in there and go diagonally across the field to the opposite corner, where you'll see three dead horses. There's a gate there, and as you leave the field bear to the right. Right there is the orchard where you'll find A Company. When you get there, report to the company commander, just so he knows you are there. His name is Major Whitley. Now I don't think there's any point in my going back up there to show you the way, do you? There's simply no way you could possibly make a mistake."

This is a bit of a disappointment. You'd counted heavily on him introducing you to the OP. All through the night, whenever you began to be a little concerned about occupying your first front-line position, you had been reassured by the thought that Stu would be leading you up and settling you in before leaving you on your own. But what he says seems so very sensible, and the pleading look in his eyes is so eloquent, you readily agree to make it on your own.

As your carrier creeps slowly down the narrow lane, dappled with the first dazzling rays of the rising sun filtering through the trees, you feel a surge of confidence after that miserable night. But it is short-lived. At the top of the lane, you come across the depressing sight of the battered anti-tank gun and the sad bodies in battledress sprawled around it.

Turning into the field, you thread your way through an entire herd of cows, all dead. Two legs on each cow point stiffly to the sky, held up by swelling bellies so grotesquely distended they must surely soon burst. In the shady far corner of the field, where horses would naturally be attracted to stand beneath a spreading tree in the heat of the day, stomping their hoofs and flicking away droning flies with their swishing tails, three poor beasts lie decaying, the flies now crawling unmolested over their bloody lacerations.

One of the horses lies directly in the laneway leading out of the field, and while it's obvious that other vehicles have had to pass over its mutilated head before this, still your empty stomach turns queasy when Saunders rolls a track over it following your hand signals to turn sharply around the corner and into the rear of the orchard.

There you halt the carrier to look around, expecting to see some soldiers in slit trenches. But you find only an empty, desolate orchard. It is positively eerie. There is not one living soul to be seen anywhere, and the whole orchard can be surveyed easily, for no foliage has been left on the trees – in fact, most of them are little more than blasted, limbless trunks. You're certain you haven't made a mistake, but check your map just to be sure. What on earth could have happened to them?

Mortar bombs start landing over on the left, among a fringe of trees at the rear of the yellow wheat fields that sweep forward along the flank of the position and across the front, dotted with black, burned-out Churchills and Shermans. You should get settled in somewhere fast.

As you hop out of the carrier and start walking up through the orchard, you wonder about the piles of branches lying here and there among the trees. It's as though the trees have just been pruned, and when you stop to examine one of the piles, you find the branches are freshly cut. Somebody has collected them quite recently.

Suddenly a chill runs down your spine as you realize you are staring directly into a pair of eyes watching you from a hole underneath the pile of branches you've been examining. Pulling yourself together – for immediately the meaning of the neatly collected piles becomes clear – you ask the owner of the eyes where to find A Company Headquarters. You reasonably expect that a head and shoulders will appear from the hole. But not even a helmeted head appears, only a hand, barely above ground level, with the index finger pointing in the direction of a grassy mound farther forward that looks like an old-fashioned root cellar. A muffled voice advises you, "Over there, in the German bunker."

Walking quickly towards the bunker, you glance around at the other little piles of branches to see if you can spot any stirrings under them induced by your presence. But the terrible menace that has turned these men into moles is stronger than curiosity, and though a whole company of infantry is dug in throughout this orchard somewhere, there is no sign of life.

Of all you've seen and experienced since coming up to the infantry, this is by far the most unnerving. And by the time you've found the entrance to the bunker (which, having been built by the Germans, faces south, away from the Allied guns and shells), you are ready to become a mole yourself.

Standing at the top of a shallow, earthen stairwell, shored up with well-weathered timbers that look as if they've been there a very long time, you call down, "Major Whitley!"

A scarecrow of a soldier appears in the opening at the foot of the stairs, and glaring up at you, growls, "Yes?"

"Major Whitley?" you inquire tentatively, hardly believing it is possible, for there is nothing about his dress to suggest he's an officer.

"Yes. Who are you?"

"I'm your new arty rep, taking over for Captain Laurie."

"Well, don't stand up there – unless you want to get your head blown off," he snarls. "You can talk just as well down here."

As you descend the stairs, you're not sure you like this guy. He's got a British accent, and you don't know yet if it's affected or real. (You can't stand Canadian officers who affect a phoney accent they believe sounds like an officer in the Guards.) But when at the foot of the stairs he reaches out and shakes your hand with a firm and honest grip, and smiles broadly at you, you're willing to give him the benefit of the doubt.

"Tom Whitley. Welcome aboard. Have to keep your head down up here if you want to stay alive . . . constant shelling and mortaring, almost continuous, since we arrived . . . and before that, I guess . . . must have been, for when we took over from the Glasgow Highlanders up here, they were so stunned, our boys had to lead some of the poor buggers out of their holes by the hand . . ."

For a moment he studies you from head to toe as though inspecting your dress, and then inquires, "Hear any bees buzzing around you up there just now?"

You admit you had heard some buzzing.

"Well," he chuckles, moving closer to you, "those aren't bees; those are bullets! Their snipers are trying to pick off our officers."

And with that he reaches over, grasps the left epaulette of your battledress blouse firmly with his right hand, and rips it out by the roots, almost pulling you off your feet.

"Got to get rid of everything that identifies you as an officer," he explains as he grabs your right epaulette and rips that out too.

As he hands you a bouquet of epaulettes, he flips your tie. "Get rid of that . . . discard your web belt and holster . . . put your compass in your pocket . . . shove your pistol in your rear pocket . . . and wear your binocs buttoned in the front of your battledress when you're not using them."

All of this is proclaimed in such an imperious way, with such total conviction (more in the manner of orders than advice), that you don't argue. In fact, you actually find yourself thanking him profusely, even as you ponder the frightening significance of his extreme agitation and outlandish appearance.

"You can't see anything to shoot at up here," he says. "Nature of the ground – falls away out of sight only a few hundred yards in front. Laurie holed up in a big shell hole – over there near the front of the position. I suggest you do the same. Just sit tight and keep your head down – we'll call you if we need you." Thus dismissed, you turn to go, but Jerry delays your departure. You flop down in the stairwell while shells crash in the orchard above, one at a time, a few seconds between each horrendous explosion and the scream of the next one coming in, as though he is using only one gun.

This bombardment – your first experience with the seemingly endless stream of shells and mortars of all calibres that will pour into this desolate acreage hour after hour, with only brief respites, during the next twenty-four hours – is awful. It gives you some idea what these poor guys have been going through up here. The tension that builds as the methodical shelling continues, on and on, relentlessly, is appalling. You've no way of knowing the calibre of the shells, but they're big ones, for the ground beneath your prone body shudders from their impact.

You visualize those poor guys out there in the orchard, crouching under their pitiful covers of brush, every man knowing that a direct hit means being blown to pieces. (This one coming in right now could be the one.) And they've been confined to those holes under this harrowing torture for more than two days now, in the hellish suspense of never knowing if this is their last moment on earth.

When the shelling finally ceases, the orchard reeks with the smell of cataclasmic violence that lingers along the ground after prolonged eruptions of high explosive. And as you make your way back to the carrier, which the crew has parked deep in the trees at the rear of the orchard, there are voices calling "Stretcher!" from over on the right, near the front of the position.

You proceed with all haste to get settled underground in the monster shell hole that Whitley referred to. Elder comes with you, carrying the remote control box and reeling out the control cable from the big No. 19 radio set in the carrier back in the orchard.

Easily located because of its size, the hole lies among the trenches of a forward platoon dug-in behind a low stone wall. Beyond the wall is a highway marking the extreme front edge of the Eterville salient, at the southeast corner of the village.

Of course, from the hole you can see nothing. But while Major Whitley may be correct that you can see nothing from *any* point up here, you have to check it out. Leaving Elder to wire up the remote control and test it, you go forward to peer over the wall, being careful to keep your head down, even crawling on hands and knees the last few feet, so as not to draw any more attention to this position than it's already receiving from Jerry.

Remembering Whitley's warning about snipers looking for officers, and binoculars being a dead giveaway, before you raise your head to look over the wall you remove from around your neck the personal camouflage netting that you've been using as a neckerchief, and drape it over your helmet, letting it fall over your face and shoulders.

This versatile little piece of lace curtain – a neckerchief in summer and a scarf in winter – dyed in random splotches of dusty, faded green and brown, not only disguises the recognizable silhouette of a soldier's head, but hides your white face and the tell-tale reflections of the sun off the lenses of your binoculars, while allowing you to see through them perfectly.

Not that you have much to use them on. Over the wall and across the road, tall yellow wheat covers the fields to the horizon, which is only three or four hundred yards distant because of the way the ground falls away and disappears down towards the Orne river about a mile farther on. Almost directly south, about the same distance, out of sight in a basin, is the village of Maltot. And on the left front, also hidden from view, about one and a half miles away, is the village of Louvigny.

Forward on the left front sit three blackened Churchill tanks, partially hidden by the tall wheat. Judging from the direction their guns are pointing, all three were headed for Maltot and were well-dispersed as they moved to the brow of the hill. But the long-barrelled 75-mm gun of a Panther or the 88-mm of a Tiger hidden among the trees of the orchards of Maltot had potted them just the same – long before they could close up to the effective range of their guns.

And over on the left, alongside the trees and just in the wheat field in front of the trees, are several Shermans. The ones with blackened hulls are obviously derelict, but those close to the trees could still be in service, judging by the way they are parked to take advantage of the shade, some with wilting, but recently cut, foliage covering gun and turret. And you recall that this morning just after dawn you heard tank tracks squeaking and squealing over this way.

For a few minutes you search the wheat to see if you can spot anything moving in it. It's certainly thick enough and tall enough to allow a patrol to sneak in close to your position without being seen, but it lies still and innocent in the glaring sun, now high in the sky. And as the minutes pass and it becomes increasingly hot and stuffy under your little camouflage netting, you finally bow to Whitley's judgement that nothing can be seen up here, and accept his advice to get in a hole, keep your head down, and wait for him to call.

By 6:00 A.M. you and Elder are ensconced in your shell hole, and are actively working on the problem of how to maintain the semblance of a sitting position on the slithering gravel walls of this funnel-like pit. Interest in this fades quickly, however, when the extreme vulnerability of the remote control cable becomes obvious on the very first bombardment after it is hooked up and functioning.

Elder, a tall, slender youth of even temperament – well-spoken, remarkably polite and considerate – is only nineteen, but before this day is out he will seem much older. And in the emotional sense, he in fact will have matured significantly. Just to pass the time crouching in the bottom of a hole, hour after hour, in these circumstances is quite bad enough – as the pitiful calls every now and then for a stretcher bear testimony – but Elder's job frequently requires him to move around above ground between enemy bombardments to repair the cable, which repeatedly is damaged by shell and mortar fragments.

It's a nerve-wracking business, for every time Elder scrambles out of the hole and goes dashing back through the broken trees with the cable running through his fingers to find where the shell or mortar fragment has cut it, he doesn't know how long he's got to splice it together and get back below ground before Jerry unloads his next lot.

It could be three minutes, five minutes, or even ten minutes. But then again it could be as little as one minute!

Sometimes, after locating the break, a lot of time is wasted locating the other end of the cable, which may have been blown some distance away. This happens to you on the only excursion Elder permits you to make on his behalf, when, after two particularly exhausting sorties in rapid succession, a third bombardment immediately cuts the line again.

And often the line is cut in several places and repairs take so long that he can't return in time and has to dive for whatever shelter is handy back in the orchard.

The first time he fails to return, the vicious, flashing blasts that rock the orchard seem to be worse and persist longer than usual. And you have visions of him having been caught running for shelter and getting shredded by the grass-cutting mortar bombs' making up this lot. When it is over, you have to prepare yourself mentally before you can go out looking for him. But just as you are about to climb out of your hole, he comes crashing in unharmed.

The hole is big enough to accommodate both you and Elder sitting opposite each other on its slippery, gravel sides, both with your heads well below ground level. Normally the remote control box rests at the bottom between your feet, except when you hear Elder thumping this way on his returning gallop. At such times, you grab it up and tuck your feet up as high as you can, out of the way of those hobnailed boots on the end of those long, thrashing legs, as he jumps and slithers down in a cascade of gravel into an exhausted heap at the bottom, heaving and gasping for breath.

With little to talk about under such conditions, when survival is paramount and all normal subjects seem irrelevant and inconsequential, his description of what happened out there on his last scramble becomes a subject of great interest. Once, he shelters in the carrier with the signaller whose job it is to maintain the big radio set (which must operate twenty-four hours a day) and make sure the batteries are kept charged by the generator driven by a one-lung Chore Horse engine bolted to the rear of the vehicle. On another occasion when he runs out of time he dives under the carrier – a very close fit, he tells you.

Around noon, he returns with the news that he found Saunders in an abandoned trench right at the rear of the orchard. Not that Saunders was lost, but not having seen him since just after dawn, it is nice to know he is still all right.

And once when Elder's return is delayed until another lull in the firing, *you* have a story for *him*. While waiting for him to get back, your unease about occupying this giant shell hole, which until now has been firmly suppressed, bursts forth into your consciousness with almost painful clarity: This damned hole is just a big funnel, and with all this stuff falling around here, eventually something is bound to land in it.

This line of thinking is probably triggered by your wondering what kind of shell can have blown a hole this size. Was it a shell from one of the 16-inch guns of the battleship *Rodney*, standing off the coast and firing in here during the first of the British attacks?

Or was it excavated by a 300-pound missile from one of the 21-cm guns the Germans are reputed to have in Normandy?

While its spaciousness is very pleasant when the bombs are not dropping – its ample mouth providing a welcome target for a frantic signaller outrunning the whisper of a mortar bomb – its very size will inevitably be its ruin. Of this you are absolutely sure. And suddenly, you become conscious of a long, deep slit trench only a foot away from the lip of your shell hole. You noticed it was vacant when you first came here, but forgot about it, assuming the owner would be back. But now, as you think about it, you can't recall having seen anyone near it the whole time you've been here.

You decide to move in without delay. You place your eyeglasses, compass, and chinagraph pencil on the ledge of earth between the shell hole and the trench, and drop your map board over into it. Then, picking up the remote control box, you struggle up the slippery side of the hole and jump down into your new nest.

You are still bent over, settling the box into the far end of the trench, as far out of the way as possible from where Elder's feet are likely to land, when you hear it coming. It's only a faint, split-second, crackling whisper, but you know the sound of a shell dead-on for line and range. You jam down into the bottom of the trench just as it lands with a terrible crash in the shell hole, blowing blackened chips and brown flakes of stone and dirt all over your back and around your ears.

You turn and peer over the ledge, now swept clean of compass, eyeglasses, and pencil, down into the hole where you sheltered, from an hour after dawn until now. All footmarks and scars have been erased from its walls, leaving them so smooth they look as though they've been trowelled. And right in the precise, geometric centre of the cone at the bottom, a little wisp of blue-black smoke still curls upwards.

More shells follow – many of them, Elder tells you later – but you are oblivious to them, caught up in wonderment at the miracle of your deliverance. A delay of even one or two seconds in deciding whether to move and you would have been blown to eternity. And why the sudden compelling urge to remove yourself from a hole in which you'd been sheltering for many hours? When you are telling Elder about it, and mention the oddity of there having been only one shell, and he is correcting you, telling you there were the usual number in the bombardment, his manner is peculiarly gentle, as though he understands your bewilderment and shares your profound sense of awe. And this, surely, is natural enough, for he must know that had he returned on schedule he might have postponed the move, and then you would have died at the same instant together.

15

"ARE THOSE OURS?"

———————————— ✳ ————————————

UNDOUBTEDLY THE BATTERY COMMANDERS AND TROOP COMMAN-ders were thoroughly briefed before they and the infantry moved in here to take over from the British units.* But you, having received no information on the tactical situation on your way up, can only guess what has been going on up here from the shattered debris and the stench of decaying flesh. Dozens of animals and more than fifty German and British unburied bodies lie scattered about the immediate area. According to the map, the road just beyond the low stone wall that marks the front of the position is a principal thoroughfare leading from Evrecy, hidden away about eight kilometres on the right, to Caen over on the left, some four kilometres northeast of here, passing through the tiny hamlet of Le Mesnil on the way.

If that road wasn't dominated by German fire and you could drive up the gently rising ground on your right about three kilometres, you would have the best view in any direction of the

————————

* At the very least they would have been aware of the attempts by the Germans to wipe out this bridgehead over the Odon, for even as the Royals were being briefed on the morning of July 11 for their takeover up there that night, the SS were in Eterville engaging the Cameronians in such ferocious close fighting that one hundred of them would die in the lanes, the churchyard, and the orchards of the village before they retired.

countryside around here, for you'd be on the crest of a broad hill of mostly open slopes, distinguished on the map by the figure 112 printed near an oval contour line at its summit, denoting its height above sea level in metres (about 373 feet). Obviously, whoever holds the summit dominates the countryside for miles around, including the village of Maltot, reputedly harbouring a nest of Tiger tanks, just out of sight in the valley down in front. And judging from the number of burned-out hulks of Shermans, Churchills, and self-propelled M-10 guns littering the wheat fields just across the road in front and up the slope on the right, the British made heroic efforts to do just that. But their efforts had been in vain, for their FDL (forward defended line) marked on your map board with a red chinagraph pencil, is only part-way up the northern slope, well down from the summit and the 112 contour line.

But what does the enemy hope to accomplish with his extraordinary expenditure of ammunition on Eterville and vicinity?

The fact this is a salient may be explanation enough, attracting showers of high explosive to ensure it is not used as a springboard for another Allied drive for the Orne. Or it could be that the Germans are engaged in a softening-up process, the prelude to a major attack designed to wipe out the salient.*

Whatever the enemy's intentions, the constant bombardment is having an effect. You are haunted by Major Whitley's description of the Highlanders' condition when relieved by the Royals, some of

---

* Historian of 2nd British Army (quoted in Report No. 58, Historical Section (G.S.) Canadian Army Headquarters, Dept. of National Defence, p. 45) unwittingly offers an explanation for the relentless bombardment of Eterville when he explains that Maltot had been made untenable to Allied attackers because of the number of German weapons sited just over the Orne on the dominant Verrières Ridge, including "not only a large number of flak guns (88's) defending the city of Caen, but a formidable concentration of multi-barrelled mortars.... At all events they were able to achieve with them something dear to the heart of the staff college

them having to be led out of their trenches by the hand after only a couple of days here. And you wonder about the condition of his own men after two and a half days of cowering in holes in the orchard under those flimsy mounds of brush. You are a witness to the fact that the commanding officer of the Royals back at tac head-quarters has lost touch with reality after the same length of exposure to the bombardment. And two of the best-trained, most highly motivated, self-possessed, and disciplined troop commanders in 4th Field asked for relief after only about thirty-six hours of it.

How much more can Whitley himself endure? Certainly he is showing signs of extreme physical and nervous exhaustion – his outsized preoccupation with snipers trying to pick off officers, for instance. When he leaned over to rip off your epaulettes, his eyes bulged so far out of his head they threatened to fall out on his cheeks, and they wore a fixed and angry stare.

From Whitley's bearing, you know he is the type of man who under normal conditions would be meticulous about his appear-ance. But now, sans epaulettes, sans tie, sans well-blancoed web belt and pistol holster – unwashed, unshaven, his tousled hair spilling down beneath the headband of his steel helmet, and his web anklets riding around backwards on the top rim of his boots – he certainly would confuse any German sniper trying to locate the company commander with his telescopic sights.

But in spite of all this, he's still very much in control of himself and his company, and you find his domineering manner and his snarling advice – proffered like royal decrees – strangely reassuring.

---

student, but so difficult to carry out in practice – denying a locality to the enemy through fire power; Maltot was that locality." Now, if true of Maltot, it should have been equally true of Eterville only a kilometre away and within range of all those same guns and mortars. Thus it would seem clear that the Germans' bombardment of Eterville and vicinity by guns, mortars, and sometimes planes, for eight days or more, was an attempt to use this "fire power" to render that village untenable.

In contrast, his second-in-command, Capt. Bob Rankin, almost bubbling with energy, shows no sign of being affected in any way by his experiences up here. At least not until mid-afternoon, when returning in his Jeep from Battalion with a load of small-arms ammunition, he chooses to "tweak the nose of the devil" in a most irrational way. With a perfectly good, hidden, route up from tac headquarters available to him (the same one you'd used to get here), he elects to emerge in no-man's-land somewhere down in the west end of Eterville. Roaring up the road in front of the position in full view of the enemy, he attracts a string of mortar bombs that land one after the other just behind the tail of his vehicle as he wheels it in and disappears in the orchard behind the bunker. The straining Jeep engine and the mortar bombs have barely stopped before you hear Major Whitley calling, "Foo! Foo!"

When you report to the bunker, he tells you that on his drive back Capt. Rankin located the observation post for the German mortars and can point it out to you. This sounds pretty exciting, until he tells you that it should be treated as a "Victor Target."

As you follow Rankin to the front of the position, you begin to think: surely Whitley was joking? You most certainly hope he was! Two hundred and sixteen guns on a German OP?

At the stone wall you expect Rankin to stop, but no, he vaults over it and positions himself in the middle of the sunlit road. And when you join him, facing southwest up the road towards the rising ground of Hill 112, dotted with burned-out Churchills and Shermans, he points out one of these derelicts about a thousand metres away, halfway up the slope, directly in line with the road. You expect he's going to use it as a reference point, but he assures you with the utmost conviction that the silent blackened hulk is the enemy OP.

Not wanting to prolong this conference out here in full view of the enemy, but terribly curious, you ask how he discovered that Jerry is occupying that tank?

His tone in replying suggests you must be stupid if you have to ask. "Didn't you see those mortar bombs landing right behind my Jeep all the way down the road?" he says. "Well, where the hell else could that OP be except right out there? So there's your Victor target. Go get it."

Of course you tell him a Victor target isn't possible, explaining it would involve every gun in the Corps – nine regiments of 25-pounders, plus the mediums, and perhaps a regiment of heavies. Surely he can see few targets would ever justify that.

He's unimpressed: "When they sent us up here, they promised us we would have the full support of the Corps artillery, and that we could call for a Victor target whenever we needed one."

You agree. Unquestionably that is true, but only when needed.

"Well," says he resignedly, "what in hell *can* you fire on it?"

You should tell him the truth, that it's only a one-gun target, but you don't dare, he might develop apoplexy. You assure him there'll be plenty of shells.

"Then get on with it," says he, and whirling around, as though he has suddenly lost interest in the whole business, he hops back over the wall and goes trotting back towards the bunker, leaving you feeling very much alone, very naked and very vulnerable.

Suppressing mightily the feeling you've been conned into a far-cical situation by a bomb-happy man, you establish as quickly as possible the map reference of that damned tank, which is relatively easy, it being on the side of the hill in direct line with the road that bends right just before reaching it. You call over the wall to Elder, now jammed in a very small trench with the remote control he's managed to drag over here, "Able Troop target – map reference 985638 – right ranging – fire!"

All you want is to see one round. If it lands anywhere close to that damned tank, you'll go into "fire for effect" – maybe five rounds gunfire – enough to satisfy Whitley and Rankin that you've shelled the stupid thing. While you have to wait no more than a minute or so, it seems interminable out there on the road.

Estimating the range from gun to target at about 4,200 yards, you figure the shell will take about eight seconds to come up from the gun when it does fire.*

And when at last you hear Elder calling out the message he's received from the guns, it sounds like: "Shot – four thousand." Meaning, of course, the range at which the shot was fired.

You start counting to yourself, "Hippopotamus one, hippopotamus two, hippopotamus three . . ." Before you reach seven, there's a sizzling overhead, and before you can get your glasses up, *wham*, there it is, an orange flash in the middle of a violent puff of roiling smoke very close to the tank. As you do a running vault over the wall, you call to Elder, "Five rounds gunfire – fire!"

Kneeling down just inside the wall, waiting, it feels so safe and secure, you decide there's no way you're going to go out there again. Somehow they let you get away with it once, but luck like that can't last. Anyway, there's no point in making corrections if the fire is off the target; it's only a dead pile of scrap steel.

But when you hear the guns thumping, you've got to see those shells land, and the only way is to jump back out onto the road. You go down on one knee and get the tank in your glasses just in time to see the shells bursting all around it. No correction is needed – in fact you almost imagine a couple of rounds hit it, not that that would make any difference to the empty derelict.

Satisfied, you take the wall in a running leap back into the orchard and join Elder in his cramped trench.

When, after a minute, the firing stops, you immediately give the order "Repeat!" as though the target really means something. A head pokes up from a hole nearby and asks, "Are those ours?" When you assure him they are, he yells, "Give 'em hell, Foo!" This

---

* At Charge *III*, a 25-pounder shell, leaving the muzzle at 1,460 feet (or 488 yards) per second, takes 2.05 seconds to travel 1,000 yards.

seems to arouse others, and by the time the second bombardment is completed, you have come to realize that these are the first Allied shells these guys have heard being fired on their behalf since coming up here. This is confirmed by their platoon commander, an unusually tall and thin lieutenant, who, standing up for a brief moment and waving a long arm in your direction, introduces himself as Len Gage.

Apparently there has been a total lack of close-in targets, and harassing fire tasks are so far away and impersonal that all they've heard are hundreds of enemy shells and mortars seeking them out to kill or maim them. Now, for the first time hearing their shells working for them, they call out to each other and to you in a kind of ecstasy. Until now you've heard no sound of human voices among the trenches in the orchard except periodic calls for stretchers. Suddenly there is a veritable hum of voices.

Encouraged, you decide to invest another forty shells in a morale-boosting effort: "Ten rounds gunfire – repeat!"

The effect on the men of your random shelling of that silent tank might at first be described as "being beyond all expectations." But as things develop a more accurate description might be "astonishing," followed by "incredible – beyond belief," ending up "bizarre" – even "frightening."

A goodly number of A Company, particularly members of the nearby Gage platoon, shower you with compliments – some of them even getting out of their holes to come right over to your trench and call down at you, "Nice shootin', Foo!"

Over and over, you advise them to get back in their holes, that you've done nothing but shell a dead tank and the mortaring is bound to start again any minute. But they don't pay any attention to you; it's obvious they don't want to believe you. Right from the start of the shoot, the infantrymen seemed convinced that something good must come from all those reverberating roars out there in no-man's-land, where the 25-pounder shells were landing just beyond their view. So when the shelling stops and quiet reigns over this section of the front, they aren't at all surprised. And while you and Elder, with your remote control box and cable, scurry back to your own, less cramped trench near the big shell hole, they sit up above ground chatting.

Five minutes go by, then ten, then fifteen, and still no enemy mortars or shells. Half an hour of unnatural peace passes. By now it seems most of A Company have climbed out of their holes and gathered around stoves improvised out of empty hardtack tins cut in half and filled with sand saturated with petrol (from God knows where, maybe from a spare jerrycan on the Jeep) and are boiling water like mad for tea while simultaneously heating cans of meat-and-vegetable stew in it.

While your intellect roundly condemns these reckless activities, which now and then send tell-tale wisps of black smoke eddying skyward over the stone wall, your less highly disciplined stomach begins to growl noisily in appreciation of the delicious odours drifting your way. Neither you nor Elder has had anything to eat since yesterday afternoon, except for a few of those nutritionless, sugarless, hard candies known as "Boiled Sweets." He volunteers to go back to the carrier and see what he can rustle up. He's barely out of sight when Lieut. Gage carries over a mess tin loaded with steaming stew.

When you protest that you mustn't eat their food, explaining your signaller has just gone back to the carrier to get you some-thing, he assumes you are lying and firmly insists you eat it, stating most emphatically, "You've bloody-well earned it!"

This is terribly embarrassing, and you tell him so. All you did was drop a few shells around a stupid, burned-out tank simply to humour a bomb-happy captain with too vivid an imagination, who chose as his *bête noire* one derelict tank out of all those derelicts lying about in the field and up the slope out there. It's all utterly ridicu-lous. Surely he can see that. And it's very dangerous for his troops to be wandering around above ground, so would he please get them back in their holes before Jerry starts shelling again.

Hunkering his tall frame down beside your trench so he can look you directly in the eye, Gage speaks with deep conviction: "Look, my friend, all I know is that from the time we came up here around midnight three days ago we've been shelled and mortared almost steadily. And whenever they left us alone for a few minutes, they shelled the troops next door. Now, ever since you worked them over out there, it's been quiet. And see those guys eating over there? They're having their first hot meal in three days. Now if your shelling didn't do this, what the hell did? You explain it."

Well, of course, you have no explanation. But you know there has to be one, and that it hasn't anything to do with you. It's as though you're sitting in the eye of a hurricane, waiting for the fury of the storm to resume.

Later you realize that if you'd carried that analogy of the lull before the storm to its logical conclusion, you might have come up with an explanation for the break in the shelling and mortaring: Jerry was preparing to attack.

16

THE GUNS

--- ✳ ---

IT COMES IN JUST AS THE SUN IS GOING DOWN, BEGINNING with a flurry of mortars, 88-mm airbursts, and a hail of machine-gun tracers lacing the orchard. The tracers are coming from the right front, but from some distance away, judging from the faintness of their staccato *bur-rup, bur-rups*, barely distinguishable among the hammering Brens and mortar explosions over on the right. And it's clear the tracers, streaking mostly through the upper remnants of the trees, are originating from a point much lower than the orchard, probably from that skinny copse some 400 yards south of here, just east of the road you earlier studied while waiting for your rounds to land – a good forming-up point, providing a concealed route almost right up to the village.

On your map you find a DF (defensive fire) target marked precisely where you want to bring down fire. But when you pick up the remote microphone to call the guns, it's dead – the line again cut by a piece of mortar or shell. Scrambling out of your hole, you run crouched over as fast as you can back to the carrier and huddle down tight against its steel flank, just outside where Kirby is sheltering. Kirby's ears are covered with big, puffy earphones, and you have to tap him on the shoulder. When he uncovers his left ear, you give him the DF target number and the order "Fire!" for transmittal to the guns. In an incredibly short time of less than a minute, shells are rustling overhead, and a great furore of overlapping, roaring explosions starts rolling up from the area of the copse. But even as you relish the response of the guns, it dawns on you with a sickening shock that in the heat of the moment you forgot that only a brigadier and up is allowed to fire a DF target.*

God! What will they do to you? Something severe, unquestionably. Under present conditions, with so much at stake, they'll be ruthless. But surely they wouldn't go so far as to cashier an officer for this, would they? You force yourself to stop thinking about it. Later, you'll have time to worry – for now, there are more pressing matters.

You notice Kirby has an odd look on his face, and is shaking his head in bewilderment. Removing his earphones, he tells you there's a strange voice on the net calling for the guns to stop firing and hands you the earphones, with dangling mike attached, so you can listen.

Putting them on, you hear, "Hold your fire, we don't need it." Depressing the pressel switch on the mike, you demand, "Identify yourself. Who are you?" But the voice ignores your request, and keeps repeating: "Stop the artillery, we don't need your fire. Stop your fire, we don't need it," until all the required shells have been fired. Again and again you try to get him to say who he is, but he refuses to acknowledge you, either during the shoot or after. And

---

* DF targets are pre-selected "defensive fire" areas that seem most vulnerable to attack. All the technical work at the guns is done in advance, so that predicted fire (not needing correction by observation) will be forthcoming with maximum speed and accuracy. Scale and rate of fire on a DF task is three minutes "intense" for field regiments (five rounds per gun per minute, or 360 rounds per regiment), and three minutes "rapid" for medium and heavy regiments.

To prevent the enemy drawing fire by feints and thus learning the artillery defensive fire plan, only a brigadier or higher rank is allowed to fire a DF target.

you and Kirby are convinced he is a Jerry trying to disrupt the defensive fire.

The machine-gun fire doesn't die immediately, but by the time you have repeated the DF target a second time (having decided it can't get you into any more trouble than you're already in), nothing of any consequence is coming into the orchard. It's then that you sense someone is behind you. Turning around, you're amazed to find Stu Laurie there. He asks you where you've been dropping all that stuff, and you confess rather sheepishly that you were firing a DF task.

"Good gawd!" says he, "Which one?"

When you show him, he snorts, "That's not a DF task – that's an SOS task. It was a DF task, but they changed it."

Is he really sure?

"Of course!"

That would account for the speed of response by the guns to your call for fire. The guns always remain laid on the SOS target, considered the most likely route of an attack, when they are not otherwise engaged. The gun crews only have to load and fire when the SOS is called for, and it can be fired by a FOO. The relief that floods through you is so tremendous, you could hug Stu. Combined with the satisfaction at knowing your guns have just squelched an enemy attack of some consequence (no more tracers skitter through the trees, and the popping and chattering of small-arms fire down in the village seem to have stopped) and the realization you are now free to go back to the guns, where you'll be able to stretch out for a few hours' sleep, your happiness borders on elation.

But this dissipates quickly when you discover that the vehicle that brought up Stu and his crew a few minutes ago, and which was supposed to have taken you and your crew back to the guns, has, in all the noise and confusion, turned around and pulled out while you and Stu were talking. It being a HUP (a soft-skinned, van-like vehicle of glass and sheet metal), you can readily understand the reluctance of the driver (Gunner Weston) to hang around waiting with all that stuff flying around the orchard. At least your crew got on board before it pulled out.

But now you are faced with the choice of walking back or staying here another night. With darkness falling, there really is no choice. To try walking back in the dark would be inviting disaster from those trigger-happy Royals at tac headquarters. The sounds of those clicking rifle bolts still ring in your head. Was that really only last night?

Your disappointment at missing the chance to get back to the guns is leavened by the reassuring knowledge that Stu is now responsible for whatever Whitley and company may require during the night. You can crawl in a hole and sleep the whole night through.

And as you realize you're free of responsibility, you are at once conscious of outrageous, staggering fatigue. After last night, even half a slit trench will be luxury, and there is always the big shell hole. But as you start to explain to Stu how you've acquired a really nice big slit trench, preferable, you think, to the big shell hole he had been using, he tells you that at night Whitley invites him to share the far end of the company headquarters bunker, and he thinks there's room enough in there for you, too. This sounds wonderful. Enclosed, with a thick earthen roof overhead, it will be not only safe, but obviously warmer than an open trench, which, you have learned since coming to Normandy, can become very cold and clammy by early morning, regardless of how hot it has been during the day.

However, at the bunker, Stu leads you to a second entrance that you weren't aware of, facing southeast in the direction of Louvigny. It's not much more than a crawl space, about four or five feet high and four feet wide, obviously designed as an emergency escape route – a shallow, inclined tunnel apparently leading into the main part of the dugout. And the main dugout must be well-filled at the moment, for Stu, who settles in first, can only get far enough in to allow you to sit across the entrance, your back against one side and your feet against the other.

While your whole right side is exposed to the night air, and whatever the fates may choose to fling about here, the relaxing effect of extreme fatigue, combined with the psychological benefits of having a thick roof over your head and an old comrade beside you, overcomes any doubts you may have of your position. Even having to slap at the odd pesky mosquito suggests a modicum of normalcy, and you're surrendering to the sweetest of sleeps when Jerry starts lobbing over something of very large calibre – much heavier than anything he threw in here during the day.

They don't whine or wail like big shells, but sound more like giant mortar bombs. You only can guess that it's one of their larger-calibre Nebelwerfers firing their rocket-propelled mortar bombs (without their usual banshee-wailing devices), one bomb at a time instead of in six-bomb salvoes, thus extending their supply of heavier bombs.*

You can hear each one coming from a long way off, growing louder and louder – sounding remarkably like a bus humming towards you at high speed on a highway while you stand at the side of the road. But just as the sound suggests it's going by, it lands with a wicked flash and a horrendous roar that makes the ground shudder and sifts sand from the bunker ceiling. And now and then one lands so close, you feel a stunning compression rather than an

----

* At this time in Normandy all three brigades of 272 Nebelwerfers (known to the troops as "Moaning Minnies") were deployed opposite the Canadians and British south of Caen. These fearful multi-barrelled (six to ten barrels) rocket mortars came in three calibres:

	Projectiles	Range in Yards
150 mm	75 pounds	7,300
210 mm	248 pounds	8,600
300 mm	277 pounds	5,000

explosion. Some concussion waves are so strong, they actually lift you and shift you a little farther into the tunnel.

Despite this, you think you could sleep soundly if it weren't for the heels of Stu's boots scrunching and kicking you in the ribs. You're so tired nothing really matters any more, but he, cursed with alertness, having had several hours' sleep back at Carpiquet, is nervous as a cat. You can't see him in the blackness of the dugout except when it's lit momentarily by a flash of high explosive in the orchard outside, but he seems to be pointed head first into the tunnel, crouching on his hands and knees. And when one of those big "express buses" starts humming this way, his feet start "digging" involuntarily – ever more vigorously as the sound grows louder – the soles of his boots grinding and banging your left hip and lower ribcage until the humming ends with a stupendous explosion.

Fortunately, his "digging" lasts only a few seconds, but no sooner has an explosion brought an end to it, than another "bus" can be heard humming this way. Then, after some ten or fifteen of them, they cease for a while. During the lull, Stu silently digs you in the ribs with an elbow to get your attention, then pokes you urgently in the chest with what turns out to be a water-bottle full of Drambuie mixed with whisky. Gratefully you take a slug, then nudge him to take it back, as you listen to Tom Whitley's voice calling into the dark orchard, and hear distant voices, barely audible, replying.

"Number One Platoon?"

"Okay."

"Number Two Platoon?"

"Okay."

"Number Three Platoon?"

No answer.

"Number Three Platoon?"

"Stretcher!"

After that you doze off until the "buses" start coming again and Stu starts digging and booting you awake. And when the bombardment ends, there's an elbow in the ribs and the same wordless ritual with the breathtaking water-bottle, while outside in the dark stillness, the Major's voice can again be heard checking out his platoons. Once more there's a plaintive call of "Stretcher!" announcing another wounded man. And this goes on throughout the night, causing you to ponder the selfless courage of the stretcher-bearers, carrying wounded men back through the menacing shadows to the MO at the battalion aid post.*

Stretcher-bearers might be described as ordinary soldiers equipped with a limited supply of bandages, sulpha, and morphine, and a minimum of training in first aid. However, ordinary men they are not. They are men of extraordinary, outsized courage, not only providing succour to the wounded, but by their very presence providing vital reassurance to all who must remain here through the night, and who may, at any moment, have need of their services. And beyond all this, by their hour-to-hour exhibition of courageous service to their comrades, they are unwittingly setting a standard of conduct for their company and their battalion which few will match, and none is likely to surpass.

In a hazy half-awake, half-asleep condition, you pass the nightmarish hours, until finally it is daylight and Jerry moves his attention to the flanks and the rear areas for a while.

Well fortified by the frequent passing of the communion water-bottle throughout the night, you decide to make your way back on foot to tac headquarters, calling up a vehicle from the guns to meet you there.

Later you'll be told that Tiger tanks accompanied last night's attack and remained sitting on the flanks until well after dawn. But you neither see nor hear anything of them as you walk back through the first rays of the rising sun, past the fly-covered, mutilated dead

---

* On December 18, 1944, Pte. J. A. Smith was decorated with the Military Medal for his outstanding work at Eterville as a stretcher-bearer.

horses, through the field of dead cows, and down the shady lane past the bodies in battledress and German grey, their upturned faces turning black from the blistering heat of the past few days.

At first it is a pleasant change to be free of the confinement of that bunker tunnel. But soon you wish you'd waited for a vehicle, for the odours hanging in the air of rotting flesh of animals and men, freshly desecrated by last night's shelling, are intolerable.*

On arrival at Royals' tac headquarters, you discover your crew never made it beyond here last night. They arrived at about the same time as the German attackers were infiltrating through the village, and the Royals' sergeant-major drafted them to help defend the headquarters. Issued rifles and assigned holes close to the vehicles, they spent the night trying to spot and shoot Jerries out of trees on the perimeter of the field, where they'd placed themselves to shoot into the Royals' trenches.

On your way back to the guns with Weston in the HUP, which now sports a round bullet hole in the windshield directly in front of the passenger seat, you try sorting what you learned on your first tour of duty in an OP.

Even as you fight off nauseating waves of exhaustion from

---

* Even after thirty years, Madame Restoux grimaced and wagged her head from side to side as she recalled for the author the day she and her family returned to their devastated farm at the southeast corner of Eterville on the road to Caen:

> There were many, many dead Germans and Tommies lying around . . . and the 450 apple trees in our orchard were just so many sticks. Our first job was to bury our dead horses and thirty-five dead cows in the field behind the orchard. The smell was terrible. The bombardment must have been frightful . . . the ground through the orchard was covered with jagged pieces of metal, and when the metal collectors came with baskets, they collected a wagonload of copper and brass fuzes.

having been denied sleep for forty-eight hours, an overpowering sense of well-being surges through you – a mixture of relief, thankfulness, and pride that you came through it without coming apart at the seams. You now know that responding to the demands of the moment can mercifully keep a man from dwelling on survival. Sustained by a deep sense of belonging to a group and responsible for its collective safety – at least to the extent of holding your end up and conducting yourself in such a manner as not to bring danger to your comrades and disgrace to yourself – a man is encouraged to assume an aggressive spirit and posture. And while no sane man can escape suffering the agony of fear, you know that under certain conditions a terribly frightened man, quite illogically, will throw caution to the winds and give in to a burning desire to wreak vengeance on the enemy.

In a static position with no enemy in sight, however, survival is everything. You've survived to see the sun go down – but will you see it rise in the morning? You've survived to see the dawn – will you survive the day? Darkness has come again – will you survive the night? And so on. Is it possible it was only the day before yesterday you came up to the Royals, that fewer than forty-eight hours have passed while you were in that godforsaken acreage of Eterville? Is not some new scale required for measuring the passage of time when you are visiting hell; when every minute is concerned with survival and you spend your time counting the number of seconds between the sound of the distant thump of a smoking tube and the arrival of its roaring missile; when your reactions must be in split seconds if you are not to die, and your greatest pleasure comes from hearing the buzzing of a fly and knowing you're still alive after the last lot? Are sixty seconds of this the same as a minute back in Canada?

17

IGNORANCE WITHOUT BLISS

---　✳　---

WHEN YOU FIRST GO INTO ACTION, UNTIL BLESSED FATIGUE dulls and stupefies them, your hyperalert senses dominate you. But, though you live with an intense awareness of every sight, sound, and smell, and every raw sensation that can be triggered in the body and soul of a man, your physical horizons are extremely limited. This is particularly true for members of OP crews up in the front line, where it is vital to remain hidden from the enemy as you peer out from a narrow hole in a wall, or from a trench with your eye barely above ground-level. And your intelligence horizons, in the military sense, are so limited as to be almost non-existent most of the time.

Sometimes, back at the guns, when it's not too hectic, you can pick up the BBC on a little walkie-talkie 38-set that operates on the regular broadcast band. And, for what it's worth, there is each morning a broadcast especially designed for the armed forces that consists of bulletins covering this and other theatres of operations, read a phrase at a time, with pauses, so they can be taken down and relayed to the troops. Using what information these broad-brushed generalities may reveal, and putting two and two together, it's sometimes possible to make yourself believe you know what's going on.

However, up in the front line – where you are forced to live in a hole day in and day out – regardless of rank, you're out of touch with everything and everybody except, perhaps, the occupants of those slit trenches right next to you. Having little or no access to official intelligence reports on the enemy, and not entrusted with even the slightest knowledge of Allied strategic plans and objectives beyond what is obvious even to the enemy, you have no way of knowing how the grand plan is unfolding and what they have in mind for you. And, of course, no one ever knows what the enemy is planning.

Thus, in addition to the overpowering sense of sinister menace lying over the front, all soldiers in a battle zone must learn to live in a dense fog of mystery.

Now and then the curtain can lift briefly on the broad picture, allowing you to experience a striking sense of relevance as you spot your own outfit and the units you're currently supporting, not buried among thousands of extras, but centre stage among the principal players. Such a moment arrives late in the afternoon of July 15, when, shortly after returning to the guns from Eterville, you are shown a copy of the first intelligence summary issued by RCA Headquarters at 2nd Division.

It's as if it had been researched especially to answer those particular questions you'd come to dwell on during the last weary hours before dawn this morning: Are they thick on the ground out there? Are they SS fanatics or regular Wehrmacht? Is it possible the chilling rumour about the Tiger tanks is correct and there actually is a herd of those reputedly invincible monsters at Maltot, just out of sight over the crest, down there in the valley in front of your Eterville orchard?

14 July 44

SECRET

RCA 2Cdn Inf Div Intelligence Summary #1

Part 1

On the division front, the main force continues to be 1 SS Panzer (Adolph Hitler) Division, whose fwd elements (1st Panzer Grenadiers) are disposed southeast of line Eterville–Le Mesnil. This regiment (the equivalent of a Canadian brigade in numbers) appears to be supported by the 102nd Heavy Tank Battalion (general headquarters troops) which is thought to have 25 Tigers; and the Werfer Lehr Regiment – 15-Centimetre Rocket Projectors (Moaning Minnies), strength unknown.

Their divisional artillery is thought to be concentrated in reserve about Fontenay-le-Marmion. 12 SS Panzer Division (Hitler youth division), that held this area before arrival of 1 SS, seems definitely to have withdrawn its broken remnants.

In front of the British 43rd Division (on 2nd Canadian Div's right flank just west of Eterville) responsibility for that sector appears to have been taken . . . by the 9th and 10th SS Panzer Divisions . . .

But to you, the appropriateness of the next paragraph is positively uncanny, providing a direct answer to questions that haunted you last night, as to why the Germans are maintaining their incessant bombardment of the Eterville salient, and whether that was just a fighting patrol in force last evening, or what it seemed to be, a serious attack that might have overrun Eterville if your deluge of shells had not descended on them so promptly because of the prearranged SOS target?

LE BON REPOS is held in considerable strength, as is MALTOT, and the orchard east of it. And the enemy is reported to be attempting to regain Pt. 112 (the hill just 2,000 metres west of ETERVILLE). In the same way the enemy is well dug-in in the orchard at 0166 (LOUVIGNY) and is attempting to regain ETERVILLE.

Anchored in FAUBERG DE VAUCELLES (a suburb of Caen) he appears determined to keep us away from the west bank of the Orne for as long as possible.

After digesting all this and more, and after studying the Counter Battery Intelligence Summary for the twenty-four-hour period ending at 6:00 P.M. last night – which identified by map reference on the Canadian front no fewer than sixty-three hostile batteries of 88-mm guns, 150-mm howitzers, and Nebelwerfers (Moaning Minnies) – you feel that you really have been put in the picture. But when evening comes, you realize nothing has changed at all; you're still completely ignorant of what is going on at every point on the compass, even only a few hundred yards away in the British zone, where it appears something big is underway.*

---

* Ignorance of what other neighbouring formations were going through from day to day in any battle zone was not restricted to those of lowly rank. Sir Brian Horrocks, Commander of British XXX Corps, in the introduction to his book *Corps Commander*, wrote: "Looking back I realize now that I was so involved with XXX Corps battles that I literally knew nothing about the operations of the Canadians, Poles and certain other British corps which fought from time to time on our left flank. My only contact with them came during the first phase of the Battle of the Reichswald, when I was under Canadian Command." Sir Brian Horrocks and Eversley Belfield, *Corps Commander* (Toronto: Griffin House), p. xv.

Just after dark, a massive artillery barrage opens up from over on the right and to the rear, involving hundreds of guns. And for some time, the sky over the dark crests in the west and north is lit with jagged flashes running back and forth across the whole horizon, much like summer heat-lightning. And the illusion of lightning is enhanced by the heavy, muffled thunder of big guns, beyond the thumping and cracking of medium and field guns just over the hill to the west.*

And even when the guns complete their firing, back along the crest in the northwest, strange lights continue wavering, reminiscent of car lights in peacetime slashing through fog as the vehicle comes over the crest of a hill. These lights are of course much broader and stronger, producing an eerie, misty scene around you as they light up the clouds of low-lying smoke drifting in from the now silent gun positions in the west. The smoke mixes with clouds of dust swirling up from the nearby sunken road, thoroughly congested with silent, marching men, tanks with deep engines and squeaking tracks, carriers dragging anti-tank guns, and armoured half-tracks and lorries moving up past the guns.

What the attack is meant to accomplish you don't even try to guess, but you're glad 4th Field Regiment guns aren't involved, for the attack has attracted German counter-battery fire on the British gun lines, and with some effect it appears.

Several fires begin to glow on the horizon – one not far away on the right, where it seems some kind of ammo dump, or a lorry loaded with ammunition, has been hit. Whatever it is, it puts on quite a show, glowing colourfully for a moment, then flaring up like fireworks, cracking and popping with spectacular vari-coloured, Roman-candle effects – rising up, falling off, and rising up again – accompanied by sporadic, heavier explosions that scatter hissing,

---

*   Four hundred guns were involved, including those of battleships in the Channel.

flubbering chunks of ragged metal far and wide over the gun positions, that sound viciously lethal and persuade all 4th Field onlookers to seek shelter below ground.

In the morning you learn the strange lights on the horizon were diffused beams of British searchlights, purposely tipped horizontally to reflect off low-lying clouds and so light the battlefield – the first time this has ever been tried in war. The wavering effect was caused by the clouds of dust and smoke, mixing with ground mists. Officially known as "Movement Light," it already has acquired the more expressive nicknames "Artificial Moonlight" and "Monty's Moonlight."

In daylight there's a lot more two-way traffic past the guns, which includes a long parade of the big van-like ambulances, marked with large red crosses, hurrying up towards some forward casualty clearing point, disregarding your sign, SLOW! DUST MEANS DEATH, and raising a great cloud of it. Of course this attracts the usual number of German shells, which routinely fall short of the road onto 4th Field gun positions. On their way back, the ambulances move more slowly, but you suspect it's not due to concern about dust, but rather an attempt to be as gentle as possible with the bundles of pain wrapped in blankets within.

Answers to inquiries of the marching troops going by suggest the attack was successful, but from the amount of firing still going on in the southwest, it is obvious the outcome is still in doubt. The sound and fury of it all is impressive, but it seems strangely irrelevant.*

The war diary of 4th Field will report that July 16 is largely

---

* Such is the density of the blanket of security spread over operations that it will be long after the event before you learn there is any connection between the forthcoming operations involving 2nd Canadian Corps and this two-corps British attack (the third attempt to expand the Odon bridgehead with slight gains at terrible cost, reminiscent of the ghastly struggles for insignificant territorial gains in the First War). Attempts by

taken up engaging hostile batteries and counter-mortar tasks, along with "observed shoots, mainly Mike targets." And mention will be made of an air-raid tonight on the area just ahead of the guns lit up as bright as day by chandelier flares drifting on little parachutes, before the bombs start to drop: "At 2255 hours enemy aircraft were over bombing and strafing. Heavy at Verson – very little on actual positions."

Nothing is said in the diary of the build-up of ammunition for an upcoming big push, though this evening the Regiment received seven hundred rounds at each gun, which must be dug in before the regular nightly visit from Jerry planes.

Troop Sgt.-Maj. Mann, bringing up the rations, narrowly escapes serious wounding or death when a shell lands beside his Jeep and a shell fragment scratches his back and another dents his helmet.

XII Corps to seize Evrecy and the struggle by XXX Corps to secure the Noyers area are timed to draw German strength away from zones east of the Orne, adjacent to Caen and south of the city, where British and Canadians are to go forth on joint operations "Goodwood" and "Atlantic" on July 18, the heaviest strike against the perimeter of the bridgehead to date.

18

WHAT A SILLY PLACE TO
PARK A TANK

———————————— ✳ ————————————

WHEN THE FATE OF BRITAIN AND THE COMMONWEALTH, AND thus of the whole world, was truly uncertain after the fall of France, when, for months on end, disaster followed disaster in rapid succession on land and sea in Europe, North Africa, and throughout the Far East, all the pacific preaching of the 1920s and 30s that war was an idiot's delight faded from social consciousness in the face of the desperate urgency to fight and win or accept enslavement or death in concentration camps. So it comes as a bit of a shock this evening of July 16 when old doctrinaire thoughts are drawn from the recesses of the subconscious simply by the sight of one of our tanks doing lonely vigil in a railway cutting nearby.

Just as the sun is setting, you venture forth on a solitary walk away from the gun position (the only time you have taken such a risk since coming here) to try to locate a barrel of cold apple cider, the existence of which you became aware this morning during a bizarre encounter with an itinerant Don R (or despatch rider). You had been squatting over a latrine hole dug in the ditch beside the road, when this passing Don R spotted you and did a most spectacular roll off his motorbike down into the ditch beside you. When he discovered you weren't bent over in the ditch sheltering from enemy mortaring, but were rather "doing your

business," as he quaintly put it, he shrugged his shoulders philo-
sophically, brushed himself off, and grinning good-naturedly
confessed that this was the second time this morning he'd made
the same mistake.

He explained that with the noise of the motorbike, along with
the muffling effect of his crash helmet and the rush of air past its ear
holes, it was impossible to hear the sound of approaching mortar
bombs. So he had been carefully noting reactions of men along the
road, and when they dived for cover, he rolled off the bike.

Before taking leave of you, he removed a water-bottle from one
of his saddlebags and insisted you try its contents. Thus you were
introduced to Norman cider. Instantly an unquenchable love affair
with that musty, acetic drink was born. Here was a wonderful sub-
stitute for that wretched, chlorinated, tepid substance currently
being passed off as water – and you vowed never to pass up the
chance to fill up as many water-bottles as possible whenever in the
future you came across an unpunctured barrel of this marvellous
beverage.

And now this evening, with all the shelling and mortaring this
area has been experiencing, you know you are being foolish departing any distance from the gun position and its sheltering trenches.
But from the moment you were given a swig of that delicious, cool,
musty nectar by that kindly Don R, and he'd told you he got it out
of a barrel "just up the road," you had been unable to suppress the
dream of locating the source, drinking your fill, and bringing back
a clutch of water-bottles full for the Command Post gang.

And you do find it, at the back of a little brick building at the
railway crossing only a few hundred yards south along the narrow,
dusty, sunken road leading to Verson from Carpiquet.

It's when you are turning to go back to the guns, having drunk
all you could and filled all your water-bottles, that you spot the
Sherman, sitting right on the tracks a short distance east of a crossing, with its gun pointing towards Caen, and the thought flashes

White armoured scout cars, like the one being loaded here on the Thames on a ship bound for Normandy, were issued to battery and troop command staffs. Providing vital radio communication, and heavy with armourplate up to 12-mm thick, protecting the occupants from shell and mortar splinters during bombardments of gun positions, they were capable of four-wheel drive and could still attain fifty to sixty miles an hour on the highway. (Barney J. Gloster, DND, National Archives of Canada, PA-145561)

Hill 112 near Eterville ravaged by constant bombardment, first by the British, then the Germans, and then by the British and Canadians. (courtesy Jean-Pierre Benamou, curator Bayeaux Memorial Museum)

2nd Panzer Corps artillery observation crew sheltering in a derelict Sherman tank on the forward slope of hill 112, overlooking British and Canadian positions about Eterville. (courtesy Jean-Pierre Benamou, curator Bayeux Memorial Museum)

Louvigny to Fleury-sur-Orne railway bridge dropped in the Orne River by retreating Germans. (F. Duberville, DND, National, Archives of Canada, PA-145560)

Mechanical flail, also known as a "crab," on front of a Sherman for exploding mines and opening a corridor through minefields. (Imperial War Museum, 137506)

Some areas of Caen were worse than this – a wasteland of rubble.
(Lt. H. G. Aikman, DND, National Archives of Canada, PA-116510)

A FOO and his crew moving up to join the Essex Scottish for attack on Verrières Ridge, July 20. In front compartment from left to right are Driver-Signaller P. J. "Pooch" Pelletier and Captain Sammy Grange. Behind them are Signaller Hans Neilson and Lance-Bombardier Ken Munro.
(G. Kenneth Bell, DND, National Archives of Canada, PA-145556)

Canadian gunners putting a 17-pounder anti-tank gun into action northwest of Caen. (G. Kenneth Bell, DND, National Archives of Canada, PA-128793)

A Hawker Typhoon, or "Tiffie." (Author's photo)

After the torrential rain on the night of July 20-21.
(Imperial War Museum, B7799)

British Prime Minister Winston Churchill, with Lt-General Miles Dempsey, Commander British 2nd Army, and General Bernard Montgomery, Commander-in-Chief of All Allied Ground Forces in Normandy, visits the ruins of Caen in the early-morning of July 22 (Imperial War Museum, 13788)

Cdn II Corps Commander Lt-General Guy Simonds and "Monty" show Churchill where the Canadians hold the corpse-strewn Verrières Ridge and the British, west of the Orne, struggle to maintain the equally blood-soaked Hill 112. (Imperial War Museum, 137879)

The German multi-purpose 88, an anti-aircraft, anti-tank, and field gun.
(National Archives of Canada, C-0004796)

to mind: What a silly place to park a tank. What if a train were to come along?

Instantly, of course, you remember where you are. There will be no train. All sane enterprise by normal people has been abandoned in these regions before the juggernaut of war. The thought lingers as you walk back to the guns: the whole world has abandoned its normal functioning to permit thousands of men to smash each other into submission or death in these fields of sugar beets and wheat. Most of the industrial might of Europe, North America, and Asia, for years now, has been dedicated to designing and producing the means by which masses of men can rage against each other in juvenile, cowboys-and-Indians fashion, right here in these fields, to decide who will run the world.

For the very first time since you donned a uniform, you realize that this is all you are now good for, having studied, trained, and practised for it for years.

And you're in good company. The best brains in government and industry have been engrossed for years in designing the most effective weapons and the most efficient methods of making and delivering them. The concentrated might of the Allied nations has been entirely focused on exploiting the most advanced technology and encouraging dedicated men and women in the teeming millions to work exhausting shifts, all for the purpose of equipping the men in this sugar beet field to overcome similarly equipped Germans in the wheat fields down the road.

Will it be believable to future generations that waging war was once the prime purpose of the world, when the needs of battle took precedence over everything else?

It's all so horribly simple-minded. You can feel, as much as you can see, that you are on the extreme cutting edge, the very culminating point of all this concentrated effort and astronomical expenditures of money. But far from being exhilarated by the idea, you are repelled that at this advanced period of history, wholesome, mature, cultivated people – including some of the best-informed and most talented people – should still be required to live like brutes, fight like brutes, and die like brutes in order to stamp out brutishness and restore civilized order to the world.

19

LIFE IN A TANK

———————————— ✳ ————————————

TANKS OF THE DESERT RATS (7TH BRITISH ARMOURED DIVISION)
use the wheat fields across the sunken road from the gun position
as an overnight parking lot, or "laager" as they say. Each morning
before first light, they move up the road towards Verson to defensive
positions with the British infantry holding the northern slope of
Hill 112 just to the right of Eterville. Exactly where they are able to
hide so many tanks up there is a mystery. But having tried without
much success, when you were up at Eterville, to spot the tanks of
the Fort Garry Horse (10th Armoured Regiment) that crawl up
each morning from wherever they laager to positions in the trees to
the left of the village, you realize it is possible.

And each evening at last light, the Desert Rats tanks come rumbling, squealing, and clinking back down the road again to curl
around in a circle in the wheat field for the night. To the gunners,
this seems a strange way to run a war – much like closing up shop
for the night and going home. What about the poor infantry? They
can't just "put up the shutters" and go to bed when it grows dark.
Aren't they being left vulnerable to a night attack by enemy tanks?
Still, until this evening no one has had the opportunity, let alone
the temerity, to question the tactics of this famous veteran division,
the pride of Monty's 8th Army, which outmanoeuvred and out-
fought Rommel's panzers in North Africa.

Just as the sun is going down, the *snip-snip* of bullets passing through the gun positions from the field across the road becomes more frequent than usual. Seemingly providing positive evidence of a sniper, long suspected of being hidden over there in one of those patches of grain still standing, uncrushed by the nightly invasions of tank tracks, it is decided he should be winkled out once and for all. Though an organized walk into the sunset in extended-line by most of the 2nd Battery gunners, carrying small arms at the ready, doesn't turn up a sniper, it does provide the gunners with a chance to chat with the tankmen, who arrive back at their laager just as the sniper-search is being abandoned in the gathering dusk. And from the British veterans they gain new perspectives, not only of tanks and the brave men who man them, but of themselves.

Tanks, being almost blind in the dark, are not only useless offensively at night, but are vulnerable to attacks by infantry carrying the hand-held anti-tank weapon known as the Panzerfaust, the German counterpart to the British Piat and the American Bazooka.

They also learn that maintenance of tanks is more easily carried out after dark behind the front, since it involves refuelling and delivery of fresh ammunition from soft-skinned lorries. And the crews of tanks, jammed into the confined space of their "bake ovens" for hours on end, are in even more need of "maintenance" than their vehicles.

Gunners, cowering in open slit trenches under bombardments of shells and mortars, might envy the tank men the protection of their mobile steel fortresses, but apparently just existing in a tank for up to sixteen hours at a stretch is such a trying experience that men must be given relief from it as often as possible. While tank commanders attempt to position their steel cocoons under trees or in the shade of buildings, few positions are that perfect, and in these days of air temperatures rising above 90 degrees Fahrenheit (32°C), and endless glaring sun, the metal by noon is too hot to touch. With five sweating men confined within the crowded space of a tank – three in the turret and two below – the hot, humid air can become foul.

Toilet facilities are non-existent, and expended cartridge cases have to serve as chamber pots, passed around among the crew and emptied out the hatch over the side. And through every minute of the day, that same confined space is filled with the perpetual, mostly unintelligible gabble of multiple, overlapping voices of signallers, with every kind of accent, spilling out of the earphones hanging around the neck of the tank commander.

But of all the information the gunners pick up, the most revealing and interesting is not about the tanks and the men in them, but their assessment of the intensity of the fighting here in Normandy. According to these veterans of North Africa and Italy, this is by far the worst they have ever encountered, and they have never seen artillery gun lines shelled like they have been here. Their actual words, which will be quoted and requoted throughout the Regiment, are: "We've never seen anything as bad as this before. The artillery isn't supposed to have to take it like this. The guns are never placed forward in full view of the enemy like they are here."

Their confirmation that this is a crazy, unusual position for guns, and the revelation that what they've been going through here is "the worst," far from having a demoralizing effect actually causes everyone's spirit to rise in a burst of pride. If what you've all been going through is "the worst," then you haven't been doing too badly under the circumstances.

20

THE HEAT IS AWFUL –
BUT GOD BLESS THE CZECHS

❄

DESPITE THE FACT THAT DAY AFTER CLOUDLESS DAY, TEM-peratures stay in the high eighties Fahrenheit – around thirty degrees Celsius – (as measured by an ammunition thermometer stuck in a shaded recess between bags of cordite propellant in one of the brass 25-pounder cartridges at Number One Gun), rising to God-knows-what levels in the sun, soldiers in Normandy wear woollen uniforms.

And even though for most there's no escape from the broiling sun from sunrise to sunset, except in the dead, sultry air trapped in a covered hole in the ground, Canadian and British soldiers wear long underwear – not the thin, cotton Balbriggans with short sleeves purveyed in more civilized times, but scratchy, thick woollen longjohns, with legs extending to the ankles and sleeves to the wrists.

The battledress, a British invention, clearly designed to combat their own cool, damp weather, retain maximum body heat when worn, according to regulations, tightly buttoned at the neck and wrists, shirred and belted in at the waist, and gathered, folded, and buttoned under anklets at boot-top level. And it is a telling comment on British weather and temperatures that, during all the years of training in Britain, no distinction was ever made between summer and winter in the matter of uniform. Battledress was worn throughout the moderate summers with little discomfort, and when combined with long underwear in winter, it was a source of great comfort to the wearer, as much when in residence in partially heated, draughty Nissen huts and clammy, unheated quarters of requisitioned houses, as when out on schemes in bone-chilling rain and fog on the South Downs or Welsh Hills.

Even here in Normandy, after the sun goes down and the chill of night descends, those confined to open trenches are grateful for all that wool surrounding them, which never seems excessive in the swirling mists that usually form around 3:00 A.M. But each day, with the sun beating down on uncovered slit trenches and gun pits, those on duty swelter, even after removing battledress blouses. While those off duty, trying to sleep under the blazing sun in open, sandy holes below grade – cut off from whatever little breeze may be stirring, bathed in sweat and itching – toss and turn and scratch and each day lose a little more of their vitality.

You have not experienced heat like this since leaving Canada, and you'd almost forgotten what a heat wave was like. But now memories are aroused of other hot days, when people alleviated their discomfort with cold drinks and light meals of salads and fruit. And your personal fantasy is the image and sound of cold water pouring freely and endlessly out of a tap.

The reality, however, is Compo rations, which, like the battledress, were designed for cold weather: meat-and-vegetable stew, steak-and-kidney pie (with its thick, soggy dough), sultana pudding and treacle pudding, all of them having to be served piping-hot to be at all palatable.

And in place of cold drinks, you have the choice of hot, sweet Compo tea, or warm, heavily chlorinated water from your water-bottle.

Oddly, no one as yet suffers from heat prostration, perhaps because they are issuing salt tablets, to be taken daily to replace the salt lost through perspiration. And it could be said the excessive heat today is responsible for actually saving a man from death.

As Gunner M. A. Killingbeck comes off the radio set in the armoured car this morning, and Kirby, his replacement, climbs up out of their slit trench – which they dug together and use alternately – on the far side of the vehicle, the sun is high in the sky and it's clear that this is going to be another scorcher. One look at that sun-drenched hole, and Killingbeck decides he can't face another day trying to sleep in a bed of sweat under the blazing sun. Enemy shelling be damned, he'll take his chances under the armoured car in the shade, reasoning that while he's above grade he'll be partially screened from shell fragments and grass-cutting mortars by the car's tires and a pile of small haversacks (stuffed with items for daily maintenance, razor, towel, handkerchiefs, socks, etc.), stored by members of the command post under the rim of the car where they are readily accessible.

However, Killingbeck doesn't tell anybody that he has changed his abode. So when Jerry starts shelling the Regiment (choosing to start off the morning by plastering Able Troop) and drops one directly into Killingbeck's trench with a terrible crash, everybody huddling in the troop command post dugout, only six feet away on the other side of the car, is certain he has bought it.

But even before the shelling stops, to everyone's relief he tumbles down into the command post, unhurt and profoundly grateful that the blazing sun had prompted him to not lie down in that trench just moments before the shell arrived. The full extent of his luck is revealed only after the shelling ceases, however, and an inspection carried out. Not only is his trench torn apart, but all the kit behind which he lay under the vehicle is riddled. Splinters ripped all four tires on the armoured car (GA), and there are holes in almost everything around and under the vehicle, including the jerrycan used for carrying bulk water for washing, tea, and all other purposes. Cans of Compo rations, clothing, small packs, and a tarpaulin are full of holes.

And in your small pack there is evidence of the lethal wickedness of the tiniest fragment of high-explosive shell. At first you think it somehow escaped damage, but when you open it, you find your socks have been turned into balls of tightly wound woollen yarn. And unwinding one of the balls, you find a tiny, ragged shell splinter inside no larger than a pea. Then you notice the end of your razor is dented and a bit of the chrome burred away, as though the tiny pea, deflected by the razor, became a buzzsaw within your pack, cutting, unravelling, and rolling up the yarn of your socks – in almost an instantaneous operation.

While everyone is still marvelling at Killingbeck's escape, he discovers, just under the front of the vehicle, inches from where his head lay, a clean, deep hole where a sizeable dud shell buried itself.

This dud and Killingbeck's fortuitous, life-saving move from his trench join a rising number of miraculous-escape-from-death stories involving members of the Regiment – most of them attributable to the high proportion of dud shells landing on the gun positions.

Over the past couple of days, on making the rounds of the gun crews, you've been shown several neat round holes in the earth in gun pits and at the end of slit trenches, drilled by 88-mm shells that failed to explode only inches from the occupants.

Despite Killingbeck's adventure, the record for the closest brush with death from a dud in this Carpiquet valley position is still being claimed by Easy Troop for Gunner C. J. Hillis, who on July 15 had the soles of his feet burned by a dud shell as it bored a hole in the side of the trench in which he was sleeping.

To excavate a dud 88-mm for examination is a major operation, since their extremely high muzzle velocity (2,400 feet per second, as compared to 1,485 for a 25-pounder at Charge III) imbeds them several feet down in the soft earth. One hole, drilled no more than six inches from the sleeping head of Gunner James Beatty, in the end of the slit trench he'd excavated in the side of a gun pit, is so deep that even when measured with a pole nine feet long the bottom can't be reached.

A couple of shells have been dug out and examined, however, and both had markings on them to show they were manufactured in Czechoslovakia. And for this reason, there is throughout 4th Field (as undoubtedly there must be in 5th and 6th Field over on the left, who've been receiving their share of duds) a truly warm feeling towards those unsung Czech heroes who are risking death from their Nazi masters each time they sabotage a fuze on a high-explosive shell to save the life of an Allied soldier. If only they could know the gratitude for their efforts, which without a shadow of a doubt have saved dozens of gunners from death or disablement in just the three regiments here in this valley.

Sgt. W. Elliott accurately voices the feeling abroad in this shell-torn valley, when, as he is showing you still another fresh hole punched by a dud near where he was sheltering, he declares earnestly, "God bless the Czechs!"

To which Sgt. Nick Ostapyck, Lieut. Ted Adams, and you must add a fervent "amen" this evening. You'd gone over to visit Ostapyck and Adams after spotting them during a lull in proceedings, standing out in front of their 14th Battery guns, staring and pointing in the direction of that distant mushroom water-tower across the Orne in enemy territory – so prominent and sinister and suspected by all of harbouring a Jerry artillery observer. You are lined up side by side, with Ostapyck in the middle, staring down across the valley, speculating on "who the hell was the idiot responsible for a whole division of guns being placed in this natural amphitheatre facing the enemy," when there is an earth-quaking thud on the very ground on which you all are standing, followed immediately by the horrible *ee-ee-ow* screech of an incoming 88-mm shell.

When you look down, there, between the toes of Ostapyck's boots, is a fresh round hole in the earth where still another impotent shell has buried itself. Once again, because a Czechoslovakian man or woman has sabotaged a fuze, in place of three mangled bodies lying on the ground, three men walk away unharmed. Ah yes, God bless the Czechs!

21

THREE–MAN SHIFTS AROUND
THE CLOCK

✳

AS EARLY AS THE THIRD DAY HERE, THE REGIMENT BEGAN TO adopt a mode of living to suit the situation, and to make noticeable amendments to drills and practices that were preferred, if not obligatory, during the long years under the critical eyes of IGs (Instructors In Gunnery) in England.

So far, most of the firing required of the guns is designed either to harass the enemy or to cool down his guns and mortars, which continue to plaster infantry positions up ahead and each gun position back here.

Hostile batteries frequently attract the attention of the Flying OP, who zooms in low over the gun positions in his little plane to undertake a shoot using the Regiment. And he promotes a good deal of satisfaction among all ranks when his target is "active enemy mortars" and he is able to report "shoot effective."

The nature of the targets and the type of response required are such that they allow gun crews to be split into two shifts of three men each – one shift working under the gun sergeant and the other under his bombardier. Of course for any fire plan or heavy firing program *all* members of the crew will be awake and on the gun.

Similar arrangements are in vogue in all command posts: the gun position officer, one ack, and a signaller on one shift; and the troop

leader (GPO's second-in-command), another ack, and another signaller on a second shift. Thus the guns are serviced around the
clock.

Camouflage nets, invariably erected on their poles over the guns
during all training exercises in England (not to do so might well
have earned a bowler hat* for the subaltern in charge), have been
taken down and will not be used again because of their proclivity to
catch fire in the dry atmosphere during periods of sustained firing.

No one would now think of sleeping above ground, and roofs of
earth as thick as possible (at least two feet thick) have been added to
all command posts, with the use of corrugated iron sheets scav-
enged from the ragged Carpiquet hangars by thoughtful ammunition numbers in the wagon lines back on the aerodrome.

Men spend almost all their time below ground. And when
anyone has to move above ground, he makes sure he's never very far
away from a hole. Most men have dug their personal trenches
somewhere close to their place of duty, and holes dot the ground
around troop and battery command posts. Gun crews have dug
theirs into the rim of their gun pit or down in a corner of it.

Each day existing slit trenches are dug deeper, and there's a
favourite saying that "anyone digging deeper than nine feet will be
considered a deserter." (Some appear to be headed there.) And new
trenches appear daily as changing tastes in design and different
theories on the direction in which they should be running to
provide maximum protection to the occupant, are put into practice. (A trench running east–west presents a narrower target to
shells coming from the south, doesn't it?) Some have dug so many
holes it's almost as if they were doing penance or presenting alms to
the god of war in appeasement.

Morale is exceptionally good and a spirit of comradeship exists
that would be difficult to surpass – though the men's vitality is

---

* Symbol of civilian life to which the officer, discharged as unsuitable
officer material, would return.

ebbing, partly because of the scorching heat and partly because everyone has difficulty sleeping in holes that bounce and are filled with dust every time the guns fire. And though you do your best to ignore it, you are always tense under enemy observation, always conscious that the next one coming this way may have your name on it.

Everyone goes about his business with an ear cocked for the first faint hum of an enemy shell or mortar. And there are clenched fists and curses when now and then, without warning, the little Air OP plane coasts in with its engine shut down, the rustle of air aroused by its wings sounding for all the world like a mortar bomb looping in, sending everyone diving headlong into holes.

One Bofors 40-mm anti-aircraft gun has been assigned to each troop in the Regiment and henceforth will travel with you. While the Allies are supposed to have complete air superiority over the bridgehead, apart from that big RAF bombing raid preceding the taking of Caen, enemy planes have been more in evidence. On two different days large flights of enemy fighters have swept up the valley before zooming over the escarpment, where lies Carpiquet aerodrome, and disappearing. The first flock of ME 109s on July 12 strafed everything in sight, but with little effect as far you could discern. Again, two days later, fifteen of them roared full-throttle up the valley, weaving back and forth, but not firing at anything – they were either on reconnaissance or headed for the coast to attack ships unloading on the beaches. On neither occasion were any Allied fighters visible, but the considerable number of Bofors throughout the valley, sounding like men shingling a hollow roof – *bunka, bunka, bunka* – spewed streams of tracers at them. They shot down at least two, adding further to the growing prestige of the light anti-aircraft gunners.

Daytime efforts of the ack-ack gunners have been impressive, but at night their guns are now silent. The NCO in charge of your attached Bofors explains they are under strict orders not to fire, since they might hit "night fighters" – radar-equipped Beaufighters up on standing patrol, being directed onto the enemy bombers by mobile radar stations scanning the dark heavens from the ground. While he, like you, has never heard the rattle of Beaufighter guns up there any night, his superiors have assured him they'll knock down every Jerry plane "on their way home." (He can't explain why they don't knock them down on their way here.) And so when, each night around 11:00 P.M., the enemy bombers, a few at a time, come droning overhead and go about their business of bombing nearby targets in maddeningly leisurely fashion, the men on the Bofors grind their teeth in frustration.

On the night of the 14th, enemy planes dropped no fewer than ten chandelier flares over the gun positions, lighting up every trench and gun pit as bright as day, causing a period of great anxiety as everybody braced themselves for the worst. But no bombs were dropped. The next night, around 11:00 P.M., they came back, dropped their flares, and bombed Verson just up ahead of your guns. But nothing landed on the gun positions. Then again just before 11:00 P.M. on the 16th, Jerry bombers hummed in very low over the guns as everyone held their breath. But they dropped their flares and most of their bombs on Verson, only a few smaller anti-personnel bombs landing out ahead of the guns.

Tonight just before 11:00 P.M., following the now normal drill, everyone settles down in holes with the thickest roofs of earth to await the sound of the approaching enemy planes. As always at this hour the whole bridgehead seems to be quiet and waiting. Minutes pass slowly as almost half an hour goes by, and it seems that tonight they aren't coming. Then at about 11:30 a faint drone can be heard in the distance, growing louder and louder until the sound of the air whistling past their wings, like a low wind, can be heard distinctly as they pass unseen at low altitude over the guns.

Immediately several poppings are heard, and glaring white flares float directly over the Regiment, lighting up gun pits and command posts with breathtaking brightness. This is it. On other nights, the flares floated just to the right or to the left of the position. But tonight they hang with ominous intimacy directly overhead. Totally unmolested, the droning planes circle around. They take their time. One feels them turning, getting into just the right position to attack.

Then, with motors humming in a fast dive, a plane comes in, and roars away, a shrill whistle growing to a shriek and a monstrous *currump!* This is followed in rapid succession by more earth-quaking blasts, each louder than the one before, until the ultimate in sound and concussion – felt rather than heard – as two bombs straddle the guns. Then, an awful silence with only the sound of heavy breathing and muttered prayers to be heard in the bottoms of holes. (Yes, prayers are uttered and later men will frankly admit it without embarrassment.)

You can hear him off in the distance wheeling around, getting into position to attack again. (To each troop it seems they're the only one being attacked, and by one plane.) This time it's anti-personnel bombs, vicious, lightly fuzed little affairs that explode so close together it's just one prolonged *r-r-r-ipp*, as they send showers of grass–cutting fragments across the positions, leaving the field swept clean of every last blade of vegetation and covered with blackened rings.

On his last run across the position, strafing with his machine guns, he causes one casualty. A bullet ricochets off a rock in front of your command post and comes in through a narrow, horizontal slit left open to oversee the guns. It bounces off the corrugated-iron ceiling with a wicked flash momentarily lighting up the dugout, and imbeds its pointed nose in driver-signaller Bill Walkden's back, with just enough force to penetrate tunic and skin.

Then, as if to add insult to injury, the departing plane drops a ten-foot streamlined aluminum case, resembling a fish, in which the anti-personnel bombs were carried. It comes down with a weird fluttering sound, landing with a hollow *thunk* on Able Troop's position.

When finally the attack is over and the damage is assessed, it's found to be unbelievably light. Though a string of six 30-foot-wide craters have been excavated in a line across Able Troop, back across 14th Battery and RHQ over the road, there were only four casualties, and very little damage to equipment. One 14th Battery gun (Sgt. Hill's) has been knocked out, some ammunition blown up, and Sgt.-Maj. Flynn's Jeep left burning. Even a wooden tripod for a director (survey instrument) left fifty yards in front of your guns – where it might be used to check the parallelism of the guns – survives. At dawn Bombardier Hossack asks you to accompany him out there to bear witness that it's still standing, within three or four feet of the lip of a monster crater.

Later you learn that Douglas "Mac" MacFarlane, Baker Troop GPO, had his hand slashed by a fragment from a bomb dropped on Eterville, where he was relieving Hunter, thus becoming 4th Field's first officer casualty.

PART THREE: JULY 18-24

Supporting Operations
Goodwood and Atlantic

22

GREATEST AIR-ARMADA
ATTACK IN HISTORY

※

IT IS GENERALLY BELIEVED THAT THE BREAK-OUT FROM THE bridgehead, so long visualized during training of 2nd Division in England, will occur just as soon as Monty decides everything is in place; that the Canadians, with their high reputation from the First World War still intact, will be among the leading assault forces; and that the fire-power Monty will bring to bear on behalf of the assault will dwarf El Alamein.

And so on the morning of July 18, 1944, it seems that the day has come. The integrated operations of "Goodwood" by the British and "Atlantic" by the Canadians – taking place simultaneously, shoulder to shoulder, principally on the other side of the Orne pointing towards Verrières Ridge and some twenty miles beyond to Falaise – have all the marks of the long-awaited break-out.

In Operation Goodwood, the centrepiece attack, three armoured divisions of British 8th Corps (the 11th, the Guards, and the 7th) will thrust south out of the shallow eastern corner of the bridgehead beyond the Orne, down past Faubourg-de-Vaucelles, the industrial suburb of Caen on the east bank of the Orne, passing along a corridor blasted by more than three thousand planes, the greatest air armada ever assembled for direct support of a ground attack.

The left flank of the attack will be protected by the 3rd British Infantry Division, while the Canadians, in Operation Atlantic, will deal with the Germans on the right flank. The 3rd Canadian Infantry Division will clear the east bank of the Orne down through the industrial suburbs of Caen (Colombelles, Faubourg-de-Vaucelles, and Cormelles), after which 5th Brigade of 2nd Division will cross the Orne at Caen to clear the bank down to Fleury-sur-Orne, which sits directly opposite the village of Louvigny, which must be taken by 4th Brigade.

The crack British tank divisions are expected to overpower any resistance remaining in the fortified villages south of Caen, secure Verrières Ridge, and exploit a break-out towards Falaise if the opportunity opens up. That these forces might fail to break their lines wide open and fall short of releasing an irresistible, liberating, tidal wave across France and the rest of Europe, is not even a consideration.

And the thousands of Allied soldiers, who at dawn will watch the bombing of Faubourg-de-Vaucelles and the fortified villages south of Caen – a bombing of enemy front-line positions, gun lines, and reserve positions without parallel in the history of war – will believe they are watching a hole being literally blown through the German army.

At about 4:45 A.M. the faint hum of the great armada of bombers coming from England can be heard in the sky north of Caen. Quickly it grows in intensity until you are enveloped in the throbbing roar of a huge flock of bombers lumbering in from the coast. They are not little specks high in the sky leaving vapour trails, as they appeared over Sussex and Kent on their way to raids on enemy-occupied Europe, but great four-engined machines, flying in from the northwest at a moderate height, plainly visible in all detail to the troops on the ground.

After years of listening to sparse reports by the BBC of bombing raids on occupied Europe, usually no more than bare-bones bulletins (such as "Several industrial targets in the Ruhr, including Essen, received the attention of our bombers last night"), leaving

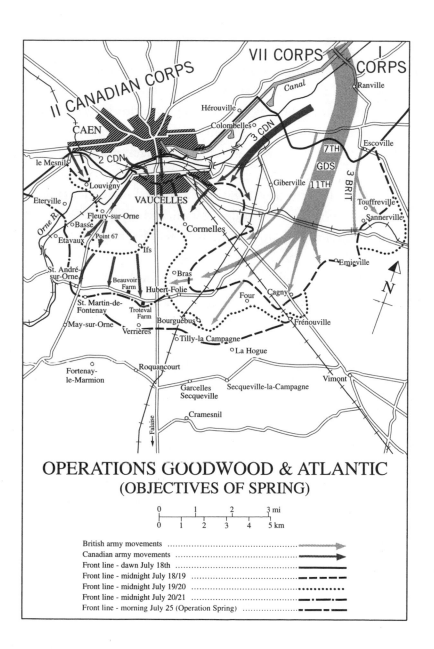

OPERATIONS GOODWOOD & ATLANTIC
(OBJECTIVES OF SPRING)

0		1		2		3 mi
0	1	2	3	4		5 km

British army movements ....
Canadian army movements ....
Front line - dawn July 18th ....
Front line - midnight July 18/19 ....
Front line - midnight July 19/20 ....
Front line - midnight July 20/21 ....
Front line - morning July 25 (Operation Spring) ....

everything to your imagination, you are about to have a grandstand view of a very large raid, the largest ever in direct support of ground forces.

As you watch the first planes turning east, lining up their run across Caen, the whole thing seems unreal, almost incongruous. RAF raids have always been at night, and your mind can't associate the obscenities of bombing destruction with this bright, beautiful, sunlit morning. But when suddenly the sky around the first planes reaching Caen is polluted with cracking, black puffs, and seconds later big bombs are tumbling down among the factory smokestacks of Faubourg-de-Vaucelles, creating earth-shaking concussions that jar your gun position five miles distant and send dense clouds of dust and debris roiling up hundreds of feet in the air, the reality is clear enough.

Soon the dust blocks out the factory smokestacks and church steeples, but not before you see a spire topple.

One Liberator, the sun glinting off it as it moves across Caen, tips over and goes down in flames. Another can be seen smoking as it swings overhead on its way back to the coast. In a few minutes all the flak disappears from the sky as the German guns are either blinded by smoke and dust or knocked out by the neutralizing fire that is now being laid on them by fifteen field regiments, twelve medium regiments, three heavy regiments, and three regiments of heavy ack-ack guns.

Now the planes streaming unmolested over their targets drop their bombs in seemingly routine fashion, wheeling around and heading back to England as though on a giant conveyor belt. For three hours the huge planes maintain a constant pulsing roar as they flow in from the coast to add their awful contributions to the thundering rumble. As the attack continues, on and on, and thick smoke and dust clouds drift across the front, all at the guns cease watching.

During the first forty-five minutes, 1,023 four-engined RAF Lancasters and Halifaxes are to drop more than five thousand tons of high explosive on factory suburbs marked by Pathfinder flares. Then 400 medium bombers of 9th U.S.A. Airforce are to scatter thousands of fragmentation bombs on the corridor of the attack. Six hundred Liberators will then hit targets east and south of the city designed to interrupt communications and snuff out counter-attacks. Finally, more than a thousand fighter-bombers will fly countless sorties over roads, farms, and villages far behind the enemy lines to prevent the Germans from moving up tanks or guns.

When the bombing ends at 7:45 A.M., almost eight hundred guns will begin laying down concentrations between the Orne river and Troarn, a village east of Caen. The Orne and Troarn are eight kilometres apart, the approximate width of the corridor down which the three British armoured divisions are to plunge.

The infantry of 2nd Division will not be involved until late in the day, when 4th Brigade will clear the right flank on this side of the river down to the village of Louvigny, so that 5th Brigade may cross the Orne after dark at Caen to begin clearing the far bank, south to Fleury-sur-Orne opposite Louvigny. The opening attack, the first by any battalion of 2nd Division since the disastrous Dieppe raid, will be by the Royal Regiment, now in reserve to the left rear of Eterville.

At first light Major Jack Anderson, acting battalion commander, and his company commanders go forward on reconnaissance to a cluster of ancient farm buildings held by 8th Recce near the hamlet of Le Mesnil and just short of the road running east from Eterville to Caen, which will be the startline for their attack. From here they sneak forward to study the ground over which they must pass on their way to taking their objectives: the village of Louvigny and its château, which is some fifteen hundred yards away down on the Orne, well screened by a tremendous orchard and grounds enclosed by a seven-foot-high stone wall.

However, they can see little of all this, for visibility is limited by a towering dust cloud drifting this way from the bombing of Caen's suburbs. Fortunately, the owner of the fourteenth-century manor farm held by 8th Recce, Jules Hollier-Larousse, is both a captain in the local Resistance and mayor of Louvigny, capable of providing the most minute detail on the layout of village and château grounds, and the best routes there.

23

LOUVIGNY

✳

THE PLAN DEVELOPED BY THE ACTING CO OF THE ROYALS CALLS
for Major Jim Fairhead's D Company to take the orchard and
château just north of Louvigny, and Tom Whitley's A Company to
follow through to clear the village itself. After this, B Company will
pass through the village and take up a position to shut off counter-
attacks from upriver.

Capt. D. S. "Tim" Beatty is in command of B Company since
Major J. F. Law was wounded two days ago in a bombing attack,
though Beatty himself has only just come back from a casualty
clearing station, sporting a dressing on a head wound caused by a
shell fragment that pierced his helmet in Eterville three days ago.
Major Ralph Young's C Company is to establish a firm base on the
high open ground overlooking Louvigny, from where a squadron
of tanks of the Fort Garry Horse (10th Armoured Regiment) will
blow holes in the seven-foot-high stone wall bounding the orchard
on three sides so that Major Fairhead's company can debouch into
the orchard.

The three field regiments of 2nd Division, including 4th Field,
will fire heavy concentrations of shells on the orchard, the village,
and the woods between the château and a nearby railway bridge
over the Orne; after which the village of Athis, from whence reinforcements for a counter-attack might come, will receive the full

attention of the guns. Other support will be forthcoming from a company of 4.2-inch mortars and medium machine guns of the Toronto Scottish, as well as from the battalion's own 3-inch mortars.

The startline, the Eterville–Caen road as it runs past Larousse's farm through Le Mesnil, will be secured by the 8th Recce Regiment.

At 6:00 P.M., while the hot July sun still glares high above the crest of Hill 112 over to the west, the divisional fire plan opens up on Louvigny and vicinity, and the men and officers of the Royals, accompanied by 2nd Battery FOOs (Laurie and Hunter) and their carrier crews, leave the shelter of the broken walls of barns and houses along the road through Le Mesnil.

Crossing the highway, the companies walk in arrowhead formation through the unharvested, yellowing wheat, down across the fields towards the flashing roar of shells now furiously lashing the big apple orchard about a thousand yards away, enshrouding it in smoke and partially hiding the main objectives – the château and the village of Louvigny just beyond on the bank of the River Orne.

Able Troop Commander Stu Laurie, who, with his carrier and crew goes in with a leading company, will recall every foot of the way of this, his first attack:

> They just start off on foot, walking across the wheat field, and immediately machine-gun fire begins to pour in – mostly through the wheat. Jesus! You wouldn't think you could miss having a foot taken off or at least wounded! But nothing like that happens. They keep on walking right along, and we're with them, until we get stuck – not in a ditch or a hole, but on a hump of earth!
>
> I won't go on the road, though there is a very good road running all the way down on the right to the objective. I won't let Ryckman drive the carrier up on it, for I think it could be mined. So we are driving along in the fields, and God it's rough –

up and down, up and down. Suddenly we get stuck right out in the middle of the field, bottomed out on a bump-up in the land, with everybody firing at us – small-arms fire coming at us like hell! And they start shelling us too. It's a miracle we get out of it intact.

Just then somebody asks me if I can't do something about all the ammunition coming our way. So I get the Regiment on the blower to bring down the guns on a target, but they say, "Sorry, the Colonel's got the guns – no use – don't bother."

So we just march on ahead with shells and mortars coming our way like crazy. And that's when 4th Brigade Tac Headquarters behind us is hit. Set up in the field just about 600 yards back, they are getting plastered. That's when Gunner Walter Chater, the CO's Don R, is killed, and Brig. Sherwood Lett, the commander of 4th Brigade, is wounded.

Then a whole bevy of wounded Germans come through on the way back . . . slits in their chests . . . bubbling blood . . . all kinds of walking wounded . . . ten or twelve of them. One officer with them is wearing a steel helmet – all the rest are hatless . . . staggering along in terrible shape, all wounded so badly . . . from our fire plan I guess.

Just then our friend Rankin (Captain Bob of A Company) comes roaring down the road in a carrier, running right over towards the headquarters they've just captured. And as we watch, his whole carrier just goes boom up in the air, and a great cloud of black smoke comes out of it . . . run over a mine, of course. Just went roaring through and that was goodbye to him and everybody else in that carrier.

In the meantime I keep asking for the guns. I desperately want them, for I know precisely where the German fire is coming from. I can keep my head up, for while they are really pouring it into Brigade behind us, we have been moving out of it as we move forward.

But no, the Regiment is still being fired by the Colonel. So I say to myself, "To hell with this, if I can't get the guns I'll go operate on my own." It's then I cross over the road on the right and go up the hill – quite a decent hill – with a young lieutenant of the Royals. And that young man is really high! I don't mean drunk, just uptight with tension, yelling and screaming at the Germans to "Come out, you bastards!" as we walk together through the wheat and brush with Ryckman wheeling the Carrier along behind us.

And, by gawd, we start digging snipers out of ditches and slit trenches around there. There are lots of trenches up there and when we go up to them, there they are, right down in the bottom of the trench, hiding. They seem only too glad to be taken prisoner. Obviously they were left behind to do this: just fire across the wheat fields until we arrived.*

A Company, with Lieut. Len Gage's platoon leading, clears about half the village before being held up by heavy machine-gun fire from the south end at last light. Then, "it being considered bad practice to try house-clearing in the dark," Whitley pulls his company back into the orchard opposite the village until morning.

The Germans mount no counter-attack, though they occupy nearby Athis and Maltot in considerable strength, including a nest of their fearsome Tiger tanks. Unquestionably the pressure still being exerted by the two British corps, in their attacks that began three days ago over on the right beyond Hill 112, has affected the German capacity to reinforce Louvigny and mount counter-attacks. And the shelling by 4th Field guns directed on the Athis flank by the CO may have been decisive.

As time goes on and more details become known, 4th Field will take some pride in the role played by their colonel who assumed

---

* Author interview.

command of 4th Brigade when Brig. Lett was wounded in the middle of the attack.*

As in all battles, no one is allowed more than a skimpy view of the struggle while it is in progress, and the outcome is not clear until the next morning, when B Company resumes the attack on the village and finds the enemy have pulled out during the night.

Only then is it clear Louvigny was won in the orchard and the château grounds, where the worst fighting took place. Some of it was truly hand-to-hand combat, one of the Royals strangling his foe with his bare hands when his Sten gun jammed just as he jumped through the hole blown in the stone wall and found himself face to face with him. There, in the relatively confined orchard of the château, while inflicting heavy casualties on the defenders and taking 55 prisoners, the Royals suffered most of their 111 casualties, 34 of them fatal, including 4 officers killed and 2 wounded.

The bitter harvest of war revealed next morning will remain forever a vivid memory for Lieut. Bob Suckling:

I was a platoon commander in D Company, but after five days in Eterville (under almost continuous bombardment that inflicted 92 casualties on the Royals) I may have appeared a bit unstable, and not to be trusted. Anyway, I was LOB [left out of battle] overnight during the attack on Louvigny.†

Next morning when I'm bringing up the D Company LOBs

---

* For his "skill and resourcefulness" in guiding the Brigade, and his "personal courage" in bringing down observed fire "while exposed to enemy snipers, mortar and shell-fire," Lt.-Col. C. M. Drury was awarded a DSO.

† "Left out of battle" is a term covering infantrymen sent back to a rear battalion area for a short rest, usually only a day or night. The term most accurately describes those routinely selected to remain out of the attack to ensure a continuity of experience and command. If the company commander (a major) is in the attack, his second-in-command (a captain) is

and we are passing Jack Anderson, the Acting CO, on the road, he asks, "How many are you?"

I tell him, "Twenty."

And he says, "Not enough!"

And he certainly is right. When I find D Company, there are only seventeen men left, out of perhaps eighty or ninety, and they are under command of Sgt. Tryon of the Support Company's 3-inch Mortar Platoon. My company commander, Jim Fairhead, is dead, and so is a fellow lieutenant by the name of Moulder. If I wasn't in a state of shock before, I certainly am now.

A little while later I learn that two other platoon commanders and Bob Rankin, Tom Whitley's 2IC, also died in the attack – and Tim Beatty, another company commander, and a Lieut. Downie were wounded.*

LOB; and if the platoon commander (a lieutenant) is in the attack, his sergeant is LOB. Because lieutenants are particularly vulnerable, a percentage are always LOB. Also, a number of privates, depending on the strength of companies, are designated LOB for the same reason: to make sure there'll be a nucleus on which to build another company.

*   Author interview.

24

TRICOLOUR RAISED ON RUBBLE
OF TOWN HALL

---------------- ❋ ----------------

ABOUT 10:00 P.M. ON JULY 18, YOU RECEIVE ORDERS AT THE guns to prepare to move. A short time later the quads come up and the guns are winched out of the pits and limbered up.* All vehicles are then lined up along the forward edge of the position close to the Verson road, Able Troop leading. There you wait for the order to move to a position near Louvigny.

For half an hour you wait, and as it get closer to 11:00 P.M. — the hour the Jerry bombers have been arriving nightly — you begin to worry that if you don't get off this position soon, the Regiment is going to get clobbered. And with all the equipment and personnel above ground, it could be a disaster. The memory of that string of bombs coming down across this very ground last night is still horribly vivid, and you find yourself sighing a great deal as you wait.

But 11:00 P.M. comes and goes and no Jerry planes arrive. You conclude that tonight he's too busy across the Orne and in the suburbs of Caen to bother with the guns back here. And judging by the fires glowing on the horizon, the muffled explosions, the continuous rumbling of distant guns and the whine of motors, which you assume are tanks, he's being kept very busy indeed.

----

* Gun trails were hooked to ammunition limbers, which in turn were hooked to the quads.

However, when the order finally does come to move up through Verson and you pull out on the road, a number of blinding-white chandelier flares burst into life and float smoking over the village. For a while, in spite of the clouds of dust your trucks are raising, you can see the terrible destruction in that poor village as the convoy picks its way over the torn roads, partially clogged here and there with rubble and burned-out vehicles.

Over the grinding truck motors, you hear the drone of the German bombers directly overhead, and for what seems an age you hold your breath, expecting that at any moment their bombs or machine-gun bullets will come ripping down on the convoy. When the throb of their engines fades away without anything happening, you pull yourself together to make what use you can of the obscene light they've left hanging over you, to read the way ahead and spot your progress along the route marked on your map board in black chinagraph pencil.

To your profound relief the planes don't come back. Evidently the Orne crossings, including one by the Black Watch from the racetrack in Caen, have the attention of the German planes tonight. When the flares burn out, they leave everything even darker than before.

It is very slow going, with several stops to make sure you are still following the right route. Once you are close to Le Mesnil you are directed right by a Don R doing "point duty" along what seems to be a farm track across open fields towards Louvigny, and you are able to move at a good pace.

Just after the track has met the road, and the convoy is passing between an orchard on the left and the looming walls of old stone buildings of Louvigny crowding the road on the right, white tracer bullets flicker across the road in front of your vehicle towards the orchard. They're German of course, for Stens and Brens don't use tracers. Immediately you halt the convoy and, jumping down, pass the order back along the line of vehicles for everyone to get out and into the ditch with their small arms.

As you crouch in the ditch, straining your eyes and ears and wondering how on earth you are going to get the Regiment out of this predicament, three or four dark figures run out of the orchard on the left and clatter across the road, disappearing among the buildings on the right, no more than twenty-five yards away. For a moment, as they are outlined against the reddish glow from burning Caen, you are able to make out the unmistakable silhouette of German pot helmets. Then, with startling intimacy and clarity, out of the darkness of the orchard, a voice shouts, "Get those vehicles out of the way — I've got casualties here!"

Instantly you recognize that slightly snarling, slightly nasal, and more-than-slightly imperious voice you'd heard so often in the darkness of that wretched orchard in Eterville only four days ago. Major Whitley's voice is hoarse with fatigue, and there is a strident, desperate note in it, but it still rings with authority, completely unsubdued by whatever has been the experience of A Company tonight. While it's disconcerting to know you are passing in front of the infantry, the sound of that familiar voice is encouraging. The guns are not up here alone, the Royals are distributed in and around here somewhere.

You wish you could be of assistance to him, but you've got your own problems. If the Germans still hold the village, and this seems clearly to be the case, then the gun positions beyond the village to which you are leading the Regiment are in no-man's-land!

The only sensible thing to do is to turn the convoy around and go back to the old position. But there is no way to turn the vehicles here, jammed between stone walls and ditches. Even if it were possible to manhandle the guns and limbers about, and inch the quads around, it would take all night.

You hear a motorbike coming this way, and wonder if it's friend or foe. As he materializes out of the gloom, you see the silhouette of a friendly crash helmet, and climb up out of the ditch to meet him. When the motor is shut off, you recognize the voice of Bill Murdoch, the regimental orderly officer. Normally Bill's a guy who strives to be blasé, regardless of how bizarre or outrageous the situation. But tonight, as you hold a low-voiced conference with him, it's obvious the situation has really got to him, for he is very subdued.

"Looks like the village hasn't been taken yet," you whisper.

"That's pretty obvious."

"But aren't our positions beyond the village, by the river?"

"Yes."

"My God, Bill, what are we supposed to do? If we could turn everything around and go back . . . but it's impossible."

"Well," he says, "they didn't shoot at me on the way back here just now. Anyway, you haven't any choice – you can't turn them round."

Of course it's true – you have no choice. And so the sooner you get out of here the better, for there's nothing more vulnerable than an artillery regiment on wheels with its guns limbered up. But knowing what must be done in no way reduces your anxiety from having to lead the Regiment forward into that dark void up ahead, which any second now may erupt into a flashing, lethal hailstorm of bullets.

Standing beside Bill, staring down that sinister road, you wish to God you were anywhere else in the world but here. And you can tell he's thinking the same way. For a moment he just sits there. Then, standing up, with one foot searching for the motorbike's cranking pedal, he declares in a hoarse whisper, "Okay, let's get the hell out of here."

But before he kicks the bike into life, he seems to remember why he came back to meet you in the first place:

"Oh, just one thing. When we get to where you leave the road, the Number Ones will have to get out and lead the guns in on foot – the position is full of frigging great bomb craters and we'll lose a gun or two for sure if we're not careful. Look for a hole in the fence – crossing the ditch will be tricky. Anyway, follow me."

With that he kick-starts the bike and it comes to life with an indecent roar. Without waiting for you to get the order to "mount" passed back along the line of the ditch and everybody back into their vehicles, he pulls away and disappears in the gloom ahead.

Though you curse his impatience, he has unwittingly provided you with something to dwell on in place of the grim spectre of a German ambush as you get the convoy underway and try to catch up with him.

Actually, the convoy barely gets rolling before the road converges with another, and right there, in front of a tall wayside shrine, barely visible in the murk, Murdoch is waiting and pointing to a field on the right. So far so good! You've made it without attracting a shot.

A sense of relief flows through you as your vehicle dips down and bounces into the field over the rough culvert of fenceposts the advance party has lain across the ditch. While fully aware that the Regiment is still vulnerable as it deploys in no-man's-land, responsibility for its fate is dividing and devolving onto a great many other shoulders of varying rank and seniority, as it splits into six distinct communities known as "troop gun positions." From this moment on, you are responsible only for your own troop.

Now if the Germans will just leave you alone until you're dug in . . . It's soft earth, but the night is hot and humid, and the air is saturated with the foul odours produced by rotting, bloated cattle somewhere nearby. On the left, near where a railway bridge over the Orne should be, mortar bombs flash and crash periodically. Otherwise the area is spookily peaceful, with only the sound of shovelling to be heard in the immediate vicinity.

Just as you are coming to believe the Germans must have been pulling back out of the village when you saw them scuttling across the road in front of your vehicle, there's the distinctive *bur-rup bur-rup* of a Schmeisser among the dark buildings over the fence and across the road behind you. Tracers streak out, but to the rear, away from the guns, towards the orchard behind the village as before.

In the silence that follows, a voice asks, "Is that a Jerry?" When he's assured that it is, the tempo of the shovelling can be heard to rise markedly on all sides.

Now and then throughout the night, during lulls in the mortar bombardment of the collapsed railway bridge over on the left, a Schmeisser *bur-rups* in the village, but never are its shots directed towards the gun position.

The first target shortly after dawn on July 19, for which no explanation is offered, is on this side of the river, just to the right of the village, at the ridiculously low range of 1,200 yards from the pivot gun of Able Troop, on the extreme right of the regimental position. Even using Charge 1 to gain maximum elevation for the gun muzzles, you will barely manage to clear the trees bordering the field and lining the riverbank along the front of the position, screening you from enemy territory on this side of the river, and to some extent the other side of the river. Actually, the trees are so close you have the gun sergeants open the breeches of their guns and look up through their barrels to make sure they can't see any tree branches before they load and fire. Shortly after, you have them do the same thing again when the SOS target is called only a thousand yards away on the other side of the river, beyond the broken bridge.

As the sun climbs in the sky, the lack of sleep begins to hit you, but you must remain alert. Information is sketchy; there's a rumour the Royals have occupied the whole of Louvigny. This would seem to be true, for Moaning Minnies begin to crash sporadically among the buildings and beyond, in what must be the château grounds. Then you get a report that when the Royals moved into the village at first light, they found the enemy had withdrawn during the night, which would explain why the Germans didn't attack the guns. If they were committed to withdrawing even before the guns came in last night, it would make little sense to men armed with Schmeissers to challenge the big guns in a duel.

In the daylight the village is a pitiful sight. Ragged buildings, torn and gutted by fire from yesterday's bombing and shelling and now damp with dew, give off a wretched, acrid smell of charred wood, joining the sickening odours coming from the dead cattle. Directly behind the guns, buildings in various states of ruin face the field from the other side of a roadway that is a tangle of rubble and drooping wires. Lying on the roadway just over the fence from your command post is a huge clock-tower, its face and hands largely intact, just as they were when it toppled down yesterday morning from the blast of a bomb that wrecked the building it graced, unquestionably the town hall.

As you stand at the fence, contemplating the terrible price Norman towns are paying for their liberation, a man of aristocratic bearing appears from the direction of the crossroads and its wayside Calvary. Following him closely is a boy, carrying, like a banner on a long staff, a large flag of France.

The man manages to march with great dignity, even as he picks his way through rubble strewn here and there in his path. The silent little parade attracts the attention of all eyes still awake and on the gun position. The man's solemn dignity is so studied, and the boy's attempt to emulate him while carrying the oversized flag so incongruous, the whole thing would in normal times be humorous. But this morning it is not; it is damned impressive.

When they reach the remains of the town hall, the man stops and directs the boy to plant the flag near the remnants of a doorway. And as the boy climbs up on the rubble and tries to fix the staff in a crack, the man makes gestures to plant it higher – still higher. When finally both are satisfied, the boy returns to the man's side, and together, standing rigidly at attention, they salute the flag.

Another bit of France is free.

The man, you'll learn later, is Jules Hollier-Larousse, mayor of Louvigny, and his flag-bearer is his son, Thierry, brought back from school in Paris before the invasion to act as a courier for the FFI (Free French of the Interior). Very small for his age – looking twelve rather than seventeen years old – Thierry was never suspected by

the Germans, though he bore them a deep hatred and had a strong
desire for revenge.

One afternoon before the invasion, a squad of Germans had
roared into the yard of the Larousses' ancient farmhouse and
demanded they reveal the hiding place of an illicit transmitter their
directional-finders had established was right there.

Just minutes earlier a family friend, Leon Dumis, another captain
in the Resistance, had moved the transmitter to Château Louvigny,
a couple of miles away. When the Germans couldn't find it, they
lined up father, mother, and boy with their hands against a wall and
told them they would remain there until 6:00 P.M. If by then the
transmitter had not come on the air it would be proof that they
were the culprits, and they would be shot.

Thierry's mother at one point spat at the feet of one of the
guards, who in response jammed her savagely against the wall and
threatened to kill her. This was when Thierry swore he'd have his
revenge if he survived.

And the Larousses had all been allowed to live, because Dumis, at
his new location, had gone on the air just before six, and the
German signaller in the nearby truck reported this fact to the
officer in charge.

Later, as the Allied invading forces drew near their farm and the
Germans ordered them to remove themselves from the battle zone,
the Larousses became for a time refugees, sometimes living in the
fields. Eventually the family managed to cross over into Allied territory, where father and son were able to help the Canadians by
supplying information on the location of German positions.

Once, Thierry, using as an excuse the need to cut hay for their
horse, went out into no-man's-land with a scythe, and until he had
noted the location of the German trenches he studiously ignored
the calls and waving arms of the Canadians on one side and
Germans on the other as they tried to warn the "stupid child" to
come in.

On another occasion some Canadians spotted a German Luger pistol in his back pocket and were lining him up for execution as a spy when a neighbour identified him as the son of the mayor of Louvigny. They allowed him to keep his Luger, and he rewarded them later by using it to release some of their buddies from a German marching them down a road near the farm. Another time near Athis, he saw German tanks churning across the Orne by way of a long-forgotten Roman ford that had become useable with the lower water level caused by the destruction of a dam downstream. He brought this crucial information to an artillery unit north of the farm. Until then, the Allies had no idea how the Germans got their tanks back and forth over the Orne without a bridge.

The day after the Chaudières overran the Larousse farm on July 10, they were relieved by the Fusiliers Mont-Royal. That day Thierry and his father returned. Immediately his father dug up in the garden a dozen bottles of prime Calvados he had saved from all he had systematically poured on the ground the day France fell to ensure the Germans would never have it. Though the soldiers were warned it was very strong – almost 50 per cent stronger than whisky – they overindulged. So all lay stretched out on the floor of the living room, dead to the world, when from an upstairs window Thierry spotted Germans poking around in the barnyard and looking in the long line of stable doors. Rushing downstairs, he went from one snoring form to another until he was able to get one on his feet. Leading the staggering soldier with a Bren outside to a vantage point along a high wall that separated garden from barnyard, he pointed down at the Germans investigating the stables. By then there were half a dozen.

The soldier tried to get a bead on them, steadying his Bren on the top of the wall, but he was wavering so much it was difficult. By the time his aim was steady enough, seventeen Germans had gathered in the barnyard cul-de-sac. He emptied a full magazine into them – then another.

25

IN THE DISTANCE THE
SKIRL OF PIPES

*

AS FAR AS 2ND DIVISION IS CONCERNED IT'S A 5TH BRIGADE show today (July 19). During the night, while 4th Field was digging in here at Louvigny, west of the Orne, the Black Watch crossed the river up at the Caen racetrack, and the rest of the brigade followed. Le Régiment de Maisonneuve are to attack down this way to clear the east bank to the village of Fleury-sur-Orne only about half a mile away, directly across the river from the guns, which by now may have been outflanked by the British armoured divisions.

Before noon, the gunners are preparing ammunition for a heavy fire plan to begin at 1300 hours with a creeping barrage of eighteen lifts on a frontage of 1,200 yards.* It will involve all 2nd Division guns and four medium regiments of 2nd AGRA (Army Group Royal Artillery).

The barrage, designed to carry the Maisonneuves 2,000 yards south from their startline on the outskirts of the factory area of Caen, takes two hours to fire. Because of the unique position of the

---

* A barrage is a belt of fire moving ahead of the advancing troops. A creeping barrage is the usual type used in support of the infantry. The fire of the units taking part in it remains in the same relative positions throughout and the whole barrage advances together in steps, or "lifts," one line at a time (usually 100 yards apart) at a pace designed to conform

guns relative to the axis of the barrage, the "lifts," which normally take shells farther away from the guns, are really switches in line to the right, with continuous slight reductions in ranges, bringing the shells closer to the guns as the infantry sweep down the river, from the left along the high ground past the menacing water-tower across from your guns.

By afternoon, ranges to targets are increasing, and while the Maisies are consolidating in Fleury, the guns engage in some heavy divisional concentrations on behalf of the Calgary Highlanders, who pass through Fleury at 5:15 P.M. on their way to taking Point 67, a bald hill about two hundred feet higher than Louvigny and plainly visible some two thousand yards away through a gap in the line of trees skirting the front of Able Troop gun position.

Just about the time the Highlanders should be arriving at Point 67, Baker Troop Sgt.-Maj. "Rod" Williams arrives at your command post in such haste he starts a minor avalanche of sand and gravel down the crude earthen stairs of the dugout. Even before his slipping, sliding descent has ended, he is begging — nay, demanding — that you come out with your field-glasses and map to range on some Germans he's spotted dashing about on a hill across the river.

When you clamber outside to look, fully expecting that whatever he saw will long since have disappeared, you are astonished to see, less than fifteen hundred yards away, three or four crouching figures begin to run hell-for-leather up the slope away from you.

Even with the naked eye you can identify them by their baggy

---

with the rate of advance of the troops it is supporting. In an infantry attack it will rarely be faster than 100 yards in three minutes, and in difficult country it can be as slow as 100 yards in five or six minutes. For an armoured attack the barrage will move at 100 yards or more a minute. The width of the barrage is dictated by the number of guns available. The fire of field guns is arranged along each line at 25-yard intervals, and for the mediums, 50 yards.

camouflaged smocks belted-in at the waist. Before they reach the crest, you have them in your field-glasses. Sharply outlined against the sky, those bent-over, leg-churning men seem so shockingly close that for an instant you are back on the Alfriston practice ranges in Sussex watching British soldiers, dressed in captured field-grey uniforms, illustrate German infantry tactics for the officers of 2nd Division and the Home Guard. Clearly visible are their potlike, distinctly German helmets and those peculiar, corrugated cans (holding respirators) bouncing on their rumps as they scurry up and over the hill to the southwest. No sooner have they disappeared than two more small groups – about a hundred yards apart – rise up and start a similar gallop up the slope.

By now it's obvious that significant numbers are involved in this strange manoeuvre. You study the map and try to figure it out. Just how far along could our troops have advanced? Are those Jerries moving into position to hit the Calgary Highlanders from the flank, or have they been driven off the hill by the advancing Highlanders and in the process of withdrawing to a defensive line from which they'll almost immediately emerge in a blazing counter-attack – as had been strikingly illustrated by those Limey soldiers that day in 1943 in that natural amphitheatre on the South Downs?

By now the Sergeant-Major is frantic with impatience: "What in hell are WE waiting for, SIR?" Then, interpreting your lengthy study of the map and apparent indecisiveness as the inability to establish a map reference for that hill over there, he inquires loudly, "Why can't WE engage them over open sights, SIR?"

While you agree it's very tempting, you point out the risk is too great. The Highlanders could appear right in the target area as you are firing, in fact they might be there already, out of sight. We simply don't know where they are and have no way of finding out.

Using the map you try to explain all this to the very frustrated Sergeant-Major, but he can't keep his eyes off that hill across the river, even though it is now completely empty of all movement.

At last, convinced a great opportunity has been lost through your timidity, he turns away, and muttering deeply under his breath stalks off in the direction of Baker Troop, wagging his head in disappointment and disgust.

As you make your way back to the command post dugout, you think you must be going batty, for over the racket of mortaring across the river, you could swear you hear the faint skirl of bagpipes.*

An ammo count at 8:30 P.M. reveals that in the past twenty-four hours more than five hundred rounds per gun have been fired. At dusk the guns take part in divisional concentrations on behalf of the Black Watch attacking the village of Ifs. By midnight they have the village and are being counter-attacked. Then it's the Calgary Highlanders' turn. Throughout the night the guns are mainly on harassing fire, and whenever you have need to leave your candle-lit dugout to answer a call of nature, the darkness along the ridge over the river is filled with flashes and rumbles. But the main concern of the gunners becomes the digging-in of 350 rounds per gun dumped by Army Service – the first instalment of 1,000 rounds per gun, which they say is to be the normal complement for guns of 2nd Division from now on.

By now it is clear the British armoured attack has bogged down without gaining the high ground overlooking the line of advance, and the heavy dumping of ammunition can mean only one thing: extraordinary demands are about to be made on the guns in support

---

* Reginald Roy's book *The Canadians in Normandy* (Toronto: Macmillan, 1984), p. 77, describing the attack by the Calgary Highlanders to clear "the hill which had permitted the enemy to overlook Louvigny" confirms this: "Eager for battle and with at least one piper playing 'The Advance' as the men swept across the fields of grain and up the slopes of their objective, the Highlanders encountered mostly enemy snipers and mortar fire."

of the infantry heading for Verrières Ridge. While the usual state of ignorance persists, there are convincing rumours the tanks have taken an awful beating. One story, delivered with the Compo rations last night by Troop Sgt.-Maj. Mann, and reputedly from an eyewitness, inspires the image of wheat fields covered with burning British tanks.

Anyone with the inclination to speculate must assume that when the tanks quit attacking, as soon they must to cut their losses, the poor bloody infantry of 2nd Division will have to take over. And the word "bloody" may well become something more than a rude description of the men who must walk across those open fields and up that sloping ground. When three British crack armoured divisions – their right flank secured by 2nd Canadian Corps and preceded by the greatest aerial bombardment ever undertaken in support of ground forces – were unable to subdue the German fire dominating those open slopes of Verrières Ridge, clearly every yard will be bought dearly by infantry battalions.

26

OF MURDER TARGETS AND

BODY ARMOUR

❋

AT NOON ON JULY 20, THREE HOURS BEFORE THE ATTACK BY
6th Brigade with Essex Scottish attached, the villages of St. André-
sur-Orne and St. Martin-de-Fontenay, sitting cheek-by-jowl down
on the right from Verrières Ridge, are subjected to a "murder
target" shelling by all field guns of 2nd and 3rd divisions and all the
mediums and heavies of three AGRAs. In just three minutes, 59 tons
of shells (60 per cent more than were fired during the Battle of
Waterloo) are sent screaming and crashing into the twin hamlets by
six regiments of 25-pounders firing 1,728 rounds, nine medium
regiments firing 648 100-pound shells, and two regiments of 7.2-
inch heavies firing 48 200-pound monsters.

A German artillery officer, captured at an OP on the hill eight
hundred yards north of St. Martin, is much impressed by the concentrated fire that descended on him shortly before he was taken
prisoner. According to Intelligence, the German "feels all troops in
the area are very shaken. Seven years in army – through Stalingrad
fight – first-class soldier – has never experienced anything like our
artillery concentrations."[*]

Those ravaged interlocking villages of St. Martin and St. André

---

[*]   2nd Cdn Corps OP "Atlantic," file 225C2.012 (D7), National Archives
of Canada.

are the objective of the Queens' Own Cameron Highlanders of Canada as they attack south along the river; while the South Saskatchewan Regiment – with the Essex Scottish in close support – attack up the slope in the centre to consolidate on the ridge at a point just over the crest; and the Fusiliers Mont-Royal thrust along the left flank bordering the Caen–Falaise highway towards Verrières, some 3.5 kilometres south of their startline at the village of Ifs.

Scheduled for noon, the attack is postponed in the hope that the black, lowering clouds will clear away, allowing the rocket-firing Typhoons to engage on call hull-down tanks as they are encountered on the ridge. And it's not until 3:00 P.M., with the cloud cover even blacker, that the infantry, accompanied by some tanks of the Sherbrooke Fusiliers, move out panting in the sultry heat behind a thunderous program of timed concentrations involving various combinations of the guns that had fired the murder target.

About halfway between Ifs and Verrières, in an otherwise bald landscape of rolling wheat fields rising gently towards the ridge, are two low clumps of stone buildings about a kilometre apart along the road leading west from the Caen–Falaise highway to St. André. On the map they are identified as Troteval Farm and Beauvoir Farm.

The two farms are the first objectives of the Fusiliers Mont-Royal, as two companies lead off, each with a 4th Field FOO, to walk across two kilometres of open country. Gordon Hunter (Baker Troop Commander) is with the company on the right that's to pass through Beauvoir Farm, and Brit Smith (Dog Troop Commander) is on foot with the company that's to clear Troteval Farm on the left about 450 metres west of the Caen–Falaise highway.

To confuse the snipers into thinking his rank doesn't deserve any special attention, Brit carries a rifle. And though it's a very hot day, his battledress collar is buttoned up to cover his tie, and his little camouflage veil is strung about his neck and wound around his epaulettes to hide the three captain's pips on each shoulder.

Adding to his sweaty discomfort, under his battledress he is wearing the body armour that was issued to all infantrymen and artillery carrier crews coming to Normandy: the fabric-covered, moulded pieces of dense plastic, designed to yield, but not break, on catching the impact of a bullet or shell fragment. Unlike the medieval variety, body armour in Normandy, 1944, is made up of separate pieces that dangle on shoulder straps, and is usually (but not always) worn underneath battledress pants and blouses. Your back is protected by one piece, an upside-down "T" across the kidneys and lungs, with the perpendicular part running up the spine between the shoulder-blades. Across the chest is a breast protector, and from it a belly-pad hangs down loosely, so that when you bend over, the two will fold. But when jumping down into a trench with knees bent, you can knock your wind out, since the lower piece is inclined to get jammed up and strike you across the belt line.

For this and other reasons – not the least of which is the very disturbing psychological effect of being constantly reminded of the vulnerability of your vital, life-sustaining, and life-giving organs – some men have quit wearing it after only a few days.* But for Brit Smith and thousands of others participating in the first infantry attack on the Verrières Ridge, those plastic pads are very reassuring when the hour comes to move out across some two thousand yards of open wheat fields, knowing there is no way to escape attracting

---

* While body armour largely disappeared from use by the end of the summer – as much left behind with the wounded and the dead as was discarded by survivors of Normandy – some men who came through it all unscathed or who actually knew they'd been saved from death by it were still wearing it in October along the Scheldt. And some looked like ghosts from the past as they wore it flapping outside their battledress – boldly, without apology, almost as if it were the mark of the long-service veteran. One soldier who wore it in this fashion was a Royals' stretcher-bearer – a man of proven, outstanding courage.

fire that can come at you with chilling suddenness: a burst of tracers out of nowhere accompanied by the distinctly nasty *bur-rup bur-rup* of a Schmeisser or MG 42 capable of 1,200 rounds a minute.

And very shortly Brit will learn that this body armour really works, that the long-fibred plastic, when hit, will stretch inwards forming a bulge that can bruise (and bruise painfully when it strikes where only a thin layer of flesh covers the bone), but absorbing and restraining otherwise lethal forces:

I'm going forward on foot with Major Mousseau [Fernand], an FMR company commander. My carrier is rolling along some distance behind, but walking with us is one of my signallers with a 38-set (a light sending and receiving radio set of limited range) with which we can send fire orders back to the signaller on the big 19-set in the carrier for relaying to the guns.

We've been told the clearing of the two farms on the way through is just an administrative move, that we are not likely to encounter any resistance simply because there's nobody there. According to a British report, the Germans have pulled back – a couple of their scout cars went through the area this morning and didn't see anybody.*

But, my God, the Germans have tanks hull-down in holes all over the place, and bags of infantry from a low-numbered division [lst SS Leibstandarte Adolph Hitler Panzer Division].

Almost immediately we encounter sniper fire. A lot of the wheat has been cut and stooked in the fields, and here and there

---

* At daybreak July 20, 4th Battalion County of London Yeomanry, an armoured regiment of the 22nd Armoured Brigade, having cleared Hubert-Folie east of the Caen–Falaise highway, was ordered to take the village of Verrières. By 10:00 A.M. a squadron had "mopped up" Beauvoir Farm, but opposition from Verrières was too strong, and it was withdrawn east of the highway. (Paragraph 195 Report 58 Historical Section Cdn Army H.Q., Dept. of National Defence)

in the stooks, are enemy snipers. So, very soon the FMRs start setting fire to the stooks up ahead, hitting them with phosphorous grenades. And when the snipers see the odd guy come screaming out of a grain stook, his uniform covered with burning phosphorus, they start popping up all over the place with their hands up.

Up to now we aren't being mortared or shelled (probably because we are passing among his snipers), and there's a lot of smoke from the flaming stooks. But when we send the prisoners running back to Ifs with their hands over their heads, shells begin to land around us.*

The foot-soldiers make it to the farm buildings [Troteval Farm] without too many casualties, but our tanks and anti-tank guns don't fare so well. Two Shermans brew up after being holed several times, and the others pull back. The anti-tank platoon of the FMRs is shot to hell. Fortunately the Germans don't waste their shots on a mere OP carrier. They let us go by, but when a T-16 carrier comes up towing an anti-tank gun, *wham!* he's gone. They knock out all the guns in that grain field from Ifs down to Troteval–Beauvoir road.

There are some stubborn SS in the farm buildings, and as they are being cleaned out, I take a Schmeisser burst along my chest that could have been very bad except for my body armour. Two 9-mm bullets leave indentations in my breastplate about an inch deep (deep enough that Quarter Stores will replace it without argument), but I'm only bruised. Once the buildings are clear, we pull out and dig in about a hundred yards away on three sides, reasoning that when he mounts his counter-attack, he'll focus his bombardment on the fixed target of the buildings.†

---

*   The Fusiliers Mont-Royal took 149 prisoners, 49 of them only three hundred yards from their startline.
†   Author interview.

However, the war diary of the Fusiliers Mont-Royal will record that they only start to consolidate about 5:00 P.M., when the newly captured positions are "for over an hour under extremely heavy mortar, shell, rocket and M.G. [machine gun] fire." This coincides with the arrival of a thunderstorm that had been threatening all afternoon, its cloud-bursting rain shutting down all air support, hampering radio communications, and bringing on early darkness to a confused and smoking battlefield. The scout platoon and one company, pushing south beyond the road between the two farms, are isolated from the rest of the battalion by shelling and mortaring, and by infiltrating enemy infantry and tanks. Then at 10:45 P.M. the company at Beauvoir Farm loses the vital support of their artillery FOO when Gordon Hunter, Baker Troop Commander, is wounded and evacuated.

Tankmen around Beauvoir Farm will later report: "The infantry cleared the top storeys of the farm buildings and reported the farm clear. One platoon was left in the Beauvoir Farm area and the advance continued towards Verrières. As soon as the advance was well-started, approximately one company of German infantry came out of the cellars of the houses and opened fire on the Fusiliers Mont-Royal from the rear."*

* "27 Cdn Armoured Regiment (Sherbrooke Fusiliers) Op 'Atlantic,' Overture to Breakthrough," p. 15, prepared by Directorate of History and held by Historical Section at Dept. of National Defence.

27

"IT'S BLOODY SUICIDE UP THERE!"

--- ✳ ---

BY THE TIME THE STORM BREAKS, THE CAMERONS HAVE GAINED part of St. André and the orchard north of St. Martin-de-Fontenay, and are holding onto the positions they have taken, though they are overlooked by the Germans on Hill 112 across the Orne, and are forced to endure merciless shelling.*

In the centre, however, the South Saskatchewan Regiment are driven to wriggling back over the ridge on their bellies through the wet grain and mud, seeking only to escape the savage machine-gunning and the crushing tracks of rampaging Panther and Tiger tanks. They hardly reach their objective (a field of peas beyond the crest, looking across at distant ridges and nearby enemy-held villages) before being hit by a hail of machine-gun fire, shells, and mortars and driven back from their exposed position into the wheat, the only available cover.

And even as they crawl through the three-feet-high wheat, the insensate steel monsters, with engines roaring horribly, follow them, trying to squash them or flush them out where their machine guns can get at them.

---

* German sources will reveal all the guns and mortars of 2nd SS Panzer Corps were directed on St. André and the orchard as though in retaliation for 2nd Canadian Corps' murder target on the village earlier in the day.

Mercifully, darkness comes early under the black rain-clouds. With their acting commanding officer, intelligence officer, and two company commanders dead, and all companies badly dispersed and riddled with casualties (66 dead, 116 wounded, and 26 taken prisoner), the remnants of the SSRs are finally able to make their way back through the Essex Scottish dug-in around Point 67, about halfway up from Ifs.

However, the sight of badly demoralized men making for the rear in disorder, many of them walking-wounded, does not help the morale of the Essex. Their spirits are already sinking from the realization they now are completely at the mercy of the German tanks, following the swift destruction of a troop of 17-pounder anti-tank guns of 2nd Anti-Tank Regiment which had rushed up the slope from Ifs to meet the expected German tank attack. In rapid succession, one after another as each came into view, they were knocked out by the German tanks: first their towing vehicles and then all four guns, killing twelve gunners and wounding eight more, even before trails could be dropped and their guns brought into action.

The memory of each grim hour of the next twenty-four on the ridge will remain forever vivid for Lance-Bombardier Kenneth Munro, a member of Capt. Grange's carrier crew in support of the Essex Scottish. They will be his last in action before being taken prisoner along with another member of the crew, Signaller Hans Nielson:

> When Capt. Parker, of Easy Troop, is killed passing through Ifs with the Essex, and we take over, we move with the leading company up the long, gradual slope south of the village to take up a reserve position behind the SSRs [South Saskatchewan Regiment].
>
> Artillery and mortar fire is heavy and it's very difficult for the infantry advancing without cover up the sloping ground. As we

move closer to the enemy we can sense the confusion ahead. Then we start passing groups of the SSRs retreating from the front – very frightened men – a large number of them walking-wounded. Then we pass some of our anti-tank guns that have been knocked out and abandoned in a hurry, clear evidence our troops were pounced on quickly by enemy tanks and never got a chance to get into firing position. None of our tanks are moving with us. So it's our men against tanks – the best tanks in the war – at the same time facing heavy mortar and artillery fire.

We see no one surrendering, for we're still not quite in view of the enemy, but the sight of the SSRs retreating from the front in that frightened, unorganized way certainly has an effect on the Essex – especially when one SSR yells at us, "It's bloody suicide to go up there!"

Surely that's what every man is thinking. And those who were at Dieppe must be saying to themselves, "Here we go again . . ." I don't see any of the Essex turn and run, but talking to them next day, they mention that some did turn back as the battle grew more intense. Anyway, when we dig in, there are no infantrymen in front of us.*

Capt. Grange's OP is near the crest of the ridge, where it is intended the Essex will be in reserve, but it immediately becomes the front line. He will tell you later:

Throughout the night and next morning I bring down considerable fire and am pretty useful in holding back the German infantry. It's here I learn the only certain way to protect yourself is to pull the guns right down on your own map reference [shell your own position]. After dark the German tanks move around

---

* This and the following quotations from Kenneth Munro are from an interview with the author.

the flanks, and when daylight comes and their attacks become more and more serious against the depleted ranks of the Essex, nothing resembling a front line is allowed to exist until the position is overrun in the afternoon.*

Meanwhile over on the left, some eight hundred yards away, driven from Beauvoir Farm and forced to give up trying to make it to Verrières, the FMRs have been able to maintain their foothold at Troteval Farm throughout the night and well into the next afternoon (July 21), only because of the intense fire from 4th Field guns.

Armed with rifles and Stens (the Bren is clogged with mud), the men of Brit Smith's crew supplement the small-arms fire from the now sparsely populated infantry trenches around them, killing many of the enemy when they work within twenty yards of their observation post. Smith repeatedly brings down all twenty-four guns in Mike target concentrations of thirty, fifty, and sixty rounds per gun:

> They have about a dozen really big tanks (Panthers and Royal Tigers) as well as about fifty Mark IVs in the two or three miles I can observe from our slit trench. But you never see them all at once, and there's a confusing number of derelict tanks lying about, both his and ours, knocked out during Goodwood. For a while we are right between his tanks on the left and ours coming up on the right. One of his with an 88-mm gun (probably a Tiger) is dug-in over in a copse near the Caen–Falaise highway firing from a hull-down position. He's so bloody close – only about two hundred yards away – that each time he fires, the muzzle blast bangs our ears together and flattens the grain all around us as the shot screeches overhead and a shower of sparks

---

* This and the following quotations from Sammy Grange are from an interview with the author.

goes up from one of our tanks up on the hill, which he keeps hitting until it brews up.

The Typhoons aren't flying because of the rain. Anyway, the Tiger is too close. (We're much afraid of a Typhoon missing its target and hitting us.) So I put a battery of mediums on him and hammer him for about half an hour. (I may not have knocked him out, but I'll bet I loosened up the bowels of that crew.) It rains a lot during the night, and some FMRs decide to go back and find their rear echelon and get their greatcoats. They haven't eaten since the day before yesterday. They marched for hours getting up to the startline at Ifs after somebody cancelled their breakfast yesterday. And without any lunch, they were sent into the attack. Everybody is soaked to the skin and dripping with mud, for the slit trenches are now just sump holes and no one even has a ground sheet. In the morning Major Mousseau says, "Some of my men are missing." And at first light the Germans begin to attack in earnest. In considerable numbers they come crouched-over alongside the tanks and it's our guns that are driving them back.*

I don't know how many casualties we inflict because they fall flat in the wheat whether or not they are hit. At first their attacks are infantry only, and we are able to cope with them reasonably well with our artillery fire, but when they begin coming with tanks, we realize the jig is up. We have no anti-tank guns, no Piat ammunition, and the FMRs are very thin on the ground.

In some haste we have to abandon our OP in a forward trench and crawl back through the wheat to the farm buildings. Here we have to keep shifting our position to take on targets. For a while we are in a hole on the right side of the farm, engaging something – then we hear somebody calling, "They're coming in from the left!"

---

* Capt. Arthur Britton Smith was awarded the Military Cross for his gallant efforts.

By late afternoon [July 21] we've stood off at least three counter-attacks, but the company is getting low on ammunition and men, and the few left have had practically nothing to eat for two days. By now I'm the only link with battalion H.Q., and the only information they are getting about what's happening to the company is through me. I keep asking, Why don't they send up reinforcements – another battalion? My God, we're a mile and a quarter in front of Ifs. Where is the reserve battalion? The remnants of one company – no more than a platoon – is now holding this farm, and no one is making any attempt to reinforce it.

Major Mousseau is wounded and captured, and the last FMR officer I talk to arrives in my trench shot through the elbow. The bullet has not gone through the bone, but the muscle is badly torn, and when we bandage him up, we tell him, "We're going to try to get our carrier out of here, so if you want to join us, we'll take you out."

It's about 4:00 P.M. The last of the infantrymen have trundled off into the grain – grey suits are materializing and tanks are starting to wander around unmolested by anything. It's clear the only way we'll get out of here is under cover of some shell-fire. So I lay the guns on the position and tell them to "Fire until you're told to stop." I figure it'll take us five minutes to get away. But when we scramble into the carrier that's parked against a high stone wall at the rear of the barnyard next to the road, and help the infantry officer into a rear compartment, Bombardier May can't get it to start. The rain has done its work. By now tank engines are roaring all around the bloody house, but all May can produce is a pitiful *rurr-rurr-rurr* . . .

We've no choice but to climb out and help the wounded infantry officer out of the rear compartment so the side cover can be removed from the engine box to allow May to fiddle with the distributor cap and the ignition wires.

Everybody is sweating blood. The only uniforms now in sight are grey, and those big engines on the tanks are terrifying. They sound as though they're right beside us! We're against one of the stone walls alongside the road, and I keep thinking, Any moment now one of those monsters is going to drive right through that wall and it will be all over. Somehow Bombardier May is able to retain his wits as he works on the engine. Unquestionably the best OP ack God ever made . . . always seems to know what you want before you ask . . . continually reminding you of something you might otherwise neglect to do, but always the courteous gentleman with a great sense of humour – putting up with horrible handicaps and hardships without flinching or saying anything derogatory of the people who have put him in that position . . .

At last the engine starts, and we all pile back in, all but the infantry officer, who has disappeared – captured I think. As we start moving out, our guns are still pouring hundreds of shells around the place, and Bill Murdoch [orderly officer and acting adjutant] comes on the blower to ask, "When are you going to stop? The paint is burning off the gun barrels." And I tell him, "Give me one more minute."

Pulling away we do our best to stay in the folds of the ground, but we attract bursts of machine gun fire. All of a sudden I am being plastered with white stuff, and I think, "Oh God, now they're throwing phosphorous grenades at us!" But then other mysterious bits of sludge start flying around. So when we get back over a little dip in the ground, I get May to stop to find out what the hell has happened to us. The answer lies in a big tin of hardtack biscuits strapped on top of the engine and riddled with holes, punched by something very heavy, like half-inch machine-gun bullets, which blew the pulverized hardtack all over the carrier. The unsavoury bits of meat splattered about are from cans of bully beef, M & V, and other Compo rations we'd stored on the front of the carrier in a long wooden box – the kind Piats are shipped in. Box and contents have been smashed to hell by the heavy bullets from the tanks, but the carrier is undamaged. The paint is chipped off, but none of the bullets penetrated its walls.

Back at Battalion I inform them everybody has been pushed out of Troteval Farm, and I don't think many will succeed in making it back. They are either casualties, prisoners, or are scattered in the grain. Then I go back up with Major White's company to try to retake Beauvoir Farm that fell yesterday after Gord Hunter was wounded. But when we get just short of the farm, we see some Mark IV tanks up by Verrières.

Then a couple of Royal Tigers – probably the same ones which an hour ago cleaned out Troteval – roll in and around Beauvoir taking no precautions whatsoever, crunching around bold as brass. And nobody can do anything about it, for they've knocked out all our tanks and all the anti-tank guns as fast as they were brought up. They have the place to themselves, and White says, "There is no way we can go in there against those guys."*

Within the hour, the two companies of Essex Scottish (just west of there along the same road running past the farms to St. André) that were able to hold out against the German attacks overnight and through most of the morning of July 22 with the support of 4th Field guns, are also overrun. But before this happens, they are subjected to a demoralizing deluge of shells and mortars, combined with direct fire from German tanks – not just from their machine guns, but also from their 88s, used as sniper rifles at ground level.

So low do those shrieking shells pass over Lance-Bombardier Munro's head, "they feel as if they could almost suck you out of your trench." According to Munro:

---

* Author interview.

The Moaning Minnies are the most demoralizing – not only because of the tremendous impact of their explosions, but the effect of the terrifying sounds they make in flight. Some men cannot take the effects of this weapon. Occasionally fellows lose their nerve and jump up out of their trench – which is their only protection – and run, just run, not knowing where they are going, but yelling for their "Mum." It's always "Mum" – not God or anyone else – just "Mum." It's very tragic. You have to feel sorry for them.

Standing up is fatal. Jerry lets you have it if he sees any part of you. Mid-morning Col. Macdonald, the CO of the Essex, hollers at one of his men in a hole about sixty feet behind me to move out and get a count of the enemy tanks that can be seen. I hear the order and I advise the fellow to stay where he is, that I have a good view and can count what looks like thirteen tanks, though four or five may be only derelicts. Anyway the fellow accepts my count, but he stands up to relay the message back to his CO. At that instant, his back is ripped open by machine-gun fire. He moans for a few minutes, then silence.

Earlier I had talked to this chap from a distance. He said he had just arrived from Canada, after only a few days in England.

Munro's troop commander, Capt. Sammy Grange, will also have cause to remember those encircling tanks:

When dawn comes, they are behind us. And at one point I actually fire short of our position to try and get some of them. I'm already firing on our position when I order, "All North 100," to move the shells slightly to our rear. Not surprisingly, someone back at the guns questions this – don't we mean South 100? And I have to reassure him I really do mean to shell the area immediately north of here. Dicey, of course, but we're sheltering in trenches, and there's no alternative – the Germans are right there and we are just about surrounded.

As things are getting extremely hot and I am bringing the guns down almost constantly, the radio goes dead – we can't get through to anybody. So leaving Munro and Nielson to man the OP, I collect Pelletier [Gunner "Pooch" P.J.] and drive back to Bill Carr [Battery Commander] at Ifs to get fresh batteries or a replacement radio set, and report to him that things are in a very bad way up here.

Now, without the fire from 4th Field guns drenching the Germans with shells whenever they appear to be attempting to move in, it is clear to Munro that things are going from bad to worse:

From the moment Capt. Grange decides Nielson and I should stay behind "because it would not look good for all of us to leave, and perhaps they'll get a telephone line up here and you'll be able to get some badly needed fire," I have the feeling we'll never get out of this position.

The Essex have no tank or anti-tank support. Two of our tanks come over a ridge behind us about half a mile from the closest enemy tank. One is hit with the first enemy shot and burns, and the other does a 180-degree turn and flees. There is one 17-pounder anti-tank gun on the position, but someone has removed the firing pin [maybe during the SSRs retreat], and so it's useless. And because of the rain and clouds, there is no air support. There's a rumour the Camerons on our right, and the FMRs on our left, are pulling back, which would leave the Essex unprotected on both flanks.

To Nielson and me it's a hopeless mess – the Essex seem doomed. From my trench I have a very good view of the enemy directly opposite, across a depression and up on higher ground. As time passes, they increase their shelling and machine-gun fire, and around noon I tell Nielson I'm going to try to get back to Col. Macdonald (the CO of the Essex) and ask his permission to leave the position on our own. This seems to me better than sitting here like dopes waiting to be taken prisoner.

By now I have no hope – only a miracle can save us. After burying my map, field-glasses, and compass, I start crawling, and I make it, wriggling very close to the ground. My suggestion is turned down flat. But when, a moment later, a member of his [Macdonald's] crew is hit, two other men are allowed to try to get him back, while Nielson and I are obliged to stay. It doesn't make sense.

Now I can't get back to my previous position, because the enemy fire has become very intense – not only machine guns, but self-propelled guns firing armour-piercing solid-shot directly at us. I can't see as well here as I could before, but I can hear the tanks inching closer. And I'm sure there are some enemy tanks and infantry behind us also.

My hope is rekindled when Major Carr crawls up here alone, and has a few words with Col. Macdonald. But when I ask if I may go back with him, I am told to stay put.

About half an hour later, a couple of enemy infantrymen come into our position. I pick up a rifle that's handy, but they holler, "Me Polski!" For a moment, no one seems to know what to do. And before a minute passes, we are overrun with German infantry The Regimental Sergeant-Major [Essex Scottish] puts up a white flag. It all happens so fast. Their tanks don't come right into our area, but three or four stand on the perimeter of the position. Thinking about it, the German infantry probably were closing in around us all day. Though from my first position, I hardly noticed any infantry.

The Germans are very noisy and loud, yelling at us to get our hands up and move. They wear the SS symbols, but what their outfit is, I don't know. Col. Macdonald isn't around. So I presume that when Major Carr came up to see him, arrangements were made to get him out.

By the time Capt. Grange gets back up to the Essex, they are overrun. Even crawling through the bushes, he can't get to where he left Munro and Nielson:

> There are Germans – lots of them – wandering around the position. Obviously the whole thing is a disaster. While I see no wholesale surrender there are lots of Germans about, and I do a great deal of crawling though the mud on my way back. When I come across a dead German with a revolver in his hand, I become quite concerned, and pull out my own revolver to be ready for all eventualities. Fortunately I have no cause to use it, for the result could have been disastrous. When returning it to its holster, I find it's plugged with the mud through which I've been crawling.

Meanwhile, over on the extreme right flank, one 17-pounder gun of 2nd Anti-Tank Regiment is engaged in a deadly dual with a number of Panther tanks about to attack the Queen's Own Cameron Highlanders of Canada, now holding the orchard on the northern outskirts of St. Martin-de-Fontenay and St. André-sur-Orne, at this time under horrendous shell and mortar bombardment from masses of enemy weapons, many of them deployed west of the Orne and hidden by Hill 112.

"A striking example of what can be accomplished by courageous and determined well-trained gunners," is how this heroic engagement between one lonely 17-pounder on an exposed forward slope leading down into St. Martin and some distant, long-barrelled Panthers, will be described in the official history of the gunners of Canada.*

---

* Col. G. W. L. Nicolson, CD, *The Gunners of Canada: The History of the Royal Regiment of Canadian Artillery, Volume II, 1919–1967* (Toronto: McClelland and Stewart, 1972), p. 299.

Having spotted a number of Panther tanks forming up in a hollow beyond the range of his 6-pounders, a troop of which is deployed in the orchard near St. André, Lt.-Col. H. E. Murray [commanding officer of 2nd Anti-Tank] brought up a 17-pounder to snipe at the enemy from a high point on the road north of the village. L/Sergeant I. L. Johnson of 20th Battery and his detachment manhandled the gun forward, putting it into action beside a knocked-out Sherman tank which was in full view of the enemy. As Murray had surmised, the Germans judged the 17-pounder rounds to be coming from the derelict Sherman, which their retaliatory shots quickly set ablaze.

Despite the enemy fire and the intense heat of the burning tank, the Canadian crew kept their weapon in action until a direct hit on the breech silenced it. By that time three of the detachment, including Sergeant Johnson, had become casualties, and Sergeant Ford had taken over firing the gun single-handedly until he too was wounded. But three of the Panthers had been put out of commission.

It was then that Bombardier G. A. Grassick of the 6-pounder troop came into the picture. When the gun he had been serving was destroyed by a German round, he crawled back from the orchard to the damaged 17-pounder, under fire all the way. Chipping away with an axe, he managed to break the semi-automatic gear and put the gun back into action. Then firing it himself he destroyed another Panther, bringing to four the number of enemy tanks knocked out by one 17-pounder.*

---

*   Lt.-Col. Murray was subsequently awarded a DSO for his part in this effective action in scattering the German tanks. Sergeants Johnson and Ford were awarded Military Medals, and Bombardier Grassick was Mentioned in Despatches.

28

GUN BARRELS GLOW RED
LIKE CANDLES

FROM THE TIME THE GUNS OPENED UP ON BEHALF OF THE Royals' attack on Louvigny two days ago (on July 18), opportunities for sleep have been rare, and for the most part non-existent. On that last afternoon at the position in the valley in front of Carpiquet, all gunners had to be on duty for the Louvigny fire plan and subsequent targets developing out of the attack. And as soon as things started to cool down, the quads came up and all were kept busy limbering up the guns and packing in for the move up to this field between Louvigny and the Orne.

There'd been some chance for sleep in the quads while they waited to move off, and during the long, slow move, but once here, all hands were needed to put the guns in action and keep them serviced while the pits were dug. And it was well after dawn on July 19 before the gunners could turn to digging personal slit trenches into which half of them might tumble for some sleep. Then the atmosphere was not conducive to sleep even for exhausted men. Every man knew he had spent the night in no-man's-land, with German burp guns (Schmeissers) behind them in the village firing tracers at the Royals in the surrounding orchards, and with the dawn, no one knew what to expect.

From mid-morning onwards all hands had to be on deck for a series of fire plans: first, in support of the Maisonneuves clearing the far bank of the Orne from up near Caen down to Fleury-sur-Orne; then on behalf of the Calgary Highlanders passing through them to attack Hill 67 late in the afternoon; and finally, in support of an attack by the Black Watch that took until midnight to clear the village of Ifs.

Shortly after midnight, the Army Service Corps arrived with those first 350 rounds per gun, making it imperative that every man remain on duty to keep the guns firing while ammo pits were being dug and shells and cartridge cases were stored below ground.

Now late this afternoon on July 20, in the middle of overlapping targets called for by FOOs around the shattered companies of the Fusiliers Mont-Royal, trying to hold Troteval and Beauvoir farms, and on behalf of the remnants of the South Saskatchewan Regiment, trying to crawl away from German tanks bent on machine-gunning them or squashing them like bugs in the wheat on the western end of Verrières Ridge, comes the torrential rain.

Hour after hour, all night long, it pours down in cloud-burst torrents, filling slit trenches and gun pits where men might have slept.

And then around 9:00 P.M., as though making certain no gun-crew member even gets the chance to rest huddled above ground under a ground sheet, Army Service arrives with the next instalment of ammo: 450 rounds per gun. A couple of hours later they come back again with another hundred rounds per gun, which they say is "a special order for 4th Field."

The field has now turned into a bog, and when the first truck sinks to its axles and has to be winched back onto the road, every case of shells and every case of cartridges has to be carried in from the road by the gunners.

With each passing hour the expression "human endurance" takes on new dimensions and meaning. Each steel case of four shells weighs 117 pounds – a weight of no great consequence to fresh, well-rested men under ideal conditions. But these gunners – already physically drained by the blistering heat and by the frequent, horrendous doses of shelling, aerial bombing, and strafing poured down on them for eight days in the previous position in front of Carpiquet – are now approaching total exhaustion from excavating tons of earth. To form a gun pit (18 feet in diameter and 3 feet deep) requires the excavation of some 28 tons, and to dig an ammo pit (12 feet wide, 18 feet long, and 3 feet deep) to receive the 250 cases of shells and 125 cases of propellant charges, representing 1,000 rounds per gun, calls for the excavation of another 24 tons of earth.

Each six-man gun crew, slogging back and forth through the mud and dark with 138 boxes of shells and 69 boxes of propellant charges, carries more than ten tons 300 yards.

By now, when weary gunners try to pick up a box of shells it feels as though it is anchored to the earth, and the very awkward twisting lifts required to lower them into the pits (and haul them out again later as they are needed) puts a wicked strain on back muscles aching for sleep.

Scarcely have the men wrestled and stacked those 18.5 tons of shells and cartridge cases down in their pits before they are hauling them up again and shovelling them into the guns at such furious rates of fire, the barrels glow red in the dark like candles, and buckets of muddy water must be poured down the muzzles to cool them off, producing spectacular geysers of steam and water.

And all the while the rain pelts down. Command post dugouts and their soil-covered roofs aren't designed to accommodate such a deluge, and technical work, demanding extreme accuracy, is carried out under miserable conditions.

Spoiled by two weeks of dry weather since arriving in Normandy, you and your staff have made no provision whatsoever for drainage, and your command post becomes a sump hole. By midnight, in spite of strenuous efforts to build a dike and dig a drainage canal across the mouth of the dugout to drain away the lake accumulating there, the muddy water, pouring steadily down the earthen steps, has risen almost up to your crotch.

At the same time the earth that was spread thickly, but loosely, over the sheets of corrugated iron brought along from the last position at Carpiquet to form the roof, is now completely saturated and dripping blobs of red mud down onto the artillery board as Bombardier Hossack tries to plot each new target. And before you can read off ranges and switches for the guns raging away outside, you must rest your battledress sleeve on the board and, with a scrubbing motion of your forearm, wipe away the mud.

Each time you expose the sparkling white expanse of waterproof talc that covers and seals in the gridded paper, you thank your lucky stars that events conspired to place you in action in 2nd Battery where you are a beneficiary of this truly marvellous invention by an ingenious ack − a veteran of the mud of Flanders in the First War. Long since posted because of his age to the reinforcement depot at Bordon, Hampshire, as an instructor. Sgt. Agner Emil Dalgas deserves to know how marvellously well his invention is working in action, and you vow to look him up one day and tell him.*

In between targets, careful not to move too quickly in the water that is now up to your buttocks, you and Hossack discuss Dalgas and this invention that curiously has not come into general use. It must have occurred to others on many occasions during training as they tried to plot their fragile white paper, huddling under the stingy little canvas cover of the board, vainly fighting to keep out the lashing rain, that artillery board gridded-paper might be covered with a sheet of translucent talc, through which the grid

---

* This was not to be. Captain Dalgas, of 1st Canadian Field Educational Section, on his way to visit 4th Field up in Germany, was killed on April 9, 1945, at the age of fifty-eight. An Engineers officer in World War One, he enlisted on September 11, 1939, with the 111th Canadian Field Battery in British Columbia with the rank of major he'd earned during peacetime service with a reserve battery. On learning he would not be allowed to proceed overseas as an officer because of his age, he resigned his commission (January 1940) and travelled to Ottawa to join the 2nd (Ottawa) Battery as a gunner. In August 1940 he came overseas with 4th Field to England, but his age again caught up with him and he was sent to #1 CARU as an instructor.

would show and on which an ack could write with an ordinary pencil. That it all could be sealed in against wet and dirt by an edging of adhesive tape and beeswax must surely also have occurred to other inventive minds. But then they must have abandoned the idea, stumped by the problem of the talc losing its waterproofing qualities by being endlessly punctured by thumb tacks securing the "arc" across the "zero line," and the pins of the metal pivot for the range-measuring arm positioned over the dot representing the "pivot gun" of the troop.

That the destructive pins on the pivot could be filed off and that renewable adhesive tape could be used to secure the pivot and the arc obviously did not occur to them. But it did to Dalgas.

Incredibly, no other battery in the Regiment adopted the Dalgas modifications, let alone other batteries of the Canadian Army. How they are managing to keep their paper dry and useable under conditions like these, you can't imagine.

Hossack locates his greatcoat from the bowels of GA (the armoured scout car) and pulls it on. It's a warm night, but the water sloshing around the thighs is cold. Signaller Harry Thorpe, a cheerful redheaded lad, who's been escaping the water by sitting cross-legged up on one end of the earthen shelf at which you and Hossack are working, sees you shuddering, and insists you wear his greatcoat. Being only a slight lad, his coat is bindingly small for you, and the sleeves only come two-thirds down your arm, but still you are very grateful for the comfort it offers.

As the night wears on, however, the air and water seem to grow colder. Your voice begins quavering when you speak, and Hossack's hands start shaking. Thorpe notices and asks if a shot of cognac would be permissible, if he were to supply a bottle?

When you both look at him with interest, he says he knows who has a bottle and he'll just "borrow" it without disturbing him. He assures you he can readily replace it in the morning, there's bound to be lots of bottles in those wrecked houses. You speed him on his way, and in a moment he's back with the bottle, performing an acrobatic feat in getting from the top of the stairs back onto his dry perch without falling in the water. And though scientists may claim that alcohol will lower the body temperature, not raise it, the shuddering ceases, life becomes tolerable again, and the irritability developing among those sloshing about this water-filled hole vanishes.

Dawn comes. Thorpe is relieved by another signaller, and off he goes on his scrounging mission with Gunner Oliver Ament, from whom he may have borrowed last night's blessed bottle. Over the past two days, enemy mortaring of Louvigny has been sporadic, but enough have crashed in there that you are no longer conscious of them landing. And so you'll never know exactly when it happened, but you're still wearing Thorpe's little greatcoat when they come to tell you that he and Ament have been killed by a mortar bomb in the village.

All morning the rain continues to pelt down, and the water rises so high in the gun pits that the breeches of the steaming guns begin to take on a rusty hue from splashing in and out of the muddy water on recoil. While this in itself isn't serious, gun platforms begin to lose their stability in the sludge at the bottom of the pits, now under almost two feet of water, and guns begin to slide so far back, their trails are jamming into the back walls of the pits. Gun crews take turns going out of action to try to stabilize, with fenceposts and railway ties, the heavy, round, steel platforms that form an integral part of the gun carriages.

Resembling a big, steel-spoked wheel, the platform is hooked up under the trail of the gun when travelling. On arrival at a new site, it is dropped to the ground so the wheels of the gun can be pulled up onto it, extending and locking in position two folding arms affixed to its hub and running up to the trail of the gun. Thus the gun is provided with not only a smooth surface for fast-traversing in action, but also a firm ground-anchor that makes it unnecessary for the trail to do what gun trails are traditionally meant to do, dig into the earth when the gun recoils. With the claws of the lower side of the platform pressed into the earth by 3,600 pounds of gun, it is usually a most stable and reliable device, giving the 25-pounder a clear advantage over every other field gun in the matter of rapid, unimpeded 360-degree traversing.

But today the rain-saturated, soupy sub-soil of the Orne flood-plain near Louvigny defeats the platform and all the wood the gunners can find to shove underneath it. After spending all morning vainly trying to stabilize the bottom of what are now pools of red sludge, the gun sergeants ask permission to pull the guns out of the pits and fire them above ground without any pro-tection against the enemy shells and mortars that every so often slam into the position.

You have no choice but to grant them permission. It seems the Germans are now on the brink of breaking through and over-running everything all the way back to Ifs. And your firing has risen to insane crescendoes, beating off SS counter-attacks supported by tanks that are decimating the forward battalions and opening holes in the line that must be plugged by your shell-fire until fresh counter-attacks can be mounted to restore it. Targets coming in from the FOOs are overlapping: "35 rounds gunfire . . . 45 rounds gunfire . . . 50 rounds gunfire . . . fire until you're told to stop!"

By early afternoon on the twenty-first, most of the 1,000 rounds per gun, built up over the past twenty-four hours, are expended. Another 350 rounds per gun have to be rushed up by regimental ammunition trucks, some from the abandoned pits in the old valley positions, and the rest from an ammo dump north of Carpiquet.*

---

* John Drewry, Battery Captain (second-in-command of 14th Battery), was given credit for organizing the trucks and ammunition details that located these emergency supplies and got them up in time to head off a disastrous situation, which could have seen the guns forced to cease firing at the very time the whole front was collapsing and when shell-fire alone was preventing the enemy breaking through to Ifs.

Before the new supplies arrive, GPOs are becoming frantic, and you are actually in the act of reporting "only 12 rounds per gun left" to Battery Command Post when they tell you to send your gun crews out to the road to carry in the shells from ammo trucks that have just arrived!

The gunners' endurance is beyond belief. Though they've not slept at all for more than forty-eight hours, and must be on the point of collapsing from fatigue, they go on loading and firing their guns without a whimper. Target descriptions – brief as they are – still leave no doubt in anyone's mind as to where their shells are going: "SS . . . Hitler youth . . . fanatics . . . enemy counter-attacking with tanks . . . scale 60 . . . repeat . . . repeat . . ."

Sit reps (situation reports) are non-existent, and the messages and queries being passed back and forth are so sparse it is impossible to get a coherent picture of what is happening. However, it's clear the whole front is in danger of being overwhelmed. Only the Camerons seem to be holding their tenuous position at St. André.

The Fusiliers Mont-Royal, seemingly overrun by tanks and infantry, are being driven from both Troteval and Beauvoir farms. And the Essex Scottish, left exposed when the South Saskatchewan Regiment were driven back from off the crest yesterday, now in their turn are being overrun and routed, and at least one company has disappeared completely.

Fully occupied with the urgency of the overlapping targets, that clearly are dropping curtains of fire across the gaps left in the line by the routed battalions, you forget about Thorpe and Ament until word comes in that the advance party that left last night to recce new gun positions near Ifs has been shot up, and that lieutenants Bill Knapp and Howard Dawson are dead – clean-cut, pink-cheeked Knapp, who won the 2nd Corps' long-distance run at Waldershare Park last month; and Dawson, with whom you'd shared officers' training, who loved his wife so very much.

When you lay on the next target, you climb out of your candle-lit dugout. Blinking like an owl, even though the sky is deeply over-cast and a drizzle is still falling, you head across the wet field towards the nearest gun, sitting in shocking vulnerability, flat up on the turf beside its abandoned, watery pit. Serviced by its entire crew, it blasts away at unseen targets on the ridge across the river.

Stripped to the waist, the gunners haul and carry shells – remov-ing safety caps, adjusting charges, loading and firing them like robots – not even looking up when a big, hostile shell lands directly in front of the troop with a horrendous roar, sending up a great, black spout of steamy mud and smoke.

The gun-layer, hunched over on his seat, his wet back glistening with the falling rain, a soggy cigarette hanging from the corner of his mouth, never takes his eye far from the rubber eyepiece on the dial-sight, as he maintains a constant rhythm, his deft hands con-stantly touching gear wheels, ensuring the lay remains on his aiming point, and pulling the firing lever each time he hears the breech-block close.

You tap him on the back, and when he looks around, you make motions for him to get up and let you climb up in his place.

Then for a long time you fire the gun in raging vengeance – almost enjoying the vicious pitch and slamming recoil of this death machine throwing its deadly missiles at the ridge over the river.

29

FOOTNOTE TO GOODWOOD
AND ATLANTIC

✳

DURING THE THREE DAYS OF GOODWOOD, BECAUSE OF THE depth of the German gun lines and the awesome superiority of their tanks, dug in on high ground with an unlimited field of fire for their long-barrelled 88s, the British lose 400 tanks, a third of their tanks in Normandy.

Late on July 19, recognizing that the German gun lines are still intact and further assaults by his tanks would be suicidal (outgunned as most of them are by the German tanks), Gen. Dempsey of 2nd British Army informs his 8th Corps he is arranging for the two infantry divisions of 2nd Canadian Corps to take over as soon as possible. At 10:00 A.M. on July 20, he issues a directive that 8th Corps is to discontinue the advance, that 11th Armoured will go into reserve when relieved by 3rd Canadian Infantry Division, 7th Armoured will complete the capture of Bourguébus, and the Guards Armoured Division will take up a defensive position on the east flank.

And when cloudburst rain descends late in the afternoon, turning the fields into a sea of mud and shutting down all support by the fighter-bombers, General Montgomery recognizes Goodwood is over and henceforth all further attacks on Verrières Ridge will be undertaken by the infantry of 2nd Canadian Corps – most particularly 2nd Division.

Students of strategy will argue for decades the meaning and intent of Montgomery's orders for Operation Goodwood–Atlantic: whether the operation was an attempted break-out, or merely a feint to hold the Germans around Caen. Monty will maintain he intended the latter, and admirers will give him the benefit of the doubt, believing that he was trying to draw the maximum amount of German armour on the Caen front to allow for his planned break-out by the Americans on their thinly held front at the western end of the bridgehead. His critics, on the other hand, will claim the weight of the British attack was so massive, it had to be an attempted break-out, and that the words of his directive – "exploiting in the direction of the Seine basin and Paris" – is a dead giveaway.

Whatever Montgomery meant, German commanders could only view the ferocious attack as complete validation of their long-held opinion that the Caen sector posed the greatest threat, and that they must continue to maintain most of their armour opposite the Canadians and British, at the expense of the western end of the bridgehead. That this conviction ultimately proved disastrous for them is irrefutable.

There is a suggestion that by the middle of July the highest military and political leaders were becoming worried that the Normandy campaign was in danger of bogging down into a stalemate – a battle of attrition such as developed after the first few weeks of fluid battles in 1914.

Certainly, to the clean-shaven, pressed-down-lapels world of Red Tabs – following the progress of the war with coloured pins on map boards and statistical summaries of expenditures of men and materials, not to mention the *Times* at breakfast – the succession of attacks initiated in June and July by both the British and the Germans along the Odon west of Verson, each ending in a blood-bath without significant territorial gain, could well have suggested a stalemate was developing.

The latest attacks by two British corps on Hill 112 southwest of Caen begun three nights before Goodwood (July 15), while achieving their tactical purpose of pinning down German panzer divisions so that Goodwood and Atlantic might develop east of the Orne, have been unable to gain significant territory. Operations Greenline and Pomegranate, by XII and XXX corps, constituting the third major attempt by the British to expand the Odon bridgehead, achieved only slight gains at terrible cost – again, reminiscent of the blood-letting battles of attrition for minuscule gains in World War One.

But all the disturbing conclusions that should have been drawn from the outcome of these and all the other attacks along the Odon and against Hill 112 – that Allied tanks simply are no match for German Panthers and Tigers – seem to have been ignored by the senior officers at SHAEF (Supreme Headquarters, Allied Expeditionary Force). And on top of this, the total failure of the thousands of RAF and USAF bombers to subdue the German gun lines and dug-in tanks along Verrières Ridge and beyond is incomprehensible to anyone watching, let alone anyone still clinging to the belief held after Dunkirk by the Air Marshal Sir Charles Portal, Chief of Air Staff, that the war would be won in the air, not on land, and the Army would return to the continent as an army-of-occupation only, the enemy's will to resist having been crushed by bombing – a belief still earnestly held as late as January 1944 by the Commander-in-Chief of Bomber Command, Air Marshal Sir Arthur Harris.*

General Eisenhower – needled by his deputy commander-in-

---

*   On August 12, 1943, Harris wrote Portal: "I am certain that given average weather and concentration on the main job, we can push Germany over this year." And in January 1944 he was still optimistic that by April 1, Germany would be driven by bombing to "a state of devastation in which surrender is inevitable." (Max Hastings, *Overlord*, [London: Pan Books, 1985], p. 48.)

chief, Air Chief Marshal Tedder, calling for Montgomery's head –
and some prominent war correspondents and instant-history
writers are shocked into a state of petulance by the inability of
Montgomery's forces to break out south of Caen.

Postwar historians, both British and American, finding this
querulous style contagious, will use it again and again to express
their impatience with the slowness shown by Canadians forces on
the road to Falaise.

However, no such thoughts enter the heads of those occupying the
slit trenches and gun pits around Caen. Not knowing what any
attack is supposed to accomplish, apart from enlarging the bridgehead, there is no sense of failure, only bewilderment that so much
high explosive, so liberally distributed, could not blow a path
through the Germans. There is no loss of confidence in the leadership or in the ability of the Allied forces to ultimately overwhelm
the enemy. It is now crystal clear, however, that it is going to take a
lot longer than anyone expected, that the Germans are prepared to
fight to the death for every foot of Normandy, and that German
tanks are vastly superior to Allied tanks.

The Sherman, the most abundant tank among the Allies, may be
fast and mechanically reliable, with a gun-turret traversing-speed
much faster than the German tanks' (allowing gun-layers to get off
opening rounds faster), but it is grossly inferior in crucial matters of
gun muzzle-velocity and protective armour. Only 33 tons – compared to the 50-ton Panther, the 63-ton Tiger, and the 75-ton
Royal Tiger – the Sherman is extremely vulnerable. It has shown
such a tendency to flash into flame when hit that it has been given
the grim nickname "Ronson" after the famous cigarette lighter.

A Tiger, armed with a long-barrel 88-mm, can sit back in hull-
down position and knock out Shermans at ranges of up to two and
a half kilometres, while the Sherman's gun can't penetrate the 80
mm of frontal armour of a Panther at any range, let alone the 102
mm on a Tiger I and the 150 mm on the slanted front of a Royal

Tiger. Even if a Sherman manages to close to 500 yards, the solid-shot from its 75-mm gun (capable of penetrating only 68 mm of steel) will just ricochet off a Tiger's 80-mm sides.

The 88-mm is a superior weapon mainly because of its multiple role as anti-aircraft, anti-tank, and mobile-assault gun. As a field gun it is distinctly inferior to the 25-pounder, because of its crest-clearance problems arising from its high muzzle-velocity and flat trajectory, which force many of its shells to be fired as erratic air-bursts. Clearly, it is as an anti-tank gun that it has earned its deadly reputation in Normandy.

Only the few "Fireflies" (Shermans converted by the British to take their superior 17-pounder anti-tank gun, allotted to Canadian tank units on the basis of one per troop of regular Shermans) are capable of knocking out the heavier German tanks. With a muzzle-velocity comparable to the high-velocity long-barrelled 88-mm, the 17-pounder, when armed with special tungsten-carbide Sabot ammunition, has superior striking power.*

Approved for issue in 1941, the gun was not mounted in a tank by the British until August 1943, and then not in a British tank, but a Sherman. Clearly the Churchill, a 152-mm frontal armour, would have been a formidable tank had its turret been redesigned to take a 17-pounder.

---

* The British 17-pounder armed with Sabot ammunition is capable of penetrating 231 mm of steel inclined at 30 degrees at 1,000 yards, compared to 164 mm for the long-barrelled 88-mm on the Royal Tiger. With Armour Piercing Discarding Sabot (APDS), the size and weight of the diamond-hard tungsten-carbide core projectile is reduced by more than half, but its velocity is greatly increased through the "choke principle." A split dumb-bell of soft alloy, taped around the projectile, shatters on point of firing, plugging the barrel and forcing an extra build-up of gases behind the slim shot before it is expelled. This rise in velocity, combined with the irresistible hardness of the slender tungsten shot, results in a remarkable increase in penetration. See Appendix C.

30

LIKE REMNANTS OF
A FALLEN CIVILIZATION

❋

AT 2:00 A.M. ON JULY 22, ORDERS COME TO MOVE FROM THE
field between Louvigny and the Orne to a field directly across
the Orne, just south of the smashed railway bridge in a bend in the
river near Fleury-sur-Orne. As the crow flies, it's no more than
three hundred yards away from where the guns now sit, but five
miles by a tortuous route bulldozed through the dark ruins of
Caen, crossing over the Orne on a newly erected Bailey bridge,
through the industrial suburb of Faubourg de Vaucelles, and south
along the high ground above the river.

To ensure at least one battery is available to respond to calls for
fire at all times, 2nd Battery is to cross over first and get its eight
guns on line before the rest are pulled out of action. As it turns out,
it takes three hours and twenty minutes to complete the move.
Passage through the appalling devastation that once was a city is
very slow, and the convoy is frequently stopped for long periods in
narrow defiles bulldozed through the rubble as traffic jams up in
both directions.

More than guns and tanks must move over the Orne at night.
Heavy trucks moving up, loaded with ammo, petrol, rations, and
reinforcements, meet ambulances and long flatbeds carrying disabled tanks coming back, and compete for bridges, roads, and
tracks leading to and from the open country south of the city,

which in a few short hours will lie exposed to enemy observation and fire.

You had wondered why the recce parties had chosen not to return to Louvigny on discovering that the new positions near Ifs were on the fringe of territory still in dispute and exposed to point-blank fire from enemy tanks. (This much you'd gathered from targets called for by FOOs when enemy attacks threatened to roll back the front to Ifs.) Now, in this stop-and-go traffic, you understand.

As time passes, you find it harder and harder to keep your eyes open. With good reason: you haven't been allowed to lie down to sleep since the morning of the 19th, almost three days ago. And you've had no sleep whatsoever since 8:00 P.M. the day before yesterday (July 20), when advance parties were called and Hutch took off to recce the next position, leaving you, like every other subaltern in charge of the guns, without a second officer to spell you off.

As if that weren't enough, just before leaving the old position, Gunner "Hank" Wilkins, your troop gun artificer, lumbered over to you with a bottle under his arm and a slender liqueur glass filled with an unidentifiable liquid, remarking, "You sure look as if you could use a drink, sir." You tossed back the breathtaking, throat-paralysing substance, which, from the taste, could have been a shot of overproof alcohol laced with hydrochloric acid. It almost sent you to your knees, struggling for air. Wilkins, roaring with laughter, said it was Calvados.*

---

* Raw Calvados, the kind most frequently found in '44, was atrociously under-aged and criminally overproof in its original state of 70 degrees alcohol, not yet cut to the legal commercial level of 45 degrees, the alcoholic level of Scotch or rye. Normandy farmers with apple orchards are the sole producers of the alcohol, which is distilled from hard apple cider fermented in huge oak barrels in their barns. It is aged for at least five to seven years, turning from white to amber and becoming as smooth as the finest cognac. Canadian soldiers, however, will remember only a throat-clutching drink, since just the unaged stuff was left above ground, unhidden from the Germans, still at its original eye-watering strength and rawness.

You try studying the map on your knees, but map-reading through Caen is impossible with its streets and intersections obliterated by the bombs. You're glad that for once Able Troop is not leading the battery, even though there's no chance of taking a wrong turn with only a single bulldozed track to follow through the city.

Stuck halfway back in the convoy, with no responsibility for its forward progress, you fight a losing battle against sleep and start dozing off for longer and longer periods. Just how long these lapses extend, you can't actually tell, as it's difficult to distinguish between dream and reality. Eerily outlined by the light of a half-moon that comes and goes behind drifting clouds left over from the rainy weather yesterday, the grotesque mountains of rubble swim in and out of your consciousness – sometimes appearing as a tumble of children's building blocks, and then as surrealistic piles of giant sugar cubes or as snowdrifts. And once, when you awake beside broken columns and arches arising from the rubble, it seems you are among the sad and ghostly ruins of a fallen civilization.

At last you surrender to total oblivion, sinking into the deepest possible sleep, from which you are rudely awakened some time later by the unbridled roar of a diesel engine spouting right beside your ear.

It's already dawn. The giant bulldozer is struggling with some rubble no more than three feet from the open window on your side of the truck.

Now fully awake and feeling quite refreshed, you pity Kirby, your driver, who has been forced to stay awake all night. But he's in remarkably good spirits and assures you he's fine and will catch some sack time later today. This is so typical of drivers, who can somehow draw on a reserve of energy denied their passengers, remaining fully alert, whether engaged in stop-and-start driving through a bombed city or hurtling over Welsh mountains with only pinholes of light from their blacked-out headlights to penetrate the fog and the rain.

And Kirby actually seems to feel sorry for you because you missed seeing Churchill – not once but twice – complete with cigar and his famous V-for-victory sign of two splayed fingers held up to the 4th Field vehicles passing him and Montgomery at some ragged intersection.

Drivers also have an uncanny knack for memorizing the routes they have been following, and with his help you orient yourself quickly. You are now across the Orne and moving south, close to and parallel with the river, but high above it on the plain.

Very shortly the convoy seems to break free of all restraints, and for a while it rolls at a good clip through a sparsely built area, broken and tumbled about from heavy bombardments. But as you close on the village of Fleury-sur-Orne, the leading vehicles slow down to a crawl as the road tips steeply down along the face of the cliff beside the river.

Over on the left, set back a short distance from the road, is the infamous mushroom-shaped concrete water-tower that seemed so menacing when studied through field-glasses from the much-tormented gun position back over there in the valley in front of Carpiquet. Now full of holes and forlorn, it has lost all its menace, and you wonder if it ever did harbour an enemy OP.

As you grind down the narrow track in bull-low, you pass the mouth of a huge cave in the cliff face, in which are assembled a crowd of men, women, and children, staring at the passing guns with discouraged, tired eyes, though some manage to nod and smile.

At the bottom of the hill you are met by a very weary, unshaven Hutch, who directs you to pass under the railway track at this end of the broken bridge, into a nice green area created by a big looping curve in the Orne.

This fresh-looking oasis, outlined by poplars marching along the riverbank, is the first relatively untouched bit of green you've seen since leaving the concentration area at Sommervieu, north of Bayeux. The vegetation has suffered very little from bombardment and has escaped the usual coat of red dust you've come to associate with Normandy battlefields, which manages to give even undamaged walls and surrounding vegetation a dried-out, worn-out, used-up, bleak, dead look. These green acres are divided into fields by drainage ditches, now dry and largely clogged with brambles, vines, and raspberry canes. Troop positions of 2nd Battery have been laid out with their backs against one of these bramble-filled ditches, and Battery Command Post is to the right of Able Troop next to the river.

At first sight this position looks too good to be true, but then you spot the 14th Battery gun markers behind you, even closer than they were to your guns in the valley in front of Carpiquet, less than fifty yards behind the ditch that runs behind your Able Troop Command Post. Obviously you will again have to get used to sleeping (if you ever get the chance again) with your head bouncing up and down on its improvised pillow each time the guns fire behind you and their muzzle-blasts pass over your trench.

When you inquire of Hutch how Dawson and Knapp got it at Ifs, you get a proper earful of old-fashioned, Prairie cussing – as lurid as it is earnest – making it abundantly clear that he holds in utter contempt those clots of senior rank who seem determined to deploy the field guns of 2nd Division, and 4th Field in particular, either up with the infantry or in full view of the enemy. However, you get no picture of what went on down there on the left, some two kilometres closer to the enemy (at positions that won't be occupied by 4th Field for another sixteen days), until you get to see Sgt. Hunt's diary at 26 Battery Command Post, now established in an underpass cut through a railway embankment nearby:

21 July 44: With first light we again set out for the new position. Arrival showed this to be a wheat field . . . A heavy rain was falling, which, with the lack of sleep, absence of breakfast, and futility of a single spade, wasn't the best preparation for the heavy shelling that followed. We took shelter in a haystack and awaited

events. Mr. Dawson left our shelter to join Mr. Knapp and Sgt.-Maj. Carlton in the latter's Jeep. It was an ill-fated move as shortly afterwards both officers were killed. Sgt.-Maj. Carlton lost a hand and received other shrapnel wounds. It was obvious the position was not tenable; accordingly were forced to withdraw [to this position].

By 5:20 A.M. 2nd Battery is in action and the other batteries can start moving. While this new position lies tantalizingly close to the old one, just over the narrow stream, it will be 9:15 A.M. before 14th and 26th are in position.

When gunners get a chance to visit the cave up the hill, they learn it's filled with refugees from Caen left homeless by the bombing. The gunners are so touched by their plight, especially by the little children, they start sneaking some of their Compo rations up to them – a practice officially frowned upon by the brass, but which, you are certain, will continue surreptitiously until the Regiment moves on, in spite of the cave eventually being declared out of bounds.

And from one of the cave-dwellers comes a possible explanation why so many German tanks, self-propelled guns, and mortars survived the saturation bombing preceding Goodwood. You are told the cave was already full of refugees from Caen, escaping the spasmodic Allied shelling by field guns and warships. But just before the heavy bombing of Caen started, German soldiers came and ordered them out of the cave, threatening to throw in grenades to speed up the process.

The refugees were forced to trek back into Caen and shelter wherever they could during the bombing. The lucky ones gained shelter in the Cathedral, which was untouched by bombs. Later many of them returned to the cave here.

This cave, and others like it around here – huge vaulted affairs capable of sheltering hundreds of people – were created centuries ago by stonecutters quarrying the granite blocks that built not only the cathedrals of Normandy, but also the Norman cathedrals in England.

One of the gunners swims over the river to collect his mess tins, which he left hanging on a fencepost, and on his return he reports that a British medium regiment has taken over the old positions and that Rear Division and Army Service Corps have established their headquarters at the Château.*

---

*   A rather vivid description of Louvigny and environs as 4th Field left them is provided by the 2nd Canadian Division Army Service Corps historian:

> The Château had been a sore spot with the Germans . . . To relieve their injured feelings, the enemy had kept the Château under observation and fire since their hurried departure to the higher ground south of Fleury-sur-Orne. From this vantage point they could discern any movement on the floor of the Orne's watercourse and Rear Div and Service Corps HQ were in for the hottest time they were to experience during the Western European campaign. The nearby village of Louvigny had ceased to exist . . . decimated by our own and enemy fire. The Château was a grisly, eerie spot when Rear Div moved into it that afternoon. Long lines of varnished wooden crosses had been erected over the graves of scores of German defenders. Shells had smashed the buildings and stone walls, and the surrounding fields were filled with the bodies of cattle decaying in the hot sun. From three sides the Germans were in a position to bring fire on the Château, still having troops around Eterville, Maltot, and along the Orne south of Fleury.

From an unpublished document held by the National Archives of Canada, RG 24, Vol. 10906, *History of RCASC 2nd (Cdn Inf) Div., June 1944–Dec 1944.*

31

FEAR AND HATRED RUN UNIMAGINABLY DEEP

✳

THESE NEW GUN POSITIONS OF 4TH FIELD SEEM TO BE LOCATED in some sort of charmed oasis, enjoying an unusual freedom from enemy shells and mortars, while all around, on both sides of the Orne, others continue to receive their grim rations.

Judging by the almost continuous round of muffled *crumps* over on the left beyond the railway embankment, where the whole area all the way back to Caen is under observation by the enemy on distant high ground, other gun positions and rear headquarters and echelons, including 4th Field wagon lines, are being shelled in rotation. While out front the Moaning Minnies regularly wind up their frenzied howling, and six overlapping, thunderous explosions lambaste the western hump of Verrières Ridge, plainly visible to the guns.

However, the only lethal metal flying about 4th Field gun positions today comes from a tank battle that develops across the river near Eterville during a late afternoon attack on Maltot by the British. While it's not possible to make out the progress of the battle, some Cromwell tanks are briefly visible – a momentary helter-skelter assembly behind a steep slope – before taking off with furious, raspy roarings that don't reach you until they've disappeared up and over the crest in the direction of Hill 112. Shortly there are some sharp *cracks* of tank guns. Then suddenly the air is filled with a weird, threatening sound of something headed this way, wobbling and swishing like nothing on earth. And tumbling end-over-end across the gun position, coming to rest in one of the gun pits under the trail of the gun, is a ricocheting solid-shot, still so hot it burns the fingers of the gunner who tries to pick it up.* And two more follow, one barely missing Gunner J. M. Millroy of Easy Troop as it digs itself in under D Sub's gun.

But the chief concern around the gun position today has been the menace of honey bees, buzzing about everybody's head in unusual numbers, suggesting their hives in some nearby apiary have recently been blown to smithereens. They show a disconcerting tendency to land on any accessible food, even when it's on the way to your mouth, thus encouraging the adoption of new eating techniques consisting mainly of waving a free hand over loaded fork or spoon until it's entirely in your mouth behind closed lips.

Fortunately the bees are good-natured little creatures without a vindictive streak, and they treat these competitions for the food as a game to be won or lost, without resorting to vengeful tactics, even though they are frequently rudely whacked by a hand frantically brushing the air space over, for instance, a hardtack cracker loaded with orange marmalade (to which they are most partial, and on which they will ride right into your mouth if allowed).

However, as the number of bees on standing patrols dwindles with the setting sun, the gunners become aware of other, more sinister buzzings, reminiscent of the bullets from out of the wheat fields across that sunken road at the Carpiquet position. The consensus is that these are coming from a stubby church tower, poking up through the trees some distance south along the river on the right.

Gunner F. C. Edwards, your ack-ack Bren gunner, asks permission to accompany Bombardier W. W. Scott over there on a patrol to try to winkle out the sniper or snipers. It could be a couple of Germans cut off by the Maisonneuve attack that went in through

---

*   Solid-shot is a steel slug rather than a shell filled with high explosive.

there to take Etavaux, a kilometre beyond. On the map the next village is Bassé, but it doesn't show a church.

The little patrol is gone less than an hour when you hear excited shouting, quickly rising to a raucous chorus that spreads throughout the whole battery position as you climb out of your command post dugout to see what it is all about. Immediately the cause is evident: marching up from the south along the riverbank, in single file with their hands behind their heads, is a column of men in blue-grey uniforms escorted by Scott and Edwards, obviously on their way to the battery command post. You count them. Nine! Nine prisoners of war! Incredible!

The tremendous excitement generated at the gun positions is at first amusing. But as you watch men dashing about, grabbing up their rifles and Sten guns before running towards the battery command post to meet the marching column of prisoners, it suddenly is most unamusing. As you follow the stampede, for that is what it turns into, you can feel around you the frightening stimulation of the mob at work. It only needs someone to shout "Kill the bastards!" . . .

You understand their feelings. Dead Germans have long ceased to be a curiosity, but these are live ones, the first seen at close quarters, and every man present feels a fierce contempt for all men in uniforms like these, an opinion formed long before the war from newsreel images of arrogant, goose-stepping bullies harassing Jews and invading peaceful neighbouring countries. It was those images that induced them to volunteer to fight the Nazis in the first place. And all these years of forced separation from home and loved ones have deepened the hatred of an enemy that seems to enjoy imposing misery on helpless people. This hatred has been aroused to white heat in recent days through the agonies of terror imposed by the Germans' shelling, mortaring, and bombing, and the ultimate shock of seeing comrades die.

As you hurry to the side of Lieut. Gordon Lennox, standing outside Battery Command Post, you can see by the expressions on the Germans' faces that they understand what is developing and are terrified. Their eyes dart here and there at the encircling mob of gunners brandishing their weapons and growling curses at them.

Lennox is obviously as worried as you. He wears that grin he reserves for impossible situations as he whispers, "Where the hell are we supposed to send them?"

You don't know, but he should get them away from here as quickly as possible – to RHQ perhaps?

Right! He grabs onto the idea, ordering Scott and Edwards to march them double-quick over to RHQ for questioning, emphasizing in a loud voice the need to get all possible intelligence out of them.

With great relief you watch the men of 4th Field stand aside to let the Germans be marched away. But it will be a long time before that terrible look of hate in the eyes of your comrades fades from memory. You find you are shaking as you walk among them back to the guns.

Over beyond the briar-filled ditch and bushes, where the prisoners are passing other gun positions, you can hear men hooting derisively and hurling insults. But here all are silent and subdued as they make their way back to the gun pits and command posts. And for the first time you notice that almost all are wearing their steel helmets! Even in their rush to meet the German prisoners they had gone to the trouble of buckling on their tin hats, which had not been in common use throughout this unusually quiet day. A strange yet completely spontaneous, precautionary act, triggered by the prospect of finally coming face to face with the supermen, still fearfully menacing even when disarmed and clasping their hands behind their heads. Could this be anything less than the result of living so long with the nightmare of invincible hordes in blue-grey uniforms and jackboots, sweeping across Europe and North Africa before the tide turned – a product of fear and hatred of unimaginable depths?

32

A NEW LIFESTYLE HAS EVOLVED

———————————— ✳ ————————————

MOST SERVICEMEN WOULD AGREE THAT LOSS OF PRIVACY IS the prime sacrifice everyone makes on joining the forces. Regardless of rank, economic class, cultural background, experience, educational level, or intelligence, all undergo in their first days in the service a traumatic experience in loss of privacy. But with the passage of time it ceases to be a matter of any real concern, as all ranks are forced to accommodate, with a show of exaggerated nonchalance, situations no one can change or rearrange.

From the earliest days of training in Britain, every man, even those of high rank and seniority, learned to abandon when necessary all dignity in accommodating normal body functions on training schemes or out on the firing ranges – dropping his pants and baring his rump to the breezes in preference to facing worse consequences. On ten-minute halts of regimental convoys, every hour on the hour, during long hauls through densely populated southern England – its 155 vehicles and 24 guns and trailers extending seven miles or more along the road – some vehicles inevitably came to a halt on the main streets of villages. This always seemed to happen at the first stop immediately following morning or afternoon tea-break (provided by Curt Embleton's Auxiliary Service YMCA mobile canteen), guaranteeing a full turnout of all ranks at roadside, including those from the most unfortunately positioned vehicles. They, gritting their teeth, had to unbutton their flies and relieve themselves against stone walls and hedges (if lucky), or into flowerbeds or onto the open village green (if they were not), in full view of all villagers, male or female, who happened to be strolling by or gazing out of their windows.

Thus the unadorned, unprotected toilet now in use by all of Able Troop on the gun position at Fleury-sur-Orne is in no way remarkable, and you probably will squat over hundreds of similar latrine holes, on overturned Compo boxes with one of the bottom panels knocked out, without retaining a lasting memory of any of them. However, this one particular throne, halfway between the troop command post and Number One gun, set well back against the bramble-filled ditch, will for you be unforgettable simply because, as you sat there today, you were handed a copy of the new Northwest Europe edition of the *Maple Leaf*, which some unsung heroes, with commendable initiative, have begun printing among the ruins of Caen.

As usual, you are alert and listening for the warning whisper of a mortar or whine of a shell that will allow you but a split second to drop flat or dive into a hole – though as you sit you wonder whether to save your life, you could actually bring yourself to take shelter in that putrid mess in the hole below you. While this is a question of some substance, familiar to every soldier of every army in every war since cannons were invented, the scene hardly qualifies as unforgettable until you come across a strikingly relevant cartoon in the little tabloid. A soldier stands in a trench, with his head and shoulders emerging from what is obviously a Compo box toilet seat, shaking his fist at a circling Air OP Auster aircraft, which, as every gunner has come to know only too well, makes a whispering sound uncannily like an incoming mortar bomb whenever it glides in low over the gun position with its motor shut down. You can't help bursting out laughing. It's so easy to identify with that poor bugger, arising, suitably adorned, from that Compo box. And evidently so can everybody else, for suddenly there are explosive guffaws arising from all the gun pits where copies of the *Maple Leaf* have been distributed and are being devoured.

Taking stock of things, it is clear that a new lifestyle has been evolving in the bridgehead. All the way back to Caen, the yellowing fields are dotted with slit trenches, guns tanks, and vehicles. Long since you've learned to live in holes in the ground, seldom getting out when in the front line, and when in the rear areas never moving far from a hole and always keeping one ear cocked for the whisper or whine of mortar or shell. You drink water that's always warm, always heavily chlorinated and smelling like bleach, drawn from the Orne, where every hour of the day a body of a man or a cow floats by. If your stomach is strong, you still spoon into your steak-and-kidney pudding or M & V straight from the can, often warmed by the sun. If your stomach heaves when you dig through the doughy mass, you might pry open a tin of sardines, or spread some marmalade on hardtack or a slice of sultana pudding. And you suck boiled sweets endlessly, smoke, and wonder who the hell is getting those Compo boxes with the canned peaches and rice puddings. You develop a love-hate relationship with boiled Compo tea, learning to drink it before it grows cold and a leathery scum forms on the top, which you wrap around a stirring finger and fling away.

And all day long the guns rumble, and the "Tiffies" dive down through the frantic black puffs of flak, releasing their swooshing rockets on targets south of Verrières and St. Martin-de-Fontenay.

Sometimes your guns are required to fire red smoke shells to mark a target identified by one of the FOOs or the counter-battery people. Targets can be anything, but most often they are tanks, and it's against these that the four Canadian squadrons of Hawker Typhoons are proving terribly effective, judging from the terse reports coming back from the FOOs.*

The planes come in at full throttle without warning, four hundred miles an hour, and sometimes you miss seeing the first one dive. But the moment he releases his rockets, everybody across the entire front is aware that the Tiffies are operating. It must make the Germans' blood run cold, for even back here at the guns, three miles from the targets being attacked, the monstrous *swoosh* of the rockets ripping the air on their way down to the ground from the straining, diving planes can cause anxiety. Even after days of hearing them, the skin on the back of your neck tenses up whenever you hear the awesome *scu-roo-ching* of the rockets descending. You never fail to watch, for each pilot puts on a truly magnificent display of courage that is silently applauded by thousands of other watching Allied soldiers.

They come weaving in from the west, one after another, with short intervals between, diving down straight at their target through a rising fury of snapping, black puffs of flak saturating the sky above Verrières Ridge – each pilot holding the nose of his plane steady on the target for some seconds until he reaches a precise distance that guarantees his eight 60-pound rocket-bombs will have lethal effect. Only then does he release them, to leave smoky trails wavering in their wake above earth-shaking explosions that can be felt all the way back here at the guns.

It's incredible any of those planes survive those dives through skies polluted with the flak of more than six dozen 88-mm ack-ack guns covering the ridge. Sometimes a plane does disintegrate in a

---

* While reports from FOOs received at the guns constantly dwelt on the success of Typhoon rockets on tanks, a 2nd Division report issued on September 22, 1944, analysing air support, declared "our own infantry say the enemy comes screaming out of trenches which are attacked by Typhoons."

ball of flames, leaving only a wisp of smoke when it's hit before its pilot can release his bombs. Now and then some poor guy, whose name you'll never know, simply doesn't reappear from his dive below the ridge, and you feel the earth shudder with the impact of his plane, and you watch for the funereal pillar of black smoke to rise above the crest.

33

THE RAVELLED SLEAVE

———————————— ✳ ————————————

IF YOU WEREN'T BENUMBED BY EXHAUSTION FROM LACK OF sleep, the supernatural intensity hanging over the bridgehead day and night would be intolerable. It's as though the grinding conflict of the immense opposing forces, exercising their colossal fire-power night and day without pause, is generating a static charge in the air about you, influencing everything you think, say, and do, stimulating and perhaps sustaining the will to carry on beyond normal endurance.

In a very real sense, Normandy has become a battle against fatigue as much as a battle for the domination of smashed and smoking villages. There are only five hours of real darkness (10:45 P.M. to 3:45 A.M. British Double Daylight Time) to inhibit matters of aggression. The interminably long days of attacks and counter-attacks and the tension and strain induced by the relentless sense of menace hanging in the dusty, foul-smelling air, combine to ensure a chronic lack of sleep and to produce this awful fatigue that afflicts all ranks. Men have learned to carry on by grabbing sleep whenever the opportunity arises, even during enemy shelling, as you did the day you came back to the guns from Eterville and bedded down in a shallow, open trench in the blazing sunlight of the treeless valley in front of Carpiquet, snoring away the whole afternoon, totally oblivious to the worst bombardment Able Troop has yet endured, according to your command post crew. Infantrymen describe falling asleep while continuing to walk robot-fashion up a road. And you know from experience a man can fall asleep standing up, having done so on more than one occasion recently while leaning over the artillery board.

For the past six days you've been largely confined to this candle-lit, primitively roofed dugout that is Able Troop Command Post, without a second officer to spell you off – Hutch having been posted to Battery Command Post immediately after being absent on that two-day advance party for the move over here. And all the while the guns have been firing constantly with only brief pauses between targets, seldom of sufficient duration (at least fifteen minutes) to allow you to grab a catnap sitting upright on a little folding canvas camp-stool, with your ankles wrapped around the wiggly, scissor-like legs to stabilize them.

Late yesterday, on the way to the latrine in a drowsy stupor, you walked under the muzzle of one of your own 25-pounders just as it fired, rendering you totally deaf so that you had to communicate entirely in writing until your hearing returned this afternoon.

Tonight you give fire orders in your sleep so convincingly you fool a new ack, Gunner William Hiltz, who just arrived today (July 23) and is on his first tour of duty. Sometime around midnight you provide the line, range, and angle of sight for a target fabricated in dreamland, only waking up after the guns begin firing. And incredibly it isn't the sound of the guns that wakens you, but your stern, subconscious reaction to hearing Hiltz break the strict code of fire discipline. In your sleep, or that mysterious state of stupefaction that passes for sleep these days, you listen without objection to Hiltz calling out over the Tannoy the fire orders to the guns as you dictate them. But when you hear him say "Fire!" – an order normally following the ordering of the range but which you withheld this time – you come up wide awake, demanding to know who the hell gave him the order to fire? Instantly realizing you are struggling out of a dream, but mystified by the reality of the guns thumping away, you ask Hiltz where he got the target. When he replies, "From you, sir," your heart almost stops.

My God! Where are those shells landing? Snatching the Tannoy mike from him, you yell at the top of your lungs, "Stop! Stop! Stop!"

You hardly dare breathe as you lean over the artillery board to swing the arm along the arc, plotting the line and range you'd uttered and Hiltz had methodically logged on his message pad. And your relief is beyond description when your pencil point dots the talc well beyond the FDL (forward defended line). Subconsciously you had fabricated a target from a mental store of ranges and switches from zero-line for the scores of harassing-fire targets you'd ordered over the past two days and nights. But the thought of what might have happened leaves you shaking.

You ask your embarrassed young ack where on earth he thinks you could get a target while sleeping over there in the dark? He explains that from time to time throughout the night they've been coming over from Battery Command Post with fire tasks, handing the slips of paper down to you through the folds of the tarpaulin that serves as a black-out curtain over the dugout stairwell. And when you started to give clear, decisive fire orders, he assumed another target had been handed in to you. Entirely logical. But please, you say, never, ever again make assumptions! Only in emergencies do acks fire the guns.

Even as you lecture him you find yourself again dozing off. To stir yourself to a modicum of alertness, you lay on the next timed target and climb out to visit the guns. To your dismay you find only one gunner serving each gun. The others lie like dead men on the floors of pits, their heads only inches away from the crashing, recoiling breeches.

Your first inclination is to rouse them indignantly. But then you check yourself. There is really no rush to get off harassing fire that is actually designed to be sporadic and unpredictable to the enemy. And these men have been digging gun and ammunition pits and shifting tons of shells around the clock for days on end. In just one twenty-four-hour period back at Louvigny, the Regiment fired 24,000 rounds. And the second-in-command visiting the guns last night reported that in the last four days 4th Field guns have consumed 40,000 shells – five hundred tons of H.E. (high explosive).

You watch the lone gunner lift out a hundred-pound case of shells, kick off the hasps, lift out a shell, place it in the breech, ram it home with the wooden rammer, slide a brass cartridge case in behind it, close the breech, mount the gun seat, check his lay through the dial-sight, and pull the firing lever. Methodically, without wasted motion, he repeats this routine over and over until he's fired the required number of rounds. Then, pitching the spent cartridge cases out of the pit, he sits down on the trail and wordlessly offers you a cigarette.

Over in the hole that is Battery Command Post, no one speaks either. They look up and stare at you a moment with red-rimmed eyes and then go back to work. For days, in incredibly dirty and cramped conditions, they've been working out targets and fire plans demanding extreme accuracy, calculating all the complicated data required to navigate shells to precise spots on the landscape, allowing for winds of various strengths and directions, and air temperatures and pressures at various strata above the earth through which the shells will loop on their way to the target – leaving only last-minute adjustments for the varying temperature of the propellant charges to the GPOs whenever extreme accuracy is called for.

They work with pencils sharpened to fine points, on talc-covered artillery boards, which they must struggle continually to keep clean of sifting dust, their noses almost touching the surface of the boards as they strain to see what they are plotting by the yellow glow of fading lamps-electric.

You hear heavy trucks milling around your gun position, and you return to find seventeen Army Service Corps three-tonners cluttering up the field among your four guns. When you inquire of the sergeant in charge if he's lost, fully believing it is a convoy that has lost its way, he asks, "Is this not Able Troop, Second Battery, 4th Field?"

When you admit it is, the softspoken man tells you he is here to drop off 640 rounds for each of your four guns. And his men could use the help of your gunners to off-load it. They spent yesterday off-loading ships and still have to make another trip back to the beaches tonight. They'd sure like to get off the road before dawn. On their way up planes dropped flares over them.

Using the Tannoy at your command post, you have the gunners, who are awake, rouse their sergeants so you can explain what must be done. As you pass the gun pits on your way back to the trucks, you hear the soles of hobnailed boots being kicked and mumbled explanations given.

What torture it must be for those men to force themselves to reject sleep for which their bodies are aching – let alone to start shifting 160 hundred-pound cases of shells and eighty boxes of cartridge cases per gun. But in the pits, where dark figures are staggering to their feet and yawning prodigiously, there's no word of complaint.

You tell the RCASC sergeant the gunners are exhausted from an awesome amount of firing during the past few days with very little sleep. He assures you he is well aware of the voracious appetite of the guns, having participated in shell dumpings the like of which, they are told, have never been attempted before: 86,400 rounds for 2nd Division alone in the past three days. Now tonight 46,000 rounds more, and before noon tomorrow another 26,000. In less than five days, 158,000 rounds for the division: 2,200 rounds per gun! Oh yes, he knows! Still, he wishes they'd move a little faster, he'd like to get that second trip wrapped up before dawn. It can get a bit uncomfortable riding in a truck with three tons of high explosive when Jerry starts bombing.

And you are reminded there is more to fighting a war than firing guns. Long after the trucks have pulled out and the first faint grey light is creeping in over the now-silent gun position, you ponder the lot of drivers who must toil night and day, moving up supplies of all kinds for the fighting troops, carrying on in obscurity, without the attention of war correspondents forever preoccupied with infantry and tank units with proud names and regional associations. Churchill said it so well before the turn of the century in his book *The River War.* "Victory is the bright-coloured flower. Transport is the stem without which it could never have blossomed."*

Denied even catnaps on your camp stool the rest of the night, you are still in a dangerously dull-witted state when you decide to leave Hiltz, slumped over the artillery board, snoring away, and go out and whip up the first brew of the day yourself. This turns out to be harder than you thought. Overnight there's been a heavy dew, and it is quite impossible to get flames to sustain among the straw and bramble twigs currently in popular use in place of petrol-drenched sand fires that characteristically produce tea tainted with oily smoke. Still, you know what to do, having seen gunners feed recalcitrant fires with spaghetti-like strands of cordite from discarded bags of Charge III propellant. Locating a blue bag from a pile thrown in an empty ammo box at one of the guns, you start adding a strand at a time to the smouldering sticks under a water-filled, square, green tin (the bottom half of a bulk container for hardtack) which rests on four stones in a cavelike firepit excavated in the side of the ditch.

---

*   Expanding on this thought, Churchill wrote: "The eye is fixed on the fighting brigades as they move amid the smoke; on the swarming figures of the enemy. . . . The long, trailing line of communications is unnoticed. The fierce glory that plays on red, triumphant bayonets dazzles the observer; nor does he care to look behind to where along a thousand miles of rail, road and river, the convoys are crawling to the front in unnoticed succession." *The River War* (London: Longmans, Green, 1899).

For a while nothing happens. And by the time this fact registers in your sleepy mind, a fair amount of cordite has accumulated under the pot. As you hunker down to see why it isn't flaring up in that sparkling brilliance others manage to produce under their boiling pots, there's an ugly, hollow roar and you are blown over backwards into a full sitting position by a violent puff of flame and soot — scorched clean, you'll soon discover, of not only your eyebrows and eyelashes, but several days' growth of shaggy beard. Fortunately fatigue doesn't dull the reaction-time of eyelids, and while you're left very red-faced (in reality as well as figuratively), sufficiently seared to require gobs of sunburn salve, your eyes are unharmed.

By the afternoon, you are so stupefied by lack of sleep that the only thing you'll recall of the entire day is passing into oblivion, with a desperate sense of relief, in the partially roofed slit trench your batman, Gunner Alexander Whitehawk, dug for you days ago in the ditch at the rear of the position.

That you had earlier in the day acted without a modicum of social grace in receiving your new troop leader (assistant GPO), you'll have to learn when Lieut. Bob Grout and you later become friends and he feels free to tell you it was with some trepidation he began his tour of duty with what was clearly a thoughtless boor. On arrival he'd asked someone to locate the GPO. And in due course a dishevelled, sandy scarecrow appeared at the mouth of the dugout growling, "Well, what the hell do you want?"

On being told, the scarecrow had simply said, "Okay, get the hell down in here and take over – I'm going to bed."

Fortunately, during the next twenty-four hours Grout is able to put your conduct in better perspective, while watching you become a source of amusement for all who come to peer in at you in your partially covered trench as you sleep the clock around, oblivious to an unending rain of dirt falling on your face from the dried-out earthen roof dislodged by the 14th Battery guns firing from only a few yards behind — each tormenting muzzle-blast, entrapped and swirling around in the roofed-over, closed end of your trench in the ditch, lifting your head and dropping it without causing any change whatsoever in the rhythmic breathing of your deep sleep. At least that is what he and others tell you when finally you come to life sometime on the twenty-fourth. And you are inclined to believe them, for you are never able to sleep in that pulsating trench again. Henceforth, when off duty, you sleep in front of GA, the armoured scout car, curled up around the stubby nest of gear shifts, your bottom on one of the bucket seats and your head and shoulders on the other.

PART FOUR: JULY 24–AUGUST 2

Canadian Units Ensure American Break-Out Succeeds

34

A FOOTNOTE TO "MAIN BATTLE
AREA OF CAEN"

✳

ON JULY 25 TWO MAJOR ALLIED OPERATIONS ARE TO BE UNDER-
taken in the bridgehead, with the Americans on the right at St. Lô,
and the Canadians thirty-five miles east of there at Verrières — with
totally different, unrelated objectives if viewed separately (the way
the Germans must view them), but fully interdependent operations
when viewed from Montgomery's perspective.

Each is vital to the achievement of a common goal: no less than
the long-awaited "break-out from the bridgehead," leading, it is
hoped, to the disintegration of German resistance on the perimeter, forcing them to retire to the Seine, where, with no bridges to
cross, they'll have to surrender or be annihilated by the bombers.

"Operation Spring," the push south of Caen against Verrières
Ridge and beyond by 2nd Canadian Corps (with two British armoured divisions available for exploitation), has limited territorial
objectives. But to the attackers, as well as the attacked, it will have
all the earmarks of a major offensive with a break-out as its ultimate
aim. This is precisely how it is intended to appear; a threat so
serious the Germans will continue to hold the bulk of their forces —
particularly their armour — on the Canadian front, thus favouring
"Operation Cobra," the American offensive Monty is counting on
to break through the thinly held western rim of the bridgehead.

All of which is consistent with German thinking that the expected American attack through the obstacle-filled *bocage* countryside can be contained with minimum forces, while a renewal of the Canadian–British offensive in the rolling country south of Caen could succeed, spelling disaster for all German forces in Normandy unless opposed by maximum forces and fire-power.

Throughout July, most of the fresh German units arriving in Normandy have been directed to the British–Canadian front. Six of eight infantry divisions and all four new Panzer divisions, including two additional battalions of Tiger tanks, have appeared in the Caen sector.

And von Kluge continues to concentrate three brigades of Nebelwerfers (Moaning Minnies) – his entire Normandy complement of these dreadful, multi-barrelled mortars – on what he perceives to be "the main battle area of Caen."* Furthermore, most of the mortars and guns that halted operations Goodwood and Atlantic (more than 1,600 barrels) are still in position to drench Verrières Ridge with fire from both sides of the Orne.

The day before the assaults begin, Field Marshal von Kluge, Commander-in-Chief of German Forces West, responding to the dual threats, reinforces the American front with a mere battle group of 2nd SS, while transferring from Caumont the full 2nd Panzer Division to a position astride the Caen–Falaise highway. At Caumont it might have made a crucial difference in shutting down the American offensive; but moved east of the Orne south of Caen to meet the Canadian threat, 2nd Panzer Division merely thickens defences already ten miles deep holding a front of less than seven miles.

The end result is that on the eve of "Spring" and "Cobra," fourteen Canadian and British divisions are pinning down fourteen

---

* From the "Templehof Papers" (an appreciation by Hauser for von Kluge, July 19, 1944) as quoted in Chester Wilmot's *Struggle for Europe* (London: Collins, 1952), p. 389.

German divisions, including elite SS divisions such as the 1st SS (Leibstandarte Adolph Hitler) Panzer Division, armed with the best equipment the German high command can supply. At the same time nineteen American divisions (Bradley's fifteen and Patton's four) are opposed by a grab-bag of German battle groups and formations totalling only nine divisions.

And because the German tanks are so vastly superior in fire-power to all American and British tanks, except a few "Fireflies" (Shermans equipped with a British 17-pounder gun), the six hundred Panthers and Tigers drawn to the Canadian and British fronts – leaving only 110 tanks and no Tigers at all opposing the Americans – will be the most telling factor in the outcome of these two operations: a decisive break-out on the American front (allowing Patton's army to drive almost unopposed in an eastern arc towards Paris) while the Canadians engage in a crushing, stalemated battle on Verrières Ridge.*

---

* The following details, showing the lopsided distribution of German tank forces between the American and Canadian–British sectors on the eve of "Cobra" and "Spring," are from page 364 of Chester Wilmot's *Struggle for Europe* (London: Collins, 1952):

On British Second Army Front (with 2nd Canadian Corps): Four Heavy Tank battalions and seven Panzer Divisions – of which five and a half are east of the Orne facing the Canadians.

On American First Army Front: Two Panzer Divisions, one Panzer Grenadier Division (with one battalion of assault guns only), and no battalions of heavy tanks.

35

"THE ENTIRE AREA LOOKS LIKE
A CHARNEL-HOUSE"

---- ✳ ----

MERCIFULLY, THE PRECISE DETAILS OF THE FORCES AMASSED
opposite them are unknown to the bleary-eyed, tormented
Canadian soldiers huddled in their sandy holes south of the village
of Ifs, awaiting orders to go forward.*

Still, a man would have to be deaf, blind, and incredibly stupid
not to be aware that the enemy is "thick on the ground" out there,
that he can whistle up swarms of tanks, including his invincible
Tigers, whenever required to crush an attack, and that "a helluva
lot" of 88s and Moaning Minnies have registered every square
metre of ground on the way to Tilly-la-Campagne, up those wide-
open slopes to Verrières, as well as the orchards and fields around St.
Martin-de-Fontenay and St. André-sur-Orne.

To the North Nova Scotia Highlanders of 3rd Division, who are
to shield the left flank by taking Tilly-la-Campagne, and the nine
infantry battalions of 2nd Division, who'll attack Verrières Ridge
and beyond, it is clear that the swollen numbers of men, tanks,

---

* Survivors of these "holding attacks" – who one day would share in
Montgomery's pride and satisfaction at the success of "his feints" in
drawing the bulk of the German fire-power east of the Orne, allowing
the Americans to break out – were, at the time, unaware that the purpose
of their attacks was simply to maintain the bloody status quo.

guns, and mortars, committed by the Germans to the defence of their dominant positions, will deal as severely with the attacking forces as they did during "Goodwood" and "Atlantic," when in a single afternoon they stopped three tank divisions cold and cut to ribbons whole battalions of Canadian infantry.

The plan for "Spring" calls for 6th Brigade to clear the startline, which will be the road running from the Troteval and Beauvoir farms, on the left, to St. Martin and St. André on the right: the Fusiliers Mont-Royal retaking the infamous farms, and the Queen's Own Cameron Highlanders clearing all of St. Martin by midnight, July 24. The first phase of the attack will go in at 3:30 A.M. on the twenty-fifth, with the Calgary Highlanders leading the 5th Brigade assault from St. Martin to May-sur-Orne, and the Royal Hamilton Light Infantry leading off 4th Brigade, attacking Verrières. At the same hour the North Nova Scotia Highlanders are to attempt to "seize" from the fanatical 1st SS Panzer Division the fortified village of Tilly-la-Campagne, which lies on the tactically important high ground to the left of the Caen–Falaise highway, some 1,500 metres east of Verrières.

In the second phase of "Spring," the Black Watch will pass through the Calgary Highlanders to capture Fontenay-le-Marmion, while the Royal Regiment passes about 1,300 metres beyond Verrières to take Rocquancourt. And when all objectives are taken, 7th British Armoured Division will push south to the height of land along the Caen–Falaise highway known as "Point 122."

Since the attack is to go before dawn, some illumination of the landscape for the troops moving into position will be provided by searchlights playing off low-hanging clouds to produce "artificial moonlight" first used in that attack by the British ten days ago west of Carpiquet, with mixed reviews by participating troops.

In the opening phase, an extensive artillery fire plan will be carried out on German positions and gun lines by nine Canadian and British field artillery regiments, and three AGRAs (2nd Canadian, 2nd British, and 8th British Army Groups Royal

Artillery) containing nine medium regiments of 5.5-inch guns and two heavy regiments of 7.2-inch guns, as well as one heavy ack-ack, four anti-tank, and five light ack-ack regiments.

At 1:15 A.M. enemy bombers come over, and while no bombs land on 4th Field positions, they create havoc among other field and medium regiments spread across the densely populated fields reaching back to Caen. Many fires are left burning among vehicles and ammunition dumps. Nevertheless, throughout the night all three divisional artilleries continue desultory harassing fire, until 2:30 A.M., when, along with the mediums, they take part in a twenty-minute counter-battery program. At 3:28 A.M., just two minutes before H-hour for the attack to go in, the CO reports Phase I has been postponed thirty minutes. (Startlines have not been cleared at either the farms or at St. Martin.) By 4:00 A.M. FOOs are reporting it very foggy, as the three divisional artilleries open on a series of timed concentrations, which 2nd Division guns will continue until 6:00 A.M., consuming 360 rounds per gun.

Any delay in opening an attack can cause confusion, as the timing of the units moving up is thrown off. And when the startline is still being fought over as the postponed attack goes in, the problem is compounded to a point where chaos threatens. So it is with the Calgary Highlanders and the Rileys when they have to subdue enemy on their startlines before they can launch their attacks and are unable to take advantage of the timed artillery program. And confusion extends to the battalions following behind, who must be in position to push on when the leading units have attained inter-mediate objectives.

With the guns raising a flashing, thunderous confusion across the whole front among the roiling mists lit eerily from behind by the low beams of searchlights, and plastered by enemy defensive fire, including salvo after salvo of Moaning Minnies crashing on the axis of advance, the Royals are forced to dig several sets of shallow slit trenches for shelter in the many hours it takes them to make it across a couple of thousand metres of grain fields – first following in behind the Rileys, and then surging forth in the van over the crest of the ridge to the left of Verrières.

"One horrendous foul-up in the dark, starting about 0300!" That is how Royals' Platoon Commander Bob Suckling will remember it.

In the infantry nobody tells you anything, which results in the birth of what are known as "shit-house rumours" – wildly exaggerated, panic-warped pieces of intelligence spread by word-of-mouth and growing with each retelling, until they are only slightly more reliable than army news despatches. And this night the rumours are particularly melodramatic. Eventually we learn the snafu is caused by somebody's failure to secure the startline. But in the meantime, we spend what seems hours in open ground in the dark, surrounded by horrific flashes and the grinding sound of tanks we're supposed to be following; not knowing why we are held up, but knowing we shouldn't be this close to the tanks.

If there is one infantry adage that should always be scrupulously observed, it is: Never follow a tank – in fact, never get close to one! The buggers draw enemy fire, and sometimes they run over you. A few of our men are lost this way after falling asleep on the ground.*

It's just starting to get light when the carrier in which Brit Smith and his 4th Field crew are moving forward with the FMRs back towards Troteval Farm, runs over a mine:

Four days before, when we were forced to bail out quickly from an OP near Troteval Farm in the pouring rain, I buried in the bottom of a trench my big 12-power binoculars and my new

---

* Author interview.

Burberry mackintosh I'd recently bought at Simpsons in London for twenty-five pounds.*

Damned if I was going to crawl through the mud in my expensive coat, with those big, awkward field-glasses dangling around my neck. So I had taken them off, and after wrapping them in my Burberry, covered them over with earth in the bottom of the trench – carefully noting its location for future reference.

Now on our way up to Troteval, I remember that slit trench is only a couple of hundred yards off the route we are taking, and decide to go over there and recover my binoculars and my rain-coat. It's still quite dark, barely light enough to see where we are going, but we catch sight of an FMR jumping up and down, waving his arms wildly and yelling something. It being impossible to communicate by voice over the roar of our barrage, I reach over in front of Bombardier May with a clenched fist, the recognized signal for a driver to stop.

Just as the carrier rocks to a stop, and I'm standing up to turn around to ask our French-speaking crew member [T. Robitaille] if he can make out what the guy is yelling, a mine blows under the track on the driver's side.

May is killed instantly. And one of my legs is shattered as I'm blown out in a cloud of sand from the layer of sandbags with which all our carriers are floored to absorb the force of just such an explosion. I go up very high, looping over before coming down in the uncut grain with an awful thump, thinking, "My God! I'm still alive!"

Immediately at least four machine guns covering the mine field open up, focusing on where they saw the flash of the mine. Bullets wham into the sides of the upturned carrier, and I, along with the two signallers (saved from serious harm by the steel

---

* About 116 Canadian dollars, equivalent to about 1,160 dollars in 1990.

bulkhead between them and the front compartment), start crawling away like mad through the grain, bullets snicking all around us. Broken leg and all, I crawl like hell for about fifty yards.

When we get far enough away to stop, I remember that Jack Thompson [the other 14th Battery troop commander] is on the move nearby with another company and should be approaching Beauvoir Farm by now. I send one of the signallers to find him and tell him we're out of action so he can pass the word back to Battery to get up a replacement crew.

While he's away, the other signaller gives me a shot of morphine, using one of my own self-contained (and incredibly blunt) hypodermic needles issued to all officers before we left England for just such a purpose. Then as he starts to rig up a splint for my leg using a rifle, I ask him if he's sure it's broken.

"Oh, it's broken all right," he assures me. "Between the ankle and knee, shards of bone are sticking through the skin."

My battledress trousers are almost non-existent, shredded by the blast and the sand, a lot of which has been driven into the skin of my legs. There's considerable bleeding, which he stops with several field dressings, including one on my neck, where a bullet, picked up as I was crawling back, is imbedded in the muscle.

After about twenty minutes, Thompson arrives showing great concern, and, before he leaves, locates stretcher-bearers to carry me out to an ambulance Jeep that can't come in from the road because of the mines.

It's only a few hundred yards, but that trip is hell. Every time a bunch of shells come in, they drop the stretcher and flop down. While I can't blame them a damned bit, it's quite an experience being dropped every hundred yards or so, and I am dropped at least five or six times. The actual wounding wasn't really that bad, but being suddenly dropped to earth from almost three feet up is pure hell.

I am also worried about the rifle they are using as a splint –
whether or not they ejected the last round from the firing
chamber before they strapped the butt to my ankle and stuck the
muzzle up under my armpit. At least three times on the way out,
I have somebody unstrap the rifle and open the bolt to check the
chamber to make bloody sure that nothing is in there.

When finally they get me to the ambulance Jeep, they put me
up on the top row, over the driver, which makes for an interesting trip as we start back along the highway towards Caen. We
have to drive right under the guns of a long column of tanks
forced to keep to the road after what happened to my carrier and
others among the mines. Their guns are depressed flat, pointing
across the fields at about a forty-five-degree angle, shooting at
God-knows-what. There is no more than a foot clearance
between their muzzles and our stretchers passing under them,
but they don't give a damn – when they decide to fire, they fire.
And it seems that every one of those damned tanks manages to
get off a round just as we are passing under its gun. Good thing
the stretchers are tied down! The muzzle-blast is incredible,
lifting and rocking the whole Jeep.*

At 4:40 A.M. the guns receive word that the North Novas are on
their objective, Tilly-la-Campagne. But as time goes on this report
appears premature. There are no reports on the progress of the
Calgary Highlanders and the Black Watch. The FMRs, aided by
tanks of the Sherbrooke Fusiliers (27th Armoured Regiment), have
retaken Troteval Farm with great dash and verve according to a
running commentary given by a tank commander and picked up
on the radio at Brigade. But Beauvoir Farm is still not cleared at
H-hour.

---

*   Author interview.

At 5:40 A.M. 4th Brigade is reported to have Verrières, but judging from the calls for fire from FOOs, this is questionable. Since first light, enemy tanks have been attacking, and clearly Stu Laurie, who with his crew went in with the Rileys, has been driven out of an OP.

As Laurie will remember it, the Rileys don't experience too much trouble gaining their objective. It's afterwards their troubles begin.

As we are approaching Verrières, going up a hill in support of the RHLI, we stop at a stone barn near the village where I can overlook the whole ridge. Immediately I see Germans running out there, and tanks coming up behind them. But when I call for the guns, I'm told, "The Major has them." This happens to me twice! And while I am waiting, in comes Colonel Rockingham, CO of the RHLI.* He has a bloody scratch right across his nose where a passing bullet has nicked it, which he ignores as he peers out the open barn door. After a moment he says, "Look, come along, we're going right into the village!"

And we do, we go right up the main street – the only street – until I find a place at the far end where I can see out across the front. The Jerry tanks don't shoot at us going in, but there's one terrifying moment when, just as we are passing under the gun of one of our own tanks, it fires at something up ahead. The muzzle-blast is awful!

Leaving the carrier back in the sunken road, I go forward about fifty yards, accompanied by MacAleer [Gunner J. R.], who as he goes unreels the remote control cable that will link us to the big radio set in the carrier behind us. We take shelter behind a stone wall where one of our anti-tank guns has just been knocked out, and the crew is lying dead around it.

---

* Lt.-Col. J. M. Rockingham had replaced Lt.-Col. W. D. "Denny" Whitaker, who was wounded at Verson on July 14.

Peering over the top of the wall, I see a great big Tiger tank just down the slope in front, with several officers standing around it directing its fire. Just then one of our tanks comes up and shows itself in the fringe of a little woods only about one hundred feet from where we are. The shot from the Tiger peels a silver groove right across its turret. And though it doesn't catch fire or anything, the metallic rip is god-awful – even at one hundred feet! What it must have sounded like to those guys inside the tank! Anyway, they get the hell out of there in a hurry.

That Tiger has control over the whole ridge where we are, and when I stick my head up to try to pin down a map reference, he starts shooting at me with 88-mm solid-shot – not at the centre of the wall, but chopping away at both ends. First he hits this end and then the other, knocking off a bit more of the wall with each shot. And he keeps this up until the wall, which was about fifteen feet long to start with, is down to about six feet. In the meantime Major Wren and the Colonel are still keeping the guns engaged elsewhere, and all I can get to use is a section [two guns] or some-times a troop [four guns].

Oh, I get some shells down, but nothing of consequence, nothing you would call real fire, before we have to leave. MacAleer and I are now alone – the few Rileys, who'd been out in the field with us, having disappeared when the tank started shooting. With our wall disappearing, our only hope is to make it back to the carrier in the sunken road.

As we get set to make the dash, I see MacAleer preparing to reel up the remote control cable, and I have to yell at him, "Forget your damned remote control and get the hell out of here fast!" And running like the devil we make it back the fifty yards or so to the sunken road where there is some protection. There we pile into the carrier and pull out with the remote control bouncing behind us.

Back at Riley headquarters the confusion is terrible. Everybody seems to be pulling back, and for a while no one seems to know what they should do – including the battery commander [Major James Wilson Dodds]. But then Rockingham takes charge. He's a wonderful guy – no question about that! When we tell him we couldn't possibly stay where we were, his advice is simple: "Go and find some place where you can stay."

And that's what we do. We take over an abandoned position along the front of a little woods to one side of the village. And whoever was here must have just pulled out, for the food they left is still hot.*

At the guns it's difficult to picture what is going on up there. Situation reports are either totally confusing, or, as in the case of the Calgary Highlanders and the Black Watch, non-existent. But all the guns on all sides seem to be firing – some plastering Tilly-la-Campagne, apparently to help extricate the North Novas from what seems to have become a disastrous situation. The guns are firing almost steadily on Mike and Uncle targets around Verrières, and at one point, to guide the Typhoons, Capt. Bill Waddell (the new commander of Baker Troop, replacing Gord Hunter) calls for red smoke to mark a clutch of enemy tanks. But the tanks are so close one of the red-smoke canisters, expelled from a descending shell, lands near RHLI tac headquarters and causes Major Dodds to complain: "Smoke fell short – our fine-feathered friends took us for the target – acted accordingly – fortunately no casualties."

By 10:30 A.M. it is clear that even though the Rileys still are heavily engaged holding off enemy attacks at Verrières, two 4th Field FOOs – Waddell and Sammy Grange (the latter in place of Laurie, who is fully occupied with the Rileys) – are going forward

---

*   Author interview.

with the Royals in the follow-through attack that is supposed to carry them over the crest of the ridge to the left of Verrières, down the slope to Rocquancourt.

Waddell and his crew are going forward in their normal carrier with a rifle company, but Grange and two of his crew are in a Sherman tank provided by C Squadron, 6th Armoured Regiment (First Hussars) that has been assigned to give close support to the Royals.

Having been delayed several hours by the late clearing of the startline at Beauvoir, the attackers are going in without the advantage of the timed artillery concentrations, which by now have all been shot. Henceforth all support from the guns must derive from the initiative of the FOOs who drench the landscape with shells, driving the German foot-soldiers to ground whenever enemy activity is spotted, and marking with red smoke, for rocket-firing Typhoons and bomb-carrying Spitfires, all visible tanks and every distant lump or scar emitting the slightest sandy puff suggesting it might be a self-propelled gun or dug-in tank.

As the Shermans approach the crest, they become embroiled in a raging battle with enemy tanks, and soon the field is obscured by black smoke, drifting from burning German and Canadian tanks. No match in a face-to-face shootout with Panthers or Tigers, let alone Royal Tigers of sixty-eight tons, only three Shermans survive. Most of the others are left flaming, with terrible consequences to their crews.

One Sherman, right up on the crest, is hit and bursts into flames just as Bob Suckling and his platoon are approaching it:

Instantly the hatch flies open, emitting a cloud of black smoke as survivors tumble out and leap to the ground. One man, in flinging himself out backwards, catches his knees on the rim of the hatch, and I watch in unbelieving horror as he hangs there, blazing like a torch, before dropping to the ground on his head, setting fire to the wheat. Stretcher-bearers have to dash forward to extinguish the flames enveloping his body, as other Royals beat out the flaming grain. And before long tanks and carriers are burning throughout the whole area.*

Lieut. Tom Wilcox of the Royals' mortar platoon, positioned in an exposed chalk pit near the Caen–Falaise highway, will later recall that when the few surviving Shermans disperse, carriers pulling the anti-tank guns become prime targets for the German tanks, and after that, anything that moves, until "the entire area looks like a charnel-house, with dead bodies and blazing vehicles everywhere."†

In one small hedge-surrounded field, nine Tigers knock out eight of the Hussars' tanks, including the squadron commander's and the one assigned to his artillery FOO. Grange isn't in it when it's hit, having gone reconnoitring on foot with the squadron commander. And though it doesn't "brew up," he finds it well-holed by armour-piercing solid-shot when he returns, and it is with some trepidation that he climbs up to peer down into it to discover the fate of his crew.

To his relief the turret is empty except for a leg with a boot on it. Cleanly severed by one of the solid armour-piercing shots passing through, it had been left by one of the Hussars manning the tank, not by Grange's ack, Bombardier Gilmour Addie, as he first thought on learning Addie had been wounded and evacuated.

Bill Waddell will forever remember his "initiation as a FOO on a hill to the left of the village of Verrières," where he is able to observe

---

* Author interview.
† C Squadron's First Hussars, commanded by Major D'Arcy Marks, brother of Major R. Marks of the Royals, lost fifteen of the eighteen tanks with which they began the attack, having lost two others to bombs dropped by the Luftwaffe on their assembly area before coming up.

the whole scene, including Grange's tank being shot up: "All hell breaks loose as Tiger tanks start shooting up the 6th Armoured tanks. Codes and formalities in wireless procedures are completely ignored as we go on the air and scream for fire on the attacking tanks."*

Seven Royals' officers are lost in the attack, and their historian will record: "Once over the ridge, the assaulting companies are struck immediately by a hurricane of fire."† In the dead ground beyond the ridge, the Germans have tanks and self-propelled 88s dug-in, invulnerable to anything but a direct hit by a big shell or a Typhoon rocket. And when the weary men of C Company, under Capt. G. K. Singleton, their ranks already seriously depleted by casualties, continue to press down the forward slope, they suddenly are surrounded by German infantry rising up and firing out of the grain on all sides. Those who aren't immediately killed or wounded are taken prisoner. Only eighteen Other Ranks of C company survive this day's fighting.‡

At this time Waddell is sheltering behind a dip in the road, peering through the wheat: "Suddenly the lad next to me gets it right between the eyes, and in that instant – for the first time I think – I fully realize the reality of war. After dark we pull back and take cover in a ditch for the night. And at one point tanks pass between us and the crest of the hill, close enough we not only can hear them but can identify them as German even in the dark."

---

* Author interview.
† Major D. J. Goodspeed, *Battle Royal* (Toronto: Royal Regiment of Canada Association, 1962), p. 429.
‡ In ten days, from July 18 to 28, the Royals were to lose twenty-one officers. Casualties among Other Ranks were equally severe. By August 3, they had received 616 reinforcements: 80 on July 20, 254 on July 28, and 282 on August 3.

36

"DOUBLE INTENSE"

---- ❋ ----

NO INFORMATION WHATSOEVER HAS BEEN GETTING BACK
from 5th Brigade since early morning, when the Calgary Highlanders were to take May-sur-Orne and the Black Watch were to
pass through to take Fontenay-le-Marmion.* When a gunner,
coming back from sneaking rations up to the civilians in the cave
at Fleury-sur-Orne, reports seeing the fresh grave of Col. S.S.T.
Cantlie of the Black Watch, who, he was told, died of wounds
suffered before dawn at St. Martin-de-Fontenay, the day-long
silence of 5th Brigade becomes ominous. Then at 7:00 P.M., when
the guns engage in still another fire plan in front of St. Martin on
behalf of the Maisonneuves attacking the same predawn 5th
Brigade objective of May-sur-Orne, it's clear the earlier attacks
were crushed.

It will be some time before it is generally known that the
Calgary Highlanders and the Maisonneuves were severely mauled
and the Black Watch virtually wiped out. The Germans were
cunningly deployed to take advantage of a network of mine
tunnels and air shafts under the whole area from St. André to

---

* As late as 7:40 P.M. on July 25, the RCA log at 2nd Canadian Corps
recorded a message from Brig. Keefler's HQ: "No news on progress of 5th
Cdn Inf Brigade attack against May-sur-Orne."

Rocquancourt, allowing them to return unobserved to positions previously cleared or reported empty by patrols, popping up in the wheat when it suited them to put advancing troops under fire from all sides. (Six days later, on July 31, Army Intelligence will produce, for the FMRs taking over in St. Martin, a map trace showing the exact positions of the mine's main tunnels and air shafts.)

The few members of the Black Watch who manage to escape the murderous fire from machine guns, mortars, and tank guns sweeping the fields from all sides, up the slope to May-sur-Orne and beyond, and who make it back to St. Martin (only fifteen out of three hundred) can provide only tiny segments of the picture. The full story of how sixty men actually made it to the crest before most of them died on coming almost face-to-face with tanks camouflaged as haystacks, will have to wait until some of those taken prisoner are freed and the ground is retaken two weeks later, allowing conclusions to be drawn from the grim evidence revealed by the number and location of the bodies, including that of the gallant acting battalion commander, Major E. F. Griffin, lying among his men, all facing the enemy.

While there is no serious fighting during the night of July 25–26, it is clear back at the guns that the front remains in a state of high alert, with FOOs and battery commanders reacting to the slightest stirring of enemy activity. And this is captured by the last terse note entered for July 25 in 4th Field's war diary: "Attack petered out, but the guns firing steadily all night on Mike Targets, Uncle Targets, and counter-mortar targets."

But on the twenty-sixth the diary recognizes both an intensification of enemy activity and the crucial role the guns are playing in the desperate struggle to maintain a tenuous hold on Verrières Ridge: "Continuous firing all day breaking up counter-attacks. All counter-attacks were successfully broken up – almost entirely due to artillery support. At 1600 hours had fired over 16,000 rounds since 1600 hours 24th."

Forward observers with the Royals east of Verrières can hear and sometimes see the enemy digging in, and 4th Field guns are frequently asked to shell the ground beyond the ridge. On one occasion Waddell fires red smoke around some enemy tanks and self-propelled guns forming up for an attack, successfully guiding the Typhoons to them.

And when the Royals, frustrated by not being able to bring their weapons to bear effectively on the enemy, decide late in the day that D Company, commanded by Capt. A. MacMillan, should move forward some four hundred yards to gain a more dominant position on the crest, the heavy concentration of shells from 4th Field guns fired in advance of the move catch a large number of the enemy forming up for their own attack. Many are wounded and at least twenty are killed, all identifiable as belonging to the elite 1st SS (Liebstandarte Adolph Hitler) Division.

Thus the Royals gain their new, advanced position without reaping additional heavy casualties. For a while after the guns finish firing, it is strangely quiet – so quiet that while Platoon Commander Suckling is establishing his men in existing trenches along a hedgerow "which apparently the Heinies have been occupying at night," he finds himself trying to identify "curious, whispering sounds of irregular pattern" passing close to his head.

For a moment I remain standing there out of sight behind the hedge, mystified, until it suddenly dawns on me I'm standing up in the beating zone of some Toronto Scottish medium machine-guns firing from some distance behind.

Then just at last light, to our astonishment a German officer and NCO come walking leisurely towards us through the wheat field, with their hands in their pockets, chatting to each other as though out for an evening stroll.

Our men are warned to remain still and let them come in so they can be taken prisoner. But only the NCO is taken alive. When the SS officer realizes what's up, he dives for the nearest trench and is shot by its occupant, a Bren gunner named Steele.

Subsequently, in the pitch blackness, their "Hitlerjugend" pals encroach within a few yards of us, and one of them with a machine gun manages somehow to get around behind us. Among the pleasantries they shout at us is: "Surrender, Canadian cocksuckers!"

Twice they counter-attack, screaming obscenities in English. And twice they are driven back. But so determined are they to retake the position that some SS actually try to dig in within ten yards of our trenches, and have to be driven off, leaving their dead behind them.*

And there the dead will lie with dozens of other bodies, theirs and ours, growing more repulsive each passing day, bloating and turning black and giving off sickening odours. No one would dream of forming burial parties on this ridge, where men in the most exposed, advanced positions are forced during the daylight hours to use the bottom of their own trenches as latrines, covering their excrement with dirt clawed from the walls of their abodes, in preference to risking a burst of machine-gun bullets above ground.

There is a conception – first inspired by the opinions expressed by the veteran Desert Rats back in the valley in front of Carpiquet – that the fighting between the densely massed forces in the confined battlefields of Normandy exceeds in intensity all other theatres. Now there is the growing belief that of all the Allied for-mations along the rim of the bridgehead, the Canadians are taking the worst punishment from Hitler's most fanatically loyal divisions

---

*   Author interview.

pledged to fight to the death for their Führer in holding a front that must be held at all costs. And the awful casualties in recent days would seem to bear this out.*

---

* To rationalize the "butcher bills" mounting at unprecedented rates in Normandy, British War Office tables known as "Evett's Rates," used by staff officers to forecast casualties and replacement needs, had to be amended. Until Normandy, the tables set out three levels of action: Intense, Normal, and Quiet. A new scale was introduced to cover the fighting in the Normandy bridgehead: Double Intense. And among the Allied forces, the Canadians suffered the worst casualty rate: 21.79 per cent of a force of 92,616 – twice the U.S. rate of 10.31 per cent of 1,220,000; and 2.6 times the British rate of 8.6 per cent of 737,384.

37

"GOD! HOW MUCH LONGER CAN THIS GO ON?"

❋

THE PAIN AND SUFFERING ASSOCIATED WITH EACH AND EVERY casualty – including the acute anguish of those who suspect they may die – is something historians tend to forget or purposely overlook.

Casualty statistics, even when shockingly high, are still only impersonal, sanitized, orderly columns of figures – so many dead, so many wounded, so many missing. All very neat and tidy: as when the South Saskatchewan Regiment was overrun by tanks on the afternoon of July 20, and listed 66 killed, 116 wounded, and 26 missing; or when next day the Essex Scottish experienced the same fate on the very same hill, suffering 298 dead, wounded, and missing. It only takes a couple of lines of type to record that four days later, the North Novas "lost" 61 killed and 78 wounded trying to take Tilly-la-Campagne; the Rileys counted 45 killed and 154 wounded taking Verrières; and on the slope just south of St. Martin-de-Fontenay, the Black Watch suffered 332 casualties, of which 123 were fatal.

Thus presented, casualty statistics suggest quite manageable situations with everything well under control, with all the blood and filth and stench of death and disablement left for stretcher-bearers, orderlies, nursing sisters, and surgeons to take care of – hidden away out of sight, as in the tents of No. 8 Field Surgical Unit, set up just northwest of Caen in July 1944.

When the wounded can be collected by stretcher-bearers, and their unit MO has done what he can for them at the regimental aid post, they are taken by ambulance Jeeps back to a field ambulance station, the first stop on a journey that can see them flown to hospital in England within hours. From Field Ambulance they are taken by regular, enclosed ambulances with big red crosses on their sides to a casualty clearing station, such as the one to which No. 8 Field Surgical is attached. There, from the endless stream of casualties, the surgeon selects for immediate surgery those so severely wounded they cannot survive further travel. Inevitably the most seriously wounded from 4th Field and the infantry battalions you support were patients at the eleven-man Field Surgical Unit, led by Winnipeg surgeon Major John Burwell Hillsman, who followed the Canadians as they moved to Carpiquet. Almost certainly his compassionate eyes were the last seen on this earth by those of your comrades who made it back that far, but no farther.

In his postwar book *Eleven Men and a Scalpel*, written as a tribute to "hundreds of patient and uncomplaining soldiers," the profound compassion Hillsman felt for each and every one of his patients comes through.* Even brief excerpts read as background notes place in heartrending perspective the appalling Canadian casualties.

Surgery, difficult enough in a well-equipped, well-lit civilian hospital, was done in a canvas operating theatre in the middle of a bare field under the strictest blackout conditions, and on occasion within the range of enemy guns:

We operated in Secqueville (five miles north and west of Carpiquet) for ten days, and covered the attack that took Caen. During those days we became veterans. We saw the tragic sights from which we were never to be free for ten long months. Men

---

* Published 1960 by Columbia Press Ltd, Winnipeg. Excerpts are reprinted with permission.

with heads shattered, dirty brains oozing out. Youngsters with holes in their chests fighting for air. Soldiers with their guts churned into a bloody mess by high explosives. Legs that were dead and stinking – but still wore muddy boots. Operating floors that had to be scrubbed with Lysol to rid them of the stench of dead flesh. Boys who came to you with a smile and died on the operating table. Boys who lived long enough for you to learn their name and then were carried away in trucks piled high with the dead. We learned to work with heavy guns blasting the thin walls of our tent.

We learned to keep our tent ropes slack so that anti-aircraft fragments would rain down harmlessly and bounce off the canvas. We became the possessors of bitter knowledge no man has ever been able to describe. Only going through it do you possess it. Above all we learned about men – about the wounded and about ourselves. . . .

When [one particular soldier] was brought in it was just dark enough for the flashes of the anti-aircraft guns to light up the horizon. I had stepped outside the operating theatre to enjoy a smoke. The ambulance drew up to the admission tent and I could see the dim forms of the stretcher-bearers quietly moving the loaded stretchers. Soon one of my men came out and told me I was wanted in a hurry. I went in. In the dim light I went over to his stretcher. His eyes were closed, his face the colour of white wax. Already a transfusion was pouring into one arm. I felt his pulse. Very weak. "How do you feel, soldier?" His eyes opened. He smiled faintly, "Fine, Doc." The eyes closed again.

I pulled back the blanket. His uniform was muddy and blood soaked the blanket. The orderly cut away his clothes. There was a large hole in his right thigh. The muscle bulged out, torn and steaming. Nothing else in front. The orderly gently rolled him over. He woke, started to speak, then clenched his teeth.

There was another smaller hole in his right back. No signs of bleeding now from the outside. Slowly we lowered him. A faint sigh of relief and the eyes closed again. More examination. He was bleeding internally from a large vessel, deeply placed.

I walked to the other end of the tent with the resuscitation officer. Almost in whispers we planned how to save this boy. Pour the blood into him fast and then a quick attempt to stop the bleeding. I went back to the operating tent and called the men together. Thank heavens they were fresh after a good day's sleep. I explained, "A desperate case. Abdominal setup. A race with a serious hemorrhage. Be on your toes." Quietly they began to prepare.

I walked outside for one last smoke. The air raid was still on and the horizon to the west was bright with flames. Must have hit an ammunition dump. I thought of the boy and his family, and wondered what they would be doing. Probably going about their quiet ways, pathetically unaware of the desperate battle we were going to wage. I silently swore to them that we would do our best.

The resuscitation officer appeared. "Blood pressure fair. Can't get it any better. Advise going ahead with it."

I went in and began to scrub. The stretcher-bearers placed him gently on the operating table. The glare of the lights woke him. I walked over. "Going to have to do a little work on you, soldier." The same slow smile. "All right, Doc."

The anesthetist bent over him. I put on my gown. The painting and draping were quickly done. I looked at the anesthetist. He nodded. A quick incision . . . Furious hemorrhage . . . I can't see! He's bleeding too fast . . . Suction quick! . . . Still can't see . . . A pack! Press hard! . . . It's still flowing . . . Big forceps, quick! . . . I'll have to clamp blind . . . Oh, God, I hope I get it . . . It's no use. It won't work . . . To the main vessel quick . . . Another incision . . . Rapid dissection . . . the vessel is tied . . . Back again to the first incision. It's slowed, but not stopped . . . Suction! Pack! Sponge! Quick! . . . I straightened up . . . A sigh of relief. It's stopped. A quiet voice said, "I'm afraid he's gone."

I looked at the anesthetist. Then I walked over and sat down. A hell of a surgeon. You stopped it all right, after he was dead. I walked outside and lighted another cigarette. The infernal din was still going on. Stretcher-bearers passed me carrying the still form in a blanket. I felt like hell. "Sorry, I'm a lousy surgeon." A tap on the shoulder. "The resuscitation officer wants to see you, another belly. . . ."

It was a tough night. I had earned a rest. As I walked wearily towards my tent, I saw a fresh mound of earth in the field and the Padre placing ropes around a blanket-draped form. I remembered the boy and felt miserable. I went over. The service began. Men slowly drifted around and took off their berets. I looked at their faces. This soldier was not alone. They didn't know his name, but he was a friend. I glanced at the road and saw some French peasants standing with their heads bowed. They crossed themselves. The boy was lowered gently and reverently into the grave. The service was ended. The soldiers shaped the mound of earth; they did it so carefully. It must look nice. Poor kid, all by yourself in the corner of a French field. Well, you'll soon have plenty of company.

As I started to walk away, I saw an old woman hobbling in through the gate. One hand clutched a cane, the other arm was full of flowers.

Painfully she knelt. Reverently she placed the flowers one by one on the grave. Several more women knelt beside her. All had flowers and soon the grave was covered. I walked over: "Merci, mesdames." I felt better.

Once, we never saw daylight for 16 days, unless you call daylight seeing the sun set as you get up and rise as you go to bed. We were working 12-hour sessions. I remember thinking one night as I walked from the operating table: God! How much longer can this go on? I sat down and took off my sunglasses. Funny, sunglasses at night. However, the barely imperceptible flicker in the lights was hard on the eyes. I listened half-consciously to the pounding of the generator. . . .

The corporal moved around setting up the table for the next case. I heard an argument going on. My assistant was hurling insults at the general duty orderly. The corporal went over and quieted them down. Then he came over and sat beside me. "The men are out on their feet, sir."

I knew. Two of them celebrated their 19th birthday here in Normandy. The things we saw were pretty tough on kids. I thought I'd seen every ghastly sight possible in civilian practice, but somehow this was different. You never got used to it. And they were tired. While I slept, these boys had to clean up and get ready for the next session. They didn't average six hours sleep out of 24. The argument broke out again. The corporal went over and they turned on him. The stretcher-bearers brought in my next case and laid him on the table. My staff stayed in a group. No breaking up into the efficient drill we'd practised.

I beckoned to the corporal. "Take over the sterilizers and send the boys to me." They came over slowly and stood awkwardly in a half circle. I got up. "Come with me." We passed through the blanket-draped passage into the resuscitation tent. I stopped and let them get a good look. The resuscitation officer and his two men were moving around taking blood pressures. From every stretcher rubber tubes went upwards to bottles of blood. I walked slowly down the double line of stretchers, then stopped before one boy. He was unconscious, thank God! He fought for air. His face was slate blue and a bloody froth ran out the corner of his mouth.

I moved on, then stopped again. Gas gangrene. The boy was awake and looked curiously at us. The gas had spread from his leg up over his abdomen. No use to do surgery here. Try the new drugs. I knew they wouldn't work though. I had tried them before.

And so the line of wax figures. Not a sound from a stretcher. All waited patiently until their turn came.

I walked back. My staff followed me into the operating theatre. They gathered round, but I didn't look at them. "Any man who thinks he is in worse shape than those boys can go to bed," I said, and sat down.

Quietly they dispersed to their jobs.

38

ALONG THE BLOOD–SOAKED VERRIÈRES RIDGE

✳

BACK AT THE GUNS, MEN LIVE MOSTLY ABOVE GROUND AND GO underground only when necessary. But OP crews, holed up with the infantry along the Verrières Ridge, risk death every instant they appear above ground. Men at the guns have a variety of concerns, but up in the slit trenches along the crest of the ridge there's one overriding concern for all ranks: survival. And to stay alive, a man must remain in a hole every hour of the day and night, only getting out when it's absolutely essential.

Thus the impressions survivors are most likely to carry with them the rest of their lives will all have to do with the sandy holes in which they shelter. Gunner A. J. "Andy" Turner came in as a reinforcement to 2nd Battery just in time to ride an old Norton motorbike up in the dark to join Major Wren's crew as a Don R at the Royals' tac headquarters near Verrières.

Turner's first fear-blurred memories will be of digging with his bare hands, tearing away the earth in the bottom of his slit trench and throwing it over the side by the handful every time a shell or mortar bomb comes whistling in:

The Major's driver, "Chuck" McConnell, and I share a slit trench, roofed over with our shovels and whatever else we can lay our hands on, with earth piled up on it at least two feet thick.

And we dig it good and deep. But no matter how deep it is, it's never enough. Even half asleep during the night, I find myself digging deeper, and always with my bare hands, for it's the activity more than the additional depth we require. For a while we're in soft earth, and every time the Moaning Minnies come over, we dig like dogs, handfuls of soil. But after we get down to the shale, it's not so easy. And worse than that, down on the hardpan, you'd swear every time those big Minnies land they're landing right beside you. The concussion wave travelling through the solid earth really shakes you up.

One night the Royals get a bunch of reinforcements. They barely arrive when the Minnies start coming down, and these new, green guys are jumping around all over the place. I grab hold of one of them – a guy wearing a big black moustache – and pull him down into our hole. And when things settle down a bit, he asks me, "Is it always like this?"

I tell him, "Well, not always, but enough."

And he says, "Can you tell me how to survive up here?"

Well, I don't know too much myself, only having been here less than a week. But I've learned something, and I tell him, "Dig yourself one of these and get into it, and don't get out for anything."

For quite a while after that, whenever I spot him, he's digging. And every time he sees me, he tosses me a pack of cigarettes. Then he disappears – wounded or killed, I guess. I never did get to know his name.*

For Platoon Commander Bob Suckling of the Royals, memories of life on Verrières Ridge will always be "a blur of unbelievable exhaustion, lack of appetite, lice, dysentery, constant noise, dust, revolting odours, and paralysing fear – just surviving day and night bombardment by shells and mortar bombs. And everywhere the

---

* Author interview.

all-pervasive smell of decaying flesh and other disgusting things. Until Verrières I didn't know the bowels of animals and men move after rigor mortis sets in."*

But amidst the awful sights of death and destruction by high explosive, and the innumerable unburied bodies turning black in the sunbaked wheat, a single image stands out to haunt Suckling the rest of his life: the sight of his batman,

> standing upright in a half-dug slit trench on the reverse slope of the ridge with not a mark on his body – dead from concussion. . . .

Sheer terror turns everyone's heart to stone. The traumatic shock of finding war at its worst, coming to believe that every day of war must be this bad, is enough to cause a number of self-inflicted wounds. And later, when conditions permit, military police interview me about a lance-corporal who shot himself in the foot right under my nose.

And my own resolve is at rock bottom, believing the best that can happen to me is to be wounded, since becoming wounded or killed is a certainty. I find comfort in an honest belief that may be God-given, that no matter how bad things are, they can always get worse. This I firmly believe, and often repeat it to others. It seems to give me some strength. And I have developed faith in the beatitude "The meek shall inherit the earth." While this doesn't seem to apply in civilian life, many a meek man displays the fortitude and resolve to carry on here, while many a swashbuckler finds the first way out.

Sharing this grim existence are 4th Field FOOs and their crews occupying holes among the forward rifle companies on the ridge. For Sammy Grange, who, along with fellow FOO Jack Thompson,

---

* This quote and the next by Bob Suckling are from an interview with the author.

returns to the front on July 26 with the reconstituted Essex Scottish as they take over the left flank of 4th Brigade beside the Caen–Falaise highway,

this period will always seem the worst of my life – just getting there, just being there, constantly subjected to shelling and mortaring!

On my way up to establish an OP somewhere on the ridge, I report to Bill Carr (the battery commander) at battalion headquarters shortly after dawn. Jack Thompson is already there, having a cup of tea. So we have one as well.

When Jack finishes, he says, "Well, I guess I'll go ahead now." I tell him I'll be right along as soon as I finish my cup. And not more than five minutes later, when I go up, he's lying dead beside a derelict tank, half in and half out of a trench.

Just as I realize what has happened, another shell lands and something gets me in the back – a shell fragment or a stone. Whatever it was, it is clearly my own blood . . . and I get quite excited about this, and retreat in some haste to my carrier, about fifty yards back in a sunken road where I'd left it to go forward on foot to improve the view. And while the view is not as good as it would have been up there, I am quite content to stay here after what has happened.

But, oh God, it's here I see a little fellow with his arm blown off who actually seems to be happy about it. He's smiling and saying, "I'm out of it now!" as he holds up the stump with the blood streaming from it. And remarkably I have no difficulty understanding him.

By now I have become quite fatalistic, as every FOO must. Death seems so inevitable after exposure to Eterville, which is etched in my mind for all time – the smashed houses, the trenches in the orchard, masses of dead cows in the field, and the unburied bodies of men. Then there was that affair with the Essex on the slope in front of Ifs, and then the move up past Verrières.

As a FOO, I know I can't expect to survive unscathed, and all the time I'm hoping it will be a wound. That is the best I can expect. That is why the little fellow who lost an arm, and is holding it up for all to see, is truly happy – he's got what he wanted.

I remain here a couple of days, usefully firing the guns a number of times. Once, Bill Carr calls up and asks, "How are you up there?" When I reply, "Slightly wounded, but carrying on bravely," there is a long, pregnant pause, after which he rephrases his question, "How is the situation up there?" He couldn't care less about my personal state.

And when, after a couple of days, I finally get the chance to visit a hospital to have my wound attended to, with visions of being sent home with bands playing and a suitable decoration hanging around my neck, they put a form of Band-Aid on it and send me back up.

Now we all get dysentery, which in front-line service presents the real problem of having to get up out of your slit trench to go someplace else and being shot at in the process. Thus it is one of the happiest moments of my life when I find one morning that someone has dug a latrine right beside my slit trench. From it you can look down into your trench as you conduct your business, and the moment you hear Moaning Minnies coming, you can dive, with your pants still down, right into your trench! Oh yes, I shall remember that latrine always!

Conditions here have proven that some of the nicest guys are cowards. One young fellow left alone up at the OP while I am visiting company headquarters a short distance away, starts calling up and repeating, "I've got to see you – I've got to see you." When I get to him, he's absolutely shaking with fear. But for no obvious reason; no shells are landing. There have been, and there will be again, but none right now. I tell him to go back to the guns, for he is totally useless up here. I don't report it, and I'll always remember him as a nice fellow, a likeable fellow. But clearly the whole idea of being shot at is too much for him. Perhaps he has no overriding sense of duty to sustain him. Most of us hate being shot at, but we're not prepared to show our comrades how cowardly we are.*

At 5:00 P.M., July 28, the Essex Scottish conduct a well-organized attack to clean out an orchard between Verrières and Tilly-la-Campagne held by the SS. Crossing open fields to hit the orchard position just as 4th Field's concentration on the objective ends, the leading platoons bring off the attack with splendid effectiveness. Not only do they rout the Germans, but they capture a waterworks and reservoir that has been supplying nearby German-occupied villages. The great success of the attack goes a long way to restoring pride and confidence to the Essex.

The FOO is Capt. W. L. Stewart MacLeod, who, until a couple of days ago, was battery captain (2nd in command) of 26th Battery, with no obligation whatsoever to go forward in the high-risk occupation of FOO. It seems, when Reg Parker was killed, he insisted on taking over a carrier crew. And when Jack Thompson bought it so soon after Parker, Dawson, and Knapp, it affected him deeply, according to those who are close to him. As MacLeod goes forward on this attack, he openly vows to avenge their deaths.

Next day (July 29) he is fatally wounded by a burst of machine-gun fire that instantly kills his driver, Gunner Geoff Byatt, a popular member of Easy Troop.

Sgt. Hunt's diary will carry a striking tribute to the gallant captain:

Yesterday afternoon we learned that Capt. MacLeod had died of wounds. This was a shock, especially since we had been under the impression his injuries were comparatively light. He joined

---

*   Author interview.

us at Horsham and went about his routine job of battery captain in the manner of a professional soldier. It was not until we got into action that something of the buccaneer emerged from under the detail of "cartridges ordinary, shorts cellular," and that law of living, "Form 1098." Reports came back from the OP that the Captain displayed an enthusiasm for engagement equalled only by his enjoyment of its execution. Farewell, blithe spirit, the men in your party thought a lot of you.

You try to imagine the state of mind of the two surviving members of that OP crew (both of whom you remember well from your years with 26th Battery in England). Only nine days after seeing their Capt. Parker almost cut in half by an 88 solid-shot and having the sad task of removing the almost headless torso of their cherished buddy Gunner Geoff Byatt from their carrier, Signaller-Ack J. W. Schneider and Signaller-Driver Ted Ford (who was also wounded that same day, but remained on duty) witness the fatal wounding by machine-gun fire of another troop commander as he crosses through the wheat to contact the CO of the Essex.

On July 29, Capt. Bill Waddell is sent to St. Martin-de-Fontenay to support the Maisonneuves in an effort to drive out the Germans, who continue to infest the village, as they have since the Maisonneuves, along with remnants of the Black Watch, were driven back there on July 25.

Sit reps (situation reports) are sketchy, but it's clear attempts to take the village church end in failure. Later, on August 6, a detailed description of these grim hours will be given to an intelligence officer by Capt. Alex Angers of A Company:

By this time the company had approximately 45 men. . . . The attack was set for 2200 hours 29 July, supported by arty [artillery] and rocket-firing Typhoons which pounded the colliery to the south. . . . As we stepped out onto the St. Martin-de-Fontenay to

Verrières road, we were met with fire from an MG [machine gun] and rifles in the hedge to the east . . . and from two or three MGs sited around the church and firing through loopholes in the churchyard wall. . . . We reorganized just north of the church in the orchard where the wall gave us some protection.

By this time we had about 30 men and tried again. Lt. Mailas 9 Platoon managed to get across the road and started to crawl for the church. He came under MG fire from the stone wall and hedges as soon as he crossed the road into the open. He had to come back after losing quite a lot of men.

I decided to wait and try again at dawn. I asked for reinforcements and received from D Company eight men, one Bren and 20 mags. By that time Lt. Valerin 8 Platoon had his strength cut down to four. This was during a second assault when his platoon managed to get two sections through by running along the road. Jerry let two sections get in and cut off the entry of the third section and platoon HQ by heavy fire. The two sections that got through ran forward and assaulted the church to find nothing in it. Of the 14 men who went in the church, only two came back. We tried again at first light, about 0500 hrs July 30. . . . So few people were left (about 15 men out of the original 40 and the 8 reinforcements), that instead of company commander I became section leader with one of my lieutenants acting as Bren gunner. We got into the road and fired on their positions, and they fired so heavily on us . . . we gave up the attack and occupied the corner house directly across from the church.*

---

* National Archives of Canada, File 145 2R6011 (D5) of Unit War Diaries covering July 1944.

39

A NOTE ON SHELL CONSUMPTION

---　✳　---

IN ELEVEN DAYS, ENDING JULY 26, THE FIELD GUNS OF 21ST
Army Group fire 1,158,490 shells – 105,317 rounds on average a
day (5,313 more a day than were fired daily during the famous ten-
day battle of El Alamein in 1942).

On July 30, worried by the enormous shell consumption,
the Major-General Royal Artillery of 21st Army Group issues a
memorandum to 2nd British Army and 1st Canadian Army pointing out that expenditures are "extremely heavy, considerably in
excess of the figures for which we have asked the War Office for
provision . . ." and "that production is not at the moment meeting
expenditure."*

The War Office had projected 62 rounds per gun per day, based
on consumption figures from other theatres, suitably inflated to
take care of the extraordinary demands of an operation everyone
knew must prove to be the ultimate clash of arms in the whole war
in the west. That this projection is proving totally inadequate speaks
volumes. These unforeseen across-the-board firing rates by the
field guns of 21st Army Group – unequalled in any theatre in the
war in terms of rounds expended per gun per day – provide not

---

* From National Archives of Canada records RG24, Vol. 10462, File
212C1.2009 (DIS).

only a truly authentic measure of the severity of the Normandy campaign as a whole, but a valid means of expressing the otherwise indescribable intensity of the clash of arms in which the Canadians have been thrust south of Caen.

And the field guns of 2nd Canadian Division, obliged to drop curtains of shell-fire, almost literally, along Verrières Ridge to stop the enemy from breaking through when battalions were overrun and driven asunder, have far exceeded the daily consumption by the field guns elsewhere in Normandy. While from July 20 to 27 21st Army Group guns were averaging 78 rounds per gun per day – the rate so worrisome to the high command – 2nd Division guns were having to draw an average of 385 rounds per gun per day. And the belief expressed by the Army Service sergeant at Fleury the night of July 22 that he was involved in an all-time record dumping of ammunition will be confirmed one day by facts recorded in a yellowing manuscript in the National Archives of Canada:

It turned out this dump (July 20) was the first of a series that would culminate in an all-time record for the dumping of artillery ammunition being established by the drivers of 2nd Div Army Service who supplied the ammunition and 2nd Div Arty who fired it.

In less than 30 hours (to 6 P.M. July 22) they had dumped 750 rounds of 25 pr [25-pounder ammunition] for each of 2nd Div's 72 guns. But the greatest job was still ahead of them – an all-time military record for the dumping and firing of ammunition was about to take place. . . . At 1830 hours July 22 the first of the record dump was initiated by HQ RCASC with the order that the formation would supply 120 vehicles for a 25-pounder draw that night from BAD [Base Ammunition Dump] at the beaches, and the lorries would make a double turn about drawing in excess of 44,800 rounds on the double haul. All night and far into the morning ammo poured into the gun sites as fast as the gunners could handle it.

And at a Quarter-Master General's conference July 28, Lt-Col Daziel reported: "Corps and Div Commanders are more than pleased. For the last show we dumped and shot off more 25-pounder ammunition than any other British division has ever done."*

Some perspective may be gained by comparing the average daily expenditure of 2nd Division guns during the last three weeks of July 1944 with expenditures per gun per day during the monster bombardments of World War One, such as the "artillery preparation" for the 3rd Battle of Ypres (Passchendaele), which, according to the official *History of the Great War*, "established a record in the number of guns employed and amount of ammo expended."† In eighteen days, ending on August 2, 1917, 2,092 field guns fired a colossal 2,967,953 rounds. This, however, was a daily average of only 78.8 rounds per gun. Then there was Valenciennes, ten days before the Armistice. According to a 1933 pamphlet by Maj.-Gen. McNaughton, head of the National Research Council of Canada, 192 field guns, backed by 104 heavies, fired "the most intensive barrage in history ... in weight of gunfire approximating that used by both sides in the whole South African War, and exceeding in tons that fired at Jutland, the greatest naval battle of all time."‡ Still, the 192 field guns, consuming 56,200 rounds in two days ending noon November 2, 1918, averaged only 146 rounds per gun per day, which would not have been considered remarkable in 1944 by the gunners of 2nd Division in Normandy.

---

*   National Archives of Canada, "History of RCASC 2nd Cdn Division, June–Dec 1944," RG 24, Vol 10906.
†   *History of the Great War: Military Operations France & Belgium 1917, Vol II, 7th June–10th November, based on official documents by direction of the Historical Section of the Committee of Imperial Defence* (London: His Majesty's Stationery Office, 1948), p. 138.
‡   "The Capture of Valenciennes," Maj.-Gen. McNaughton, *Canadian Defence Quarterly*, Vol. X, No. 3, April 1933.

The twenty-four guns of 4th Field alone fired 93,000 rounds over a twenty-day period, ending August 1, averaging 195 rounds per gun per day. For three consecutive days they actually averaged 469 rounds per gun per day, and in one twenty-four-hour period, ending the afternoon of July 21, 1,000 rounds per gun were fired.*

---

*   For comparison, 3rd Field in Italy, assaulting the Gustav and Hitler Lines in the Italian campaign, averaged 132 rounds per gun per day for eleven days. Col. G. W. L. Nicolson, CD, *The Gunners of Canada, Volume II, 1919–1967* (Toronto: McClelland and Stewart, 1972), p. 235.

40

"A DAY IN THE LIFE OF A GUNNER"

─────────────── ✳ ───────────────

SOMEHOW THE CANADIAN ARMY FILM UNIT HAS BECOME AWARE of the record firing by the field guns and has decided it should record the business for posterity. One of their cameramen visited 4th Field a couple of days ago to arrange to spend a day here at the guns, shooting footage for a film with the working title "A Day in the Life of a Gunner."

He is scheduled to come back with his camera this morning, and you are looking forward to appearing in the film, however briefly, knowing how much your wife back in Canada would enjoy seeing you at an actual gun position in France. However, it is not to be. Just as you're coming off a midnight-to-dawn stint in the command post, preparing to hit the sack for a few hours, a signal comes from RHQ: you are to take over Able Troop OP crew and go up to relieve Bill Waddell at St. Martin-de-Fontenay, where the FMRs have taken over from the Maisies.

When the carrier arrives from the wagon lines, you are glad to see Ryckman, a most experienced driver, hunched down in the driver's seat. As you climb in beside him, you do your best not to let your nervousness show, but you don't relish having to make the trip up there. It would be bad enough going up after dark, but going up in daylight over a completely exposed ridge and down a long slope into the village seems simply to be courting disaster.

Every so often during the past eight days, alerted by the distant howling of Nebelwerfers, you've looked up to watch another six-bomb salvo of those violent rocket bombs plough the western hump of Verrières Ridge, some fifteen hundred metres south of here. Always they seem to land along the crest, near where the road south from Fleury-sur-Orne disappears over the ridge and (according to the map) heads down the slope straight as an arrow for St. Martin-de-Fontenay and St. André-sur-Orne, lying side by side in the valley.

Just after sunrise this morning (July 30), as you were brewing up the first "cuppa the day," that familiar, insane chorus wound up, and as you looked, black geysers of smoke and dirt billowed up from that same corner of the ridge, generating a deep roar that rolled back over the gun positions like thunder. As always you wondered what Jerry thought he was accomplishing, whacking away at that bald hill, which, as far as you know, is not occupied. Well, now you are going to get the chance to go up and find out. When you call in at RHQ to find out the safest route up there, Capt. G. M. "Tim" Welch, the adjutant, hasn't a clue. He suggests you "drop in" on the CO at Brigade on the way up.

Though it's a good three kilometres out of the way, you feel you have to get the advice of the CO. You find him in a particularly desolate corner of the parched and dusty landscape, standing in a ragged, gravelly hole that would hardly qualify as a trench, in the lee of a broken stone wall – a remnant of a shell-demolished farmhouse or barn just to the left of the Caen–Falaise highway. As far as he knows the whole Orne valley has been cleared all the way down to St. André. But he can't say how far the Brits have cleared the menacing high ground on the west bank. He doesn't suppose any route along the east bank of the Orne is very "healthy" in daylight.

Before you can ask why the hell 4th Field is keeping 5th and 6th Brigades supplied with FOOs, he draws your attention to a string of mortar bombs following a dust cloud rising in the distant fields

behind a motorbike roaring this way from Verrières Ridge.
Laughing, he throws up his glasses to his eyes to follow the despatch
rider's wild and woolly progress, remarking "That will be Wren's
Don R," as though that's explanation enough for anyone.

Not that it matters, for you have more important things on your
mind. And as a black-haired, dusty Don R (Gunner Andy Turner)
comes rolling up, grinning from ear to ear, you pull out towards Ifs.

Passing west beyond the village, you get a broad view of the low-
lands down along the Orne. The sight is not reassuring. Derelict
vehicles of all kinds – half-tracks, scout cars, carriers, Jeeps – lie
burned out, dead, unmoving in the wheat fields.

You decide you'd better try making it by the road over the crest.
Perhaps if you sneak up the slope as quietly as possible until you get
to the top, then tear down the other side into the village, you'll
make it before they wake up and get a bead on you.

When you tell Ryckman that once over the crest he'll be in full
view of the enemy all the way down into the village, and that he'll
have to "tramp on it" if he is to make it, he merely shrugs as if to
say "what the hell," and starts grinding the carrier slowly up the
slope at an angle meant to gain the greatest concealment before
turning onto the road itself. The cool, deliberate, and remarkably
quiet way he manoeuvres the sluggish machine up the slope is very
reassuring. But when the carrier at last tips over the brow of the
ridge and noses down, the breadth and depth of the sunlit
panorama lying before you is even more startling than you imagined it would be. In the clear morning air, you can see for miles, far
beyond St. Martin, now laid out below you two kilometres away.

And it's clear that if you have an unobstructed view, so must all
the Germans' dug-in tanks and camouflaged 88s out there – each of
them capable of destroying you with one shot from distances far
beyond that first crest and the high ground they still hold over on
the right, across the Orne. It's as though you're riding a shooting-
gallery duck as the carrier dodders over the crest, almost stopping as
Ryckman changes gears from the bull-low used to climb quietly up

the steep route – for though he's highly skilled and moves smoothly and swiftly to change up to high gear, it still takes time to get a sluggish carrier rolling.

Even when he has it roaring down the slope with accelerator pressed to the floor, you know you're offering an easy target for guns that fire missiles faster than the speed of sound. The way is as straight as a Roman road all the way down to the village, without a house, a tree, or anything to obstruct their guns' view. And on all sides there is chilling evidence of their accuracy: the slope on the left is dotted with burned-out tanks; and down on the bottom-land on the right, close to the Orne, is an appalling clutter of burned-out half-tracks, carriers – and even a smashed Jeep.

You find yourself holding your breath. Ryckman has the carrier roaring wide-open now, passing very close to the edge of a yawning cavity along the left side of the road, a quarry or gravel pit clearly marked on the map.

You're halfway there. . . . Then suddenly there's a heart-stopping, metallic *wham!* Ryckman involuntarily lets up a bit on the accelerator before realizing it's only one of the tracks taking a slap at the underside of the carrier body. Before he gets full power back on, to take up the slack in the tracks, both of them are slamming away at the undersides of the carrier, making a terrible racket. If the Jerries have been dozing, they surely are awake now, and hastening to man their guns.

But the village with its sheltering buildings is getting close. The stubby church tower over in the southeast corner, near the map reference you're headed for, is plainly visible.

Now you're passing a large orchard on the right. Only three or four hundred yards more and you'll be among the first buildings. They must be withholding their fire until you get so close that they'll be absolutely certain not to miss. You find yourself breathing, Oh please, not now . . . now that we've almost made it!

Suddenly, from the orchard on the right, a soldier leaps out onto the road, directly in the path of the carrier, and waves his arms over his head, frantically signalling you to stop.

Even at a distance, the tall, rawboned man with a great shock of jet-black hair that no helmet could completely hide, is instantly recognizable as Gunner Lewis Milton Bryan, a member of Waddell's crew. As the braking carrier rolls up to him, barely halting in time, he's jabbing his left hand urgently towards a track leading off to your right. And when Ryckman skid-turns in that direction, Bryan hops up on the front of the carrier, depositing one hip on the fender in front of you, yelling urgently, "Get going! Back in there among the trees. Fast! You're under observation here – he still holds half the village."

Ryckman tramps the accelerator, rocking the carrier down the track towards the centre of what must have been a lush orchard extending west about 800 metres towards the Orne, but now leafless and forlorn. After ninety metres or so you see, parked deep among the scarred and blasted trees, to the left of the track, a carrier with the number 42 painted on it. Gesturing, Bryan directs Ryckman to park beside it. Jumping down, he yells, "Get out and find yourself a hole – quick!"

There are a couple of slits to the left of the carrier, and you and Ryckman promptly follow his advice. You're barely underground before you hear the banshee yowling of Moaning Minnies winding up just beyond the village, growing horribly louder and louder as they loop directly overhead and down into the orchard, crashing so close to where you are sheltering, the hot, hurricane blasts blow sand and bits of branches into your trench. After they land you start to get up, but a hand on your shoulder restrains you, and you hear Bryan's voice:

"Wait, he usually sends over a couple of lots."

And he's right. There is another salvo. Then, as you wait to be sure he's finished, Bryan, smiling quizzically, remarks, "I just happened to see you coming over the ridge, and went out to the road to make sure you found the track in here. But the way you were coming, you looked like you were going to drive right into the village!"

You tell him, you were — to join a company located near the church.

"They may be there, but Jerry still controls that street. Anyway, Capt. Waddell can tell you. He's at their battalion HQ, over there in that German bunker."*

Down in the bunker, which turns out to be remarkably deep, you find Waddell, who introduces himself and then the acting CO of the battalion — a Major Sauvé — and a couple of other officers you can barely make out in the gloom of the bunker, having come directly down out of the blazing sunlight. As your eyes adjust and you are able to take in the scene, you are struck by the uncanny resemblance to a stage-setting for the First War play *Journey's End*.

The Major, seated behind a little table with a map spread out before him, illuminated only by a guttering candle stuck in a black bottle, is the picture of outrageous fatigue. As he lights a fresh cigarette from a smouldering butt, he makes no effort to hide the fact he's fighting utter exhaustion if not despair. He has no idea what has happened to the company you've been ordered to join in the southeast corner of the village. In fact, he has been out of radio contact with all his companies since before dawn. And of course it is impossible for you to join a company whose status is unknown — and which may no longer exist.

Waddell tends to agree with him, suggesting you stop here at Battalion Headquarters. However, being new to the game and having received orders to go to a specific map reference, you feel obliged to try to get there.

————

* Bryan, who unquestionably saved you and your crew from certain disaster, and who survived the war without a serious wound, was decapitated a few years later when he ran his snowmobile under a guy wire attached to a hydro pole one wintry night outside of Ottawa, where he was employed as a city police officer.

At this point, an officer you take to be the adjutant informs the CO that a runner has just come back from the lost company of FMRs in the village. On hearing this, the acting CO is highly indignant, demanding to know why he has not been told this before and ordering the runner to be brought before him at once!

While he waits, he confides in you that it is a very, very bad spot up here – the units they replaced suffered severe casualties, the Black Watch particularly. Actually, his own regiment is already dangerously under-strength in case of a major German counter-attack.

After a minute or two, an unassuming young soldier is ushered down the bunker stairs before the CO, who questions him intensely in French for several minutes. Satisfied the company in question is reasonably intact, the CO asks the soldier in English if he thinks he could "take this artillery officer up there?"

The boy shrugs, pursing his lips and rocking his head from side to side, as if to say, "I suppose so . . . if it must be done."

With that, the CO orders him to act as your guide. As you are leaving, he requests you give first priority on arrival up there to restoring radio contact with him, and has the adjutant provide you with the current wireless frequency on a piece of paper, suspecting there is some confusion in this regard.

You stop at your carrier long enough to don your sheepskin vest, in anticipation of the inevitable chill when darkness descends tonight, and to stuff your pockets with bully beef and hardtack, before slinging the walkie-talkie 38-set around your neck. Then, turning to your young guide, who has been waiting patiently, you follow him to the southeast corner of the orchard, imitating his bent-over, cautious approach as he sneaks along a stone wall covered with dried-up, dusty vines marking the southern boundary of the orchard, and hopefully hiding you from the enemy. He kneels down where the wall ends, just short of the road that you used coming down from the ridge and which constitutes the main street of St. Martin-de-Fontenay, leading south to the next village, May-sur-Orne, about a mile away across a shallow valley.

By the time you kneel down beside him, you are sweating profusely, and not just because the day is well on its way to becoming another muggy scorcher. The brooding terror that hangs in the sinister silence of this desecrated place is almost visible out there in the empty, sunbaked stillness of the rubble-cluttered street, leading off to the right between shattered buildings.

"I will go first," the FMR soldier whispers. "Wait until I am across . . . then you follow. Run like hell . . . we lose six men crossing here this morning."

With that he jumps up and squirts across the road like a scared rabbit. Sheltering behind a broken wall of a smashed house, he beckons to you to follow.

Taking a deep breath, you raise yourself up into the crouch of a sprinter, clutching your map board tightly under your left arm and pressing your right across the 38-set dangling from your neck to prevent it bouncing on your chest as you run. Then, with the soldier's words ringing in your ears – We lose six men crossing here this morning! – you run with every ounce of energy you can muster across that menacing gap.

Even before you reach him, he takes off, running a weird obstacle course through partially demolished stone buildings. Already drained by your lung-bursting dash across the street, you do your best to keep up, leaping here and there over the rubble and through broken walls, until you trip attempting to hurdle through a tall vacant window of a roofless house.

The spring having disappeared from weary leg muscles, the heel of one of your hobnailed boots has caught on the low sill, and you tumble head first down into a deep, rubble-cluttered cavity within a house that has largely collapsed into its own cellar, creating a most horrible racket as you roll into a tangle of rattling tin rubbish at the very bottom.

Lying perfectly still, face up in the blistering sunlight amidst what appears to have been furnace pipes, very conscious of your sticky underwear sopping with sweat, and fearing the consequences of having alerted every German within a mile, you struggle to get your breath. Then, worried you'll be left far behind, you disengage yourself from the rasping tin and crawl up out of the crater.

He's waiting. But as soon as he sees you, he takes off again, though now at a much slower pace. He picks his way cautiously and stealthily – at one point leading you in a crawl through one cellar window, down into a dank cellar and out another window on the other side of the house.

Arriving in a garden surrounded by a high stone wall, at the rear of a substantial stone house which appears to be more or less intact, you notice with relief that for the first time your guide walks confidently upright as he leads you to the back door. You've made it!

The enclosing wall gives you a wonderful feeling of security. Only a nearby church tower overlooks the garden. Abutting the kitchen door is a low, flat-roofed, concrete shelter (reminiscent of the blast-shelters placed before the doorways of London buildings), forming an entryway about ten feet long. Inside, you wait in the shade while your guide disappears in the house to find his company commander.

A soldier lies stretched out asleep in the shelter, face down in the dust on the bare concrete floor. Beside him is an 18-set radio, but there is no sound coming from the earphones hanging on its aerial. At first you assume the batteries are dead, but when you bend down to see the frequency at which it is set, you discover it's turned off! No wonder they couldn't be raised. And when you check the setting against the frequency they gave you back at Battalion, you find it's nowhere close.

The officer who arrives at the kitchen door seems awfully glad to see you. Georges Brégent – a pleasant, softspoken, earnest man – shows you such deference you find it difficult to believe he really is in command of the company. Catching you staring at his epaulettes, which carry only the two pips of a lieutenant, he readily volunteers he was a subaltern only five days ago, but with the heavy casualties he became an acting-captain, and now he's the company commander – an acting-major, he thinks.

You find his limited experience disconcerting, considering his company is hoping to survive in what, for all practical purposes, is no-man's-land, currently the worst battle-zone in all Normandy, where whole battalions have been shattered in vain attempts to drive out the SS. However, his frank and modest manner is so appealing, you like him instantly, and find yourself wanting to help in any way you can.

A minute ago, you were looking for reassurance yourself. Now you assume a pose you hope will reassure him, for you suspect from his manner he needs this more than anything else. It certainly wouldn't do him any good to know how limited your experience is.

He wants your opinion of a plan he has for when it gets dark, for "using the knives very quiet" to "destroy" the Germans in the house next door. He explains it must be done stealthily so as not to alert the Germans in the house next to them, who, in their turn, will have their throats slit quietly without arousing other Germans beyond them, and so on down the street. He wonders if you think it is a good plan.

You tell him it sounds like a wonderful plan, if he can find men with the nerve to carry it out. But even as you try to involve yourself in his problem, you can't take your eyes off the weary soldier in the dirty, rumpled battledress lying on the floor. A red hen has been killed and plucked, and the feathers are everywhere. In his restless sleep, the soldier has rolled in them and is covered with them. They even stick to his face. Somehow he typifies the utter exhaustion and endless misery which is the lot of the infantryman. Reduced to accepting the barest subsistence level, snatching food for his belly and rest for his aching legs whenever and wherever he can, he waits for the next orders to go forward.

Worried that you unwittingly may be encouraging Acting-Major Brégent into doing something really suicidal, you change the subject to the vital need to restore radio communication with his battalion tac HQ back in the orchard. You suggest he wake up his signaller and get him to net in his 18-set to the battalion frequency you've brought along with you.

He readily agrees, explaining, as he wakes the soldier, that he approved of the 18-set being turned off to save batteries only when they were unable to raise Battalion this morning.

Once the signaller is sufficiently awake and alert to what you're trying to tell him, it takes him only a couple of minutes to get in touch with Battalion using the new frequency. Then, using your 38-set and the call letters the signaller provides for the other companies, you search the dial until you locate each of them in turn, providing them with the new Battalion frequency. Thus, within minutes, full radio communication exists throughout the battalion, you're feeling awfully proud of yourself, and Company Commander Brégent is much impressed.

When you ask him where you can observe the zone, he leads you into the house and up two flights of stairs, through a tangle of broken lumber and plaster chunks, to the attic, now entirely open to the sky.

At first it seems like the perfect OP. While large sections of roof have collapsed in tangled waves of beams and refuse covering most of the third floor, the southeast corner must have been blown away completely for it is relatively free and open. You can walk right up to the chest-high, thick wall of dressed stone that remains intact around the perimeter of the whole house like a parapet.

Following the lead of the young Major, whose only concession to concealment is to drape his little camouflage net over his head and shoulders before rising almost fully upright, you take up position on his left and peer over the stone wall towards the rolling, sunbathed fields south of the village.

As at Eterville, you are struck by the deadness of no-man's-land – the complete absence of movement of any kind. You can see for miles, but no living creature moves anywhere out there, no smoke rises from any chimney, and roads and fields and barnyards are empty.

For the moment your companion is silent, and you have time to sweep the valley with your field-glasses, examining in minute detail the opposite slope leading up to May-sur-Orne, searching for the slightest tell-tale sign of movement. But you find none, and in that eerie deadness, you feel the sinister menace you've come to associate with the front line.

At last, your companion points south across the valley to haystacks on the side of the hill, which he suspects are camouflaged tanks. (If they are tanks, they're close enough to thread your needle, and, feeling the need to make yourself less conspicuous, you pull your head down into your shoulders like a turtle.)

Then he points to the factory-like minehead and hoisting tower just beyond the southern edge of the village, explaining it's connected with the network of mine tunnels and air shafts that are being used by the Germans to pop up in positions previously reported clear. (You lower your head a bit more.) Then he points to the church tower over on the left, so close you feel you could almost hit it with a rock, and tells you the Germans have at least one MG-42 machine gun in there. (You now stoop until only your eyes are peering over the rim of the parapet.)

Finally, he reaches out beyond the rim of the stone parapet and pointing directly down towards the ground, says, "And of course the house next door is full of them." Staggered, you drop down behind the wall. My lord, he really meant it when he referred to Germans in "the house next door"! Perhaps his plan "to use the knives very quiet" after dark isn't so crazy after all.

When he suggests you join him in some lunch downstairs you readily agree, pleased to have an excuse to get off this open deck for a while. There has been altogether too much arm-waving going on up here; it couldn't help but attract attention unless every damn German out there is sound asleep. Eventually they're going to loop over a basket of mortars. Why they haven't already done so is a mystery. And if there really is an MG-42 in that church tower over there – and your informant seems to know – why didn't they let fly a burst and cut you both down when they had the chance? Again it begs the question you kept asking yourself all the way down the hill in the carrier this morning: What are they waiting for?

Acting-Major Brégent volunteers a possible answer, suggested by the Maisonneuve company commander he relieved here this morning, whose company was reduced to only fifteen men by attacks yesterday and the day before on the church: "Jerry tends to keep his machine guns quiet, not giving away their position until you attack and then *pow!* He ambush you."*

Lunch turns out to be a can of Compo M & V (meat-and-vegetable stew) he'd left on the window sill to warm in the sun. Spooning out half the contents into a tin cup for you, he proceeds to eat his share out of the can, remarking with notable sincerity, "These Composite Rations are really very convenient, and *plutôt appêtissantes*, do you not think?"

Appetizing? Of course you think he's joking. But then you see he really means it, and for a moment you have doubts about his sanity. It occurs to you that due to the general unreliability of messing for front-line infantry – deriving as much from their being perpetually in isolated and exposed positions, as from the capricious and inconvenient timing of their attacks and enemy counter-attacks – he simply hasn't had the chance to consume enough Compo rations to grow tired of them.

Now and then the methodical hammering of a Bren in short bursts can be heard from upstairs. Brégent explains it is merely his

---

* The Maisonneuve company commander, Capt. Alex Angers, in an intelligence report dated August 2, mentioned this phenomenon: "We noticed during these engagements that Jerry is willing to keep his automatic weapons silent for days if necessary in order that, when finally launching a big attack, we will be surprised by fire from unexpected sources." From File 145 2R6011 (D5) of Unit War Diaries covering July 1944, National Archives of Canada.

men ensuring the area is dominated by our fire. Having seen only a handful of men upstairs, you inquire where the rest of his company is located. He says that most of them are concentrated in the house. But he has a couple of outposts over on the left, along a hedge lined with dead Maisonneuves, killed yesterday in attempting to take the church.

During the afternoon, alone at the parapet in the open attic, you poke around enemy territory with one of your 25-pounders – first punching some holes in the church tower with H.E., then the minehead building, then some suspicious chalky scars that could be trench-work on the distant slope. And just as you are about to start bracketing one of the haystacks that could be a camouflaged tank, you get the message to return to the guns.

Greatly relieved that you will be able to get a night's sleep tonight, but not relishing the thought of having to retrace that harrowing route taken by your guide this morning on the way up, you bid farewell to Brégent and start back.

Hating every step of the way, fearful you may miss a landmark, you hesitatingly pick your way, trying not to break the menacing silence. Each time you dislodge a bit of rubble, you cringe in anticipation of something coming your way.

With mixed feelings you locate the cellar window out of which you crawled this morning; most grateful you recognized the damn thing, but feeling foolish as you worm your way back in and drop down into the dank gloom, merely to cross over and clamber out a window on the other side. Somehow you recognize other landmarks, including the open pit into which you'd tumbled among the furnace pipes, and at last you make the final dash across the road into the orchard where your carrier sits next to tac headquarters.

There you inquire of the 6th Field FOO who is replacing you what route he used coming up from the guns. He says straight across the fields along the river from Bassé that lies just south of Fleury. And though derelict vehicles dot the field in ominous stillness on all sides, Ryckman brings the rocking carrier back to the guns without incident, arriving just before the sun goes down.

The motion picture cameraman, a cheerful fellow named McGaughey, is just packing up to leave, very disappointed by the small amount of firing the guns have been called upon to deliver this day.

Bob Grout explains that the only target of any urgency was the one at about 9:00 A.M. when some fast but abbreviated fire was required on those "robot tanks in front of Verrières."

Robot tanks?

"Well, whatever you call them. You saw them of course?"

Saw them? Until now you hadn't even heard of them.

"Oh? Well, the attack must have occurred while you were in transit."

The description sent back to the guns was that the things resembled Bren carriers – tracked, but slightly narrower than a carrier. Within eight hundred yards of our lines they were abandoned by the drivers, and when their motors stopped, the things exploded with terrific blasts. But as the blasts were mostly upwards, and all out in the open, there was very little lethal fragmentation.

The machines were sent under cover of 88-mm air bursts and mortar fire. Our guns shelled them, but since the things were meant to self-destruct, it was impossible to tell if any of them were destroyed by our shells.

This new secret weapon appears to be rather a joke in its total ineffectiveness, but of course it was no joke to anyone up there this morning, including 4th Field carrier crews, when those strange things were crawling towards their holes.*

The fact that all of this took place beyond Verrières Ridge, out of

---

* For his courageous work on Verrières Ridge during this novel German attack, Lance-Bombardier J. W. Schneider, with Easy Troop carrier crew, was later awarded a Commander-in-Chief's Certificate. With the infantry calling for SOS fire, and the remote cable leading to the

sight of the lens of cameraman McGaughey, has added to his
general frustration. With no major attacks to support, or large
counter-attacks to cool down, the guns were reduced to a leisurely
harassing-fire program and brief, periodic bursts, called for by FOOs
inspired as much by suspicion as by any actual observation of
enemy activity – shooting up scars on a distant hill that might be
enemy trenches, a minehead useful to the Germans, and a ragged
church tower harbouring a machine gun and possibly an artillery
observer.

The disappointed man recalls that when he was assigned to shoot
this film, he was told your guns were engaged in record-breaking
firing, that during a four-day period ending July 22, your regiment
averaged ten thousand rounds a day. And a couple of days ago, when
he came up to make arrangements with you to film your guns, there
were enormous piles of spent cartridges beside each of your gun
pits. He recalls watching in fascination as a gunner cleared them
from the floor of one of the pits, creating a veritable stream of
ringing brass as he pitched one after the other onto a growing
mountain outside the pit. And when some of them began to tumble
back down into the pit, the gunner climbed out and attacked the
slithering pile with tremendous vigour, driving an upraised, hobnailed boot against it and pushing mightily until it shifted enough
that the peak tipped over and an avalanche cascaded down away
from the gun pit. What a shot that would have made for his film!

Now, even those mountains of brass, which could have provided
mute testimony to the record-breaking firing, have been packed
away in boxes and neatly stacked up.

He's very concerned that what he has captured on film is so very
unrepresentative of life at the guns of Normandy as to be utterly

---

radio in the carrier cut by a mortar bomb, he left the shelter of the OP
trench, in the midst of airbursting 88-mm shells and crashing mortar
bombs, to carry target information from his FOO back to the carrier
parked some distance away for transmittal to the guns.

silly: a man (Sgt. Nick Ostapyck) diving off the nearby newly built Bailey bridge into the murky Orne; another (Gunner E. G. Kent) paddling a patched-up canoe in the river unusually clear of human and animal bodies, which he had heard were always floating by here; a GPO (Lieut. Walter James Faber of Baker Troop) calling fire orders into a Tannoy mike; a gun getting off a round or two; a fleeting shot of a despatch rider (Gunner Turner) passing by on his motorbike; and finally, some men eating out of mess tins and drinking tea from enamelled mugs. Hardly the makings of a dramatic film – and certainly not representative in any way of what the gunners have been going through up here.

As he's pulling out, you inquire if this means that the film will never be released, that relatives back in Canada will never get the chance to identify their long-absent loved ones on the movie screen?

Oh no, not at all. Knowing the way the brass love to hide the dark side of the war and show only smiling faces to the folks at home, he expects it'll be released as a short for the theatres in Canada.*

But what makes for a dull movie, makes for a pleasant existence here at the guns. Overnight, life has become remarkably relaxed, even though harassing-fire programs can extend for hours – as today, when the guns sporadically shelled selected areas between May-sur-Orne and Rocquancourt.

Though Jerry continues to drop thousands of shells and mortars across the whole front, and nightly his bombers visit much of the rear areas reaching back to Caen, including 4RCA wagon lines and the guns of other regiments, causing damage and casualties, he continues to spare this small oasis in the bend of the Orne as though balancing things out after those wretched days in the valley in front of Carpiquet. Today, they tell you, there were only a few airbursts,

---

*   *A Day in the Life of a Gunner* was never edited for release.

the most disturbing being a premature from a Baker Troop gun, bursting with a terrible crack just after leaving the muzzle. Fortunately it caused no harm.

And with less demand on gunners and command post crews, and more opportunities for sleep and relaxation, everyone seems to be "coming up for air."

They've even adopted a mascot over at Baker Troop: a scrawny, long-legged, freckled pullet picked up back in the rubble of Louvigny by Lance-Bombardier Ralph Hughes and Gunner W. J. Brewster. The original idea was to keep it just long enough to fatten it up for a feast. But now that it has been given the name Hardtack, in recognition of its principal diet, it's clear no one would dare suggest a chicken pot pie – certainly not in the presence of any of its guardians, who now number most, if not all, of Baker Troop.

As you are dropping off to sleep in the gathering dusk, curled up on the bucket seats of good old armoured scout car GA, you ponder how different all this is from life up in St. Martin-de-Fontenay. This brief interlude of comparative ease for the gunners ends shortly after midnight, just after you are awakened by Bob Grout to take over "the graveyard shift" in the troop command post. By 6:00 A.M. 4th Field guns will have consumed 390 rounds per gun, while taking part in bombardments by the field guns of 2nd Division and 4th Armoured Division, and by the mediums of 2nd Cdn AGRA (Army Group Royal Artillery).

At 1:00 A.M. the guns provide support for a company of the Lincoln and Welland Regiment (10th Brigade, 4th Division), conducting a feint against the tiny hamlet of Tilly-la-Campagne from the northeast, while the Calgary Highlanders form up in the northwest along the Caen–Falaise highway to attack at 2:30 A.M. Supported by a squadron of tanks of the Royal Scots Greys (4th British Armoured Brigade), the Calgarys attempt to take that desolate confusion of rubble and broken walls, still firmly held by swarms of SS and still covered by as many machine guns,

Nebelwerfers, self-propelled 88-mm guns and dug-in tanks as were required to maul the North Novas so severely a week ago.

Early reports have the Calgary Highlanders in Tilly. However, as time passes, it becomes clear they have been driven back, when well after daylight the guns are called upon to support a second attack on Tilly by the Calgarys accompanied by the Scots Greys' tanks.

As in the first attack, there is a report they have gained the village. But again it becomes evident the violent fire from the German guns and mortars has forced them to relinquish their tenuous hold of the village, when at 2:00 P.M. the guns are called upon to fire another bombardment in support of a third attack by the survivors. This time there is no report of early success. Nor is there when the Lincoln and Welland Regiment attacks Tilly from Bourguébus just before midnight.

Sit reps are equally silent when a final attack by the Lincoln and Welland, supported by the guns, is undertaken at 2:45 A.M. August 2.

Tilly-la-Campagne, which could have provided the Canadians with an improved launching position for the next big push while denying the Germans their superior overview of Allied territory all the way back to Caen, is still in enemy hands. And the war diaries of 6th Brigade, the Calgary Highlanders, and the Lincoln and Welland Regiment will provide the reason as they document the devastating effect of the awesome fire-power 1st SS (Liebstandarte Adolph Hitler) Division was able to bring to bear in repelling five determined attacks on this one ragged hamlet in just slightly more than twenty-four hours.

Against the Calgarys' first attack, "the enemy gave battle with anticipated violence, laying down intense defensive fire with guns and mortars."* And while they failed to prevent some elements from gaining a foothold in the village, their fire, "mistaken by the

---

*   Calgary Highlanders War Diary, August 1, 1944, Unit War Diaries Section, National Archives of Canada.

distracted riflemen for that of our own artillery, was so accurate, our troops were forced to retire and dig in along the railway."

When the Scots Greys tanks were ordered to go forward in day-light with the Calgarys on their second try, "elements again fought their way into the village, but severe losses of both infantry and tanks again compelled a withdrawal. At about 1000 hours, the strag-gling remnants of the Calgary Highlanders fell back under heavy fire, through a company of the Royal Regiment which was ordered to dig in along the main road [Caen–Falaise] to meet an expected counter-attack."

When incredibly the Calgarys mounted a third attack they were stopped only a few hundred yards beyond the startline. "Depleted, exhausted, and unable to move in the face of the concentrated fire of machine-guns, mortars and tanks, the Highlanders dug in, and supported by a squadron of the Fort Garry Horse and a company of the Royal Regiment, held their ground."

When the Lincoln and Welland Regiment, in their first attack in Normandy, moved out in a "silent attack" through the gloom from the direction of Bourguébus, at fifteen minutes to midnight, "their advance across 700 yards of open ground towards the village was broken up by heavy fire from machine-guns and mortars." And the same fate awaited them in the fifth and final assault on Tilly-la-Campagne: ". . . a second attempt was again defeated, and at dawn the project had to be abandoned."*

By now the brass mountains of expended cartridge-cases piled up at each gun pit have grown by another 100 rounds, to 490 per gun. But, of course, there is no photographer in sight.

During the day you learn the FMRs, taking advantage of the heavy diversionary fire distributed by the guns around St. Martin-

---

* Page 2, Report No. 65, Historical Section (G.S.) Army Headquarters, Dept. of National Defence, Dec. 23, 1953.

de-Fontenay during the first attack by the Calgarys on Tilly, conducted a totally successful assault on the church in St. Martin. You find yourself wondering if Acting-Major Brégent had any role in the assault. Did he and his men get the chance to use their knives and slit the throats of the Germans in the house next door?

With that infamous church and tower finally clear of Germans and firmly occupied by the assaulting company, led by Major Dextraze, the battalion's exhausted acting CO, Major Sauvé, should now manage to get some sleep.*

When you learn that the 6th Field FOO (Capt. D. E. McRae), who replaced you in time to take part in the assault on the church, was killed, you are swept by conflicting emotions: regret that such an obviously nice guy should have bought it, but humbly thankful it wasn't you.

During the eight-day period beginning July 25 and ending at 6:00 A.M. August 1, the guns of 4th Field alone fired more than 41,000 shells, averaging 5,210 a day, and consumption rose to 9,360 rounds the first day and the last day. Then for six days after the Tilly-la-Campagne affair, demands on the guns and the gunners cool down remarkably.

However, the lull in offensive operations – providing a much-needed period of rest for the gunners and maintenance of their weapons – does not improve, to any appreciable degree, the grim existence of front-line riflemen and the artillery FOOs and their crews huddled in sandy holes among them. And this fact, easily overlooked by history touching only on the highlights of a campaign, is recorded by the war diarist at 6th Brigade, who, in an inspired burst of descriptive prose, captures with supreme accuracy

---

* Major J. M. Paul Sauvé survived the war and, following the death of Maurice Duplessis, became Premier of Quebec until his own death one hundred days later. Major J. A. Dextraze remained in the army after the war, fought in Korea, and eventually became Chief of the General Staff.

the never-ending anxieties and risks of men in forward battle lines:

> The noise of the conflict echoes across the fields from dawn to dusk, only to be taken up in new and uneasy tones as darkness closes in. And while losses never reach the proportions of the 25th of July (1,500 killed, wounded and missing), the static battle costs the Canadian Corps 100 casualties a day.*

———

* 6th Brigade War Diary, in Unit War Diaries section, National Archives of Canada.

41

A SEPTEMBER '39 ORIGINAL
RETURNS AS CO

---- ✳ ----

IF ANY WORD TRICKLED DOWN FROM RHQ THAT LT.–COL. DRURY left the Regiment July 28 to become G1 (general staff officer, grade 1) at Headquarters 2nd Div, it never registered in your sleep-starved brain. And so when Bombardier Hossack shakes you awake around 4:00 P.M. this afternoon, on August 2, and you disentangle yourself from your camp-stool just in time to see a long-legged lieutenant-colonel slithering down the steep earthen steps of your troop command post, you are more than a little puzzled. And when he introduces himself as McGregor Young, your new CO, you really start to worry.

Commanding officers hardly ever visit gun positions. Even the fussiest of fuss-pots back in England left harassment of gun positions, if there was any, to his second-in-command. What the hell could he be looking for? Had he seen you sleeping? Should you explain that you are still trying to catch up on sleep lost over a period of several days when you were without a second officer to spell you off, and have survived with catnaps sitting on that crazy camp-stool?

But before you can start in, to your relief he makes it clear he only stopped by to get directions to RHQ. Your gun position was simply the first he encountered after coming down off the steep hill from Fleury. And after you tell him the best way to get there, and he does a cursory inspection of the layout of your cramped dugout, he turns to climb out. It is then you notice the extra ribbon on his chest – a DSO (distinguished service order), no less – and are much impressed.

But then he pauses at the foot of the dugout steps and inquires why you haven't left an opening in your dugout wall – the part above grade – through which you could keep your guns under observation for purposes of fire discipline?

Oh gawd, you think, not one of those guys!

As politely as you can, you explain that you took an instant aversion to open ports in command-post walls back at your very first position in the valley in front of Carpiquet, when you'd had a man wounded by a bullet from a strafing plane that ricocheted off the ground and in through a port you'd left open in the front of your dugout so you could see the guns. He was the only man wounded by that strafing plane. You go on at some length to point out that at night you can't see the guns anyway, and in the daytime you can always move up the steps and watch them better from there than through a restricted port.

By now, another type of senior officer (several of whom you have known), would have told you to shut up and get on with the reconstruction of the whole damned command post. But your speech leaves this man pursing his lips, raising his eyebrows as though in recognition of a novel concept, and rocking his head back and forth in a way, you think, shows he appreciates your plea for common sense. Then smiling broadly at you, he turns and climbs out of the dugout without further comment. As you follow him up and watch his long legs striding off to the waiting Jeep, you decide you like the new CO very much.

However, early impressions of another CO having proven wrong once before, you are curious as to what Bombardier Hossack thinks the reaction of the men will be towards his appointment as CO?

Good, he thinks. As far as he knows, everybody was sorry to see

"Mac" leave the Regiment when he was promoted second-in-command of some 3rd Division outfit in 1943. This, of course, means he's been in Normandy since D-Day, which would account for that DSO ribbon.*

Hossack is surprised you didn't recognize him – after all he was one of the 1939 originals of the Toronto 53rd Battery. You can only conclude that though you joined the Regiment in 1942, a year before he left for 3rd Division, you never met simply because until the tent camp in the backyard of Arundel Castle in the summer of 1943, 4th Field was never together as a regiment except during schemes or training camps.

----

* Over the months ahead you would witness firsthand the cool courage of this unassuming man. And from time to time you would hear fragmentary references to his heroism on D-Day and on other desperate days right after the landing, when the charged-up "Hitler Youth" of 12th SS Panzer Division were determined to follow their Führer's direct command to drive the Canadians back into the sea. And one day you would get an eyewitness account of one of his exploits among the assaulting forces from a new CO of the Royals (Lt.-Col. Lendrum), who was with the Canadian Scottish during those first days ashore. When a leading company was cut off, communications non-existent, and the enemy about to overrun the infantry battalion headquarters, "Mac" took charge of one of his regiment's 105-mm self-propelled guns. Directing it to push ahead with gun blazing, he opened a corridor through the SS to the desperate company, from whence he was able to call down such concentrations of fire from his other twenty-three guns on the surrounding enemy, the Germans were forced to withdraw.

PART FIVE: AUGUST 3–11

1st Canadian Army Ordered to Break Through to Falaise

42

A FOOTNOTE TO THE BREAKING

OF THE HINGE

———————————— ✳ ————————————

SUPREME ALLIED COMMANDER GENERAL EISENHOWER, IN AN attempt to place in perspective the extraordinary strength of German forces facing the Canadians relative to those facing the Americans, will one day say, "ten feet gained on the Caen sector was equivalent to a mile elsewhere."[*]

And as the Canadians have gone on holding Panzer Group West in close and deadly combat around Verrières Ridge, the American Operation Cobra, bursting through the thinly held western rim of the bridgehead, is, by August 1, a full-fledged break-out exploited by the newly arrived mobile army of General George Patton, south and west towards the ports of Brittany.

By August 3 the Brittany peninsula (apart from some key cross-roads and garrisoned ports) is said to be controlled by the French Maquis: some fifty thousand men distributed among numerous guerrilla groups, some led by British and French paratroopers of the Special Air Service, and most of them equipped with arms dropped by the RAF.

With no coherent front opposing Patton, Gen. Bradley, Commander of 12th U.S. Army Group, directs him to thrust south

———————

[*]   *Canadians at War 1939–45, Vol. Two* (Montreal: Reader's Digest, 1969), p. 481.

and east to Le Mans in the "wide sweep" envisaged by Montgomery
in his original plan.

As Patton turns east on August 4, Montgomery issues a directive
reinforcing the purpose and intent of his strategy: "Once a gap
appears in the enemy front, we must press into it and through it and
beyond it into the enemy's rear areas. Everyone must go all out all
day, and every day. The broad strategy of the Allied Armies is to
swing the right flank towards Paris and to force the enemy back to
the Seine."

Montgomery counts on the Germans doing the militarily sensible thing: pulling back to a major water barrier to establish a line.
The American break-out will deny them a retreat to the Loire,
forcing them back to the Seine. There, encircled and pocketed
against that wide river, without a single bridge standing and no adequate alternative means of getting themselves and their equipment
to safety, the Germans must surrender or be annihilated by the
Allied air forces.

However, on Hitler's orders the main German forces still press
insanely north and west, as Patton's army races unhindered far to
the south of them towards Paris, covering seventy-five miles in
three days, almost reaching Le Mans by August 7.

Now the "Caen hinge," which the Germans have continued to
defend with fanatical tenacity, and which they have been encouraged to shore up and buttress at the expense of other parts of the
front, has to be broken to allow the northern, British–Canadian
wing of this great encirclement to start east to the Seine.

To this purpose, on August 3, Montgomery orders Crerar's 1st
Canadian Army to "break through the enemy positions to the
south and south-east of Caen."

"Operation Totalize" will involve: (1) the improvisation of new
equipment; (2) the unconventional application of regular equipment; (3) specialized training for the assault troops, tankmen, and
drivers of the improvised armoured troop-carriers never before

used in action; and (4) the unprecedented use of tanks and heavy bombers in support of an attack in the black hours of the night.

But in spite of all the special difficulties – not the least of which is persuading RAF Bomber Command to cooperate in bombing in close support troops on the ground, where an error by Pathfinder planes could be disastrous – this most demanding and complicated operation will be launched by 1st Canadian Army at 11:30 P.M. on August 7, a mere four days after receipt of the warning order.

This is possible only because General Crerar anticipated as early as July 29 that the Canadians would be called upon to smash out towards Falaise, and wisely turned over the planning of the attack to one of the ablest of Allied field commanders, with perhaps the most creative, original military mind of any general on either side in this war: Lt.-Gen. Guy Simonds, Commander of 2nd Canadian Corps.*

Anything less than Simonds' imagination and boldness of spirit applied to the problem of devising a way to break out of the suicidal deadlock in front of Verrières Ridge, and "Totalize" must certainly become a disaster surpassing Dieppe. A conventional frontal assault in daylight along the lines of British operations Epsom and Goodwood, or the U.S. Operation Cobra, against the fire-power

---

* Chester Wilmot, on page 410 of his postwar book *The Struggle for Europe* (London: Collins, 1952), recognized as the definitive work on Allied operations in northwest Europe in 1944–45, judges ex-gunner officer Lt.-Gen. Guy Simonds to have been "a most able, forceful and original soldier." Conceding that he was "ambitious, reserved and ruthless" and "not an easy man to serve, for he was intolerant of minds less capable than his own," in Wilmot's judgement, "he certainly commanded confidence and respect. Like Montgomery, his approach to problems of battle was that of a scientist. Both were perfectionists, but whereas Montgomery was primarily the expert implementer, Simonds was a radical innovator forever seeking new solutions. Simonds' originality was strikingly evident in the plan he devised for this operation which was given the code name Totalize."

arrayed in such depth at this narrow front at Verrières, must end in failure, producing casualties far in excess of even the July rate for the Canadians on this front, already the highest rate for all of the Allied armies. And if, under pressure from on high (inevitably ferocious with the whole course of the war in the west at stake), a conventional assault were pursued for many days, 1st Canadian Army would cease to exist as a fighting force.

By July 31, Simonds and his staff have assessed the problem and worked out possible solutions. It isn't sufficient to break through the German line running from the southern outskirts of St. André-sur-Orne and St. Martin-de-Fontenay on the right to Tilly-la-Campagne on the left. There is another line five miles farther south – running from Bretteville-sur-Laize on the right to St. Sylvain east of the Caen–Falaise highway – that will have to be breached and rendered ineffective if a true breakthrough is to be accomplished. All attacks against the first line towards May-sur-Orne and Rocquancourt have been bloodily repulsed up until now, and Simonds recognizes that even if it is possible to break through those first defences, the Germans will just regroup at the second line unless it too is overrun.

Assuming there will be available air and ground bombardment equal to that which opened Goodwood, Simonds has to find a way to get his tanks – this time closely supported by infantry – through the first line of defence and crushing into the second line before the initial stupefying shock of the bombardment wears off. Then, unlike Goodwood, he must maintain a constant flow of air and artillery support to the spearheads exploiting the breakthrough. In Goodwood, the British armoured divisions left their infantry far behind, outran their artillery before they got to Verrières Ridge, and although the German gun lines remained intact covering the ridge no provision was made for continuation of the aerial bombing into the second day.

However, surprise – a fundamental condition for any successful military operation – can hardly be attained here, after all the intense and purposely threatening attacks Montgomery has had the Canadians make in this sector over the past three weeks to scare the enemy into moving a maximum number of men, tanks, and guns onto this front.

And the awesome losses during these attacks have pointed up the ultimate problem of getting tanks and infantry across open country that affords the enemy outstanding observation of Allied fields and roads all the way back to Caen and provides him with tremendous, unobstructed fields of fire for his guns, heavy mortars, and machine guns. Even if the assault troops are transported in armoured personnel carriers to reduce casualties from machine guns and mortars, the enemy's long-barrelled 88s – deadly accurate and lethal to Allied tanks at more than two thousand yards – can destroy the relatively thin-skinned armoured personnel carriers as fast as they are driven into view.

But what if they were not driven like shooting-gallery targets up and over the ridge in daylight, but were moved forward under cover of darkness, immersed in a column of tanks plunging forward behind a rolling barrage – taking advantage of the utter confusion left by a colossal bombing of front-line targets and bypassing all village strongholds still able to offer resistance? Might they not have a chance of driving miles into no-man's-land and establishing a series of firm bases before daylight, from whence full exploitation could be carried out by armoured divisions following in behind through the ruptured lines?

Simonds believes it possible, and surprisingly he is able to gain the confidence of tank commanders, who traditionally believe that tanks, being blind and ineffective in the dark, should be left hidden away from the battle in laagers at night. And perhaps even more surprisingly, he is also able to win the cooperation of RAF Bomber Command, which has never before attempted to bomb front-line targets at night in close support of an armoured breakthrough. While RAF strategic bombers are accustomed to flying in the dark to targets marked by Pathfinders, the need for accuracy has never been so critical. To ensure RAF Pathfinders do not make a mistake, the artillery is given the job of firing flare shells onto targets just before the Pathfinders are timed to arrive. And just to be sure it will work, the RAF insists on testing the effectiveness of the artillery-placed flares up near Ouistreham, on the coast north of Caen, the night before the bombing is to take place.

Once these key elements – Bomber Command and tank divisions – are sold on the idea of the novel attack, the principal problem is getting enough armoured carriers to transport the infantry. The White scout cars of a 4th Division motorized regiment are available, and many can be borrowed from the artillery regiments of 2nd Division, but to fill much of the need, Simonds has to come up with an improvised vehicle, and one of astonishing effectiveness is brought into being almost overnight.

He gets permission from the Americans to remove the 105-mm guns from the seventy-two Priests (the self-propelled guns on tank chassis borrowed by 3rd Division for the D-Day assault), and modify each open steel chassis to carry twelve infantrymen and their weapons. Four officers and 250 tradesmen, from twelve different units, are brought together for the job. The first carrier, immediately dubbed a "Kangaroo," is finished at 7:00 P.M. on August 3.

Modifications call for the removal of the gun, mantlet, seats, and ammunition bins, and for the welding of armour-plate over the opening at the front. When all available armour-plate is used up, pieces of lesser steel, scrounged from a variety of sources (some say even from landing craft stranded on the beach waiting for the return of high tide), are welded in layers two inches apart, and the space between is filled with sand. Working round the clock, they "defrock" the last Priest by 10:00 A.M. on August 6, allowing just enough time for the infantry to learn how to board and disembark at the ready, and for drivers to practise manoeuvring them in the fields behind Louvigny. Thirty-six Kangaroos are allotted to the Royals, while an equal number of armoured half-tracks are loaned the other two battalions (RHLI and Essex Scottish) by the engineers, recce, and artillery units. The other thirty-six Kangaroos are allotted to the British assaulting brigade.

Most of the drivers of the Kangaroos are the 3rd Division men who drove them as self-propelled guns. But twenty-eight drivers and four NCOs from Army Service volunteer to take over the twenty-eight new armoured half-tracks sent over from England to increase the pot of thick-skinned vehicles divided between Canadians and Brits.

The assault forces opening "Totalize" are the 51st Highland Division to the east of the Caen–Falaise highway, and 2nd Canadian Division to the right of the highway, supported by the 2nd Canadian Armoured Brigade which consists of 6th Armoured (1st Hussars), 10th Armoured (Fort Garry Horse), and the 27th Armoured (Sherbrooke Fusiliers).

The Canadian assault battalions will go forward from Troteval and Beauvoir farms over Verrières Ridge in four tightly lined-up columns: the Essex Scottish on the right, the RHLI in the centre, and the Royal Regiment on the left, with 8th Recce on their left. Leading each column will be a "gapping force," made up of flails (tanks with rotating drums out in front to which are attached heavy, logging chains slapping the earth as they move) exploding any mines lurking in the path of the advancing column. Then the tanks and AVREs (Churchill tanks of the Royal Engineers fitted with short-range heavy mortars known as Petards, and various devices for bridging), which this night will be marking corridors with white tape. And each column will have two troops of M-10s, self-propelled guns supplied by 56th and 33rd batteries.

43

ARMOURED BULLDOZERS DIG GUN PITS

FOR OPERATION TOTALIZE, THE GUNS MUST BE MOVED FORWARD to gain as much range as possible for support of the assault columns expected to gain the high ground seven kilometres farther along the Caen–Falaise highway. For 4th Field, to gain two thousand yards in range means a move of about four kilometres east and two south, to a field just in front of Ifs.

On the afternoon of August 3, Major Gordon Savage, the second-in-command, leads the three battery CPOs (Les Hutcheon, "Stevie" Stevenson, and Ted Dack) up there to recce positions. Included in the party are the regimental surveyors under Survey Officer Len Harvey, who, from data supplied by 2nd Corps Survey Regiment, must establish pivot gun markers to the accuracy of "theatre grid"– a most unusual state of readiness for guns that won't even start moving up until 10:00 P.M. the day after tomorrow.

After dark all three batteries and RHQ send up digging parties to prepare gun and ammunition pits and command post dugouts, with the help of an armoured bulldozer supplied by the Engineers. The CRA 2nd Division (Brig. Keefler) deems this necessary because the new positions between thirty-metre and forty-metre contours are still under observation from the ragged pile of broken walls that is Tilly-la-Campagne, just three kilometres distant on a seventy-metre contour. So it is with some uneasiness your troop leader, Bob

Grout, accepts responsibility for the eighty-man regimental detail going up to dig the pits. And it does his peace of mind no good to discover, close to where Able Troop will deploy, the lonely crosses marking the place Dawson and Knapp died.*

After dark it's really weird — gun-fire lighting the horizon in front and behind, and shells whining overhead in both directions. And now and then there's a sound that I can't immediately identify, like the crack of a whip. After establishing where the pits for 2nd Battery are to go, and leaving a sergeant in charge of a digging party, I'm leading the other two sergeants to the locations selected that afternoon, when a plane flying low overhead drops parachute flares. We flop down flat on the ground. However, they drop nothing near us until just as the flares are dying out, when with a strange howling a large metal container about the size of a coffin, complete with lid [a disposable carrier for anti-personnel bombs], lands a few feet from us.

The plane is still above us, so I suggest we make a dash for some slit trenches I spotted in the afternoon on the other end of the field. But before we get to them, there are more flares. The sergeants make it to a couple of trenches with roofs. But the one convenient to me is open to the sky. This time the plane dives and makes a pass right over us, dropping a string of anti-personnel bombs. There's a close bracket across my trench, and for a moment I think they contain gas because the fumes are choking. Again he comes back — this time strafing with machine guns, and I thank my lucky stars I spotted these trenches before dark.

Later, when the planes have departed and the bulldozer comes up to the third position to start digging, the operator suddenly jumps down and runs for cover in a ditch. When I get to him to ask what's wrong, he says bullets are ricocheting off his dozer.

---

* They had been buried by Black Watch padre Honorary Capt. E. C. Royle, who "came across the bodies still seated in their shattered Jeep."

Then I hear more of those whip-cracks. Suddenly I remember where I heard that sound before: working the targets in the rifle butts at Petawawa. Bullets coming close, from only a couple of hundred yards away, sound like that. There is a clump of trees out in front just about that far away that could be sheltering a patrol. After a while they appear to pull back, probably believing they have come up against a tank from the sound of the bulldozer engine. Anyway, the work on the pits is allowed to continue. When at dawn I report all this to RHQ, they're surprised I wasn't told to be on the look-out for a Heinie patrol in the vicinity of Ifs last night.*

During the night regimental ammunition trucks move up the first instalment of ammo: 3,242 rounds from Fleury (143 rounds per gun).

Back at the guns things are exceedingly quiet – the quietest since coming into action. Still, with Grout up at Ifs, you are stuck on duty in the command post all night. To pass the time you decide to get down, on the nice clean piece of musical-staff paper Hiltz scrounged for you in the village, the words and music of a new song you composed to send your wife for your third wedding anniversary, coming up on August 30. It will be the third you have missed sharing with her:

From your pictures you're adorable, my dear.
From reports you are the lady of the year.
From those in the know these days I've heard,
You're beautiful to see –
You twinkle like the candles on an anniversary!
From informants you would seem to be immortal –
They have booked the hall of fame and burst its portal –

---

* Author interview.

From "enchanting" to "alluring"; from "endearing" to "enduring,"
But from memory, you're just swell my dear!

For a non-musician, self-taught composer, arranging harmony without a piano by imagining the keyboard is devilishly hard, and having to work by candlelight, scribing musical notes of varying value, whose precise position in relationship to the staff lines is critical, using a "straight" pen dipped in India ink, calls for the patience of Job. But around about dawn it's finally finished – every last dot, stroke, and wiggle has been inked in. Right then and there you should have returned the cork to the ink bottle sitting on the artillery board next to the finished manuscript, so that if and when a target came in, it wouldn't get knocked over. But you didn't, and in the scramble to clear the deck, it happens: one whole page is blotted beyond repair.

It takes well into the afternoon to construct a new page, and then locate the glue to paste it in place ready for mailing home. *C'est la guerre!*

At 9:30 P.M. on August 4, half an hour before 26 Battery is to lead off the move to the new positions over at Ifs, 5th Field reports heavy shelling of the area, and the CRA stops the move. Then at 10:00 P.M. the move is on again, and 26th Battery manages to get into position just after midnight, 2nd Battery at 2.30 A.M., and 14th Battery at 4:00 A.M.

When daylight comes, all ranks expect the Regiment to be hammered as it was back in the amphitheatre positions in front of the Carpiquet escarpment, but nothing of consequence occurs. In fact there's very little shelling activity in either direction all day. Some large calibre duds thud into the position, which would have caused damage to men and guns if they had gone off. One, landing on Baker Troop, drills a hole so deep that the bottom can't be reached with a fifteen-foot pole.

Still being able to see high ground occupied by the enemy makes everyone uneasy, and the gunners have plenty to do on their gun pits and ammunition pits before they have them to their satisfaction. While grateful for the excavations scooped out by the bulldozer before they arrived, the gunners find the holes are pretty ragged, and much pick-and-shovel work is required before the ammo pits are ready for the first instalment of the 857 additional rounds per gun that will be brought up during the next two nights by Army Service Corps.*

---

*   In thirty-six hours 2nd Corps Army Service moved up 205,000 shells, 152,000 gallons of petrol, and 130,000 rations for Operation Totalize. By then a troop of ninety tank-transporters, modified to carry ammunition, could lift 2,700 tons of shells, as much as could be carried by ten transport companies using three-tonners. (Reported in Arnold Warren, *Wait for the Waggons* (Toronto: McClelland and Stewart, 1961).

44

IS 4TH BRIGADE TO BE SACRIFICED?

APART FROM THE USUAL LIGHT HARASSING–FIRE PROGRAM CALLED for each night, there is very little demand on the guns during the first two days up here, just north of Ifs. And on August 7 the guns are again quiet throughout most of the day.

Just after 6:00 P.M. great swarms of Kangaroos and other armoured personnel carriers, transporting the three assault battalions of 4th Brigade, which for the past two days have been involved in manoeuvres in the fields west of Louvigny, suddenly appear on the sloping ground south and west of the gun positions. So suddenly do they "sprout" in the fields in front, some at least must have used the old Roman ford at Athis to cross the Orne instead of the new Bailey bridge at Fleury.

By dusk it is obvious that tremendous forces are about to be unleashed. Not only are the nearby slopes on both sides of the highway leading to Falaise covered with tanks, flails, Kangaroos, and other armoured carriers taking up position, but out of sight behind Ifs and down in the low ground in front of Fleury-sur-Orne there's been the creaking and clanking of tracked vehicles assembling all evening.

The tanks of 2nd Canadian Armoured Brigade will be with 4th Brigade, and east of the Caen–Falaise highway the British 33rd Armoured Brigade will lead another three columns of armoured personnel carriers with a brigade of the 51st Highland Division aboard.

Well aware of what 2nd Canadian Division infantry has been through in taking and holding the ground lying out there just ahead of the muzzles of your guns – the two kilometres from Ifs to the Beauvoir and Troteval farms and the last blood-soaked kilometre from there to Verrières – you can't help wondering if two brigades of infantry and two brigades of tanks could possibly accomplish anything significant in the way of a breakthrough beyond the ridge that forms the southern horizon.

In a message to the troops, it is clear Lt.-Gen. Crerar believes so. He obviously expects remarkable gains from a successful plunge by 1st Canadian Army through the German defences: "We have reached what very much appears to be the potentially decisive period of this five-year World War. I have no doubt we shall make August 8, 1944, an even blacker day for the German army than that same date 26 years ago."* A First War veteran, the General is referring to General Ludendorff's statement that August 8, 1918 – the day the British offensive began east of Amiens – was "the blackest day of the German army in the history of the war."

All the guns having been moved as far forward as possible to increase their range and extend maximum support for the attack, both during the barrage and afterwards, and the infantry having been pulled back from their most forward positions for safety reasons before the bombing begins, great masses of troops and vehicles have been compressed into a relatively small area. Brig. Keefler, CRA of 2nd Division, has decided, under the circumstances, to issue route maps and mark these routes on the ground with white tape so the masses of transport following the assaulting columns, and the two armoured divisions that will follow along still later, will not literally overrun the gun pits of the six artillery regiments in the

---

* Chester Wilmot, *The Struggle for Europe* (London: Collins, 1952), p. 411.

immediate vicinity of Ifs. Thus the forming–up areas for the leading tanks, flails, and armoured troop carriers end up very close to the guns. And in the gathering dusk, command post personnel, having completed all the preparatory paperwork on the barrage, amuse themselves trying to spot their own armoured scout car among the other armoured cars loaned by the Regiment and the other field regiments of the Division to provide additional thick-skinned vehicles to carry infantrymen forward.

Yesterday afternoon, as your car, GA, was being completely emptied out, and a great clutter of equipment and personal kit was being dumped onto the ground in a pitiful-looking mess, a rising tide of irritation among your command post gang was suppressed only when you reminded them that the big, five-ton, armour-plated touring car – eighteen feet long and six and a half feet wide – would be providing protection against small-arms fire and shell splinters for at least ten infantrymen tonight as they go forward behind the barrage blasting a gap through the German lines.

While the armour–plate encasing them is not thick, as in the Kangaroos, it still is of hardened steel ranging from six to twelve millimetres thick, and will certainly deflect 9-mm Schmeisser bullets and shell and mortar splinters.

All who normally ride in GA fervently hope she survives, for she has many proven virtues as a command post vehicle. In addition to being roomy, she's much less vulnerable than a conventional sheet metal truck sitting on a gun position. And though equipped with four-wheel drive to pull through rough country and heavy mud, she's capable of reaching fifty-five miles an hour on good roads, if given a chance to get rolling.

For an hour or so there is an unnatural atmosphere abroad – quiet, but full of tension. Surely all of this activity this evening, at least some of it under observation, will have alerted the enemy that something very big is about to burst on them.

While it's impossible not to be impressed by the vast herd of armoured vehicles, forming up nose to tail on all sides, you'll wait and see what happens to them before becoming excited about the prospect of an early break-out. After all, these initial assault forces don't come anywhere near the size and fire-power of the British–Canadian forces involved in the integrated operations Goodwood and Atlantic, when the three best British tank divisions were brought to a flaming halt before this ridge only eighteen days ago, and 2nd Canadian Division infantry was left to take the ridge and withstand the enemy's counter-attacks, suffering the highest rate of casualties of all Allied divisions in the bridgehead.

You realize you've become more than a little sceptical of the promises held out for big attacks around here. And as you visit the men in the gun pits – now removing safety caps and stacking hundreds of shells in readiness for the long barrage – you realize this feeling is general here at the guns, so vastly different from the way it was at the beginning of Goodwood–Atlantic, when everyone truly believed that no resistance would exist after all that bombing and shelling.

With the obvious purpose of raising morale, Major Gordon Savage, the second-in-command, visited the gun position late this afternoon. After explaining to the troops that the Canadians have had to keep up the pressure on this front to hold the main German forces here on the eastern end of the bridgehead while the Americans broke out on the far western end, Savage explained what tonight's big show is supposed to accomplish.

While everybody earnestly hopes it will succeed, no one really believes that a single blow, regardless of how heavily it is delivered, can accomplish a significant break-out on this front; too many attacks have ended in bloody disarray along the Verrières Ridge for anyone to be optimistic about another. So the question naturally arises, "Is this really meant to be a break-out or is 4th Brigade merely going to be put through the grinder again to hold the

German tanks and guns here while the Americans continue to expand their break-out?"

And tonight, you feel the concern throughout the Regiment is legitimate, for over there, waiting, lined up in those columns on those dusty slopes, are a lot of friends: six FOOs and their crews in Universal Carriers, along with three battery commanders and their crews in White Armoured Scout Cars.

Some of the gunners have picked up a rumour that 4th Brigade is to be "a sacrifice brigade"; and they are comparing tonight's charge through the enemy gun lines to the Charge of the Light Brigade.

As in all predicted fire, after all the measurements of the line and range to each lift of the barrage are made for each troop on the artillery boards in the battery command post, and angles of sight are calculated for differences in the height of the guns and the height of the terrain over which the barrage will flow, there still remains the matter of the "correction of the moment." As close as possible to the time of the firing of the barrage, adjustments must be applied to all ranges and switches to compensate not only for the temperature of the propellant charges, but also for variations in air temperatures, air pressures, and the speed and direction of the wind at various levels through which the shells must loop on their way to target. These last figures are based on meteorological data in the "meteor telegram" produced by the Survey Regiment and received at the guns at frequent intervals throughout each twenty-four-hour period. These corrections are now applied to the gun programs just before they are handed out to each gun sergeant.

Then comes the call to the phone for synchronization of watches for H-hour, which for the guns is 11:30 P.M. – thirty minutes after the bombing begins and fifteen minutes before it ends at 11:45 P.M. At 11:00 P.M. coloured-flare shells, fired by some regiment nearby, start glowing on the horizon – red on the left and green on the right of the Caen–Falaise highway – designed to mark the target areas for RAF Pathfinder aircraft leading the 1,020 Lancaster and

Halifax bombers from England, which even now can be heard approaching from the coast. And as the wavering glow builds from more flares dropped by the aircraft, the roaring mass of bombers can be heard coming up from behind Caen.

Though the infantry has been pulled back outside the danger zone of two thousand yards, they've been issued wads of cotton wool for their ears, from bales flown from England earlier in the day. Presently, the first wave of bombers is passing low overhead, and the first of the 3,500 tons of bombs start to land with rumbling, thunderous flashes and earth-shaking *crumps*, seemingly just beyond the crest, though you know they are being dropped no closer than May-sur-Orne and Bretteville-sur-Laize.

Then at 11:30 P.M., the roar of eight hundred engines, in tanks and flails and armoured carriers, revving-up for their move to start-lines, adds to the enveloping din. You begin to worry the gun sergeants may not be able to hear the order to fire when it comes time to start the barrage fifteen minutes from now. (Corps calculates it will take that long for the mobile columns to move up and get in position on their startlines.)

But you need not have worried. The overpowering crash of guns on all sides in response to yells of fire from GPOs is beyond anything you've experienced before in Normandy. Not only are there 720 guns of all kinds supporting Totalize, but so concentrated are they that their thunderous roar makes voice communication impossible. Even shouting directly into another man's ear is ineffective, and the only sure way to communicate anything important, even down in the command post dugouts, is to write it out.

And so it is for the next hour as the stupendous bombardment straddling the Caen–Falaise highway ploughs a swath four thousand yards wide and six thousand yards deep. Every two minutes the guns lift two hundred yards. And the mediums are superimposed four hundred yards in depth.

Some 312 guns, including the heavies, will fire a twenty-minute intense bombardment on "known hostile batteries" an hour and forty minutes after H-hour, and then repeat this seven hours after H-hour.

Once the guns have completed the fire plan, they become available to respond to "concentrations on call," predetermined, code-named targets of possible trouble-spots along the ground over which the spearheads will pass on their way to their objectives.

When at last the barrage ends, and the noise drops to some distant rattles, pops, and burps here and there in the direction of glowing fires silhouetting Verrières Ridge, and the high-pitched whine of straining tank motors grows fainter and fainter, the whole front (at least from the perspective of the gunners) assumes an unreal calm unlike anything experienced before in Normandy. For the first time you actually feel the front receding into the distance.

Whether the German guns have been destroyed by the bombs, or are confused by the breakthrough and are scrambling to pull back, or are simply overwhelmed by the number of targets presented by the assaulting columns, they are inactive as far as the gun lines around here are concerned.

For the present there is nothing to do, which offers a glorious opportunity to catch up on sack time. But no one wants to sleep; all are too keyed up, their nervous systems still pulsing and agitated by the hammering roar of the colossal air and ground bombardment just ended. Everyone is hungry for some word as to what is happening up forward, but there are no sit reps coming back from the FOOs. Radio silence has been imposed on them until they are on their objectives, or until dawn, whichever comes first, so as to reduce radio interference with the radio directional beams guiding the columns.

Still, the gunners gather in little groups around the troop command posts to talk and speculate on what may be happening to 4th Brigade and their friends from 4th Field moving with them.

While the fantastic fury of the bombing and the gun barrage, which lit the sky for miles, all the way back to Caen, encouraged optimism that a break-out might occur this time, few are really confident that this won't be just another bloodletting for modest gains.

"Monty's Moonlight" is working well – at least here at the guns. The steady beams of the searchlights, disappearing far away in the smoke and dust on the horizon, light the gun positions brightly enough to read by. To prove it, someone from the command post produces the list of code names for the attack that uses the names of seventy-seven film stars, to cover the startline (Crawford), boundaries (Barrymore and Flynn), report lines (MacDonald, Laughton, Dressler, Valentino, Henie, and Lombard), and all the woods, high points, towns, and villages all the way to Falaise. And for a while those gathered at the command post amuse themselves discovering what Hollywood personalities have been attached to what: Verrières (Marx), Rocquancourt (Pluto), May-sur-Orne (Allen), Bretteville-sur-Laize (Faye), Falaise (Donald Duck).

And all night the red, jewel-like tracers on the 40-mm Bofors ack-ack shells – fired in groups of six every four minutes – sail gracefully in silent arcs across the sky overhead, resembling fantasy necklaces, following the curvature of the earth to oblivion.

Shortly after sunrise, concentrations are called for on behalf of the walking battalions attempting to clear the villages bypassed by the mobile columns immediately beyond the Verrières Ridge. For a while the fighting up at May-sur-Orne and on the left at Tilly-la-Campagne is so sustained you wonder if anything of consequence was accomplished by all that effort last night. When several open-topped half-tracks come back this way, packed with prisoners for deposit in a barbed-wire compound just behind Ifs – the first time anything like this has been seen in this sector of Normandy – you are encouraged to conclude the attack was truly a success.

However, what went on during the night in those undulating fields along the Caen–Falaise highway in the direction of Point 122 and Gaumesnil will remain a mystery until there are reunions with carrier and battery commander crews.

"King" or "Royal" Tiger tank abandoned near Vimoutiers. (Author's photo)

Firefly tank – a Sherman with a British 17-pounder gun.
(DND, National Archives of Canada, PA-37171)

St. Martin-de-Fontenay, looking north towards Hill 67. (G. Kenneth Bell, DND, National Archives of Canada, PA-145562)

Tilly-la-Campagne after endless Canadian infantry attacks that failed to gain a foothold against fanatical resistance by 1st SS Adolph Hitler Liebstandarte division. (courtesy Jean-Pierre Benamou, curator Bayeaux Memorial Museum)

The inferno created by RAF heavy bombers opening 1st Canadian Army drive to Falaise. (National Archives of Canada, PMR-82060)

Flaming crests on the road to Falaise. (G. Kenneth Bell, DND, National Archives of Canada, PA-132963)

The RAF bombing short at Hautmesnil quarry. (National Archives of Canada, PA-132825)

A Nebelwerfer or "Moaning Minnie." (Imperial War Museum, B7785)

The road ahead – always forbidding. (National Archives of Canada, PA-131344)

The guns passing through Falaise. (G. Kenneth Bell, DND, National Archives of Canada, PA-145557)

The main square after the battle for Falaise. (National Archives of Canada, PA-116503)

German column caught by the "Tiffies" as it tried to flee the Falaise Pocket. (Imperial War Museum, CL909)

The remnants of more than two thousand German vehicles on the west bank of the Seine at Rouen. They were smashed by Allied aircraft and artillery before they could be rafted across. (Canadian Army Overseas Photo, National Archives of Canada, 39642-N)

Fortified houses covering Blue Beach and the defile leading up to Puys, north of Dieppe. (Canadian Army Overseas Photo, National Archives of Canada, PA-60391)

45

PATTING A PANTHER IN THE DARK

———————————————— ✳ ————————————————

ACTUALLY, NO ONE SEES VERY MUCH DURING THAT WILD DRIVE — wild not because it is fast, for much of the night most of the columns seem to be sitting still or barely crawling along, but wild as a hurricane or an inferno is wild, with dust and flame and flashing, thundering bombs and shells penetrating over the roar of hundreds of straining engines in tanks and troop carriers massed on all sides as they move forward.

Dense dust clouds are raised by the bombing and the rolling gun barrage, blasting the earth just in advance of the "flails" beating the same trembling earth, followed by the churning tracks of hundreds of tanks, troop carriers, FOO carriers and half-tracks tearing up the dirt as they play follow-the-leader over tinder-dry wheat fields. These impenetrable clouds, combined with smoke shells fired by the enemy to thicken up the ground mists already forming in the valleys, completely frustrate the efforts of searchlights to illuminate the battlefield in a useful way, at least in the early stages of the assault.

Navigators and drivers are so blinded and bewildered by the dust and smoke that each is reduced to trying to follow the dim taillight on the vehicle ahead. Though as time goes on the arrows of ack-ack tracers are a help in pulling them back into the right general direction, the armoured columns frequently shift to the right and left, and in the process disintegrate and reform, and not always with the same battalion column.

Diversions begin in earnest once the surviving German gunners recover enough to start brewing up the odd leading tank or vehicle. Using the flaming wreck as a reference point, they spray the area with mortars and small-arms fire, and hole, with 88-mm solid-shot, any other vehicle that shows up in silhouette as it tries to move past.

And the progress of the British columns east of the Caen–Falaise highway is equally slow, involving many collisions. Some vehicles straying from their course attract the fire of their friends, while others run into strong points they are meant to avoid. Within the first mile, three navigating tanks are ditched in bomb craters, and in trying to avoid these the advancing column loses direction and cohesion.

The commander of a British column will later report: "... chaos indescribable ... the blind leading the blind." A semblance of order is restored when officers dismount and lead small groups of tanks on foot, while the CO fires Very lights to show the way.*

Under such conditions, all sense of dash disappears from the attack, but they all go forward in the right direction. As do the Canadian columns over on the right of the highway, where similar conditions prevail and one column is temporarily halted and others forced into wide detours.

The RHLI columns, instead of passing to the right of Rocquancourt, as they are supposed to, are diverted by an active 88-mm that starts knocking out tanks and half-tracks in the Essex Scottish column on their right flank, first by random fire into clouds of dust and then by the light of the burning vehicles. This forces the Essex column to split up in confusion, and to escape a similar fate, the Rileys edge to the left and find themselves eventually in close-packed columns among the cobbled streets and lanes of

---

*   Quoted in Chester Wilmot, *The Struggle for Europe* (London: Collins, 1952), p. 412.

Rocquancourt, pulling along with them B Company of the Royal Regiment, at that moment straying from their own battalion axis left of the village.

At this point in the strange affairs of the night, 4th Field FOO Capt. Len Harvey finds he is out of contact with the Royals' B Company, which his carrier has been following, and that now, he and his crew are quite alone, passing in their carrier along the blackness of a narrow village street. Suddenly Harvey sees a wall looming up on his left – so close, the side of the carrier is about to scrape it. He yells at Ryckman, his driver, "Keep right! Keep right!" When Ryckman protests that the carrier can't be scraping the wall on the left as it is already scraping the wall on the right, Harvey puts out his hand to be sure, and feels not cold rough stone, but warm smooth metal, vibrating under his hand! As he passes his hand over the metal and peers intently through the gloom to try to distinguish what it is, a brief flicker of light from an airburst or a wavering beam of artificial moonlight momentarily penetrates the dust cloud. His heart almost stops! He is patting a German hash-mark cross on the side of a tank! Fortunately, the occupants of the Panther, which is just sitting there with its engine running, are as confused as everybody else as to who is friend and who is foe, and Ryckman is able to guide the carrier past without scraping and slink off undetected into the swirling dust and smoke of the flashing, roaring night.

The confusion of the Germans is matched by that in the Essex Scottish columns as most of their armoured personnel carriers become separated from their leading company and the tanks they are following. For a time the ensuing chaos is horrendous, as official historians will later describe:

Some of their half-tracks and tanks were hit and burst into flames. Other vehicles turned, or backed, or collided with those behind, throwing the column into disorder, which increased as vehicles straying from other columns tried to join company. A platoon sent to deal with an 88-mm gun was driven off by machine-gun fire. By this time their commanding officer was missing, and Major Burgess, 2nd-in-Command, ordered the infantry to get out of their vehicles, deploy and dig in while the column was reformed. This was reported to Brigade at 0357 hrs.*

Attached to the Essex Scottish this night is another 4th Field FOO, Sammy Grange, of Fox Troop. He is riding, not in his carrier like Harvey, but in a tank supplied by 2nd Armoured Brigade at the rear of their column of tanks, immediately ahead of the infantry in their armoured personnel carriers. His tank is a dummy, designed not to fight, but to carry an artillery observer. Apart from its fake gun, however, it is a regular Sherman, indistinguishable from the other tanks in the squadron leading it. This will have significant bearing on the course of events for A Company of the Essex and for Capt. Grange during a bewildering, agonizing night, when it appears to him that he has led an entire infantry battalion astray.

By the time we are told about "Totalize," I am pretty jaded about war. I am convinced that death is inevitable – that it is only a matter of time. So on hearing about this great attack we are to make, I say to MacGregor Young, "Do you think there's any chance of success?"

He is shocked that I feel so gloomy about it. But that is the way I feel. Every time anyone has tried to go through here they got a bloody nose. Why should this be any different?

And that is what I am thinking as we take off – again in a tank – at the end of a column of tanks leading the armoured infantry carriers. We trundle over Verrières Ridge and down towards Rocquancourt, which we are to bypass on the right and carry on, following our tanks guided by white tapes the engineers are

---

* Page 25, Report No. 65, Historical Section (G.S.) Canadian Army Headquarters, Dept. of National Defence, Dec, 23, 1953.

laying down up ahead. But in the dust, the other tanks get away out of sight, and I am lost.

Of course I carry on, but go the wrong way. And then to my horror I find all the infantry Kangaroos and armoured carriers following me. We all end up in Rocquancourt. Fortunately the village is in the process of being abandoned (or at least that is how it seems to me), with them going out the back way as we are coming in the front, probably believing they are surrounded from the great numbers of people passing by them. Anyway, where I am, there is really no fuss. In fact I am surprised at how little opposition there is. Some shots are fired, but none from my tank I can tell you. And after it's all over, I find my tank is the only one there – all the others have gone to the right place. On top of everything, my tank is just a dummy – its gun couldn't fire anything! Then, when dawn comes, I discover huge quantities of infantry have followed me instead of the right people.*

So when later I get a call to go and see Bill Carr, my battery commander, I think, This is it! I'm going to be court-martialled and I deserve it. There is absolutely no defence I can offer. I just wasn't paying attention when I got lost. But when I get to see him, he says, "I just want to tell you, the infantry have asked me to commend you. You were the only tank that stayed with them – the rest buggered off!"

Vastly relieved, I don't tell him the truth that I led them astray. Nor do I reveal to the Essex that my tank, whose imposing presence had given them such comfort, had only a rubber gun.†

All those going forward in the bodies of Kangaroos – surrounded by a wall of steel, clouds of dust, and stunning noise –

---

* Some of the "huge quantities of infantry" may have been members of the South Saskatchewan Regiment, which suffered fifty casualties clearing the village that morning.
† Author interview.

are completely dependent on the drivers getting them where they are supposed to go, for they can see nothing but the flashing shells of the stormy barrage they follow for six kilometres. Gunner Turner, Major Wren's Don R, who on the Major's orders has tied his motorbike on the front of the scout car and climbed inside, sees even less, for he is forced to lie prone on top of equipment piled up under the canvas roof. While the position offers little protection, it still is preferable to riding his old Norton in the choking dust amidst the crush of tanks and vehicles pressing forward in roaring confusion.

Moving with one of the three companies of Royals that have been able to follow the leader and arrive in good order at their dispersal point before all other battalions in the attack, is Baker Troop FOO Bill Waddell. Just before first light, the Royals' column is halted to allow the company commanders to confer.

By now the effects of the spine-stiffening, pre-attack rum ration, and the excitement that helped sustain everybody during the initial charge through the enemy's forward lines, have faded – replaced by a growing sense of vulnerability as they peer about in the sinister, dark silence and reflect on how deep they are in enemy territory. They have no idea where the Jerries are or what may happen when dawn arrives.

Still, the Royals and their arty reps know where they are on the map, and so far have the advantage of surprise over the enemy. Since it will soon be light, Col. Anderson decides that A Company should move as fast as possible onto its given objective, D will take the objective formerly allotted to B (the missing company), and C will move up in reserve. And in spite of some enemy shelling and small-arms fire, the intrepid drivers of the Kangaroos take the three companies right up onto their objective on Hill 122, where they pile out and move into tactical positions best suited to defend this dominating feature.

By 6:00 A.M. the other battalions are still not on their objectives, and there is no sign yet of the 51st Highland Division, though there is now considerable evidence of unsubdued enemy troops in the area.

The first enemy attack develops at 8:30 A.M., when two Panther and two Tiger tanks move up the Caen–Falaise highway, and another group of them on the far side of Cramesnil opens fire. Firing heavily, several actually penetrate to within a few yards of the Royals' tac headquarters, which is on the east side of the road.

On the west side is the Royals' mortar platoon, along with some carriers and medium machine guns of the Toronto Scottish. All are still digging in when, suddenly, screeching, armour-piercing shots begin hitting the Toronto Scottish carriers. Then one after another the Royals' mortar platoon carriers are hit. As the carriers take fire, mortar bombs begin to blow up and the Germans spray the area with machine guns. The Tor Scots lose all their carriers and medium machine guns, and all seven of the Royals' carriers, along with all their mortars and ammunition, are destroyed.

In the midst of this threatening uproar, which grows more dangerous by the minute, Bill Waddell, the 4th Field FOO with the leading company, pinpoints the location of the German tanks and goes back on foot to lead up a troop of Sherbrooke Fusiliers tanks into position where they can get clear shots at them. And when he gets them close enough to be effective he directs their fire, knocking out at least four.*

Major Ralph Young, second-in-command of the Royals, an eyewitness to Waddell's heroism, will have difficulty later (even forty years later) finding words to describe it: "This guy is standing out in the open, all by his bloody self, pointing out a German tank here, another there, yelling at our tanks, 'Hit the goddam thing!' or words to that effect. Those are his fire orders. Oh yes . . . incredible! With him pointing and the tanks shooting, they knock out three, maybe

---

* Capt. William James Waddell was subsequently awarded the Military Cross.

four, of them – one or two self-propelled guns, and a couple of tanks. Oh, I remember Waddell! He doesn't last long after that, as I recall."*

By noon the RHLI are dug in close to their objective on the right, the Essex Scottish are in the process of occupying Caillouet, and east of the highway elements of British 154th Brigade have come up. At 2:00 P.M. the Royals push on another 1,700 yards to Gaumesnil, where they find Sherbrooke tanks awaiting them. They now are seven kilometres south of their startline at Verrières, at the head of what clearly is a massive breakthrough, and their casualties have been extremely light; only four killed and thirty-four wounded, clear vindication of Simonds' innovative attack, particularly his improvised armoured troop-carriers.†

---

*   Author interview.
†   German Field Marshal von Kluge reported "a breakthrough has occurred south of Caen the like of which we have never seen." And after the war the commanding general of 12th SS Division, Kurt Meyer, described how he, in the early hours of August 8, stopped the rout of his troops down the road to Falaise before the thundering barrage and the growling tank columns – the first German troops he had ever seen running away in panic. Placing himself in the middle of the road and lighting a cigar, he inquired of the sheepish men if they were going to leave him there alone to fight the enemy – even as his own legs were shaking and he was bathed in cold sweat. In the morning he sent a tank force up the road from Falaise to wipe out the spearhead before it could consolidate. There they met up with 4th Field's Waddell and the squadron of Sherbrooke Fusiliers tanks commanded by Major S. V. "Woppy" Radley-Walters. Among the dead left about Hill 122 was a Captain Michael Wittman, Germany's foremost tank commander, celebrated on the Russian front as the most successful panzer ace of the war, with a record of 117 tanks before he was posted to Normandy to continue his cavalier ways. At Villers Bocage (west of Hill 112) on June 13, using a Tiger, he destroyed five Cromwells, two Fireflies, and the half-tracks of an entire motorized rifle company of the 4th County of London Yeomanry. British writers attribute the demise of Wittman's last Tiger to Shermans of the Northhamptonshire Yeomanry.

46

WHEN THE DUST SETTLES
THEY ARE WAITING

———————— ✳ ————————

TO NO ONE'S SURPRISE, RESISTANCE TO THE WALKING TROOPS exists in every village bypassed by the mobile columns, but most particularly in Tilly-la-Campagne and May-sur-Orne, and throughout the morning the guns take part in divisional fire tasks. (During one of these, Sgt. "Lefty" Phillips asks Troop Leader Grout to time his gun crew with a stopwatch. They succeed in getting off an astounding seventeen rounds in one minute.)

The dust confronting the walking troops of 5th and 6th Brigades, who were withdrawn one thousand yards for safety at the outset of the RAF bombing, is horrendous as they move up to their startlines. Sent roiling by the bombs hundreds of feet in the air over the dark battlefield, and fed by the creeping barrage and the churning tracks of vast herds of vehicles, the dust is impenetrable. And so it remains for what "seems like hours" to Capt. J. E. "Elmo" Thibault, of the FMRs, leading his men up to a startline in the south end of St. Martin-de-Fontenay, near the church and the house. From here Thibault's D company and Acting-Major Brégent's B Company will go forth to clear May-sur-Orne.

Waiting for the dust to clear enough to see where they are going, the FMRs are very conscious they are about to cross fields where the Calgarys were shattered, the Black Watch virtually wiped out, and the Maisies severely mauled two weeks ago. Capt. Thibault mulls

over a question that will haunt him the rest of his life: In the preparations for Totalize, why weren't the mine tunnels taken care of? By
now all know of the network of tunnels under the field (some
1,200 feet deep, offering incomparable shelter from shells and
bombs) and are aware that the air shafts allow the Germans to reoc-
cupy positions from which they were driven. Why haven't suitable
measures been taken to eliminate them?

When the dust settles, the Germans are ready and waiting (just as
they were for the Black Watch and the Maisies), having arisen
unscathed from their underground labyrinth and reoccupied their
old positions, including the minehead building from whence the
shot comes that kills Acting-Major Georges Brégent whose
company is passing that way.

Not until after daylight – when the Crocodiles (flame-throwing
Churchill tanks) dragging immense supplies of fuel in trailers
behind them, are brought up to disgorge, with horrible, roaring
blasts, huge balls of liquid fire across that dilapidated minehead
structure and many other known and suspected enemy positions –
do the FMRs make headway. Then it becomes "a walk-in."

At 1:00 P.M., an hour before 4th Canadian Armoured Division and
the Polish Armoured Division are to take off on follow-through
attacks exploiting the break-out, the first of five hundred heavy
bombers of U.S.A. 8th Airforce begin to drop 1,500 tons of bombs
beyond the now distant spearheads on potential trouble spots,
including Bretteville-sur-Laize.

After last night's spectacular RAF show by twice as many
bombers (1,020), dropping more than double the weight (3,500
tons), right out in front, no one shows much interest. Until suddenly bombs start tumbling down from a low-flying Liberator
back near Caen. Everyone stares in disbelief as, one after another,
twenty-four U.S. Liberators and Flying Fortresses, the sun glinting off their silver bodies, drop bombs on the mediums deployed
around Colombelles, at least 1,500 metres back of here, and on

Faubourg-de-Vaucelles, where 3rd Division is also concentrating for their move up.

It's all over in a matter of minutes, but an immense dust cloud is left drifting, and among the rising pillars of black smoke there are sporadic, muffled explosions and the faint, hoarse cries of desperate men.

What a terribly demoralizing experience for divisions preparing to enter battle, the two armoured divisions for the first time! Sgt. Howard Hill asks the question that is on everybody's mind: How in God's name could that have happened? Only last night in the pitch dark, the RAF bombed so close they had to issue our infantry earplugs, but not one bomb fell short. Now, in broad daylight, the Yanks drop their loads ten miles behind where they are supposed to!

Just how many casualties were suffered back there no one can learn, for all ranks are confined to their own areas, and the brass are not anxious to spread bad news and evoke despair. But rumours of awful carnage begin to circulate – even the 3rd Division commander, they say.*

---

*   North Shore Regiment alone lost one hundred officers and men to the bombs. Many at 3rd Division Headquarters were wounded, including the division commander, Maj.-Gen. Keller. Of the 65 killed and 250 wounded among the Canadians and the Poles, a very high percentage were artillerymen – 44 killed and 137 wounded. Fourth Medium, waiting on wheels to move, had 12 killed and 28 wounded, as eight guns and five tractors were destroyed; 7th Medium, firing on a target at the time the American bombs tumbled down on them, destroying three guns, had 11 gunners killed and 18 wounded; 2nd Counter-Battery had three killed; 2nd Survey Regiment, 13 killed and 20 wounded; 8th Light Ack-Ack, four killed and 49 wounded; 3rd Light Ack-Ack, three killed; and 3rd Division Artillery HQ, four killed and two wounded, and all their vehicles destroyed. From Col. G. W. L. Nicolson, CD, *The Gunners of Canada, Volume II, 1919-1967* (Toronto: McClelland and Stewart, 1972), p. 318.

47

VERRIÈRES

--- ✳ ---

WAITING FOR THE GUNS TO COME UP TO THE NEW POSITION JUST to the left of the smashed village of Verrières, you wander alone among slit trenches of the recently vacated infantry position. Here and there in the wheat and sandy holes lie crumpled sacks of battledress which a few days ago were men. You pause beside the body of a captain, lying face down, half out of a slit trench, his head resting on one arm as though asleep. Curious as to whether he was RHLI, Essex Scottish, or Royal Regiment, you bend down and read his shoulder flash: 4 RCA. With a shock you realize you have stumbled onto the spot where quiet, gentle Jack Thompson died. He was one of the very few chosen for long-service leave just before D-Day, and you recall how eagerly you questioned him when he got back to England. What was it like for a man to return to his wife after many years of separation? "Incredibly beautiful," he said reverently, and his eyes glowed with the memory. But then he frowned and added, "But I don't know whether these leaves are good or not — you see, I left my wife pregnant."

As you turn away from the sad remains of this kind man, you wonder if your eyes are wet for Jack's baby, who will never see her father, or for your own little girl, whom you've never seen.

On your way back to where you planted the four banderoles to show where your four guns are to be placed — in the lee of a row of scrubby trees, not much more than bushes, running across the front of your position – half a dozen Sherman tanks come roaring back over the crest, down through a gap in your bushes, passing between the markers for Number One and Number Two guns, and continuing on back towards Ifs, following a track across the wheat fields.

Their passage worries you. Obviously this is a favourite tank route – the depth of the single tank track already worn across the parched field plainly tells you that. You have laid out a gun position directly across an "elephant walk." The image of a herd of clanking monsters, half-blinded by dust, ploughing through your position flashes through your mind. The risk is only too real. Still, you hate to move your markers. If you shift them enough to get rid of the problem, two of the guns will be out beyond the hedgerow and in view of a distant ridge, the occupancy of which you are uncertain. While you are still pondering the problem, another group of tanks (having replenished their fuel and ammunition) come roaring up from Ifs, following their preferred route.

Desperate for advice on how you might divert tanks from using this route between your guns, you try waving one down. To your surprise the first one stops. By yelling strenuously you're able to communicate your problem to the tank commander, who's standing in the open hatch.

The solution, he tells you, is quite simple. Erect any kind of barricade, regardless how flimsy, around your position and the tanks will respect it. Once the new diversion is marked by a few tanks, the barricade will no longer be necessary. Tanks meticulously follow a well-established track because of their fear of mines. Show him where you want them to go and he'll start the new track.

You lead him around the right end of the bushes, and the others follow him as he cuts back onto the track leading up and over the crest.

From then until the guns arrive just after dark, you tug and pull bits and pieces of old farm machinery into place along the back and front of the position – shafts off a broken cart, a relatively whole high-wheeled hayrake, a couple of barrels on which poles can be laid – anything you can find around the nearby farm that can be moved by one man. When finished, your barricade doesn't look like much, but it proves effective when a convoy of half-tracks come back over the ridge. Without hesitation they swing west, around the end of your position, and curl back behind you to take up the track again to Ifs, like the tanks that pioneered the bypass.

The first couple of half-tracks pass without incident, but then *pow* – a mine explodes under the right front wheel of one, just as it is passing around the end of your position. A soldier tumbles out onto the ground beside the smashed wheel, collapses face down, and doesn't move again. The drivers of the two half-tracks following stop and are examining him as you come up. Their verdict: Dead. Quietly they return to their vehicles and continue on to Ifs, leaving their dead comrade lying beside his disabled half-track.

Though it is dark when the guns arrive, Monty's Moonlight is again in vogue, and it helps facilitate deployment. But after the quads have wheeled about in their normal fashion, dropping guns and trailers, and have left for their wagon lines, a string of Hawkins anti-personnel mines, of the kind used by infantry to secure their positions, is discovered lying in the grass right across where guns and quads have just passed and repassed. Bdr. Don Finnie spotted what he thought was a signal wire, and when he tried to shift it so it wouldn't get sliced by a jabbing spade, up popped the mines, bobbing at intervals along the wire's length and recognizable as khaki-painted Johnson Wax tins, loaded with explosive, carrying TNT detonators in saddles soldered on the front of each tin.

How all those wheels and feet thrashing about here just now were able to miss all those mines is inexplicable, and provides fodder for discussion as the digging of gun pits and ammo pits begins.

It's a good thing the guns are not required to fire anything of consequence during the night, for the reserve regiments of 4th

Armoured Division move up past the position raising dust clouds so dense that gunlayers cannot see lighted aiming posts beyond ten yards. Even in the command post – constructed by turning a huge, round, cast-iron watering trough upside down over a normal command post trench – the dust is so bad you can hardly see the artillery board. How many tanks and vehicles pass, you do not know, but for more than an hour tanks, carriers, and armoured cars play follow-the-leader around your bypass before the dust is allowed to settle.*

Then, just as you are breathing a sigh of relief, as well as some dust-free air, and visiting the half-finished gun pits the men have been digging as the dust clouds rolled over them, your attention is drawn to two exceedingly bright lights – as bright as a pair of prewar American car headlights, coming from the direction of Ifs. At first you think they belong to some sort of heavy-equipment mover, for, though you can hear its diesel straining for power, it is moving at a snail's pace. But when finally it arrives, the vehicle turns out to be just an armoured bulldozer engaged in removing the soft topsoil from the track worn by the tanks, preparing a road to be used as a supply route from Caen to God-knows-where.

The problem is, the dozer operator is following orders given him by one who clearly is imbued with the Roman road-building principle of proceeding in a straight line come hell, high water, or 25-pounders. Nothing short of shooting him dead will divert him, and while this is tempting, it probably wouldn't be seen as justifiable by a court of inquiry. So gunners with poles hold Tannoy wires high overhead as he passes under them, and you stand waving a lamp-electric on the parapet of Number Two gun pit to ensure he doesn't fill it with earth.

At dawn, fighting the nausea you've come to associate with

---

* Some eighty tanks of the Governor General Footguards and eighty-four armoured carriers and half-tracks of the Lincoln and Welland Regiment, as well as dozens of support vehicles.

extreme fatigue (more pronounced than usual from eating dust all night) you can't face a breakfast of M & V. And when Hiltz suggests there may be something interesting to be found among the victuals left behind in the disabled half-track abandoned so summarily yesterday, you jump at the idea. But before you get to look inside the vehicle, you and he come upon what is left of the body of the poor man you saw fall dead here yesterday. It lies directly across what became during the night the path of hundreds of 4th Armoured Division tanks and vehicles. You and Hiltz return to the troop command post, empty-handed and retching.

48

FOOTSLOGGERS OFFER A
HUMBLING TRIBUTE

FROM THE MORNING OF AUGUST 9, UNTIL THE REGIMENT LEAVES for a new position, the guns are silent. The calm produces a strange feeling after all that has gone on here on Verrières Ridge since it first became a concern of the guns way back at Louvigny at dawn on July 19, at the start of three grim weeks of bloody battles of attrition.

Still, the gunners will leave here with a sense of satisfaction, knowing all German attacks (and there were so many that brigades lost count) were shattered largely by concentrations laid down by the guns. Of this all ranks were aware, even as the struggles ebbed and flowed, simply by following the pattern and intensity of the fire requested. And the gunners recognize (though Intelligence won't confirm it for some time) that even the most fanatical German soldiers are showing a reluctance to attack in daylight when they know each attempt will be met with an instantaneous deluge of high explosive produced by Mike, Uncle, and Victor targets. Any remaining enthusiasm of the elite SS for launching attacks must surely have died during the last days of July on the slopes about here under gunfire of an intensity exceeding anything they had experienced before, according to statements volunteered by prisoners.*

---

* A July report by 2nd SS Panzer Division opposite the Canadians east of the Orne confirms this: "The incredibly heavy artillery and mortar

The ability of field artillery reps attached to the infantry (even the FOOs at the company level) to concentrate on a single target all the guns of a regiment, a division, or a corps, or even all the guns of the entire army, within a few minutes, has led to widespread belief among the German rank and file that 25-pounders are hopper-fed.

Prisoners, taken in the first hours of the breakthrough and brought back to the prisoners-of-war compound at Ifs, asked to see "your supergun – the automatic 25-pounder." These included two prisoners who were being used to raise buckets of water by windlass from an exceedingly deep well, at a house near your guns, to fill an endless line of water cans for their fellow prisoners behind the barbed wire. When they were told that 25-pounders must be loaded one round at a time, they merely smirked in disbelief, nodding their heads in a knowing fashion, as though to say of course we know you have to lie for security reasons.

This is understandable. Never having encountered on the Russian front anything like the ad lib concentrations of Mike, Uncle, and Victor targets, whose fury can erupt about them without warning, like spontaneous combustion, they have to have

---

fire of the enemy is something new for the seasoned veterans as much as for new arrivals from the reinforcement units. The assembly of troops is spotted immediately by enemy reconnaissance aircraft and smashed by bombs and artillery directed from the air; and if nevertheless the attacking troops go forward, they become involved in such dense artillery and mortar fire that heavy casualties ensue and the attack peters out within the first few hundred metres. Losses by the infantry are then so heavy that the impetus necessary to renew the attack is spent. Our troops enter battle in low spirits at the thought of the enemy's enormous superiority of *matériel*. The feeling of helplessness against enemy aircraft operating without hindrance has a paralysing effect; and during the barrage the effect on the inexperienced men is literally soul-shattering. The best results have been obtained by platoon and section commanders leaping forward uttering a good old-fashioned yell. We've also revived the practice of bugle calls." (WO219/1908 British Imperial War Museum.)

some explanation. And since their own artillery has never seen fit to develop a system capable of rapid concentration of great numbers of guns on a single target, they suspect a super weapon, not a superior system of fire control providing the effect of a giant machine gun beating a zone.

The idea of a supergun comes easily to a people nurtured in the Krupp tradition.* It's hard for them to entertain the possibility that the superiority of British and Commonwealth field artillery is traceable to the speed and accuracy of their surveys — linking every troop of every artillery regiment with every troop in every other field regiment in the theatre of operations in total accuracy — so that a FOO can call down instantly on a target of his choosing one troop or all of them, as required.†

Unquestionably the Germans were prevented from breaking through to Ifs, and perhaps beyond to Caen, by the awesome concentrations fired by both field and medium regiments, but most particularly by the 25-pounders of 2nd Division, responding with extraordinary scales of fire that sometimes overlapped on Mike and Uncle targets, occasionally combining with the guns of 3rd and 4th

---

* Krupp's superior steel and design (first rifled guns and breechloaders) were directly responsible for Germany's fragmented states becoming a united country that defeated France in 1870. Henceforth Krupp's guns were considered the key to victory.

† Non-gunner Lt.-Gen. Sir Brian Horrocks, in a postwar book *Corps Commander*, wrote: "The core of the Royal Artillery was the fantastic accuracy of their Survey Units. . . . Neither the Germans nor the Russians, nor the French, who were always supposed to be the masters of artillery fire systems, could approach the accuracy or the weight of concentrated fire power which . . . I had at my disposal. If a target was sufficiently important to warrant all or most of Corps artillery to be fired . . . in a matter of minutes, about 400 guns could be brought into action where I wanted them . . . made possible by good surveying, good communications and a high degree of flexibility at the guns." Sir Brian Horrocks, Eversley Belfield, and Maj.-Gen. H. Essame, *Corps Commander* (Toronto: Griffin House), p. 177.

divisions on Victor targets. And at the most desperate moments, FOOs even pulled down fire from their own guns on their OP positions to flush out Germans swarming over the infantry they were supporting.

No senior officer or instructor during the years of training in England, including the walking-encyclopedias of gunnery, the Instructors in Gunnery of Larkhill and Senneybridge, ever once gave the slightest indication they knew, or even suspected, the terribly persuasive fire-power placed in the hands of FOOs by the invention of Mike, Uncle, and Victor targets.

In an OP in normal circumstances, when the rumble of neighbouring artillery or local enemy activity is not interfering with your hearing, there's a familiar sequence of sounds through which you follow your shells onto target. First comes a distant, faint thumping somewhere back behind you, then nothing for a few seconds. Suddenly overhead there's a sinister sizzling and crackling, followed by an abrupt, split-second silence, then a fury of cataclasmic flashes erupting in the target area amidst violent black puffs of smoke and dirt. This rapidly builds without pause into a hellish cauldron that gives off the reverberating roar of the wicked, overlapping thunderclaps that only 25-pounder shells pelting a Mike target can create.

Horrifying enough when viewed from a distance of three or four hundred yards, but until you have lived through the terrible screams of 25-pounder shells arriving on target, and experienced the distinctive, jolting whacks of their explosions around you, it is impossible to conceive of the full horror of a Mike Target to which attacking Germans are subjected again and again on a regular basis.

In the sweltering, dispiriting, dusty heat of the late afternoon of August 10, the Regiment is ordered to move south from Verrières about eight miles as the crow flies, to a new position a mile and three-quarters northwest of Bretteville-sur-Laize. Following the now well-established procedure designed to provide continuous support for the infantry, 2nd Battery leads off at 6:00 P.M., with the other two batteries following at one-hour intervals.

And you leave not an hour too soon, for the neighbourhood is changing rapidly, and not for the better. When ex-gunner Lt.-Gen. Simonds' 2nd Corps Headquarters settled in close by, 14th Battery was told to move its noisy guns a few hundred yards to the left rear. While unflattering opinions of the delicate sensitivity of high-level ears were expressed abundantly in tones loud and clear by gunners and officers alike, they promptly complied with the request. (In sharp contrast, you would later learn, to the reaction of a platoon of the FMRs when asked by an advance man of 2nd Corps to give up the only reasonably intact large house in May-sur-Orne, which they'd chosen as their bivouac after the war moved on from that godforsaken village. That they were in the midst of their first civilized meal since coming to Normandy – combining freshly fried chicken and champagne from the cool cellar – may have had something to do with their total lack of cooperation. When Lieut. Noel Meilleur inquired of the staff major if he was carrying a weapon, and the haughty man replied, "Of course!" he was quietly advised: "Well, you'd better be prepared to use it, for the only way you're going to take over this house is to fight for it the same as we did.")

As your 2nd Battery convoy crosses along the ridge to move down the Caen–Falaise highway past burned-out and derelict Allied tanks and vehicles, through what was no-man's-land for more than eighteen days, you are struck by the number of unburied German dead strewn across the shell-blasted fields, their upturned faces blackened by the sun and bloated by the torrid heat – many of them, unquestionably, the victims of the guns now rolling along behind you.

And for the first time you see disabled German tanks in numbers, some with their turrets blown right off and lying upside down on the ground, providing mute testimony to the accuracy and blasting power of Typhoon rockets. How often during the past three weeks you watched them go into a vertical dive straight down through the black puffing flak, releasing their rockets with terrible, hair-raising *scrootch*es, before disappearing below this ridge. The earth-shaking explosions that followed produced the derelicts lying here.

Surely the Typhoon is proving to be the most effective weapon of all in combatting the superiority of the enemy's armour, particularly his irresistible Tigers. Without the Typhoons, the Allies might never have subdued his armoured divisions to the point where a break-out became possible. They must seriously inhibit, if not entirely prevent, all movement of his armour in daylight.

After you turn right, off the main road and onto less-travelled tracks, with fewer derelict vehicles around which to detour, you come upon more infantrymen trudging forward in single file along the side of the road. It's very hot and exceedingly dusty along these powdery tracks, and your heart goes out to those weary footsloggers.

Even moving slowly, your vehicles, guns, and limbers raise swirling clouds of dust that sift up into the cabs of the vehicles and drift over the sweating infantrymen plodding along right next to them. At one point you slow the convoy to a crawl as you pass a company of men who have been broken off to rest at the side of the road. Since they are sitting and lying along the top of the bank of the sunken roadway, they are almost eyeball-to-eyeball with the men riding in the trucks. What with the wretched dust raised by your trucks roiling up around them, and the fact that you are riding while they, the indisputable *crème de la crème* of all who wear the King's uniform, are forced to walk, loaded with packs and weapons and ammunition, makes you very self-conscious. You half-expect them to call out some derisive remark, as they used to in England when they saw the artillery riding by, and are totally unprepared for what one of them calls out: "Keep it up, fellows. You're doing fine!"

Then another voice pipes up, "Good show, Arty! Keep it up!"

And then one of them stands up and starts to clap, and the first thing you know, a lot of them are standing up and clapping too.

It's so entirely unexpected, you feel tears welling up in your eyes. You want to call back to them, Bless your dear generous hearts, we should be clapping you! But you don't, of course. You sit there embarrassed until you pass out of sight of all of them. Only then does your driver, Gunner Art Harder, show any sign he heard or saw anything unusual. He turns and, in a low voice, husky with emotion, says, "My God, did you see that? They were clapping us! The infantry – clapping us!"

And you know every man in every truck in the battery is feeling that way, for they have come to look with awe upon the infantry-man, fully aware of the appalling casualties all battalions of 2nd Division have suffered in the past month and the extraordinary depth of courage a man has to muster to keep going forward, when the best he can expect is a clean flesh wound to get him out of it.

Harder, who was slumping with fatigue and the effects of dysentery, which now afflicts a large proportion of the troop, is sitting bolt upright, with shoulders back and head held high, as he drives on at a lively clip now there are no marching troops along the road ahead.

49

EXCAVATING GUN PITS IN
SOLID CHALK

✳

THE NEW POSITION NORTHWEST OF BRETTEVILLE–SUR–LAIZE IS ON high land just off a road running along the left bank of the river. But to get there you have to pass through what remains of that poor village, which died under tons of bombs two days ago, on the first day of Totalize. After seeing Caen and village after village smashed to ruins, you should be getting used to it, but the desolation is so complete here, you experience fresh feelings of shock and regret. The huge bomb craters and the clutter of broken stone and rubble – requiring extensive shifting and filling by the engineers' bull-dozer crews, struggling to provide some kind of base for a vehicle route through the town – have obstructed the natural course of the river. The diverted water runs whichever way it can, forming great muddy pools and turning the newly formed road into a sludgy causeway.

As your vehicle bumps slowly through this melancholy place, you feel for the poor people who called it home, and who must soon return here to begin life again. Reddish muddy water flows through the tumbled stones and broken walls, and a sickly smell of charred wood fills the air. With relief, you leave it behind and start up a winding road with a sparkling, fast-flowing shallow stream on your left and lush greenery cascading down steep slopes on your right. And soon you are directed to turn right, up a chalky road to a gently sloping plateau, where the air is remarkably cool and fresh.

At first sight the stubble field high above the river promises to be by far the most pleasant gun position in France so far. Here is a beautiful landscape, untouched by war and free of that eternal layer of dust that coats everything in Normandy. The only hint of the furies existing elsewhere is some tangled webs of silver-backed, skinny strips of paper lying here and there on the field and drooping like Christmas decorations on nearby bushes and trees. These are the remains of a blizzard of foil (known as "window") dropped by Pathfinder planes to confuse enemy radar the other night when bombers were operating over Bretteville.

To the right, a ravine full of bushes runs down the steep hill to the Laize river babbling softly over rocks and sandbars. And over the river and up a slope, a wide sweep of forest extends right and left, all the way to the horizon. It's so remarkably quiet and peaceful. But the position loses all its charm once digging begins.

Little more than a foot below the surface is solid chalk. Every shovelful has to be picked loose, and the pick shows a nasty tendency to stick with a frustrating *thunk* in the damp chalk, resisting all but the most strenuous efforts to pull it out.

Dysentery is now rampant, and its debilitating effect doesn't help the pace of the digging, which becomes maddeningly slow as the hours pass. You were one of the first to be afflicted back at Fleury, and are pretty well over it, but it still saps your energy.

When, dripping with perspiration and ready to drop from fatigue, you notice that everything on the position has suddenly become visible in the misty, grey light that precedes the dawn, now appearing as the faintest glow on the eastern horizon, you declare the command post finished. It still isn't deep enough to provide proper headroom for a standing man when it's roofed over, but if everybody else feels as utterly done in as you, it will damn well have to do.

When you visit the gun detachments, half expecting to find they have given up long since, to your amazement you find they have picked and shovelled gun pits of respectable depth. Some are still working, surrounded by great, greyish-white rings of chalk chips, but they move as men completely worn out by their effort. No one wants to engage in any chit-chat this morning.

Shortly after sunrise, you take a phone call from RHQ requesting volunteers to go on a patrol over the river to winkle out a sniper, or a nest of snipers, periodically producing menacing *phut-phut* sounds across the gun positions.

In spite of everyone having been up all night and aching with fatigue from digging, there is no problem getting volunteers. But you accept only four, making sure to include the troop ack-ack Bren gunner, Fred Edwards, who with Bombardier Scott brought in those prisoners back at Fleury. You figure the smaller the group the better. If it's only one sniper, a few men stalking him as unobtrusively as possible would seem preferable. If it turns out to be a pocket of enemy with no intention of giving up, then no matter how large your patrol, it'll be in deep trouble. Gunners are not trained or mentally tuned to infantry work, and you've had a minimum of training in infantry tactics, consisting mainly of a little common-to-all-arms training while at Brockville Officers' Training Centre. According to the map, that forest over there, Forêt de Cinglais, stretches two miles along the river and runs southwest about four miles. Directly across the valley from the guns there's a cul-de-sac in the forest, about three hundred yards wide at the river, extending about seven hundred yards up the slope into the trees. The consensus at RHQ is that the sniper is up the hill in the trees, at the far end of the cul-de-sac.

Crossing the shallow stream on sandbanks and rocks, and leaving Edwards at the riverbank to provide covering fire with his Bren if required, you and one man go up through the fringe of the woods on the right-hand side of the open field, while the other two winkle up through the trees on the left.

Halfway up the hill you realize that the woods could be full of snipers and you'd never find one. Only a sniper who wanted to give up would give away his position to a patrol wandering around looking for him. And when you stop and listen in the utter stillness, it occurs to you that if there were anything more than a single sniper up here, they would by now have let fly at you, for your progress through the woods has hardly been silent. Convinced you'll find no Germans on your objective, you move along at a good clip for the last hundred yards, and fortunately, your hunch turns out to be correct.

But they were here very recently, in large numbers, well dug in and camouflaged. Just within the treeline there is a long string of trenches, each shored-up with logs.

How different it would have been if you'd tried coming up here yesterday. It's not something you care to think about. For a hundred yards or more along the edge of the forest there are slit trenches and log-covered dugouts strewn with bits and pieces of equipment, including gourd-shaped aluminum water-bottles covered with moulded and varnished wood veneer, and a splendid black leather case that could have held a valuable instrument of some kind.

These trenches have not long been abandoned – probably only last night. Everywhere there are items of partially eaten food that insects, birds, and animals have not yet got around to cleaning up. And the way the open tins and eating utensils lie about suggests the occupants of these trenches left in a great hurry in the middle of a meal. There are loaves of black rye bread, as heavy as lead, some partially consumed and some whole, showing no sign of mould, still fresh enough to eat. There's a jar of ersatz coffee, and in another trench you find a package of highly aromatic tobacco and a blue pack of French cigarettes with some still in it – precious items to any soldier, not likely to be left behind except when pulling out in an awful hurry.

Though your patrol returns without a sniper, it doesn't come back empty-handed. Everybody seems truly pleased you got back at all, and are very interested in the German things. Those who try the black bread with marge and marmalade declare it quite good, if a bit rubbery. But there's no enthusiasm whatsoever for the cigarettes and ersatz coffee.

There's been no call on the guns to fire today, and the exhausted gun crews have been able to get some sleep. And now that the sniper scare has been settled (at least to the satisfaction of 2nd Battery), many go down to the river to bathe themselves and do some washing.

Your priority is sleep. But before you can climb into GA and curl up around the gear shift (now your favourite place to sleep), your attention is drawn to a low-flying Typhoon coming back from a sortie over enemy territory with a faltering engine that roars for a moment then flutters out, roars up again and then cuts out, sinking lower all the time. Suddenly he fires a raucous, chattering burst of his cannons and machine guns, and for a moment you wonder what he's shooting at. But when he turns his plane over and he falls out, just as he's passing over the guns, you realize he was warning everybody below his plane must soon crash. A wisp of white cloth streams up from his falling body, and you hold your breath, waiting for his chute to open. It doesn't. He lands with a sickening thud just behind the position. His plane crashes with a roar just a bit farther on, sending a black pillar of smoke billowing skyward like a funeral pyre.

Everyone is filled with that mixture of horror and inner rage that prevails each time you are witness to a particularly outrageous aspect of the brutality of war. That poor young man, whose broken body lies out there in the field, was a complete stranger, but you feel you knew him, for he took the time to warn you that he had to abandon his plane. In that instant he established himself as a caring person and sealed a bond of human fellowship with everybody watching on the ground below.

It all seems so damnably unfair! The poor guy, struggling to bring his plane home, had made it to friendly territory only to have his chute fail to open because of the low altitude. If he had not wasted time and altitude by firing that warning burst, perhaps . . .

At 6:00 P.M., the Regiment begins a move of some nine kilometres southeast, to take over positions from 23rd Field of 4th Armoured Division in a great stone quarry near the village of Hautmesnil, just to the right of the Caen–Falaise highway. To ensure continuous support of the guns, the batteries are moved forward one at a time, at one-hour intervals, 26th Battery leading. The new positions are well-forward among the reserve infantry battalions of 4th Division. And just before you enter the new gun position, there's an ominous sign:

THIS ROAD IS UNDER OBSERVATION FROM 88S

When 2nd Battery – the last one to move up – arrives about 8:30 P.M., the self-propelled guns of the battery that you are supposed to be relieving are firing furiously, and you have to sit and wait.

In contrast to the last position – which seemed so remote from the conflict, with its river of clear water babbling through its verdant valley untouched by war – here, in this vast, barren, dusty quarry, amid these strange guns hammering away, there is again the smell of urgency. And you feel rising within you all those familiar tensions with which you've had to cope since coming to Normandy.

When the SPs finish firing, they don't move out as expected, but continue to sit in position. On inquiring, you learn that the order "Prepare for tanks" is now in effect, enemy tanks having been spotted roaming around out there beyond the railway embankment that lies just along the southwest fringe of the position.

It seems 8th Brigade, attempting to get the drive moving again today, has been bloodily repulsed by self-propelled 88s and tanks in-festing Quesnay Wood, a large forest of irregular shape (according to the map) about two kilometres wide and the same deep, lying astride, but mostly east of, the Caen–Falaise highway. While nothing develops locally, a tank battle does seem to be taking place on the distant height of land forward of the position, for a few high-velocity solid-shot scream overhead and thud nearby.

When the 23rd RCA gang finally does pull out, they leave behind two vehicles with wireless sets netted to two of their FOOs out ahead there somewhere with 10th Brigade, so that 4th Field guns may respond to any calls from them for fire, until their own guns are deployed in their new positions. This is most unusual, but seems to you an eminently sensible arrangement. Their FOOs, however, don't take advantage of it. Very soon one of them comes in, and the other remains out of communication until the two signal vehicles leave to catch up with their unit.

At last light you are told to make sure your guards are on the alert tonight. There's a possibility that, with all the reshuffling presently going on among divisions and units preparing for the next big push towards Falaise, virtually no friendly infantry or tanks are directly out in front of the guns here.

And this may well be so, since the infantry have not shifted over to the east in accordance with the move the guns have made. All three battalions of 4th Brigade and all 4th Field battery commanders and carrier crews are still way back in the area of Bretteville-sur-Laize, six kilometres to the west and two kilometres to the rear of the guns.

Unconcerned that their artillery is unprotected, the infantry are preparing to lead off an attack tonight by 2nd Division, supported by 2nd Canadian Armoured Brigade, in a sweep southwest from Bretteville-sur-Laize designed to clean out a large pocket of Germans assembled in that area. This information, arriving at command posts and guns deployed in and around the quarry, is more than a little worrisome, particularly when only recently German tanks were seen roaming around over there beyond that railway embankment a few hundred yards up ahead. And so suitable preparations are made for all eventualities.

On orders from RHQ, you establish an OP on the railway embankment immediately in front of the guns, and settle down out there, staring into the gloom and listening all night. However, apart from some desultory mortaring and a few airbursts, the night passes without enemy interference with the Regiment's harassing-fire program. Still, with most of the targets requested of the guns off to the west – up to 90 degrees from the zero-line and almost 180 degrees from the targets the SPs were engaging over to the east before they pulled out – some are wondering just who the hell is in a pocket – the Germans or us?

Rumours are rampant, left behind, you suspect, by the SP signallers, that the follow-through attack, expected to carry the armour all the way to Falaise, is in real trouble – that yesterday the British Columbia Tank Regiment was ambushed and virtually wiped out, along with two companies of the Algonquins, riding on the backs of their tanks.*

Clearly, German armour can still be overwhelming when concentrated to hold or retake a locality deemed vital by their commanders.

---

* On August 10 the B.C. Regiment, lost and cut-off, had forty-seven tanks knocked out, and suffered 104 casualties, sixteen of them officers. Of the forty who died, seven were officers, including the commanding officer, Lt.-Col. D. G. Worthington. Sharing in the tragedy were the two rifle companies of the Algonquin Regiment that had gone forward on the backs of the tanks. They were able to muster only seventy-nine men "fit for duty" after the battle, which took place on a hill (MR 143490) east of the village of Estrées, about two kilometres east of the Caen–Falaise highway, and twelve kilometres north of Falaise. (Report No. 65, Historical Section [G.S.] Canadian Army Headquarters, Dept. of National Defence, Dec. 23, 1953, pp. 33-38.)

And with each passing hour it becomes ever more clear that Bill Waddell's initiative on Hill 122 – directing, with incredible bravery, the Sherbrooke's Firefly to victory over 12th SS's self-propelled guns and tanks – saved the Royal Regiment from a disaster equalling, if not surpassing, that suffered by the B.C. Regiment.

PART SIX: AUGUST 12−13

2nd Division Outflanks
Enemy Positions

50

A FOOTNOTE TO CLOSING THE
FALAISE GAP

❋

AT THE OUTSET OF OPERATION TOTALIZE, THE PURPOSE OF THE
Canadian drive, as seen by General Montgomery, Commander-in-
Chief of all Allied Ground Forces in Normandy, was simply to
break the Caen "hinge" on the left or east side of the German door,
which he expected would swing open by the force of the American
break-out gathering momentum from the west flank.

And an August 6 directive issued by Lt.-Gen. Crerar to 2nd
Canadian Corps and 1st British Corps, attached to 1st Canadian
Army, made it clear that British 2nd Army, driving from the west,
was expected to take Falaise, after which 1st Canadian Army would
"then swing to the east" and pursue the Germans fighting a rearguard action to the Seine.

But when Hitler not only refused to let his commanders pull
back to reform their line at the Seine as Montgomery expected, but
committed all possible German forces on the offensive towards
Mortain (even as an American spearhead was wheeling south and
east towards Paris against no organized resistance), the Canadian
push, only then nicely started from Verrières Ridge, took on
tremendous new significance.

On August 8, as the American spearhead neared Le Mans,
seventy miles south of Falaise, Supreme Allied Commander

Eisenhower recognized that Hitler was presenting the Allies with an incredible opportunity to entrap the German armies in Normandy in a more confined and deadly pocket of destruction than Montgomery had envisaged, if Allied forces could cut across their rear before they began their inevitable retreat to the Seine. Telephoning Monty from headquarters of Lt.-Gen. Bradley, commander of American 12th Army Group, Eisenhower suggested Patton be ordered to peel off a force from his drive for Paris and send it north towards Argentan to meet the Canadians now on the move towards Falaise. Monty agreed, as long as this diversion of forces did not hinder Patton's drive to the Seine, which he still saw as being of greater consequence at this point.*

Thus, overnight, the Canadian offensive turned from "hinge-breaking" to closing off the mouth of a pocket entrapping armies, the most vital action in the pivotal battle of the Falaise Gap, which in retrospect will be seen by Sir Brian Horrocks, commander of British 30th Corps, as "unquestionably the turning point in the whole war in the West."

By August 10, with the Germans in full retreat from the western extremities of the pocket before the main British and American forces hammering at them, it was clear that time was of the essence. All roads east out of the pocket had to be shut off as quickly as possible.

But then General Bradley decided to halt the American spearhead thrusting north at Argentan, fifteen miles south of Falaise, concluding that the forces available to Maj.-Gen. Haislip's xv U.S. Corps of Patton's Third Army weren't strong enough to close off the German escape route and keep it closed. Thus the whole responsibility for closing the gap devolved on 1st Canadian Army, still eight miles north of Falaise.

---

* Facts and quotations, vital to the development of this chapter, are derived largely from Report No. 65, Hisotorical Section (G.S.) Canadian Army Headquarters, Dept. of National Defence, Dec. 23, 1953.

In his postwar book *A Soldier's Story*, General Bradley would provide a reasonable explanation for his decision, which was approved without criticism by both Field Marshal Montgomery and General Eisenhower:

> Although Patton might have spun a line across that narrow neck, I doubted his ability to hold it. Nineteen German divisions were now stampeding to escape the trap. Meanwhile with four divisions, George [Patton] was already blocking three principal escape routes.... Had he stretched that line to include Falaise, he would have extended his roadblock a distance of 40 miles. The enemy could not only have broken through, but he might have trampled Patton's position in the onrush. I much preferred a solid shoulder at Argentan to the possibility of a broken neck at Falaise.*

In effect, the commanding officer of all American forces in Normandy said, It's more than we can handle – the honour is all yours, Canada. And Montgomery, chief of all Allied ground forces in Normandy, recognizing the realities, issued a directive on August 11 to 1st Canadian Army that, after wresting Falaise from the Germans, it should complete their encirclement by driving east and south towards Argentan: "Canadian Army will capture FALAISE. This is first priority and it is vital. It should be done quickly. The army will then operate with strong armoured and mobile forces to secure ARGENTAN. A secure front must be held between Falaise and the sea facing eastwards."

Thus, for the second time in the course of a week, the priorities changed for the Canadian Army's push towards Falaise.

And now, with the Americans restrained at Argentan, the Canadians must not only fight miles beyond Falaise to link up with

---

* Gen. Omar Bradley, *A Soldier's Story* (New York: Holt, 1951), pp. 376–77.

them, but must make it without the benefit of an equal pressure on the Germans from the south by the Americans.

Coinciding with this rising need for a sustained drive by the Canadians, however, is clear evidence that their spearheads, so spectacularly driven through the German lines by Totalize, have now been contained, and that a new operation must be mounted to regain the momentum.

General Eisenhower, reflecting on the state of his armies on the night of August 13, in his memoirs, *Crusade in Europe*, will recognize what the Canadians have been going through and what still faces them: "The Germans were still fighting desperately just south of Caen where by this time they had established the strongest defences encountered throughout the entire campaign. The Canadians threw in fierce and sustained attacks, but it wasn't until August 16 that Falaise was captured."[*]

Directly facing 2nd Canadian Corps are parts of four infantry divisions, supported by elements of 12th SS "Hitlerjugend" Division. Along a line through Quesnay Wood and a string of hamlets about a thousand yards north of the Laison river, Divisional Commander Kurt Meyer has assembled fifty or more 88-mm guns and 110 tanks, including twenty Tigers. To build up his depleted forces, other regiments on his west flank, not so badly depleted, are "cannibalized, and the motley crews so acquired . . . injected with small numbers of SS men for stiffness."[†]

The new Canadian operation, which must destroy these newly formed lines, is given the code name Tractable. Scheduled for August 14, it will use much the same tactics as employed in Totalize, leading off with the bombing of close-in targets by a huge air armada of 811 heavy and medium bombers. Two main assault

---

[*]   Dwight D. Eisenhower, *Crusade in Europe* (New York: Perma Books, 1952), p. 313.

[†]   Report No 65, Historical Section (G.S.) Canadian Army Headquarters, Dept. of National Defence, Dec. 23, 1953, p. 62.

columns, with one brigade of infantry in each, mounted in Kangaroos, will follow spearheads of tanks and flails in tight columns behind an artillery barrage. And following on foot will be the two other brigades, cleaning up any resistance left in villages, farms, and woods.

There is one principal difference from Totalize: the attack will go forth in the daytime. In place of darkness, which hid the attackers so successfully from the enemy gunners, a giant smoke screen will be laid down by the artillery and sustained for at least the time needed for the armoured columns to plunge through the enemy gun lines.

All of these factors, combined with the recognition of the tremendous consequences of the operation, will ensure its place in history. But few students of musty archival files will ever note the significant contribution to its success produced by the preparatory attack and the fierce fighting involving 2nd Canadian Division on August 12 and 13.

51

A MAN OF SIXTEEN ON
THE ROAD TO FALAISE

——————————— ✳ ———————————

THE BUSINESS OF WIPING OUT POCKETS OF RESISTANCE AND
conducting diversionary attacks, often far away from the main
thrust, will always be dealt with in cursory fashion, or ignored completely, by the historian. And when the operation is not even given
a name, but called a "reconnaissance in force," it would seem destined for oblivion.

Such is the attack by 2nd Division that goes in on August 12. But
during the next two days, this nameless operation will move the
right flank of the Canadian front so far forward on the west side of
the Caen–Falaise highway – outflanking the Germans by three
miles – that it will guarantee the success of Operation Tractable,
lining up east of the road.

Without the benefit of heavy bombing preparations, and supported only by the tanks of 2nd Canadian Armoured Brigade, its
own division artillery, and two AGRAs, 2nd Division will drive a
wedge six miles deep down to Clair Tizon, almost three miles south
of the German stronghold in Quesnay Wood, the first major obstacle Tractable will have to overcome.

The attack is on a single thrust line, with 4th Brigade leading and
the RHLI in the van. After a night of manoeuvring for the startline
under mortar and shell-fire, the Rileys move out at 7:30 A.M.,
accompanied by a troop of tanks. At first they experience no

difficulty as they pass among the farms and woods towards Barbery, a tiny hamlet five miles southwest of Bretteville-sur-Laize, halfway to the ultimate objective of Clair Tizon.

Barbery, a mere collection of deserted houses and barns where nothing stirs, is bypassed and left for the 8th Recce to occupy. The Rileys continue south, with Major Joe Pigott's company wading through unharvested wheat on the left of the road, and Major "Huck" Welch's company proceeding on the right.

For a while all is peaceful for the sweating men ploughing through the dense, yellowing grain and the rumbling Shermans following them. The still fields and woods offer no hint of what is in store for them, and for the Royal Regiment, who with their accompanying FOOs will pass through the wounded, dead, and dying Rileys among burning tanks and carriers on their way to capturing the next village of Moulines.

The Germans are waiting for the Rileys about one thousand yards beyond the seemingly deserted village of Barbery, at a point where the woods close in on both sides of the road. And as Pigott's company draws near, it comes under a burst of fire from the copse on the left.

At once all companies are "enveloped in a storm of bullets and shrapnel" which their intelligence officer, Lyle Doering, will record as "the most intense mortaring and shelling the unit ever witnessed." And the German Panzer grenadiers are so aggressive, Pigott will remember them as "fanatical devils" who engaged his troops in hand-to-hand fighting as they came "running out of their slits, firing rifles and grenades."*

Forced to consolidate well short of their objective, the Rileys are digging-in when a private in Welch's company, pausing in his labour for a moment to peer at the woods, calls to his company commander:

---

*   Quotations from Doering and Pigott are from *Semper Paratus*, the history of the RHLI, published by the RHLI Historical Association, 1977.

"Sir, are those our tanks over there?"

"Of course they are," says Welch, not bothering to look up.

"Jesus, they don't look like it to me!" says the private.

When Welch straightens up, trundling towards him is a Tiger tank.

The Shermans are no match for the massive Tiger that concentrates on knocking them out while accompanying Panthers spray the position with machine-gun fire. Though the German tanks stay back, well out of effective Piat range (which for tanks is about a hundred yards), the Rileys are pinned down by continuous fire, and by late afternoon are in bad shape. Then a shell scores a direct hit on their tac headquarters, wounding five, including their Col. MacLachlan and 4th Field's Major James Wilson Dodds, leaving them without an arty rep at the battalion level until Battery Captain Jack Drewry can make it up from 14th Battery wagon lines.

When the Royals, and their supporting troop of tanks, try to pass through the Rileys on their way south to the next village of Moulines, they find the going equally sticky. Their route takes them through the same open grain fields without cover from the fire of the defenders, and after only about eight hundred yards, they run into heavy machine-gun fire from a barn and copse on the left that drives them to ground. Still, A Company, supported by concentrations fired by 4th Field guns, is able to work its way up to some woods near a crossroads.

But here, plastered by mortar and shell-fire, they suffer many casualties. While there are some holes available, most have to find what cover they can in mere folds in the ground, for, with the intense and accurate sniping, it's impossible to dig in.

Sherman tanks come up and try to knock out the 88-mm firing from the right flank, but the leading tank is hit as it advances along a sunken road, and when it brews up, the others withdraw.

For a time Capt. Bill Waddell's carrier, moving with the forward company, is pinned down by the same terrifying, point-blank fire from the German gun. And for a sixteen-year-old signaller on his crew, there is a heart-stopping moment when an armour-piercing

88-mm slug rips in one side of the carrier and out the other, with a bloodcurdling, metal-tearing screech, unique to solid-shot drilling a hole through armour-plate at three thousand feet per second.*

It's Gunner Bill Knox's first tour of duty in a FOO's carrier crew moving with the infantry, and each terrifying minute will be remembered in infinite detail:

We're going through this slightly wooded area in a sunken road. Everybody along the road is wounded, and as we come up, one of the infantry guys jumps out in front of the carrier and yells, "Get the hell off this road! Everybody here is wounded or dead! The German artillery has got the road taped!"

So we pull off the road and get in behind some bushes in a field. That's where the 88 hits us, and everybody piles out as fast as they can into a nearby depression – everybody except me. I am on the left side of the carrier, the side exposed to the hill where the 88 is, and for a moment I bend down over the 19-set to collect my wits before climbing out. I still have my earphones on, and I hear "Blackie" Bryan, our driver, over in the depression, telling them back at the guns that I am dead. He is using the microphone with the long extension cord that Wally Driemel [the other signaller] took with him when he bailed out over the right side of the carrier. He's reporting we've been hit, that there is a hole in the carrier and one man is dead – meaning me.

---

* Gunner William J. Knox was born March 16, 1928. In the fall of 1942, he hitchhiked from Toronto to Montreal to join the army. Turned down, he hitched a ride to Ottawa, where he again lied about his age and was signed on by the artillery in the old Regal Building. He was fourteen years and nine months old. After training as an ack-ack gunner on the East Coast, he was shipped to England in the fall of 1943. There he was trained as a signaller in time to go to Normandy with a unit formed especially to man a relay station passing signals from shore to warships lying off the coast. When the need for this disappeared, Knox was posted to 4th Field, where he volunteered for duty on a carrier crew.

I yell, "I'm okay," and jumping out make it to the depression.

Capt. Waddell says we should run the remote up to that ridge ahead of us. So he and I go up there and fire Mike targets down into a town [Moulines] that we later take and where Major Wren is killed next day.*

While 4th Field carrier crews come through the day unscathed, the Royals suffer sixty-seven casualties, ten of them fatal, trying to cross open grain fields under fire from tanks, mortars, and machine guns. And the RHLI suffer even more grievously: twenty dead and one hundred wounded.

The last assault against their riddled companies comes late in the afternoon, the enemy's tanks moving in for what appears to the Rileys – now out of Piat ammunition – to be the *coup de grâce*.

Watching them come, Major Welch is astonished at the cool arrogance of the German tank commanders, standing up "exposed in their turrets, looking for targets through their binoculars, their guns traversing all the time." Suddenly they stop, make one last sweep with their machine guns, then turn about and disappear from the field of smoking hulks and dead and wounded men. The only possible explanation is that they are out of ammunition.

Back at the guns, apart from the odd airburst whacking overhead now and then, there's been no enemy activity to endure. Still, those spine-jolting, ear-splitting reports arriving unannounced, followed a split-second later by the shrieking rip of their coming, have been keeping everyone on edge; particularly after Gunner Don Kirby, on duty at the radio in GA, is wounded in the face with a bit of shell fragment and is evacuated.

It's been a long tiring day in the sultry air in the quarry. There is no protection from the dazzling sun reflecting off the vast acreage of stone shelving, and the great barren basin unmercifully amplifies

---

* Author interview.

each reverberating roar of the guns getting off an unending parade of Mike targets called for by the FOOs and battery commanders, trying to quell enemy shelling and mortaring pinning down the infantry.

This quarry at Hautmesnil will be remembered long after most gun positions are forgotten, but few will recall it with the pleasure of Sgt. Bruce Hunt in his diary: "Moved command post from house at cross-roads to a cave – a shrine of German ingenuity! Here we work in comfortable security while concentrations from the artillery massed around us blast away."

Bombardier Hossack's bleak note in his log is probably closer to the experience of the majority: "A built-up railroad obscures the enemy's view of us, but he finds our line and range with mortars and shells during the night."

Around 3:30 P.M., 4th Field receives two divisional fire plans: one to support 4th Brigade, and the other to support 5th Brigade, indicating the Colonel and CRA are taking a hand in affairs. Heavy concentrations by all seventy-two guns on Moulines and vicinity in advance of the 4th Brigade attack seem to work wonders. At 5:30 P.M., when the Royals try again to move into the village, they find most of the enemy have pulled out.

52

NO MEDICINE LEFT FOR
ENTERIC DISORDERS

✳

WHILE OVERNIGHT 4TH FIELD GUNS WERE TAKING PART IN AN intensely noisy divisional harassing-fire program designed to keep the enemy awake and anxious, an order came down warning that advance parties would move off shortly after dawn. The new positions are two and a half miles farther south, near St. Germain-le-Vasson, reconnoitred yesterday by Major Savage and Regimental Survey Officer Lieut. Jim Nesbitt under rather "dicey" conditions. Though no harm came to them, the situation offered some interesting possibilities, since the nearest infantrymen (5th Brigade) were near Mesnil-Touffrey, a good mile and a half to the rear and to the west of the new gun area.

Even at dawn today, with 5th Brigade two and a half miles farther south, the axis of advance of 2nd Division remains one and a quarter miles west of the new gun positions. In between is terrain extensive enough and rugged enough to hide a whole division, as the Calgary Highlanders discover at dawn, when the overnight deluge of high explosive by 2nd Division guns on enemy territory is replaced by a barrage of propaganda leaflets expelled from gently popping 25-pounder smoke shells that have had their smoke canisters removed. A veritable flood of Germans, with hands high in the air, present themselves to the astonished forward companies, induced to surrender by the promise contained in the "Guarantee of Safe Conduct Certificates," fluttering down on woods and gullies by the thousands. Every Jerry coming forward to surrender clutches a certificate in one of his upraised hands.

At the guns, encouraging rumours are circulating of large numbers of Jerries surrendering to the infantry – the first from the "pocket." And one wild rumour will later be corroborated by a vivid description of the event in the Calgary Highlanders' war diary: "Prisoners simply poured into our cage and looked like a queue going up to the ticket office at a theatre, with the Intelligence Officer acting as doorman. Each and every prisoner had an Allied 'Safe Conduct' leaflet assuring him of good treatment if taken prisoner."*

As you go forward with 4RCA advance parties at 5:30 A.M., you are inclined to take seriously the warning "The area may not be entirely free of Germans." However, all is peaceful and deserted as you and Bombardier Hossack wander about getting the lay of the land, now bathed by a brilliant sun that, even at 6:00 A.M., is beginning to bake the stubble of a vast field dotted with stooks of grain marching hither and yon.

To the left rear of this rolling, golden plateau, there is a very broad, shallow valley, beyond which you can make out the Hautmesnil quarry, where the guns can be seen puffing away at some target far ahead in another valley, creating a delayed rolling rumble reminiscent of distant thunder announcing the coming of a summer storm.

Out of sight beyond a hedge and a thick orchard, which will become the wagon lines of 6th Field deploying on your right, is a village that could be either Le Bout Roussin or St. Germain-le-Vasson, depending on how you interpret the placement of their names on the map. The second-in-command of 6th Field confirms the area still harbours at least one German, after the gas tank of his

---

* Calgary Highlanders' War Diary, Unit War Diary Files, National Archives of Canada.

Jeep collects a bullet hole on the way in here. It's likely a lone sniper, however, for there is evidence the Germans pulled out of this area in a great hurry. In the orchard just over the hedge, they left behind a troop of their precious Moaning Minnies – completely armed with rocket bombs, ready to fire.

There's always the possibility, of course, that once they discover they were startled into retreating by a mere artillery recce party (if that is what happened), they'll decide to come back to rescue their weapons. At any rate, 6th Field – uneasy that all 2nd Division infantry units are still far off on the right, and moving not this way, but south towards Clair Tizon – decides to establish an OP in the nearby church tower poking up among the trees on the right.

While this is probably a very sensible move, you wonder how they can spare the manpower. You and Hossack are fully occupied. The gun position allotted Able Troop is a broad, open field with no ditches, and there is no problem with crest clearance with the ground falling sharply away out in front, so it takes no time at all to plant gun markers, choose a distant aiming-point on which Hossack can orient his director, and get down to what you have come to believe is the real purpose of advance parties: the digging of the troop command post.

Ever since Fleury-sur-Orne, six gun positions ago, you and Bob Grout and your GPO acks have taken turns going on advance parties so that the digging might be more fairly shared. Continuous artillery support being a must these days, when the front is in such a state of flux, batteries move forward one at a time. In this case they are going to allow half an hour between each move, and with 2nd Battery not moving until 10:00 A.M., your guns won't arrive until at least 10:30. This means you and Hossack have more than three hours – plenty of time to produce a respectable command post ready for roofing, a pleasant surprise for the rest of the command-post gang when they come up.

Command posts for Able Troop have become of fixed design: two slit trenches, each about six feet long and two feet wide, dug parallel to, and about two and a half feet from, each other. While these trenches are dug below grade only about four feet, the excavated soil, dumped around the perimeter, builds up about three feet above grade, allowing headroom when the whole thing is roofed over with corrugated-iron sheets (your old friends from Carpiquet) carrying a couple of feet of earth. On one side of the earthen column or ledge left standing between the two trenches, the GPO is able to stand with Tannoy mike in hand overseeing his GPO ack at the artillery board. In the opposite trench the signallers carry on their duties, which, in inclement weather, include brewing tea and heating Compo rations.

Hossack starts on one trench, you on the other. It has suddenly become oppressively hot. The first foot or so of topsoil is easy to work, but then you hit chalk, solid chalk – not a chalky conglomerate of chips and stones, but solid, damp chalk that allows the head of your pick-axe to bury itself up to the handle with an encouraging, substantial *thunk*, but then refuses to allow you to withdraw it, regardless of how hard you tug, until you have wiggled and rocked it a discouraging number of times. And when it does come free, you find it has produced less than a cupful of loose chalk.

You soon abandon the idea of completing two trenches, and both of you concentrate on the one on which you've been working. By now the sun is high in the sky and broiling you as you sink in the pick and wiggle it, pry it, wiggle it, and wrestle it until you can pull it out, just so you can sink it in again. Hossack takes a turn on the pick, and for a while it seems he is managing a bit better, but the procedure soon exhausts his patience, which normally is considerable.

The effect on the depth of the trench after your combined labours are applied for more than an hour is almost imperceptible. You can't remember ever having been so discouraged about anything.

You and Hossack had looked forward to finishing the digging and retiring to the shade of a green grove of trees surrounding a farmhouse to the left rear of the position – perhaps even finding a barrel of cool cider. But after another hour of intensive effort, the trench is considerably less than two feet deep, and you are considering giving up and waiting for the others to come up and take over.

While you are over your dysentery, it has left you somewhat less than vigorous, and in this heat, the picking and scraping-out of each shovelful of chips is not just wretchedly frustrating, but physically draining.

It must be plain torture for poor Hossack, enfeebled by the debilitating malady now at its worst stage for him, as it seems to be for most of the afflicted members of the troop. And when he shows signs of the disorientation you are starting to experience, you call it quits and lead him over to a spot of shade under a tree along the hedge. Lying there, the war seems to fade away. Though the guns go on rumbling in the distance, there is only the hum of a bumblebee to disturb the silence here. And this is where Bob Grout and the rest of the troop command-post gang find you both, stretched out sound asleep, when the guns arrive.

While they don't dare say too much about the insignificant scar the GPO and senior GPO ack have gouged out of the chalk after all those hours up here, they manage to make it clear they are not impressed. But when they take over, with a great show of vigour and enthusiasm, they soon discover that this is the worst digging yet, and only a basin of mortar bombs dropping nearby – impressing on all the continuing need for a good deep trench – keeps them going at all. And then it is one man, and one man alone, who really sees the job is done. Whitehawk puts everyone else to shame with his grinding determination to see the job through.

Long after the others have begun to find excuses to avoid their turn on a pick or a shovel, Whitehawk continues his measured pace, seldom stopping to take a breather. His endurance is incredible. But just how incredible you fully appreciate only after he has finished and taken you aside to request, almost apologetically, that he be evacuated as a dysentery casualty: "Sir, I feel awful sick. Can you send me back to the MO so I can get some medicine?"

Your heart sinks. Oh, God, you think, if ever there was a man in this whole army more deserving than Whitehawk of getting the last drop of medicine for this cursed plague, you don't know who he might be. But you have to tell him that the MO has used up all the medicine he's been able to get his hands on, and has issued instructions that no more cases are to be sent back to the regimental aid post.

With deep hurt showing in his eyes, your friend points to his lips, grotesquely swollen and cracking, and pleads, "Please – I really feel rotten – I'm really sick – the doc must have something that would help."

You go to the phone and get the MO on the line. You know Doctor Dunham to be a most kindly, concerned, understanding man in normal circumstances. But this dysentery (he prefers to call it "enteritis") epidemic obviously has got him down.

When you plead with him to make a special case of Whitehawk, he turns severe, and you end up shouting into the phone something to the effect that it's about time he and the other sawbones got off their collective asses and demanded they fly over from England whatever the hell is necessary to treat this epidemic before the whole damned army comes to a full stop. When he hangs up on you it makes you even madder. And while all this does nothing to help Whitehawk, at least he knows you tried, and you are able to send him back to the wagon lines, where it should be a little quieter.

Then much grimmer news snaps you back to the realities of the bitter fighting, which is still going on over there, among the wooded hills and valleys, for little, insignificant villages, the names of which will not likely be remembered by any of those men who from minute to minute are risking death to secure them: Bill Waddell has been wounded and captured.

Then comes a report from the CO at Brigade that Major Gordon Wren has been fatally wounded.

No details are immediately available, because (as you later learn) the radio in his scout car was knocked out during the shelling of the Royals' tac headquarters in Moulines. But Lieut. "Hank" Caldwell, the battalion anti-tank officer, will one day tell of seeing "Major Wren standing in that Moulines farmhouse courtyard beside his command vehicle when the shell landed." It is an image he will carry in regret the rest of his life, for Major Wren made a very deep impression on him during that "ghastly learning experience at Eterville."

> Back in those early days under almost continuous bombardment, we all were trying to act like soldiers should under fire, with our helmets pulled down over our ears, but inwardly despairing: If this is war, how on earth are we going to put up with it? Then one day Major Wren went back to his regiment overnight, and when I saw him next day, in one glance he changed my capacity to endure what was going on. He was wearing a beret! He said that after seeing the battle maps, etc., back at his headquarters he felt like a different person. And I caught the spirit from him. Bless him! Does that sound crazy? Well, it was a tremendous lift for me, and I hope I was able to help those under me to feel a little better about our plight.*

Turner, the Major's despatch rider, the last to speak with him, will remark on the fact that even as the Major was dying he was concerned with the welfare of his crew, that they should return to the guns. Turner will never forget that on the night of the big break-out from Verrières, Wren had him dump his motorbike on the bumper of the scout car and ride inside.

---

*   Author interview.

53

HOW DO MEN SUSTAIN THE
WILL TO CARRY ON?

✳

FROM THE POUNDING TAKEN BY 4TH BRIGADE YESTERDAY, August 12, it's clear that resistance has stiffened, that the Germans have no intention of allowing the Canadians to cut off their avenue of retreat and engineer the destruction of their armies in Normandy.

And while the Rileys were able to move through the Royals at Moulines during the night and take some high ground a mile southeast of there, the Essex have been unable to make any headway in taking Point 184 two miles farther on.

So in the early hours today, when the Royals are ordered to take over the offensive, with Bob Suckling's D Company leading, accompanied by a troop of tanks and 4th Field's Bill Waddell and his crew to ensure artillery support, all know it won't be any more "a piece of cake" than the day before.

Like the men of all battalions aiming at Falaise, relentlessly urged forward these past five days – particularly those units that were chewed and decimated along Verrières Ridge before Totalize even began – Suckling and company are carrying on in a state of utter exhaustion, both mental and physical.

The long marches, weighed down with personal equipment, shovels, weapons, and extra ammunition for the Brens and Piats; the frantic digging-in at each stop to get below ground as fast as possible to gain shelter from shelling and resist the inevitable counter-attack; and the never-ending tension that comes from living, minute to minute, alert and ready to react to every rustle of air, knowing that the worst could happen at any moment – all combine to guarantee that those who do survive attack after attack after attack exist at the outer limits of their endurance, in a state of fatigue that defies description.

In the six nights since assembling on the evening of August 7 near the village of Ifs for the beginning of Totalize, there's been only one night when Suckling's men have had a chance for what might be called restful sleep – as restful as sleep can ever be for a man fully dressed in his filthy clothes, complete with boots laced up on swollen feet, huddled over or hunched up in a gravelike, sandy hole that shudders and sifts sand on him every time a mortar bomb or a shell lands nearby.

Of course there was no sleep whatsoever on the first night of the opening attack, during the nerve-wracking, thunderous drive through enemy lines, enveloped by the fury of the bombs and the great gun barrage preceding them.

And shortly after dawn on August 8, the enemy counter-attacked the isolated spearheads, keeping everyone busy all day. That night, with the front still fluid and with little known of the enemy's whereabouts or strength, all units had to remain alert throughout the hours of darkness.

On the night of the ninth, the Royals finally got a chance to rest in reserve position. But the next night they were surrounded by Allied guns firing until dawn: 25-pounders, 5.5-inch mediums, and a battery of the big American 155-mm "Long Toms" fresh from the Cherbourg siege, required to fire fifty rounds per gun on Falaise during the night.

After dark on the eleventh, the Royals resumed the routine of no sleep at all when, after marching more than three miles southwest over to Bretteville-sur-Laize, they were sent trudging on another two miles south under intermittent shell and mortar fire to deploy astride the axis of advance near the village of Favrolle, north of Barbery.

From there they started out on an all-day attack stretching into the night of August 12 – marching and running and crawling and digging in – as they penetrated another two miles in the direction of Falaise and cleared the village of Moulines, at a cost of ten men killed and fifty-seven wounded. And today two more Royals will die and another forty-two will be wounded, taking an obscure hill about half a mile south of Moulines, known only by its elevation above sea level, "151." And in the process their artillery representative at battalion will be killed and the FOO with the leading company will be wounded and captured.

Suckling will always identify this day as

> . . . the time one of my lance-corporals in the midst of a mortaring bombardment, with tears streaming down his face, gets up out of his hole and, like a hunted animal, darting this way and that, disappears from my world forever.
>
> On top of everything else, dysentery is rampant, with everybody suffering to some degree from stomach cramps and nausea associated with loose bowels. For some it is dreadful: one of my platoon commanders has diarrhoea so bad it shoots five feet out of his rectum when he bends over.
>
> Everybody is now having to scratch continuously, for we all are crawling with lice picked up from the slit trenches and those splendid dugouts abandoned by the Krauts. And as if all this weren't enough, I am tormented with the burning itch of watery blisters on my face from impetigo [a highly contagious skin infection] I've managed to pick up somewhere along the way.*

---

* Author interview.

The first attempt by Suckling's company to reach Point 184 comes to an abrupt halt even as they are moving up from a reserve position. An 88-mm knocks out the leading Sherman, causing the others to pull back, leaving the Royals scurrying for whatever cover they can find in ditches and folds in the ground as mortars and machine guns search for them. The enemy fire is so sustained, and from such close quarters, that Lt.-Col. Jack Anderson decides to pull the leading companies back four hundred yards to allow 4th Field guns to "stonk" the German positions and cool down their withering fire.*

But before this can be arranged, Anderson's tac headquarters in Moulines suffers the direct hit that fatally wounds his arty rep, Major Wren, and disables his command post vehicle.

Only the barest details get back to the guns, and as the awesome events of the next twenty-four hours unfold, dominating all thought, it will be some time before you hear the story (from Col. McGregor Young himself), of how Gunner Turner, the battery commander's despatch rider, keeps communications open between the Royals and 4th Brigade until Capt. Laurie is able to get forward to take over. The crucial situation reports Gunner Turner gets back to Brigade allows the CO to lay down fire from 4th Field guns so effectively the Royals take an intermediate hill, from which the enemy fire has been originating, and capture sixty Germans, thereby shutting down the fire of twelve machine guns, and opening the way for the Essex to take Point 184.†

And this encouraging success is built on by 5th Brigade, when

---

* A "stonk" involves the guns being laid in such a way as to ensure their shells land in a straight line along a selected map grid-bearing representing an elongated target such as the outer fringe of an orchard or hedgerow. The twenty-four guns of one field regiment could effectively stonk a target 840 yards long.

† The citation, signed by Lt.-Col. Young and Maj.-Gen. Bruce Matthews, that resulted in the Croix de Guerre with Bronze Star being awarded Gunner John Andrew Turner some months later, stated in part:

the Calgary Highlanders pass through to gain a small bridgehead over the Laize River at Clair Tizon, three miles west and half a mile south of Potigny, visible to the left rear on the Caen–Falaise highway.

For this attack across the river, there's an elaborate set of artillery tasks, involving not only 4th, 5th, and 6th Field, but also heavy bombardments by the mediums and heavies of 2nd and 9th AGRAs. The attack succeeds, and the guns earn a nice commendation from 5th Brigade: "We got exactly the fire we wanted, when we wanted it."*

When the Maisonneuves attempt to expand the bridgehead at last light, and are bloodily repulsed by very strong forces, it is clear the Germans are reacting to the threat 2nd Division poses to Falaise. Thus on the eve of Operation Tractable to entrap the German armies, 2nd Division has accomplished the full diversionary purposes of the so-called "reconnaissance in force," outflanking the German-filled Quesnay Woods by about two and half miles, and virtually guaranteeing the success of the final drive to Falaise and beyond.

However, 2nd Division battalions are left riddled with casualties and on the point of collapsing from exhaustion. By now you've come to feel sorry for all infantrymen you see, whether you are merely passing them on the road or moving with them. How they sustain the will to carry on day after day, risking death or crippling wounds, is a mystery.

"On one occasion south of Bretteville-sur-Laize, when enemy shelling was particularly heavy and his Battery Commander became a casualty, this gunner took charge of the remainder of the party and continued the necessary artillery support . . . the disregard of personal danger and the devotion to duty was an inspiration to all that worked with him. . . . his conduct under fire had a direct bearing on the successful outcome of the battle."
* Col. G. W .L. Nicolson, CD, *The Gunners of Canada, Volume II, 1919-1967* (Toronto: McClelland and Stewart, 1972), p.320.

Long after, reflecting on what he considered "the greatest problem, the constant fear and anxiety which dulls the mind and is absolutely unshakeable," Major Suckling will declare:

> For me the fear of what was behind was greater than the fear of what was in front. Over the years I had been well indoctrinated with army discipline, and I'm sure this kept many other people going too. I've always admired the resolution of men who carry on solely because of their commitment to a cause of righteousness. In my own case, it was simply that I was more scared of what was behind me than what lay ahead of me – which is the best reason I know in favour of discipline. Weeks would pass before I got over the shell shock or anxiety neurosis, and it was much later before my mind settled down somewhat. While my body, even at the age of twenty-six, became increasingly weary to the point of exhaustion.*

And in *Battle Royal*, the story of the Royal Regiment, historian Major D. J. Goodspeed, marvelling at the capacity of men to carry on in spite of agonizing fear and grinding fatigue, will produce this vivid image of infantrymen and their supporting arms on the road to Falaise:

> For brief or intermittent periods we may with justification speak of the "bright face of danger," but prolonged exposure to mortal peril brings not uplifting of the spirit, but rather a dull and almost despairing fatalism. . . . Some men broke under the strain and none can blame them. . . . The overwhelming majority plodded on, doing their duty, finding (incredibly) that extra spurt of energy when it was required and when the Regiment needed it. . . . Before the fighting, most men would not have believed that they could have been so tired and still survived. Night after

---

*   Author interview.

night passed without sleep and day after day was spent with no more rest than was afforded by the odd cat-nap. Men fell asleep as they drove carriers along a road, as they plodded in single file with their sections, or as they huddled in slit-trenches under bombardment. Weariness built up until it laid its hand upon the very spirit. Men went for days on end in a sort of dazed mental stupor, in which they could not remember the events of an hour before, and in which they were utterly incapable of speculating upon the future.*

---

* Major D. J. Goodspeed, *Battle Royal* (Toronto: Royal Regiment of Canada Association, 1962), p. 460.

54

THE QUALITY OF MERCY

———————————— ✳ ————————————

ARTILLERY FOOS, BY THE VERY NATURE OF THEIR OCCUPATION and the awkward conditions under which they must practise their trade, are bound to accumulate strange experiences, but none could be stranger than that of Capt. Bill Waddell today.

Certainly it will always seem out of place among the dismal stories of death and destruction to which every hour in Normandy is dedicated, for it is a heartening tale of mercy – a rare commodity in these hellish days, almost incredible in the face of the enemy's well-established reputation for brutal viciousness, now accepted as normal in the Normandy fighting, including the shooting of unarmed Canadian prisoners by Hitlerjugend of 12th SS Panzer Division.

Waddell will recall that at an orders group called by Col. Anderson at 6:00 A.M. he is assigned to go along with Suckling's D Company of the Royal Regiment and its supporting squadron of tanks:

The RHLI having passed through during the night, we are sup-posed to be in a reserve position, but as it turns out, when the leading company of the Royals move up along the front edge of some woods, they find Jerries, not Rileys, on the startline.

Of this I am not immediately aware, for when I get back from the O Group to my crew, they are just making something to eat, so I decide to take a minute to have some too before joining the Royals – knowing we can easily catch up, since we'll be riding and they'll be walking. And when eventually we take off down the road, we are not warned by anyone at all as to what we are getting into.*

What Waddell and his crew are getting into is an unplanned reconnaissance well in advance of the infantry, since the Rileys are nowhere to be seen and none of D Company of the Royals are visible either, having been forced to take cover only five hundred yards down the road when they came under intense machine-gun and mortar fire and the tanks were fired on.

Only the abandoned Sherman – holed by an 88 and still in the process of brewing up, its exploding ammunition puffing smoke rings from its turret – is to be seen along the road. Once past that, Waddell and his crew are driving in no-man's-land, right into German territory. And this he begins to suspect when he notes the complete absence of tank tracks in the sand.

I halt my crew and go forward on foot to reconnoitre. Not seeing any fresh tank tracks, I am worried. Then I spot one or two Jerries in the wheat field, and I turn and take off, running for my carrier. That is when I am wounded. My crew is being attacked too, and have no chance of getting to me, so they turn back to the Canadian lines.

The bullet went through my right cheek and jaw. Fortunately it came out in front of my left ear and through my helmet. Two Jerries pick me up and I am taken into the hedgerow, where I lie for some time, during which we are shelled by a few rounds from our own 25-pounders. (I later learn that when my crew got back

---

* The quotations from Bill Waddell in this chapter are from an interview with the author.

and told Col. Anderson where I'd been captured, he had Major
Wren fire some rounds up there to prove to the RHLI they'd
given a wrong map reference for their position.)

After this I am led away blindfolded to a small village, which I
believe is called Clair Tizon, or some such name. There, in a
house, they sit me in a chair. Beside me is a Jerry, shot through
the stomach. He can speak some English, and we both think that
war is a rough deal. The doctor bandages my head. He tells me
the bullet removed five teeth and part of the jawbone. He asks if
I want a painkiller? I say no, because I don't know what is in it.
Eventually he comes around again, and asks if I wish to go back
to Canada. Naturally I say yes.

So they put the blindfold on again, give me a white flag, and
lead me out to the point where I was hit. There they take the
blindfold off. A German lieutenant comes out and a soldier as
well. The latter takes off my Rolex watch as I am talking with the
lieutenant, who is reluctant to let me go. I strongly tell him that
the "Captain" told me I could go back to the Canadian lines.
Eventually he lets me go, and I take off. But not before warning
them not to shoot me in the back.

It is a long, slow walk, not knowing if they will shoot me in
the back or not. Eventually a Jeep, flying a Red Cross flag,
appears and I jump in. Turning on a dime, it takes me back to
Royals battalion headquarters where Col. Anderson informs me:
"You've been AWL for a few hours!" Then I am advised the
battery commander Major Wren has been killed. And later I find
out that my replacement lasts only long enough to go back with
me from an advanced casualty clearing centre.

Royals' Lieut. "Hank" Caldwell, will never forget Waddell
arriving at Royals' tac headquarters with "holes in both cheeks. I
watch fascinated as he asks for a cigarette and tries to take a puff,
but draws only air through his cheeks with gurgling noises. He

obviously is much distressed because he can draw no smoke – a brave guy with guts to match."*

Waddell will remember leaving the Royal Regiment, sitting up in a Jeep, holding a cup of hot, sweet tea.

> From now on I am on some sort of painkiller. I pass through the casualty clearing station and am admitted to Bayeux Hospital, where I'm X-rayed during the night. Apparently they find that an operation is not immediately required, so I am sent back to England about 6:30 A.M. The DC-3 (Dakota) carries twenty-one stretcher cases and three walking-wounded. It is wonderful to see England again.†

When the details of Waddell's story finally filter back to the guns this evening, everyone experiences a lift. It's such a satisfying, dramatic story – and very, very welcome at this juncture, providing everyone with something to dwell on besides the heat, the damned sand fleas, and the accursed dysentery, which continues to devastate the troop.

Waddell was with the Regiment and Baker Troop just twenty-

---

*   Author interview.
†   Lt.-Col. Anderson of the Royals joined Waddell within a day in the same hospital at Basingstoke, England, after being shot accidentally in the knee by his own German P-38 automatic pistol when it fell out of his battledress blouse onto the slate floor of a farmhouse. He was able to report that after Waddell left he sent a German prisoner back to those same enemy lines to tell the Germans they were surrounded, but that if they would come in with their hands up they would be treated fairly. About 110 took advantage of the offer and marched in, following his POW emissary, and Waddell would always assume there was a direct connection between the humane treatment given the German and the subsequent surrender of so many.

four days, and during that time only a handful of people in the Regiment ever saw him, for almost continuously 4th Brigade was heavily engaged, and FOOs are obliged to spend their time with the infantry when they're in the line. But, though he's unlikely ever to become aware of it, he's already well on the way to becoming a legendary figure in 4th Field – as the story of his being shot through the jaw, captured, treated by the Germans, and then released back to our lines is told and retold.

It is almost irresistible to combine the image of him walking back through no-man's-land from the enemy lines, head swathed in bandages, with another image of him standing out in the open, directing the fire of our tanks on enemy tanks, and brewing them up one after another on Hill 122 – for, though that tank engagement took place five days ago on the first morning of the breakout, it is only during the last day or two that eyewitness accounts of his heroism that morning have begun to make the rounds.

55

THE NEBELWERFER BOOBY TRAP

———————————— ✳ ————————————

IN THE COOLING TWILIGHT JUST AFTER THE SUN GOES DOWN, AS
you are enjoying a gentle, fresh breeze, after a wearing day of heat
and digging and firing, the air is suddenly filled with a blast of
blood-chilling sound: the wailing and screeching of a whole herd of
Moaning Minnies, as though the sky is full of those horrible missiles, descending directly onto the gun position.

Everyone dives for cover, pressing face and body tight to the
earth. But as the banshee wailing continues, growing fainter and
fainter until it ends in a distant, thumping salvo, you gradually
realize what has happened. Those captured Nebelwerfers, which
were left in the orchard just over the fence all loaded up and ready
to fire, have been turned around and unloaded on enemy territory
by 6th Field gunners.

But even as most of the troop are still climbing out of holes and
scrambling to their feet, grinning and bantering back and forth in
relief as they speculate on the possible effects on Jerry of this
curious event, the sound of another herd of Moaning Minnies can
be heard winding up. This time, however, the volume is rising, not
falling. By the time everybody realizes they are coming this way,
there's barely time to hit the ground before the ungodly howling
ends with earth-shaking blasts very close: just over the hedge in
the orchard where the abandoned Nebelwerfers stand, where

inevitably a crowd of curious 6th Field gunners will have gathered to examine the strange weapons and exchange views on the spectacular event of their firing.

In their bloody fashion the Germans have shown why, when forced to abandon their weapons for lack of transport, they left them intact and ready to fire. They knew the invitation would prove irresistible and that a great crowd would collect to watch the firing. All they had to do was lay other Nebelwerfers on the precise map reference where they'd abandoned them and wait.

Almost immediately there is a call on the phone from RHQ ordering you to collect half of all the shell dressings in your troop and take them to the wagon lines of 6th Field. They assure you the MO will replace them before the night is out. (Every soldier, regardless of rank, carries a shell dressing buttoned into a big pocket on his left front thigh, and another on the left lip of his steel helmet underneath a camouflage netting.)

As soon as the announcement is made over the Tannoy, a flood of shell dressings begins to arrive at the command post, and Troop Sgt.-Maj. Mann, who has just come up with rations and mail, is seconded to drive you and armfuls of dressings over to 6th Field by a tortuous route behind the positions. It is dark by the time you find the stone barn where the casualties are being treated. Inside is discouraging, dismal gloom, hardly penetrated by one hissing, smoking gasoline lantern and some hand-held lamps-electric moving about, briefly casting a vague yellow glow on white faces and red-stained uniforms.

The doctor (identifiable only because the gas lantern is being held in position for his benefit) and a couple of stretcher-bearers bend over the wounded, doing what they can to stem the flow of blood, dust sulpha on wounds, and now and then administer hypos to what seems to be a disastrous number of dark forms lying on blankets down on the ground, stretching into the darkness along both walls of the barn.

You are struck by the silence. Though the barn floor is covered with wounded men all crowded together, there is seldom a sound other than the odd cough or clearing of a throat. The doctor and his assistants hardly exchange a word, and when they do, they speak in very low voices. There is an air of deadly seriousness here that is totally unnerving. It is clear that you are witnessing a race with death, as the MO tries to assess the nature of the wounds and the chances of survival, and issues instructions to his helpers.

You can't possibly interrupt them, but as a folding table is being set up as an operating table, you get the chance to ask a stretcher-bearer where he wants you to put the dressings you have brought them. He gets another stretcher-bearer to help him pack them in a hamper he locates somewhere. And while they are filling it from the Jeep, you ask them how many of their guys were casualties. They say that at least eight are dead and about double that wounded. A sickening feeling of utter helplessness you have been fighting to control sweeps over you, and you find yourself cursing out loud at the terrible waste of men's lives.

Then realizing you aren't helping in any way, and could even be hindering, you return to your command post, thankful beyond words that your troop didn't find those Nebelwerfers. If the Germans had booby-trapped them they couldn't have been more devastating. And in one sense they actually had turned them into booby traps.

Long after you're back in the comforting familiarity of your dugout, surrounded by friendly, unwounded, whole men, you continue to live with that horrific scene in that gloomy barn among the dead and dying gunners.

PART SEVEN: AUGUST 14–23

Renewing Attack to Entrap
the German Army

56

UGLY SOUNDS OF
HORRIBLE MEANING

※

MOST SHELLS AND MORTARS SOUND A WARNING BEFORE THEY arrive, and throughout every waking hour, you, like everyone in the forward areas of the Normandy bridgehead, regardless of what you are doing, go about with ears cocked continually for the sound of something coming. Early on, you learned how to distinguish from the sound which of them were going to land close by, which were going to land well beyond you, and which were completely off line and would land harmlessly some distance away to your right or left. This saves a lot of needless diving into holes and flopping down in the dirt.

Moaning Minnies are in a class by themselves in providing warning with unearthly animal sounds, sometimes suggestive of the agonized bellowing of a herd of cows hurtling through the sky with butcher knives buried in their rumps, and at other times sounding like the very hounds of hell itself might sound, baying and howling with growing intensity as they descend around you.

Designed to alert the whole front, and keep everybody in dreadful suspense as to where the salvo of six big bombs of tremendous blasting force is going to land, they daily and nightly accomplish their purpose.

In contrast, the enemy's conventional mortar bombs, the more frequent visitors, signal their coming with very abbreviated swishing or buzzing sounds, of varying intensity and pitch, depending on their size and velocity. Spinning shells moan, hum, whine, wail, shriek, or emit only an air-rustling whisper before landing. The most dangerous, those dead on line, provide the least warning: only a faint, vicious hum, screech, or crackle, then *wham!* And, of course, you don't actually hear the explosion of the one that lands really close to you. You feel it, but the shocking intensity of a shell or bomb exploding close by is so entirely overpowering, your eardrums, stretched to the point of bursting by the compression, can't register it. You feel the concussion, you feel the ground shake, and you see the flash even through closed eyelids, but you don't hear it.

Among the weapons sending projectiles this way, two are in contention for the title Most Demoralizing, but for entirely different reasons: the Moaning Minnie, because of the length and intensity of its bloodcurdling warning, and the 88-mm gun because of the total absence of warning, with the final vote probably going in favour of the 88.

The 88-mm shell, being faster than sound, flashes a paralysing explosion before you hear it coming. Suddenly, with no warning, there's a wicked *wham* from a black airburst puff over a crossroads or above the gun position, followed instantaneously by a metallic screech, a chilling, banshee *yee-ow!* that could only be duplicated by a giant ripping asunder a piece of boilerplate. And so, in rapid succession, it's *Wham! – Yee-ow! . . . Wham! – Yee-ow! . . . Wham! – Yee-ow!*, until Jerry decides he's thrown over enough for the moment.

The shocking crash of an 88-mm shell landing without warning beside a slit trench may be the cause of heart failure of those men who now and then are found dead in trenches with no mark on them and whose deaths are usually attributed to "concussion."

Even an armour-piercing, 88-mm solid-shot, passing just over your head in the open, is a deadly sound. But when one drills through

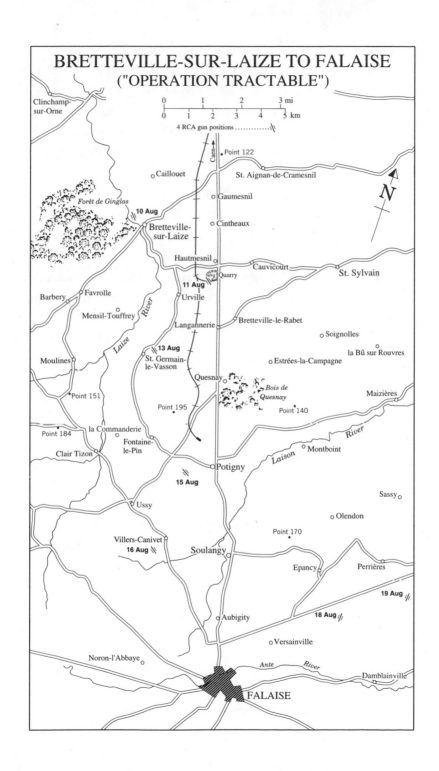

BRETTEVILLE-SUR-LAIZE TO FALAISE
("OPERATION TRACTABLE")

Clinchamp-
sur-Orne

0   1   2   3 mi
0   1   2   3   4   5 km

4 RCA gun positions ....\\\

Point 122

Caillouet

St. Aignan-de-Cramesnil

Forêt de Ginglas

Gaumesnil

10 Aug

Bretteville-
sur-Laize

Cintheaux

Hautmesnil

Cauvicourt

St. Sylvain

Quarry

11 Aug

Favrolle

Barbery

Urville

Bretteville-le-Rabet

Mensil-Touffrey

Soignolles

Langannerie

la Bû sur Rouvres

Laize River

13 Aug

St. Germain-
le-Vasson

Estrées-la-Campagne

Moulines

Quesnay

Bois de
Quesnay

Maizières

Point 151

Point 195

Point 140

Point 184

la Commanderie

Fontaine-
le-Pin

Laison River

Montboint

Clair Tizon

Potigny

15 Aug

Ussy

Sassy

Olendon

Villers-Canivet

Point 170

16 Aug

Soulangy

Epancy

Perrières

19 Aug

18 Aug

Aubigity

Versainville

Noron-l'Abbaye

Ante River

Damblainville

FALAISE

the stone walls of a house in which you are standing – in one side and out the other, in a deafening split-second *rip* – it produces still another heart-stopping effect. And this morning Jerry, by design or accident, provides this experience while you are visiting a little stone barn currently serving as regimental headquarters at the left rear of the guns, down a rather steep slope exposed to distant ridges still held by the enemy.

At dawn, just after you've climbed into your sack in your trench along the hedgerow, and are luxuriating in those delicious final moments of consciousness before drifting off, you get a message from RHQ. You are to go back several miles to 2nd Division Headquarters to pick up a fire plan and overprinted maps related to the support expected of the guns during the opening of the final drive through to Falaise.

Since your involvement in the aftermath of 6th Field's disastrous Nebelwerfer affair kept you awake until you went on duty at midnight, you had a totally sleepless night, and your humour is foul as you drive back many miles to a map reference not far from your second-last gun position, on the high ground along the river northwest of Bretteville-sur Laize.

Still, as you drive west on the quiet road, in the open Jeep with the rising sun behind you, you can't help recognizing a truly beautiful morning. While it will probably develop into another hot, muggy day, the early morning air is a tonic – cool and fresh, smelling sweetly of the dewy vegetation along the slopes of the Laize valley, which still manages to retain its charming green untouched-by-war look, in spite of an obvious increase in the traffic through here.

You find the Division HQ trucks and caravans sitting in a peaceful, leafy orchard dappled with early-morning sunlight. Pinned to a board on an easel is an impressive large-scale map showing the developing Falaise pocket, which, if closed, will trap the whole German army. A couple of clean, well-pressed, beautifully turned-out officers are examining it with obvious excitement verging on gaiety. Conscious of your sandy, rumpled battledress, you get away from them before they can notice you and go looking for the major you are supposed to see. You find him, stripped to the waist, shaving from a folding, green canvas sink before a real mirror hanging from a tree. You study his clean, pink back and wonder what your own back looks like, as you haven't had your clothes off for more than six weeks, and have been scratching a great deal lately, having missed the delousing parade, when all ranks had had an anti-flea powder blown inside their tunics and pants through a tube inserted at their collars and waistbands.

You catch sight of a dirty, unshaven face in the mirror. With shock and guilt you realize it's your own, and involuntarily hide your filthy hands behind your back as the Major turns around, drying himself with a sparkling white towel. He's in high spirits as he pulls on a clean shirt. And as he leads you over to his caravan for the maps and plans, he tries to engage you in conversation as to "how things are going with you chaps up there. You know, if you can speed it up, we could end the war right here." But you snatch the roll of papers from him, and get away as quickly as possible before you run into the General.

It's while you are delivering the plans at regimental headquarters that a stray armour-piercing tank shell tears through the back wall and out through the front, with a hell of a *rip*, leaving a hole just above the sleeping adjutant's head. And strangely this makes you happy as the devil as you go back up to your guns.

Overnight there were massive movements of troops and tanks, as formations repositioned themselves for the attack, principally 3rd Canadian Division, 2nd Canadian Armoured Brigade, 4th Canadian Armoured Division, the Polish Armoured Division, and the 79th Armoured Division, that special British division equipped with various "funnies," including the tanks carrying fascines (enormous bundles of densely packed tree branches) meant to be dropped into the Laison river at shallow spots to provide causeways for tanks and recce cars.

And though a heavy harassing-fire program was conducted by the guns to cover the sound of whining motors and squealing tracks, the noise aroused a great deal of attention from German guns and mortars. So when the Polish Armoured Division became neighbours of 26th Battery in the early hours, attracting Moaning Minnies and 88s, the newcomers were not entirely welcome.

Still, few expressed their antagonism to the extent of one Gunner G. C. Henry, who, on awakening to the sound of encircling armour and crashing shells, had a dark figure drop in his trench uttering words sounding most Germanic to untrained ears. Hardly surprising that Henry (as Sgt. Bruce Hunt duly recorded) "laid violent hands on the importunate Pole, who, doubtless having heard of the more uncultured pursuits of his new comrades-in-arms, took off in haste, 88s notwithstanding, shrieking, 'Me Polish! Me Polish! See my hat!'"

Far over to the northeast, just short of the horizon, tanks of the 2nd Armoured Brigade are lined up in what an army historian will call "parade-ground order." Behind them are the armoured cars of 7th Recce, and then the 9th Canadian Infantry Brigade in Kangaroos. Behind them is 7th Brigade, and still farther east in the valley south of Cauvicourt, are the columns of 4th Armoured Division. In front are the flails of the 1st Lothians of the British 79th Armoured Division, who will pound a way through mine fields, leading the 21st and 22nd Canadian Armoured Regiments of 4th Armoured Brigade (each formed up almost track to track in four lines), with the 28th (British Columbia) Regiment and the Lake Superior (Motor) Regiment arranged in equally solid formations at the rear.

At 11:25 A.M. all the guns for miles around open up in a crashing roar, some firing red smoke to mark targets for the first wave of bombers. No one at the guns will be able to follow the course of the confusing operation, made even more confusing by bomber errors as the day progresses. But Canadian Army historians will later reconstruct an unusually vivid picture of the opening phase:

> ... the din grew to unbelievable proportions as noon approached on this glittering August day – the guns adding to the thunder of exploding bombs as the artillery opened up with its concentrations.
>
> The resultant smoke and dust was soon obscured by grey-white billows of smoke pouring from the bursting canisters of 25-pounder smoke shells and filling the valley south of Estrées-la-Campagne [five kilometres east of the guns, beyond the Caen–Falaise highway and Quesnay Woods] with a misty, impenetrable blanket.
>
> At 1140 hours the suspense engendered by wireless-silence was broken with the words "Move now!" and the armoured brigades came on towards the startline to begin their daring and spectacular advance. Punctually at noon, under the canopy of bombers, our columns crossed their line between Soignolles (on the left) and Estrées-la-Campagne and, at 12 miles per hour, began their long crawl to the Laison River.
>
> And as they moved south they gradually disappeared behind the continuous screen into which the white puffs of smoke (roiling from the 25-pounder smoke canisters) had merged. Almost at once drivers found it impossible to keep direction; they could merely press on into the sun with accelerator pedals pushed to the floor. Running blind behind their clumsy fascines, the Churchills began to stray stupidly among a welter of Shermans, carriers, Crocodiles, and Flails – each trying desperately to get back onto the required direction, with the heavier monsters trying to keep the head of the column.
>
> Units lost formation and in less than an hour the almost ceremonial array of the forenoon had degenerated into a

heterogeneous mass pouring down into the smoke-filled valley against a current of prisoners streaming to the rear.

In spite of the dust which obliterated land marks and made visibility extremely poor, obstacles were surmounted, mine-fields marked and by-passed, and after each brief halt to check direction the lumbering vehicles lurched forth again to disappear with a roar into the mist-like smoke, acrid with the stink of engines. . . .

Blinded by the smoke and dust, the enemy gunners frantically "searched" their defensive fire zones, but with comparatively little success. Many enemy infantry, deafened by the blast and bewildered by smoke, realized the utter uselessness of trying to resist the weight of steel bearing on them from every direction. . . . As the attack gained momentum, prisoners became so numerous that they were merely sent back along the centre line unescorted.*

That the assaulting columns succeed in all their objectives, crossing the Laison after sorting out massive confusion along its near bank as units pushed this way and that for fording places, is not something to which people in the rear areas give much thought as the afternoon progresses and the thunder of bombs being delivered miles behind the lines mounts to an awesome crescendo. Even Corps Commander Simonds, for a while at least, can't help being preoccupied with matters other than what is going on up front, as his armoured car is rocked violently to and fro by the concussions of errant 500-pound bombs landing around and about the quarry at Hautmesnil, where he has chosen to view proceedings.

---

* From pp. 66–67 Report No. 65, Historical Section (G.S.) Canadian Army Headquarters, Dec. 23, 1953, subtitled "Tractable: The First Phase (14 Aug)," based on unit was diaries.

57

RAF TAKES A TURN AT BOMBING
THE CANADIAN ARMY

※

IT'S A BRIGHT SUNNY DAY, WITH ONLY WISPS OF CLOUD IN THE SKY, and they're bombing the Germans again just over the hill in front to get Operation Tractable, the final drive, moving towards Falaise.

The new offensive, involving 3rd Division infantry this time, got underway at noon, covered by the giant smokescreen fired by four field regiments across a front of more than three miles, moving forward in lifts like a creeping barrage to a depth of about two and a half miles, staying abreast of the advancing columns of tanks and armoured personnel carriers full of infantry.* The column on the right is led by 2nd Armoured Brigade with two brigades of 3rd Division following, the 9th in Kangaroos and armoured half-tracks and the 7th following on foot; while on the left, 4th Armoured Brigade conducts the 8th Infantry Brigade of 3rd Division in carriers, with 10th Brigade following on foot.

Fifteen minutes before H-hour (a little more than two hours earlier) guns of 23rd Field marked targets with red smoke shells for seventy-five medium Mitchell and Boston bombers, attacking gun and mortar positions along the wooded Laison river valley, while

---

* After observing from six hundred feet up in an Auster OP plane, Lt.-Col. Frank Lace, GSO 1 to Brig. Brownfield, BRA Canadian Army, reported he was very satisfied with the quality of the smoke screen.

Tiffies and bomb-carrying Spitfires attacked whatever they could find. Now eight hundred Halifax and Lancaster heavy RAF bombers, including those of No. 6 Royal Canadian Air Force Bomber Group, have begun to drop 3,723 tons of bombs, on targets bypassed by the assaulting columns, around Potigny, two and a half miles south of here, and Quesnay Wood, just a mile and a quarter east of your guns. Though dropping considerably less than the 5,200 tons dropped on German positions south of Verrières a week ago to start off Totalize, today's bombers will still unload 1,300 tons more than were dropped on Hamburg on the night of July 27–28, 1943, in what has become known as the "deadliest RAF raid of the war" because of the awful fire storm created.

Your guns are now silent, having participated in the timed concentrations on targets selected for ten minutes of drenching fire by four divisional artilleries and two AGRAs five minutes before H-hour. And now, having no part in the big smokescreen, all here at the guns have become spectators of the vast, roaring air armada swarming in from the coast, wave after wave of great black planes with bomb bays open, moving relentlessly, without any apparent enemy interference, towards the two dust clouds forming out front.

The concussions are monstrous. The ground shudders and blast-waves shatter and wrinkle the lacy clouds overhead, as stones might if tossed into a pond of milk.

As a towering black dust-cloud billows hundreds of feet in the air, you experience a creeping sense of horror at the depths of hell being sounded in that valley in front, where the targets are not war plants or concrete forts, but men sheltering in shallow holes.

Then suddenly they start bombing several hundred yards behind, and before the dust blackens out the scene, you see men running frantically as black bombs tumble down on them. Some bombers still stagger out of the dust cloud behind and pass over towards the dust cloud ahead, the menacing bombs clearly visible through their open bomb bays. Someone remarks that our carrier crews with their infantry battalions are back there somewhere, for only this morning 4th Brigade was pulled out of the line and marched back there for a few hours' rest.

Units of the Polish Division, some of which are parked alongside 26th Battery, are down there where the bombs are dropping, and you assume the men you see standing on tanks dotted about the valley floor, frantically waving swatches of yellow celanese cloth to identify themselves as friendly troops, are Polish troopers. Some have lit yellow smoke-generating canisters, and the smoke is drifting in gaudy streaks across the sunlit valley.

You wonder how many other units, including artillery outfits amassed to provide maximum support for this big push, are now being plastered in that dust-cloud.

A terrible disaster is taking place, and you are powerless to intervene. You think you're going to be sick to your stomach if you don't start doing something, even if it's only walking around in circles. There's a farmhouse almost hidden by trees to the right rear of the guns, a couple of hundred yards away. Maybe there's a barrel of cold cider there.

As you walk across the stubble field, between the stooks of yellow grain, you feel the earth tremble and shudder beneath your feet from the thunderous *crump, crump, crump* of the bombs landing on the slopes near the Hautmesnil quarry about a mile away and down on the valley floor covered with tanks and vehicles only four or five hundred yards away. Inexplicably some bombers still resist the temptation to add their bombs to the inferno in the valley below, and continue to lumber out of the dust and smoke with their bomb bays still loaded with big black bombs, passing overhead towards the towering dust cloud in the valley in front of the guns.

Then you see a little Auster aircraft, the kind used by artillery air OP officers, flying right up towards the bellies and the open bomb bays of the huge bombers, firing off red Very lights at them.

You, along with thousands and thousands of others watching from the ground, earnestly wish that brave man luck. If one of those bombs raining down round him strikes his little plane, there'll be just a split-second atomizing flash, and he'll be no more. And he obviously knows it.

Still he flies his tiny, fragile craft round and about, right up underneath the open bomb bays, waggling his wings and looping smoky red baubles from his Very pistol across the flight path of the great roaring bombers.

Seldom, if ever, have so many been witness to such a splendid display of courage by an individual as is now being displayed by that man in that fragile little plane up there.*

---

* Eversley Belfield, of the Royal Artillery, serving as a flying OP officer with the Canadian Army, recorded in his diary something of the extraordinary action he took on this afternoon of horror: "The weather was perfect as the first wave of heavy bombers plastered Quesnay Wood which had been holding us up for so long. Everybody felt very elated and excited and we were all congratulating ourselves on their accuracy, but the second wave arrived. . . . Suddenly to the east of where we were sitting on the open ground watching this attack, there was a vast billow of black smoke and the earth rocked as more and more Lancasters dropped their bombs there. Then some began to come over us at 3,000 feet, their bomb doors open and the bombs plainly visible. We dashed for some nearby German slit trenches, fearing the worst, but all the bombs seemed to land the other [east] side of the road. There was a lull and then I saw a third wave of bombers approaching. I leapt into a Jeep with one of the mechanics and made for one of the Austers (which were parked nearby). As he started it up, he offered to go up with me, but I refused, as his extra weight would have reduced the climbing performance. I climbed at full throttle; and with great difficulty (for I had forgotten how it worked), I fired off a red Very cartridge at about 2,000 feet and another at 4,000 feet. At about 6,000 feet, I was just below a large formation and twisted and turned to get their attention. I am certain that none of the third wave bombed our own forces, as I was in the midst of the stream of planes and noted, when one formation passed just above me, that I could plainly see the large bombs in the open bay. I was very fearful of bombs falling on me, as I was over the area that they had been bombing earlier." Quoted by Sir Brian Horrocks, Eversley Belfield, and Maj.-Gen. Essame, *Corps Commander* (Toronto: Griffin House,), pp. 44–45.

You find the farmhouse occupied by a command-post crew of another artillery outfit. Astonishingly, they are so absorbed with the progress of a fire plan, they're oblivious to the fact that bombs are falling short behind them. Feeling like an intruder, you retreat to the yard. In the shade cast by some trees are two kitchen chairs. On one sits a portable wind-up gramophone. Sitting down on the other, you pick up from the ground two recordings, one labelled *Blanche-Neige et les Sept Nains*, and the other, *J'Attendrai*.

Blowing the dust off *J'Attendrai*, you put it on the turntable and, for the next hour or more, play it over and over – only half-listening as you reset the needle and wind up the machine when it runs down – on and on like an automaton, so preoccupied are you with the bombing. Surely they'll discover their error before they start filling in the gap still remaining between the two gigantic dust clouds. Still, if they can bomb miles behind their actual strike zone, they have to believe it's enemy ground between that dust cloud back there and the one in front. Mechanically, you pursue your ritual of keeping the machine wound up and the record playing as you stare skyward, over the house and trees, at the undersides of passing bombers, clusters of bombs hanging in their bomb bays like monstrous black grapes.

Just how long you sit there, playing *J'Attendrai* over and over, you'll never be able to say, but finally you become aware that the thunder of bombs has ceased and only the fading drone of planes remains as the last of the bombers head for the Channel and their bases in England. As you abandon your gramophone, you wonder if any of those bomber crews know yet what they've done. When they're back in their messes in England tonight, having a Scotch-and-soda before dinner, will they become fully conscious of the disaster in which they participated, and get totally sloshed before going to bed and attempting to sleep?*

---

* General Guy Simonds, in a postwar lecture attended by the author, explained that the ground forces had been told yellow celanese or smoke

Unquestionably many have died back there, and you despair for friends in the 4th Field carrier crews and battery commander crews attached to 4th Brigade infantry who had only hours ago been pulled out of the line and sent back there for a rest.

Stu Laurie, who is attached to battalion headquarters as their arty rep since Major Wren was killed yesterday, barely arrives back with the Royals in their rest area near Hautmesnil when it becomes the epicentre of a torrent of bombs. Days later, it will still be an ordeal for him to recall the horror of having a bright, sunny day suddenly turn inky-black amidst a string of stupendous explosions.

Surrounded by a god-awful cacophony of four-engined planes roaring overhead and bombs screaming down to earth-quaking blasts, sweeping him with concussion winds of hurricane force loaded with sand and pebbles and larger hunks of debris, Laurie crawls about on his hands and knees in total blackness, convinced he has been blinded. Determined not to return home blind, he pulls his pistol from its holster, but before he can use it the dust cloud opens briefly, allowing a flicker of light to show him it isn't his eyes that are the problem, but the density of the dust.

I'm out in the open in a field when the bombing starts. We are all just standing around, watching the bombing out front. Then they start bombing to the rear. And for a while we watch everybody else taking it. They plaster the Poles – they're running in all

---

would be recognized by the airforce as the mark of friendly troops, and should be displayed whenever they were fearful they might be mistaken for the enemy by strafing aircraft. The airforce were told that yellow celanese or yellow smoke would mark the front line. Thus, when nervous units, bombed by the U.S.A. Airforce back at Caen a few days before, displayed yellow celanese miles behind the lines, it appeared to mark the front line to some airmen, who should have been, but were not, timing their run from the coast to their designated targets.

directions. I don't know what to think of this. But then they start to drop what seems like thousands of bombs down on us.

I crawl around on my hands and knees in the dark for what seems like all afternoon. You can't see anything. Finally I find a hole to crawl into. It turns out to be a hole in a mound – a great big ruddy mound – full of men.*

Earlier in the day Major Ralph Young, acting CO of the Royals, on arrival at Hautmesnil "for a few hours' rest before going forward to fill a gap between 3rd Div and 51st Highland Division later in the day," had discovered this huge German bunker and designated it his "alternative battalion headquarters."

The regiment is distributed among the houses of the village with battalion headquarters in a substantial farmhouse. Behind us is this sunken road, and beyond the road is this hell-of-a-great bunker, a really big thing which you enter from the road.

The support company is deployed around the perimeter of this field – carriers, mortars, anti-tank guns and vehicles, all of them parked in the shadow of the hedgerows.

It is a beautiful warm day, and the guys have taken off their equipment and most of their clothing, and are lying about relaxing in the sunshine, or down the hill at a mobile bath that's been set up nearby, when this thing starts north of Hautmesnil and progresses south until eventually the bombs are landing right on our position.

I am at an O Group at Brigade with my intelligence officer, David Henry, when I get an S.O.S.: "Bring back yellow smoke – we're being bombed three hundred yards north of us." Somebody produces a box of yellow smoke, and we take off. But when we get there, A Echelon has just arrived and is strung out

---

*　Author interview.

along the road, blocking it all the way up the hill. Henry goes one way with an armful of smoke bombs and I go another. When I get to battalion headquarters there is a great hole outside the farmhouse and two pioneers lying dead on the rim of the crater. So I go to my alternative headquarters in the bunker. Half the battalion seems to have collected there – most of support company anyway – at least fifty people. It's a big room, maybe twenty feet by fifteen.

All of a sudden, bang . . . bang . . . bang – a string of huge explosions! Everything goes dark and pandemonium almost breaks out. I am more or less at the entrance to the bunker, and I, along with everybody else, think a bomb has buried the entrance, entombing us. This sets up quite a feeling of panic. It is starting, it is coming, but I am able to stop it by making them aware of a second exit, a ventilation opening at the other end I discovered when I was checking out the bunker as a possible HQ. As it turns out when the dust clears, the entrance is clear.*

Bob Suckling, commander of D Company, will also carry frightful memories of what it is like to be under the worst concentration of bombs ever dropped on troops by Bomber Command, for the Royals were at the very centre of that high-explosive hurricane today – a day that began so pleasantly for him:

We have just marched back some miles from a forward position to a little village [Hautmesnil] on the Caen–Falaise highway. I am now a company commander. In a matter of five weeks, I've been elevated from lieutenant to acting-captain to acting-major! Unable to locate within the battalion any "crowns" [embroidered shoulder-insignia identifying a major], I seek them at Brigade HQ, finally getting a pair from Jim Knox, the brigade

---

* The quotations from Ralph Young are from an interview with the author.

major, who fired me as liaison officer in England. He is surprised, and I am glad!

But then in the afternoon we are bombed intermittently for an hour and a half by Lancasters and Halifaxes of the RCAF and RAF at low level. For sheer terror, this is an afternoon of a lifetime.

I'm waiting in the south end of the village to meet our blanket truck and other soft-skinned vehicles to show them to the company area, when the bombing starts. The men mostly flee the village into the surrounding wheat fields – though it's impossible to know which way to run.

At one point I am in a partly dug slit trench, just deep enough that when I double up, the top of my head is at ground level – which is not very reassuring. A little later, having moved between bomber waves, I find myself in a bomb crater with Padre Harry Appleyard.

At the south end of the village there is an open space of about two hundred yards between us and a very large stone quarry. There I see some Royal Canadian Engineers, each holding a corner of an enormous piece of yellow chiffon [celanese] so the bombers can see it. They do. Their bomb bays are open approaching from the north. The bombs are released. They come down screaming over our bomb crater and land absolutely squarely on the yellow chiffon. The earth and stones blasted in the air make it seem like midnight on a bright sunny afternoon. And when all the crap settles back to earth, there is not a single vestige of yellow celanese or the four engineers to be seen.

By now the whole battalion area is ablaze, though most of the stone houses in the village are still surviving to some degree.

At one point I find my way to tac headquarters in the basement of a stone house, where I see a Toronto Scottish sergeant – his face pock-marked by sand and gravel – coming down the stairs with tears streaming down his face.

My company area is an apple orchard full of mature trees. Our company carrier was left parked alongside a stone fence. When I get back, there is not a tree standing – the whole orchard is under a foot or more of fresh earth. There isn't a sign of the carrier, though the nearest bomb crater is thirty or more yards away. Finally I find part of a bogey wheel about fifty yards away, but that is all. I keep thinking, all that armour-plate couldn't just disappear. But it has.

Support company vehicles are all on fire, and mortar ammunition and pioneer platoon supplies carried in them explode for hours.

My company [when collected] is practically naked, and only a few of them have weapons, simply because most of them were stripped down when the bombing started, and ran into the fields in their underwear.

Located in the big stone quarry just south of the village, in the turret of an armoured car with our corps commander, Guy Granville Simonds, watching his planes carry out their great bombing attack, was Air Marshal Sir Arthur Coningham, Commander-in-Chief RAF Tactical Forces. Even he couldn't do anything to stop them. I'd like to know what he was thinking as he bounced around inside that armoured car during that hour and a half!*

When the bombing finally ends and Major Ralph Young comes outside the bunker, he sees no one:

The battalion has disappeared. My adjutant and I walk around the area and meet no one. All our carriers, mortars, and anti-tank guns are destroyed. The field where they were parked is a total shambles. A smashed carrier is upside down in a hedgerow. Then we discover Jack Stothers's company in a cellar under a house.

---

*   Author interview.

Gradually others begin drifting in from the fields and up the hill from the mobile bath. And after a while to our relief we find we have lost only fifty-six – a grim enough toll, but nothing to what it might have been had they not scattered into the countryside.

But the Royals have lost most of their clothing, personal equipment, blankets, ammunition, and weapons, including six anti-tank guns, fifteen mortars, seventeen machine guns, twenty-nine wireless sets, and twenty-four vehicles of various kinds.

And in the aftermath, 4th Field FOOs and their crews, who shared this dreadful afternoon with the Royals, will be left with indelible images: of half-naked, stunned men, some in bare feet, straggling back to the village and wandering aimlessly across freshly turned earth of neighbouring fields, searching in vain for any sign of the vanished equipment or clothing; of stretcher-bearers wending their way around giant craters searching for the wounded; of the endless parade of ambulance Jeeps assembled from other units, flying Red Cross flags and loaded with blanket-wrapped soldiers, threading their way back along the traffic-choked roads to casualty clearing stations in the rear; and of the silhouette against the setting sun of a burial party, with the padre carrying out the sad duty all padres must perform as the battle dies away and the furies recede.

After so many nerve-wracking days of plodding forward – fighting to secure another rise, only to be ordered on again to fight for yet another, indistinguishable from the last – for this to happen now is almost too much for men to bear. Morale is about as low as it can go, before a rum ration is scrounged and a supper of sorts is put together for the haggard men.

By midnight the Royals' quartermaster, Capt. Dan Wilkie, manages somehow to procure replacements for much of the lost weapons and vehicles, and has outfitted the men with enough clothing to allow the battalion to move out in the morning to fulfil its obligation to the left flank of the final drive south towards Falaise. But seriously under-strength, the battalion is a very ragged-looking outfit, with most of them still lacking battledress blouses. The troops that Stu Laurie (now acting-commander of 2nd Battery) accompanies down the Falaise road in the morning are armed only with shovels.

No unit within or close to the perimeter of the maelstrom will establish a list of casualties for at least twenty-four hours, for when the bombs began to tumble down, scores of men, including men from the 4th Field wagon lines, ran from fields that appeared next in line for the carpet bombing then moving south. Some ran in terror until they dropped from exhaustion, and won't reappear until after they are listed as missing.

An accurate casualty count will never be possible because of the difficulty in separating casualties of the bombing from other casualties on August 14. Next day's estimate of four hundred casualties – 150 dead and 250 wounded – must serve as a final count, but to those who were within sight and sound of it all, those figures will always seem to understate the facts. To anyone watching, it will always seem a miracle that anyone emerged alive from that horrendous rain of bombs.

Coming only six days after the Americans bombed behind you south of Caen, causing 380 Canadian and Polish casualties – many among the same units as were bombed today – this tragic error is, for many, unendurable. In the opinion of "Hank" Caldwell, the Royals' anti-tank officer (shortly to become a company commander), "the wounded of the bombing consisted almost entirely of men who were left nervous wrecks. Afterwards I saw General Guy Simonds standing by the roadside as truckloads of such casualties went by."*

Clearly the official casualty toll, grim as it is, will never tell the true story, for no count will ever be made of the untold numbers of

---

*   Author interview.

men, who, though they came through the day with no visible wounds, discover their nervous systems are so shattered they will never recover the emotional resilience necessary to survive shelling and mortaring without losing their grip and breaking down.*

---

* Months later in the Rhineland, the author saw Royals, recently returned from hospital after recovering from "battle exhaustion" induced by the Hautmesnil bombing, break down again under heavy shelling.

58

GUNNERS LYING ABOUT AS THOUGH DEAD

✳

THERE ARE ALMOST AS MANY THEORIES AS TO THE CAUSE OF dysentery afflicting the Canadians on the highway from Caen to Falaise as there are cases. Perhaps most suspected as the culprit is polluted drinking water, which from mid-July until now has been drawn from the Orne River, where bodies of dead men and animals lie in stagnant backwaters or drift slowly downstream and out to sea.

Certainly, all those in 4th Field who watched the parade of water wagons at Fleury-sur-Orne, backing up to the river near the collapsed railway bridge right behind the gun position, to fill their tanks with the turgid liquid, could easily believe that water is the cause.

Gunner Saunders is not likely to soon forget a 4th Field water wagon with its suction tube inserted in the river only a few feet away from the upturned, glistening bottom of a German body, caught in a weedy backwater. At first he thought the shiny, blueish-black object was a bladder out of a football – until he poked it with a stick.

But when you raised the matter of water quality with Gunner Tommy Dodds, the 2nd Battery water-wagon man (trained to add the contents of this bottle and that bottle to his tank, and conduct tests on the water until he deems it safe to drink), he assured you,

"That water is so loaded with chlorine, you could sell it as bleach back in Caen. No germ could ever live in it."

And from the smell and taste of the water in your water-bottle, you are inclined to accept his verdict. Furthermore, though dysentery made its appearance at Fleury, it wasn't really widespread until after Ifs, where the Regiment feasted on the clear, cold water from a deep well behind the guns on the outskirts of the village. This, of course, has inspired the theory the Germans dropped something in the well.

Another theory attracting a great deal of support is that the dysentery is caused by flies fresh from feasting on the abundant decaying flesh of men and animals, alighting with polluted feet and proboscises on food even as it is being carried on a spoon from mess-tin to mouth.

Certainly there are millions of flies. The first morning at Ifs, you were conned by Bombardier Hossack and Gunner Hiltz into walking some distance over to a farmyard to examine a shiny, black-enamelled two-wheel cart – after they had drawn you into speculating as to what it possibly could be used for, it being the only well-painted cart so far seen in all Normandy.

They, of course, had already been over to it, and watched with amusement as you went over and discovered it wasn't painted, but was completely covered with shiny black flies – every detail, from the shafts to the box, including the spokes of the wheels, the rims, and the hubs, every visible square centimetre, hidden under a seething mass of flies.

Oh yes, there are lots of flies here. And it's easy to accept the theory that with the abundance of decaying bodies lying around unburied throughout all of July – not to mention the tons of human excrement in thousands of uncovered latrines throughout the bridgehead – very little in the way of food is consumed that has not been touched by a fly that has just flown in from some foul spot.

Still, there are others who believe that because some men have not succumbed at all, or have been only lightly afflicted, the illness may have its origins in a lowered resistance caused by extreme fatigue or anxiety. But if this were so, then on this unusually quiet day today at the 4th Field guns, you might have expected that there would be some improvement in the dysentery problem, since today has been given over to maintenance and rest here at Able Troop, as 3rd and 4th divisions carry the attack east of the Caen–Falaise highway, with obvious success following yesterday's bombing of enemy positions by those planes that did manage to land their bombs properly on target. However, the perverse affliction seems to flourish in relaxed bodies – at least the debilitating effects seem to become more pronounced when men are relaxing and catching up on sleep. This you discover in dramatic and disturbing fashion early in the evening.

Late in the afternoon recce parties are called to go forward to line up new gun positions about five miles farther on towards Falaise – a few hundred yards to the right and just beyond the town of Potigny. And at about 8:00 P.M., the order comes from RHQ to limber up and form up in regimental convoy out on the road behind the position, ready to move off. This you pass on to the guns in routine fashion over the Tannoy speakers just as the gun quads are rolling onto the position to park in attendance at their respective pits to receive limbers and guns.

But when the command post has been dismantled, and everything is packed into GA and TL (including the two long strips of corrugated iron from Carpiquet aerodrome used to support the earthen roof), and you look around the position expecting to see the guns hooked up to the quads waiting patiently the order to pull out, you can hardly believe your eyes.

The quads sit there devoid of limbers and guns. Absolutely nothing is going on. The guns still rest in the pits. And near them you see men lying on the ground, unmoving as though dead.

The scene is unnerving! You start conjecturing wildly: your first thought is that you have a mutiny on your hands. . . . All that digging they've had to do recently, three gun pits and three ammunition pits in three days, all of them in solid chalk! But why on earth would they want to do this now, when they've had practically nothing to do but sleep all day? That they're drunk is a more likely possibility. . . . Somebody must have discovered a cache of Calvados somewhere, and in their weakened state that overproof stuff has knocked them out. As you hasten towards the nearest gun past a quad, you notice the driver is leaning forward over his steering wheel, head down, as though sleeping. Oh no, not the drivers, too! You recognize him: Ross Wilcox, a most dependable man. You stop and call up to him, "Wilcox . . . what the hell is going on?"

Raising his head he stares at you a moment before replying laconically, "Just suffering the shits, sir – like everybody else."

Is it possible? Has the dysentery that has plagued the troop for days, and for which the MO has no medicines, culminated in this?

Confirmation comes from Sgt. Carl Mayhew when you lean down to question him as he lies on his back beside his gun pit, his arms folded over his eyes. No odour of alcohol rises from his puffy, feverish lips as he uncovers his eyes and laboriously rolls over until he's kneeling before you. For a moment he looks at you blinking, as though trying to comprehend what you are asking, then, in a weak, husky voice, says, "Sir, we're all too sick."

This of course is unacceptable. And you can tell by the way he says it (not in defiance, but as a plea for mercy) that deep within him he knows it, too. It is clear what must be done, but how to accomplish it is another matter. Barking out orders and threatening to put men on charge will not work here – not with men such as these, who for interminable periods during the past month have carried on beyond human endurance without a growl or complaint. But if those guns are to move tonight, they must somehow be persuaded to get up on their feet.

Convincing men, who are so sick they don't know what's going on around them, into getting up and limbering up guns is something beyond all your training and experience. But you count on the character of these men, whom you've come to admire so much, reasserting itself with a little encouragement.

You start with Mayhew, talking encouragingly as you grasp his hands and pull him to his feet, reminding him of the one thing no gunner could ever refuse, a call for help from the infantry. They are depending on these guns for support, and unless they are moved forward, they'll be out of range and unable to bring down fire to break up counter-attacks. Surely he doesn't want to let those poor bastards down now – now they're so near to closing off the pocket and capturing a whole German army, and maybe ending the war right here.

And when Mayhew's up on his feet, you go to each of the other three sergeants and do the same, saying whatever comes into your head that might encourage them into making what, for them, must be a superhuman effort to get their guns winched out of the pits and hooked up to limbers and quads, reminding them over and over how much the infantry is depending on them. And then you watch as the astonishing leadership of the gun sergeants begins to work its magic. Soon every man is on his feet and moving, albeit slowly.

You will never admire men more. While their conscience leaves them no choice, you know what they are going through, for you were one of the first to suffer the convulsive cramps and cold-shuddering fever associated with this damnable scourge just before the break-out from Verrières.

They move, but they move like men who are dying on their feet – so slowly the Regiment (with surprising good grace) accepts your report of the situation and leaves you and your troop behind, to find your own way later to a map reference about a mile southwest of Potigny.

And when finally the four guns are limbered up, and you are moving off in the dark into a thickening fog, you think what an indescribable nightmare it must be for infantry suffering dysentery even to drag themselves over hill and dale for miles laden down with weapons, ammunition, trenching tools, and the like, let alone dash here and there for cover on the way, dig in on their objective, and then brace themselves with what little will and strength they have left to resist the inevitable counter-attack. How do men summon up the necessary physical and moral courage to continue doing this, day in and day out, when the best they can expect is a flesh wound that will release them from the obligation of going forward against the enemy?

The fog becomes a real pea-souper just about the time you enter a corridor that's been cleared through a very deep mine field.

A cursory reconnaissance on foot, after you spot a sign warning of mines nailed to an old German "ACHTUNG MINEN" sign, reveals a corridor some twenty-five yards or more wide, marked by wisps of white tape tied on the tops of steel posts planted every fifty yards or so along each side.

But the night is so black and the fog so dense, you can never see more than one festooned guidepost at a time, and for long intervals you lose sight of both the post behind and the one ahead as you crawl forward, staying as close as you dare to the right side of the corridor. Fearing your scout car may drift out of the corridor, leading the troop to disaster among the mines, you get out and walk ahead of it, now and then stopping the column until you locate the next post on the right.

After much stewing and sweating, you and the guns make it across without mishap. Near the new gun position, you are met by Bob Grout, who warns that the whole area is dotted with huge, yawning bomb craters, and that the gun sergeants will have to lead the quads in on foot. Baker Troop has had to winch one quad, limber, and gun out of one.

Your guns make it without mishap. But now it starts pouring rain. Tempers are short, and one of the gunners on an ammunition truck takes umbrage at something said (or the way it was said) by the bombardier in charge of the detail, and hangs one on him. Of course he is put on charge, and eventually he'll face a court martial.

This is damned unfortunate, for both are men of high character who have been doing a hard job for days on end, moving untold tons of ammunition forward from position to position each time the guns move – five new positions in seven days, three of them requiring digging gun pits in that chalk. Clearly the incident is the result of fatigue bordering on outright exhaustion, and you vow to make this clear at the court martial.*

Your command post is in a little stone farmhouse – the first time it has been set up in a building of any kind since coming to Normandy – and it's nice and dry. But the outlook for your dysentery-ridden gun crews, too weak to dig gun pits, is bleak, until you decide to break with the normal drill and keep the quads on the position to provide them with shelter from the pelting rain. This turns out to be a good move, for there are no calls for fire of any kind all night.

---

*   With his GPO appearing as a character witness to describe the extenuating circumstances, and defended by Adjutant Sammy Grange, who one day would become a judge of the Supreme Court of Ontario, Gunner William Wright escaped without a conviction to mar his war record.

59

WAR BECOMES A BLUR FOR MEN
BEFUDDLED BY FATIGUE

※

SO OFTEN DO THE GUNS MOVE (SEVEN TIMES IN NINE DAYS, ending August 19, and usually at night), and so often are you forced to remain awake all day, either with recce parties or covering off the command post while your troop leader takes his turn going forward with advance parties, that fatigue becomes chronic, and in your befuddled state you will remember almost nothing of the two days just before Falaise is taken, and will always be dependent on a hodgepodge of images provided by others.

Among these is the startling picture of a group of women, carrying great bouquets of flowers, marching in from no-man's-land to greet the advance guard of the Polish Armoured held up by the Germans at Potigny. The village is a unique community made up of people of Polish origin, families who long ago had migrated here to run the iron mine. When some women of the village overheard Allied prisoners speaking Polish as they were being marched down the road by their German captors, they rushed over to them and engaged them in excited conversation. And on learning there was a whole Polish division of many thousands of men coming this way with the Canadian Army, the women returned home, filled their arms with flowers, and in spite of dire warnings from the Germans, marched up the Caen–Falaise highway to welcome their liberators.

And there's the strange sight of Poles in British battledress giving cigarettes in welcome to Poles in German field-grey uniforms right after they've been taken prisoner and before they change into Canadian battledress and join in the drive to close the Falaise Gap. The alacrity with which men can change sides, and how swiftly others are able to extend forgiveness to their fellow countrymen – at least on the battlefield – brings forth expressions of dismay in Sgt. Hunt's diary.

Unaware that captured Poles must become a source of badly needed reinforcements for the Polish Division, Hunt wrote bitterly on August 15: "The Poles take some prisoners, snipers from the nearby woods. For this we are grateful, but when the Poles give the snipers cigarettes we give the Poles . . . well, I mean to say, what? It seems the prisoners are, by birth, Poles. Even so, one wonders how many Canadians fell before these mercenaries surrendered to smoke Canadian cigarettes."

Then there is the unforgettable image of a Hitler Youth of the 12th SS refusing to surrender, though his covered hole is overrun. He has to be dug out and shot like a groundhog.

The company of Royals with whom Len Harvey and his carrier crew are moving saw him disappear in a covered dogleg trench as they came up, but when they call to him to come out with his hands up, he yells back, "Come in and get me, Canadian bastards!"

Twice they toss grenades into the open end of the trench, but he is able to duck around the corner of the dogleg and escape the blasts, leaving him unscathed and snarling defiant obscenities. Finally the Royals unlimber their shovels and remove enough of the roof to shoot him dead, leaving him there like the animal he'd become – rather than the boy he might have been.

Then there's the bizarre duel between a sniper in a tree and a company commander of the FMRs on the ground, conducted with both bullets and grenades.

Though 2nd Division has been in action only a month, casualties have been so high, infantry companies now look like platoons when on the move, and the FMRs are no exception.*

Because of the need to maintain a roster of experienced officers to help boost sagging morale, wounded officers sometimes feel obliged to spend the later days of their convalescence with their units in the line. Capt. Noel Meilleur of the FMRs is one of these. Hit by shell fragments on July 20 at Beauvoir Farm and evacuated to a British hospital in Bayeux, he discharged himself after two weeks and hitched a ride back to his unit at St. Martin-de-Fontenay, where, still limping, he took part in the big push on August 8.

Now, on August 15, Meilleur's company has been chosen to take the principal strong point along the axis of advance on Falaise, a large house known as "*la Commanderie*," eight hundred yards north of Clair Tizon, simply because his company, with a complement of forty other ranks, is currently the strongest in the battalion.

Officers being prime targets for snipers, Meilleur has removed his epaulettes with their tell-tale officer's pips, carries a rifle, and is draped with khaki-cotton bandoliers of bullets criss-crossing his breast and overlaying the two Bren-gun magazine pouches fixed to his webbing and bulging with tins of bully beef, hardtack, a change of socks, and smokes. He thus presents an authentic image of an Other Rank.

As he sends a section this way and another that way, Meilleur gives unobtrusive hand signals, but still he attracts the attention of a sniper, hidden up in a big, leafy tree in the backyard of the house. The sniper gets him in the leg with a bullet before he can make it into an abandoned trench. Then, peppered by grenades dropped from above, he escapes from two successive slit trenches as grenades

---

* By August 17, Canadian infantry casualties having reached 76 per cent and reinforcements being insufficient, the nine battalions of 2nd Division – the hardest hit of all Allied formations – were almost 2,000 under fighting strength of 5,040 (9 × 560).

roll into them and explode. But when he rises up to see where a third grenade has gone, the explosion gets him full in the chest, wiping away not only the bandoliers of small-arms ammunition and bully-beef-packed Bren pouches, but also his battledress breast pockets, filled with letters and snapshots from home, wads of Compo toilet paper, and other precious possessions.

Though he suffers blast injuries to his face that will cause him the loss of one eye, he is saved from death by the body armour which remains intact under his shredded clothing. But left with "the granddaddy of all headaches," he is so enraged he throws caution to the wind and, hopping about on his good leg, goes searching for his grenade-tossing tormentor. Moving around the bottom of the tree, he spots him up among the thick foliage, and shoots him dead.

And there are Bombardier Hossack's diary notes for these days:

The troop moves up to a German-vacated wheat field over-looking the burning city of Falaise. The roads are rough and dusty, and lead through villages of destroyed and burning houses where the smell of death is very evident. Cows have been left unattended at a farmhouse adjacent to the guns and our farmers-turned-soldiers milk them for us daily. . . . Enemy planes put on a very fine daylight show of aerobatics, but their continual weaving and turning to avoid ack-ack fire disrupts their aim and their bombs and machine-gun bullets land mostly in unoccupied fields. The BBC news tells us that the Americans are in Paris. Our joy is greatly overshadowed by that of the natives when we tell them, "Les Americans dans Paris."

Finally, a striking little image supplied by Sgt. McEwan's diary: "As we advance through a village completely destroyed by our bombers, beside a house that is merely a shell is a small garden a few feet square. In it, not touched one iota by the blast, are three beautiful spurs of gladiolas and a few dahlias, forming an odd contrast to the destruction around them."

60

FALAISE IN FLAMES

---　✳　---

THE MORNING OF AUGUST 16 ARRIVES CLEAR AND FRESH, AND there's an early move away from the moon landscape of giant bomb-craters to a sun-bathed position among stooks of grain in a stubble field enclosed by green hedgerows untouched by war. There, the new battery commander – a Major Don Cornett, who seems a decent sort – drops by for a chat on his way up to the Royals to take over from Stu Laurie, who has been acting as their arty rep since Major Wren was killed.

You hear that Bombardier Jim Fraser and Lance-Bombardier Russell Green of 26th Battery, reported missing a couple of days ago when they failed to return from a scrounging expedition on a motorbike somewhat beyond the established FDLs, have been found dead. Sad news indeed. They were good guys. To you, Fraser always seemed to suggest the spirit of Huckleberry Finn, and he'd occupied a special place in your heart since that cold, wet day a couple of years ago when he offered you a steaming piece of chicken from a pot he had boiling on a Primus stove in the back of a moving truck in the middle of a regimental convoy.

You were on a motorbike, "riding herd" on the regimental convoy headed for Wales, when you picked up the delicious odour of cooking chicken as you roared up past the moving line of guns and vehicles to get to the head of the column to direct traffic at the next crossroads. Tracing the tempting smell to its origin, you found yourself riding behind one of your own troop's 15-hundredweight trucks, face to face with Fraser, who was looking out from under the canvas hood right next to the tailgate.

For a moment he attempted to look dumb and brazen it out, but then deciding bribery was his best move, he broke into a wide grin. Leaning down, he speared a chunk of chicken from a pot and brought it up where he could examine it with a critical eye, while beckoning you to move in close to the tailgate. Fully aware there was no way he could have acquired a chicken without "borrowing" it from a henhouse along the line of march, and that winking at this wanton act, while countenancing the use of a lighted Primus stove in one of his majesty's trucks in a moving convoy, made you equally if not more culpable, the smell of the chicken suppressed all considerations of good order and discipline. Nudging your sputtering Norton forward, you were just able to grasp the tender morsel from Fraser's precariously extended fork.

Fraser loved life, and he loved good grub, and he and Green may well have been looking for a chicken or two when they bought it.

Still it was madness for them to go junketing through countryside not totally clear of the Germans. In the fluid conditions existing before Falaise, with no clearly defined front line, there is no telling where you may bump into pockets of enemy troops, or from what quarter you may be fired on. To this, Stu Laurie can attest when he returns to resume his duties as battery captain:

Somewhere south of Potigny I was walking with Ralph Young [acting CO of the Royals] when we saw an 88, no more than ten feet away, sitting in a field just inside a gate through a hedge. Of course we all went over to look at it. It appeared undamaged except it had been stripped of its gears. And right beside it sat a Tiger tank, also undamaged as far as could be seen, and which only recently had been abandoned, for when we went around it examining it and feeling it, it was still nice and warm.

Someone should have poured petrol over it and thrown a grenade at it to set it on fire, but we just moved on and left it. And this turned out to be a mistake. Next day we couldn't settle down anywhere but a bloody 88 was shooting at us. And we never could tell where the fire was coming from: first it was from behind us, then from the side, then from the other side. But it was that Tiger tank all right, for when I was on the way back to the guns, I looked in on that field and it wasn't there!*

That Falaise is still occupied by determined enemy troops, Fox Troop Commander Sammy Grange is able to report when he goes well beyond the FDLs to establish an OP in the town's northwestern outskirts. And while recognizing that the real liberators of Falaise are 6th Brigade units that attack the town next day, wiping out many of the last of the 12th SS Hitlerjugend fanatics (up to one hundred of them dying in the flames of a walled monastery or school that burned over them as they fought to the death), Sammy will always lay solemn claim to having been "first in and first out of the birthplace of William the Conqueror." "In on the 15th, out on the 16th," is the way he puts it when he gets the chance to tell you of it:

I think it was Bill Carr's idea to send me up accompanied by a dozen or so Essex Scottish to provide protection. I never really understood the purpose of my expedition. All he said was, "I'm going to send you into Falaise. . . . We don't know what's in there. . . . No one has been in there yet. . . . I'll get a section of the Essex to go along with you to protect you." About a dozen Other Ranks came along, and while it was nice having someone there concerned with my protection, I would have preferred to be there alone, for all they did was draw fire.

---

*   Author interview.

We were right in the outskirts of Falaise, in some farm buildings looking down from a hill. The view was excellent – I could
see the whole town. While I couldn't see any Germans, there
were snipers all around. And of course my infantry guards started
to draw fire when three or four of them exposed themselves (in
the military sense), chasing a hen round and about with the
object of killing and plucking it for the pot. At least two of them
were hit, one serious enough I had to go out and bring him in.
So much for their concern for my safety!

Normally I would have brought down neutralizing fire, but
we were then beyond the range of our guns. They were supposed to be moving up closer (at least Carr had given that
impression), but they didn't. It was then I realized there was
nothing more useless than this patrol. It turned out to be my last
tour of duty as a FOO before becoming battery captain and
turning over Fox Troop to Jack Cameron, the CPO."*

Next day 6th Brigade attacks Falaise, and the following day
(August 18), when 4th Field advance parties pass through, the town
is still burning, new fires having been started the previous night by
Luftwaffe bombers.

The flames are so fierce in places, the searing heat raises blisters
in the paint on the side of the 2nd Battery command post scout car
as it is guided gingerly through the rubble-cluttered streets by
Driver George Bracken, with all its armour-plate shutters in place
over windshield and side windows because of snipers. Incredibly,
the Provost Corps has already erected signs: LOOTING: PENALTY
DEATH.

Positions south of Falaise are laid out and surveyed, but never
occupied. The guns are redirected to a wooded plateau, high in a

---

* Capt. S. G. M. Grange's thirty-eight days as a FOO during the worst
fighting Normandy could offer from Caen to Falaise was recognized
when he was later awarded the *Croix de Guerre avec Étoile de Vermeil*.

range of hills (Les Monts d'Erain) southeast of Falaise, overlooking what the BBC is calling the Falaise gap – that narrowing corridor, still open to the retreating Germans, between the Americans in the south and 1st Canadian army pushing towards Trun and Chambois. Up here in a stump-filled clearing, it is impossible to dig in, but there are plenty of logs to build up protective bulwarks to form command posts, gun "pits" and "slits."

Waiting for the guns to come up in the evening, you watch a battle raging on another hill one thousand yards away that gives every appearance of being the main thrust by the Germans in their attempt to keep the pocket open. There's a feeling that this may become a hot place, but, with Jerry guns and planes preoccupied elsewhere, the night passes quietly, if uncomfortably. For those off-duty and able to bed down, there is not a square yard of level ground devoid of roots, stumps, and stones.

Around midnight there are some tense moments when low-flying planes throb overhead and start dropping parachute flares – more and more until the sky is filled with orange, white, red, and yellow flares, lighting up the landscape in all directions in noonday brilliance. When they buzz off without dropping anything else, it is assumed they are Allied planes lighting up the gap, especially the Polish position on another hill now cut off and needing to be supplied from the air.

Before dawn you are aroused from a lumpy bower and sent forward to establish an OP and listening post down over the brow of the hill, only a few hundred yards in front of the guns. There has been a report of Germans heading up this way. But nothing happens, and when dawn comes, though it is a grey morning with scattered showers, you bring up your NCOs to see what they can see. This must be a very disappointing experience for them, for while it is possible to see at least fifteen miles from up here – a complete overview of the pocket – there is absolutely nothing to be seen moving down there. The only things at all suggestive of the destruction and carnage the BBC broadcasts now claim is being visited on the Germans in the pocket are some Tiffies and Spitfires flying past almost at eye-level and diving on unseen targets, adding muffled *crump*s and rumbles to the faint thundering roar of shells landing far off, and a vast pall of smoke drifting across the landscape from numerous fires including those in Falaise.

An evening move on August 19 takes the guns to Perrières, near Vicques, which Hossack's diary calls "a heap of rubble that once was a village." Enemy air activity is impressive:

Darkness brings planes and flares. It is the enemy this time and his bombs and bullets put us to earth. In response to ack-ack fire, an enemy plane's machine guns can be seen to flash back at the gun sites. The downward streak of enemy fire presents a dramatic picture against all the tracers racing upward, and the plane's position above the flares is momentarily revealed. In a fanatical effort to knock out one nearby ack-ack gun a plane roars very low overhead – the noise is deafening and we hug Mother Earth as we seldom hugged her before. The flares twinkle out and the rain starts.

Everyone not on duty is sleeping under canvas [tarpaulins], although little protection is gained for all the tarpaulins were pretty well shrapnel-ventilated back at Carpiquet. Blankets and clothing are soaked. Morning reveals last night's enemy planes made an effort to drop supplies to their hard-pressed comrades in the Falaise Gap, but their map reading was poor – the food supplies fell to the nearby Polish Division and the petrol rations landed on 26th Battery's position.

61

A SMOKY HAZE HANGS OVER
FALAISE POCKET

SENT UP TO THE FRONT, NOT TO REPLACE A FOO, BUT TO ADD another pair of eyes watching for any sign of Jerry attempting to break through here, you find it difficult to establish an OP and be sure you are observing hostile territory – or are even looking in the right direction. It is impossible to obtain a clear picture at any given hour of the perimeter of the ever-shrinking pocket as the Yanks press against the southern shoulder, the British push in from the west, and the Canadians, with elements of the Polish Armoured Division now in the van, drive south.

And while much of the Polish fighting strength is immobile, cut-off and surrounded on a nearby hill, there's a report that some have been able to link up with the Americans at Chambois, south-east of Falaise.*

---

* Two Polish regiments did get through on August 19 to join up with an American division at Chambois, where they found the enemy in terrible shape: among piles of their dead from air attacks and artillery bombardments. Still, the Germans continued to prevent reliable communication between American and Canadian armies until the Canadian 4th Division tanks linked up with the Poles at Coudehard on August 21. At the same time, two thousand Poles and seventy tanks, cut off from all ground-delivered supplies of food and ammunition from the 19th, until rescued

However, the pocket is still open, and with the Tiffies and Spits handicapped by low-lying clouds and the smoky haze hanging over the pocket from the fires smouldering in the misty rain, the guns are now expected to play a major role in shutting down the escape routes.

Eventually you find a place where you are reasonably certain you are overlooking, if not enemy territory, no-man's-land. Your ack, Gunner John Elder, who was with you in your first OP in that hellish orchard back at Eterville in July, is twenty today, August 19.

Of the terrible drama unfolding in the pocket, nothing can be seen here, and your most satisfactory target of the day is found, not way out in the hazy panorama, but in the immediate vicinity of the Royals, who are now securing some bridges over the Dives river against use by the Germans. A Lieut. Ross, recently made responsible for the Royals' reconstituted scout platoon (which through casualties had ceased to exist), turns out to be an old friend from collegiate days. Colin, or "Hefty" as he was known to most everybody in those far-off times, was one of the first to enlist with the Cameron Highlanders in Ottawa on that sunny Sunday that Britain declared war. The Monday sports pages had made much of the fact that a perennial stalwart of the Ottawa Roughriders would be lost to them just as the season was about to start. You'd lost track of him until 1943 in England, when he again briefly donned football togs to help a hastily assembled Canadian Army team beat the American

---

by the Canadian Grenadier Guards on the 21st, held "Maczuga" ("the mace"), as they dubbed their dominant Hill 262, overlooking the main escape route to Vimoutiers, driving back attack after attack by Germans trying to push east out of the pocket, while resisting attacks from the east by a newly arrived 2nd Panzer Division brought down from Abbeville–Amiens area to help keep open the corridor (not to be confused with 2nd SS Panzer Division caught in the pocket). In the drive for Falaise and the closing of the gap the Polish Division suffered 1,450 casualties, 450 of them killed.

Army football team in an exhibition game in Wembley Stadium, London.*

Today, when you come across him, he and his scouts are just back from five days of improvised training for their precarious occupation, and are moving up through your position to take on their first assignment: ensuring a house out in no-man's-land is clear of snipers. While you are glad to see him, you can't help feeling sorry for him, for no infantry subaltern lasts long here – and scout officers least of all.

Since there is a total lack of cover leading up to the house they are supposed to clear, he and his men are delighted when you suggest your guns have a go at it before they risk trying to get across that open ground. And to the obvious relief of all, a few rounds of high explosive poured into the house from a single gun of Able Troop, blowing holes in roof and walls, produces fast results: a white sheet at a window. And when you stop your shelling, half a dozen Jerries march out with their hands up.

However, in your search for troops attempting to escape the pocket, only once do you see anything moving: a distant line of men and horse-drawn wagons, barely visible in the misty rain that falls most of the day. A lack of identifiable landmarks out there makes accurate map-reading difficult, and corrections are needed to bring the shells onto target. By then they have scattered, but you think you discern remnants of wagons and horses among the debris left behind.

Even though it remains cloudy and drizzly throughout the day, Spits and Typhoons continue to fly low-level sorties, strafing, bombing, and rocketing, without having to face any enemy ack-ack as far as you can see. Unquestionably, desperate engagements are taking place, for the sounds of battle can be heard in the southeast and southwest, but along here, there is only a smouldering, ominous stillness. You shell some likely places on the assumption that even

---

* Other stars of the "Big Four" on the team were: Major George Hees, Toronto Argonauts half-back; Lt.-Col. Denny Whitaker, Hamilton Tigers quarterback; and Major "Huck" Welch, a famous punter.

random shelling at this stage can hardly miss causing havoc, with every road and track in use by some vehicles and desperate foot-soldiers seeking cover in every bush and gully as the British snap at their heels from the west and hourly the pocket shrinks.

After dark you can see fires burning, and all around the horizon guns continue to flash and rumble. By now there are at least three thousand guns within range and firing from three sides into the pocket, and the BBC continues to tell of the awesome slaughter taking place.

It will be weeks, however, before you get any real concept of the extent of the carnage – not until you receive a firsthand account from an officer you'd known at the Brockville Officers' Training Centre, who after the battle is put in charge of a party collecting bodies for burial, combing the gullies and the thickets. He will tell of fields and woods littered with dead, hundreds in field-grey uni-forms, sprawled in black pools of dried blood carpeting the ground, filling in some ditches and lying in layers in gullies. Horrible, bloated things expelling a stench so powerful Air OP pilots retched as they flew low overhead.*

---

*   That he did not exaggerate will be born out by General Eisenhower: "Roads, highways and fields were so choked with destroyed equipment and with dead men and animals that passage through the area was extremely difficult. Forty-eight hours after the closing of the gap, I was conducted through it on foot to encounter scenes that could be described only by Dante. It literally was possible to walk for hundreds of yards at a time, stepping on nothing but dead and decaying flesh." (Dwight D. Eisenhower, *Crusade in Europe*, New York: Perma Books, 1952, p. 314). Besides the destruction wrought by shelling, 2nd (British) Tactical Airforce destroyed 210 tanks and 3,000 motorized and horse-drawn trans-port, 115 tanks and 1,500 other vehicles on August 19 alone. Between August 10 and 25, 25,000 Germans died in the pocket and 40,000 were taken prisoner. In Normandy, the Germans lost 400,000 men, of whom 200,000 were taken prisoner, 135,000 between July 25 and August 31.

62

COMRADESHIP

———————————— ✳ ————————————

COMRADESHIP – THAT SPECIAL RELATIONSHIP BETWEEN PEOPLE who share awful conditions and whose lives depend on mutual support – will always be a source of fascination. You used to think that it was just another word for friendship, but you know now that the most caring, sharing, selfless comrades can be men you've never met before and who will remain forever nameless, unless you meet them again under more civilized conditions someday, when in all likelihood, you'll not recognize them after the war, for their eyes will be cold and impersonal, not filled with the compassion and understanding you see in them here.

Phrases like "tightly knit unit" and "*esprit de corps*," which you once thought meant something significant, seem to have lost all validity, at least among the infantry. Battalions have been so riddled with casualties that officers, NCOs, and Other Ranks are largely strangers to each other. It can hardly be otherwise when a battalion has to replace 100 per cent of its fighting strength over a period of only a couple of weeks as the Royals have done, absorbing 80 reinforcements (six officers and seventy-four other ranks) on July 20, another 254 on July 28, and a further 282 (two officers and 280 other ranks) on August 3.*

———————

* D. J. Goodspeed, *Battle Royal* (Toronto: Royal Regiment of Canada Association, 1962), pp. 425, 432, 435.

And more often than not, these reinforcements are brought up in the middle of the night, introduced to holes already dug for them (two to each slit trench) by officers or NCOs whose faces they can't see, and told to stay in those isolated, separated holes regardless of what happens. Some will be wounded and shipped back down to hospital never having had a chance to make an impression on anyone in the whole battalion, let alone nurture friendships. And some will die right there in their first trench, and later be buried by a padre who never had an opportunity to look upon their living faces.

When the Royals were on Verrières Ridge, nine reinforcements were brought up one night after dark to Jack Stothers' platoon and placed in previously prepared trenches. By dawn all were lying dead in the wheat. Stothers blamed this tragedy on the reinforcements' lack of training and discipline; choosing not to follow his orders to stay in those holes until dawn, regardless of what happened. When the Germans infiltrated between their positions and spewed tracers around, giving the impression the platoon was overrun, they left their holes to escape and were promptly cut down by other Royals following orders to shoot anything moving above ground.

While the sense of comradeship in the front line is very real, particularly during the more hellish periods, it tends to be on a spiritual level of mutual support, rather than social, for there is little opportunity, and even less inclination, for socializing. Just having to remain constantly alert while on duty, forever preoccupied with matters of survival, in an inexplicable way absorbs all the time left between those brief periods of intense activity that periodically arise. And off duty, sleep takes priority over everything else. All normal interests tend to be held in suspension by these overpowering preoccupations. And so men occupying slit trenches only thirty feet apart for days on end can remain total strangers, even as they remain committed to dying for each other if necessary.

During the long period of training in England, there was so little contact between artillery and infantry, it could hardly be said that they had any relationship, good or bad. Even on big training schemes, like Spartan, involving all the various branches of service, gunners were never really concerned whether the infantry was theoretically successful or defeated in their "attacks." And when on rare occasions they did come in contact with the infantry marching along the verges of a road, the footsloggers, jealous of the gunners riding by in their gun tractors and trucks, would hoot at them in derision.

But since coming into action, a very special relationship has developed between gunners and infantry. The gunners, totally involved and following every minute of the terrible battles that involve the infantry and tanks they're supporting, have come to hold front-line soldiers in awe. At the same time the gunners have won the profound gratitude and respect of surviving veteran infantrymen, who have seen how effective the guns can be in breaking up counter-attacks and softening up the enemy before they attack.

And this special relationship is sometimes expressed in a most touching way:

A company of the Royals has broken off to bivouac in a barn for a couple of hours, to sleep inside out of the rain before moving forward again. The 4th Field FOO and crew attached to the company, having had to make a detour for rations and petrol back along the line of march, arrive at the barn after everybody has settled down, and every inch of floor space is covered by prone infantrymen, their packs, and their weapons. The artillerymen stand hesitatingly at the door as they swing the weak beam of a lamp-electric over the clutter of sleeping forms and their equipment.

Always now, regardless of circumstances, gunners tend to show tremendous respect for the infantry, and they are especially conscious of not wanting to disturb their rest this night, knowing how far they have walked and how desperately tired they must be. But as they turn to go out, they are spotted by a hoarse-voiced sergeant, who calls out from the darkness: "The FOO and his boys need some room to rest, too, lads."

That's all he says. It's not an order. It's only an appeal to decency and generosity, but it works wonders. There's a general shifting of the whole floor of bodies. Many are already asleep, but their neighbours nudge them awake, explaining, "The arty guys need some room." There's no grumbling, no discussion, only a low murmur now and then. And, miraculously, enough room appears on the floor beside the door that four members of a 4th Field carrier crew can lie down and stretch out in dry comfort, while the rain lashes the barn roof.

At dawn, as the company is preparing to move on, the French farmer appears with a pail of steaming ersatz coffee and a mug to portion it out to the yawning men. A truly good-natured man, it would seem, for last evening (according to Company Commander Capt. Jack Stothers), while you were back picking up rations, these same Royals uncovered and consumed the man's entire stock of *prime vieux* Calvados, which he'd been able to keep hidden from the Germans throughout the occupation, dug-in in the barnyard, a bottle here and a bottle there, their corks just below the surface of the earth. When Stothers had broken off the weary men to bed down in the barn, and they were dragging their feet across the yard, one of them stumbled over something in the ground. Curious, the man had bent down to see what had tripped him, and poking around discovered it was the neck of a bottle. Of course when a full bottle was pulled out and brushed off, everyone began to examine the ground and dig around. And in minutes a dozen bottles were raised and being consumed when the farmer appeared. Taking in the scene, he grabbed his head, exclaiming in awe: "*Mon Dieu! Les Boches sont ici depuis quatre ans et ils n'ont jamais trouvé mon Calvados. Les Canadiens arrivent et dix minutes plus tard, ils ont trouvé toutes mes bouteilles!*" (My God! The Germans were here for four years, and they never found my Calvados. The Canadians are here ten minutes and they have every bottle!)

Now the smiling man is serving coffee to the hung-over looters – albeit ersatz, and so awful-tasting it may be a form of revenge.

Back at the guns Bombardier Hossack's diary will record:

> Ordered to move on the morning of August 20, we drive along vehicle-littered roads in teeming rain to a large apple orchard. . . . Few targets are called for. The nearest town, Grand Mesnil, is almost totally destroyed. Refugees walk the roads, and a small shelter nearby houses 24 French people. They have no sanitation and human excrement is all around. "No lights" [meaning not even the faintest glow from the tiny holes in blacked-out head-lights] is again the order as we move on the night of August 20–21. The objective is Vimoutiers. The drivers do a remarkable job of nursing their vehicles along in the "pea soup" fog. The roads are busy with two-way traffic and the convoy is split up several times as lead vehicles speed up, make wrong turns and fail to see dimly lighted route signs.

For some reason Hossack chooses not to record a fog-related incident involving Sgt. Ernie Offord, about which everyone is still talking when you return from the infantry. It seems that when the guns were coming in here last night in the rain and dark, the sergeants were unaware that scattered about the fog-enshrouded field were unburied cows that had been dead for some time – their legs held up in the air by bellies hugely distended to the point of almost bursting. And when Offord, intending to guide his gun to its marker, jumped down from the high door of his quad, he landed squarely on one of those cow bellies, bursting it and almost disap-pearing inside the gruesome cavity.

Enveloped by its horrible contents and gagging on its revolting gases, the poor man struggled free and, screaming, started off on a crazed run into the fog and dark. As soon as his comrades were able to grasp what had happened, they piled out of the quad and set out in pursuit, fearing he might kill himself running blindly into a tree or some other obstacle. When, after a bizarre chase through the foggy night, they were able to locate and capture him, they conducted him to the farmyard pump, where they washed him clean and settled him down.

For such a thing to happen to anyone would have been shocking, but for it to happen to Offord – the epitome of good grooming and personal hygiene, always the best turned-out soldier in the battery if not the whole Regiment – seems particularly horrifying. Your heart aches for him when you seek him out to see how he is getting on. Obviously he's very depressed. But in the bright light of morning, nothing is ever so bad as the night before, and he manages a wry grin. And you honestly feel that what is now bothering him most is that he looks as crummy and unkempt as everybody else, in his newly washed-and-dried battledress, a bit shrunken and a mass of wrinkles.

63

BOULEVARD OF BROKEN DREAMS

———————————— ✳ ————————————

OFFICIALLY THE FALAISE POCKET WAS CLOSED TWO DAYS AGO, on August 19, when units of the Canadian Army reputedly linked up with the Americans at Chambois. However, groups of determined Germans, riding on tanks or in half-tracks, or moving with a single self-propelled gun, are still roaming just outside the pocket – either escapees from the trap or holdovers from 15th Army units rushed down here from the Calais area to help keep escape routes open. Whoever they are, they may be encountered in varying numbers on any road leading east. To inhibit their escape to the Seine, 2nd Division units are sent wheeling east on August 21, crossing behind the last bitter struggle by 4th Division and the Polish Division to seal off the pocket about Chambois, Trun, and St. Lambert.*

That night 4th Field recce parties, laying out gun positions within a mile of Vimoutiers to support the infantry engaged in shutting off the Trun–Vimoutiers–Orbec road, the main German

———————

* It's at St. Lambert-sur-Dives, during three days (August 19–21) of fierce fighting to contain Germans desperate to escape the Falaise pocket, that Major David Currie, South Alberta Regiment, an armoured recce regiment of 4th Armoured Division, won the V.C.

escape route, begin to have serious doubts as to who is in possession of what. Sporadic bursts of Schmeisser fire near the lonely positions keep them alert and standing-to most of the night, until the guns move up.

And when the Regiment moves again at midday the next day, it is along a sunken road that only a short time before was plugged solid with smashed German vehicles, dead horses, and dead men. Bulldozers have been used very recently to push everything helter-skelter up onto the banks on both sides of the road, and some wagons and motor vehicles still smoke and smoulder and flame up as you pass through mile after mile of awesome refuse. All along there are dead horses, torn and bloody, still harnessed to wagons with broken wheels, for the long column of transport, caught in this deeply sunken road and unable to scatter from the fighter-bombers, was largely horsedrawn.

Still amongst the horses are broken half-tracks, self-propelled guns, towed guns, staff cars, civilian cars, lorries, and at least two Red Cross ambulances overturned at the roadside. Bodies of men are everywhere, some spilling out of vehicles, and some half-covered with refuse as though tossed onto a garbage dump. And over all is the stench of death.

Passage along the road, which, as you proceed, looks increasingly like a refuse-strewn trench, is very slow, with drivers having to thread their way between derelict vehicles. And so you are able to take in every detail of a scene the like of which you never expected to encounter and never expect to see again, except in a nightmare: a pageant of destruction beyond anything imagined by the most extravagant film director looking for a way to make still another statement against war. There is something reminiscent of the imagery of Napoleon's retreat from Moscow here, the same sugges-tion of retribution you always sensed in paintings and films de-picting the slow death of *la Grande Armée* on its way home. When someone suggests the name Boulevard of Broken Dreams for this corridor of death, it seems entirely suitable – the words "of world conquest" being implied, of course.*

---

*   Among the troops shredded in the pocket were remnants of the 12th SS "Hitlerjugend" Panzer Division, marked men from the day after D-Day, when they rolled into battle so arrogantly and then began killing unarmed 3rd Canadian Division prisoners in their frustration at not being able to drive the Canadians back into the sea, even conducting a mass murder in a walled garden of the Abbaye d'Ardenne, where SS Standartenführer Kurt Meyer had his brigade headquarters. After Falaise, 12th SS could muster only ten tanks, no guns, and only three hundred of the twenty thousand young fanatics with which it had begun the Normandy campaign. Likewise 2nd SS "Das Reich" Panzer Division had earned its destruction without mercy by its action on June 10 on the way up from southern France at Oradour-sur-Glane, fourteen miles north-west of Limoges, where it shot all the men of the village after herding them into six barns, and murdered four hundred women and children in the church, in reprisal for the disappearance of the colonel of the 4th SS Grenadier Regiment. After Falaise they counted only 450 men and fifteen tanks.

State of Panzer Divisions as Reported by Army Group B, August 22–23.
2nd Panzer: 1 infantry battalion, no tanks
21st Panzer: 4 weak infantry battalions, 10 tanks
116 Panzer: 1 infantry battalion, 12 tanks, 2 batteries guns
1st SS Panzer: weak infantry elements, no tanks, no artillery
2nd SS Panzer: 450 men, 15 tanks, 6 guns
9th SS Panzer: 460 men, 25 tanks, no guns
10th SS Panzer: 4 weak infantry battalions, no tanks, no artillery
12th SS Panzer: 300 men, 10 tanks, no artillery
(Panzer Lehr and 9th Panzer were wiped out by American Operation Cobra and in German attacks at Mortain.)

[The foregoing statistics are from page 101 of Report No. 65, Historical Section (G.S.) Canadian Army Headquarters, Dept. of National Defence, Dec. 23, 1953, p. 101.]

64

4TH FIELD SUFFERS WORST
ONE–DAY CASUALTIES

***

NEXT DAY, ON AUGUST 23, THE THRUST FOR 2ND DIVISION IS north towards Thiberville, at the junction of the Lisieux–Rouen highway and the road leading up from Vimoutiers, both main escape routes for the Germans. This, of course, means the infantry and supporting artillery units start cutting across other less distinguished but equally useful German escape routes leading northeast to Elbeuf and the Seine. Thus, even as FOOs with 4th Division and the Polish Division — left to contain the Germans in the pocket — are firing concentrations south and west on desperate groups of Germans trying even in daylight to probe the perimeter for weak spots, FOOs with 2nd and 3rd Divisions, moving away from the pocket, are firing north and east on Germans heading for the Seine.

Three or four German half-tracks or tanks can roar across a road right in front of an Allied convoy without a shot being fired. Or they can cut through the middle of an infantry column with their machine guns spewing fire, leaving artillery FOOs and anti-tank gunners (their anti-tank guns rolling along limbered up) mentally pawing the air in frustration.

They can join the end of a convoy at night by mistake, or on purpose as a means of camouflage to get them as far as possible towards the Seine before being discovered, and leave again without firing a shot, as though they are out of ammunition. Or they can use up the last of their ammunition shooting up the rear vehicles in the column as they wheel about and disappear up a side road.

The Royals experience all these variations in the frantic but determined withdrawal tactics of parties of Germans during two or three confusing days and nights when they themselves are almost continually on the move, first east towards Orbec and then north towards Lisieux. In fact during this one day, August 23, they have three or four variations in separate encounters, including one with remnants of 1st SS.*

The most serious encounter occurs in the black of night during a heavy rain when the battalion intelligence officer (Lieut. R. E. C. McCaul) and three ORs are killed by fire from two half-tracks mounting ack-ack guns that come up against the rear of the regimental column, just when the Royals are in the process of debussing from troop carriers. When the German half-tracks are taken on in a shootout by a platoon of Toronto Scottish machine gunners riding at the rear of the column, they turn their headlights full on, wheel around, and go tearing back and up a side road.

This grim incident of flashing and rattling confusion occurs just after four German tanks suddenly burst through the column and roar across the road at full speed with guns blazing, causing at least four casualties, and just before four more tanks appear at the rear of the column, but leave without firing a shot – out of ammunition.

Earlier, while still daylight, at a crossroads in a wooded area,

---

*   General Kurt Meyer, who escapes the pocket by forcing a French civilian to guide him, joins what is left of 1st SS Panzer Corps on August 20, and is saddened by the state of his beloved Liebstandarte: "I couldn't help the tears from running down my face. Thousands of my comrades lay dead in the Norman earth. . . . Our expulsion proves that west of Seine there remains no stable front." (Tony Foster, *Meeting of Generals* [Agincourt: Methuen, 1986], pp. 397–98.) Meeting up with Field Marshal Model at Rouen he is put in charge of an improvised fighting group to delay the Allies at Elbeuf and in the Forêt de la Londe.

where Battalion tac headquarters' vehicles halted briefly to allow a reconnaissance to be carried out along the forest tracks, three German tanks came up a side road so casually they appeared to believe they were joining friends. And they might have driven right through the men and vehicles clustered around a house at the cross-roads, without anyone realizing they were German, if one of them, standing up in the turret of his tank, hadn't shouted out in German a warning to the other two when he discovered they had joined an Allied column.

Gunner Knox, the sixteen-year-old Baker Troop signaller, was standing out in the road in front of the house, "chewing the fat" with buddies Purvis Vickers (the driver) and Lorne Garrow (the other wireless operator) when the three tanks pulled up next him, and he heard a voice yell, "*Englander! Englander!*"

When we all look up and see the cross on the side of that tank, we get the hell out of there, but fast. I make it to the other side of the building, but Garrow and Vickers dive under the carrier.

As the German tanks roar off up the road, the last one opens up with his machine gun. Vickers is killed and Garrow is wounded in the head.

Next day we're in a field supporting the infantry, and there are four of our tanks about us. Suddenly they start getting picked off, one after another. As each tank is hit, the crew bails out and runs for cover. But when one takes fire it produces the most shocking sight I've seen so far. A man in the turret is on fire, and when he rolls out over the top of the turret and falls on the ground, both his feet are gone.

This really has an effect on me – makes me ask myself: Why am I here? I could go home; I only have to go to someone and confess I am still three years under the legal age. But then there is no way I could do that. I have a duty. . . . I have to see this thing out. And when I hear Smitty, a Royals' stretcher-bearer, giving the trooper first aid while waiting for an ambulance to come to take him out, assuring him he will make it all right because the burning cauterized the stumps of his legs preventing bleeding, I feel somewhat better. Smitty is a wonderful guy. They say it isn't beyond him to go ahead and talk to the Germans to see if they have any wounded they want taken care of.*

Meanwhile the guns, pointed at Orbec and deployed at the village of Friardel near its substantial church, come under the worst shelling since Carpiquet. Last night 6th Field guns on the left flank were shelled and fifteen were wounded. And now, at 2:00 P.M., shells begin to arrive on 4th Field gun positions and wagon lines, and before it's over, the Regiment suffers twenty-two serious casualties, two of them fatal.

Dead are Gunners Patrick J. K. Harty and Charles Kolesar. Among the wounded are Lieut. John Gerby and Easy Troop Sgt.-Maj. Jim Hart.

The shelling is so accurate everyone is convinced they are under observation. But from where, no one can guess. The only spot an observer could get an overview of fields obscured by hedgerows and woods is in the church now in the possession of 26th Battery, with their battery command post in the house of the *curé*. Still the accuracy is unnerving – three vehicles, including the petrol truck, are immediately set ablaze, sending up pillars of black smoke and attracting even more shells. And before the other vehicles can be moved, thirty-two tires are slashed by shell fragments.

Memories of such hours must always be scanty, limited to what eyes can see when blurred by anxiety bordering on terror, particularly when your face is only a few inches above the earth, buried in a thick bed of marigolds alongside some hollyhocks at the front door of a little farmhouse. For the rest of your life, you know that every time you catch a whiff of the pungent odour of marigolds, a confusing blur of what was August 23, 1944, will return: those first

---

*   Author interview.

whacking airbursts leaving black puffs over the trees you had thought were hiding your guns; the ripping geysers of earth spouting among the tombstones of the churchyard; the burning vehicles sending up pillars of smoke and attracting even heavier shelling; the uncanny accuracy with which the enemy's shells follow the guns and wagon lines as you move in haste to new positions; and, when finally it grows quiet, the urgent needs of the wounded and dying.

PART EIGHT: AUGUST 24–SEPTEMBER 5

Being Welcomed
as Liberators

65

YOUR ADVANCE PARTY
LIBERATES BOISNEY

———————————— ✳ ————————————

AS 2ND DIVISION TURNS NORTH TOWARDS LISIEUX, THEN EAST towards Rouen, there is clearly no line of defence. Groups of enemy, some of them small and others large and strongly supported by guns and tanks – either troops brought down from Calais to hold open the gap, or units that escaped before the gap was closed off – are competing for all roads leading to the Seine.

Today you liberate the crossroads village of Boisney, on the main highway from Lisieux to Rouen, some five miles in advance of all Allied troops. This happens when you are given an incorrect map reference for the rendezvous of recce parties and run out of radio range before they get around to sending out a correction. The fifteen-mile stretch of highway from Lisieux to Boisney is a white stretch of concrete as straight as an arrow, inviting you to find out just how fast a five-ton armoured scout car can go. Never before have you had such an opportunity, and you tell Bracken, your driver, to push it to the limit. It takes miles to get the sluggish vehicle up to a shuddering sixty miles an hour. By then you have to start slowing Bracken down, for there is the crossroads rushing at you.

Parking directly opposite the side door of the crossroads café, you wait. Not a soul is in sight. Peculiar, you think. But then your party had made a special effort to pack up and leave in a hurry so as to be first at the rendezvous. Just to make sure you didn't made a mistake, you check your decoding of the map reference. It is correct, and this crossroads is unmistakable. You ask the signaller to get RHQ on the blower, but he is unable to raise them or anybody else.

This being the first intact, operating café you've come across in Normandy, Dunsmore thinks a cool beer would go down well. But when he tries the door, it is locked. He bangs on it, but there is no response. Convinced that the publican, a Monsieur Morin according to the sign, is within, he continues to bang on the door. Finally you see the lace curtain move slightly, and immediately a bolt is pulled, the door opens, and a hearty, middleaged man flings himself out the door at Dunsmore, embracing him and yelling, "*Bienvenue, Tommy! Bienvenue, Tommy!*"

"Non-non! Canadien, dammit!" protests Dunsmore.

"*Canadiens! Canadiens!*" Monsieur Morin repeats in rapturous joy, as he hugs each of you and kisses you on both cheeks as one by one you pile out of the scout car. Then he calls to his son, who has just appeared, to go into the backyard and dig up the special bottle of Calvados hidden from the Germans for this day.

Once the bottle is uncorked, the son runs off up the street to ring the church bell and his father starts pouring out little glasses of the amber liquor. Toasts are drunk to France, to Canada, to Britain, to the United States, to *soldats Canadiens*, to Tommies, to Yankees, to sailors, to airmen, to de Gaulle, to Churchill, to Roosevelt, to Stalin. By now the church bell is ringing madly, and people are swarming into the street.

Someone reports that the Germans are up in trees down the road, but no one takes this seriously. You are getting worried, though, that no one else from 4th Field has shown up. Then, far back down the road along which you came half an hour ago, you spot a recce car creeping this way, the head of its commander, who has field-glasses to his eyes, barely visible above the turret. Leaving the crowd now growing in front of the café, you walk out to the centre of the crossroads and beckon him on. As he comes rolling in, now standing erect in the turret, he can hardly wait to ask what the hell you are doing miles in front of everybody, and whether there are any Germans around here. You tell him that a Frenchman claims they are just down the road a bit. Has he seen any vehicles with unit sign "42" on them back there along the road anywhere? He says about five miles back there is a "42" arrow pointing north along a side road.

When you get back to the guns, deployed in a field off a road parallel to the main highway, but several miles north of it, the battery is in a ferment of excitement. One gunner from each troop has been chosen to accept an incredible invitation from a farmer living in a house some distance across the fields. According to your troop leader, Bob Grout, the ecstatic farmer, his eyes shining with emotion, had come across the fields carrying ten gallons of fresh milk, apologizing for such "*une expression chetif*" of his family's pro-found gratitude to their liberators. Though the fresh milk was tremendously welcome, and his pails were speedily emptied into the gunners' cups, the farmer continued to apologize, and just before leaving – obviously convinced his gesture had been entirely inadequate – asked Sgt.-Maj. Mann to select "two worthy soldiers to honour his home by sleeping with his two daughters."

Grout assures you the chosen ones' sergeants have accepted responsibility for seeing they are aboard their quads if the battery has to make a sudden move during the night.

Now surrounded by most of the troop as he shaves, washes, and combs, Able Troop's selectee is besieged with offers of aftershave lotion and ribald advice.

Believing there may be a gross misunderstanding of the farmer's intent due to language difficulties, you quietly warn Able Troop's ambassador, as he leaves, to proceed with caution.

Days later, when he chooses to give you a report, he will tell you that there was no mistake – though at first he thought there had been, when, after dinner, the family sat around chatting. But when bedtime came, he and his pal were escorted upstairs with their respective girls and shown to their bedrooms by the mother, carrying lamps.

While this form of gratitude, expressed with the blessing of all members of a family, must certainly be rare, if not totally unique, the Regiment becomes aware over the next few days of a remarkable change in the reception people along the way are giving the passing troops. Now that you are outside the areas of severe destruction, where people, if seen at all, were grim refugees totally concerned with survival, the residents of untouched villages and unscarred farms of green fields and live cattle, are exuberant in their welcome as the guns roll by.

When one day you try to set down a record of these days, there's a kaleidoscope of images: "madly cheering French civilians lining the streets of villages gay with tricolours as at Thiberville . . . the refreshing green, rich farmland and apple orchards . . . the barrels of apple cider . . . tomatoes, apples, and masses of flowers pressed on the vehicles . . . weak, ersatz coffee, sometimes laced with all-powerful Calvados and cognac . . . urchins begging, '*cigarette pour papa – chocolate pour mama*' . . . the freedom-fighting Maquis with red, white, and blue arm bands and the inevitable Mauser rifles slung over their shoulders . . . laughing women yelling '*Merci Canadiens*' . . . and church bells ringing . . ."

These are exciting days. The Germans seldom are seen in strength, and the infantry are moving as fast as possible, using whatever transport available, forcing the guns to make up to four moves in a twenty-four-hour period. The result is that small groups of Germans are left in buildings and woods, and it is no longer unusual to see a gunner marching three or four bedraggled Germans, hands clasped behind their heads, out of a field being laid out for a gun position by an advance party.

So briefly are the guns in position in most spots, that digging is being restricted to personal slit trenches, and very infrequently are these needed. And it's a good thing, for you no longer carry the slabs of corrugated iron taken from the hangars at Carpiquet aerodrome for the roofs of command posts. Before setting out on this "chase" to the Seine, the Regiment was ordered on August 19 to get rid of all excess baggage, and reluctantly those old, rusty, mud-caked friends, which had held roofs of protective earth over some eleven successive dugouts, were abandoned.

66

SHOWERS OF STEEL SHARDS
IN FOREST

---- ✳ ----

FORÊT DE LA LONDE, TEN KILOMETRES LONG AND FOUR WIDE AT its widest part, lies next to the west bank of the Seine, which snakes its way with countless horseshoe bends past Rouen on its way to the sea, and provides dense cover from the air for Germans assembled in there waiting to be rafted over the river after dark. From the fierce fire the RHLI and the Essex attract at railway underpasses in the forest, it is clear that the Germans intend to retain command of forest and hills (some with sides of clifflike steepness) until they get all they can over the river.*

Not only have they placed guns and mortars and machine guns at strategic points, covering railway underpasses and forest openings,

---

* According to German generals quoted by Chester Wilmot in *The Struggle for Europe* (London: Collins, 1952), in terms of equipment lost or abandoned, the rearguard action from Falaise to the Seine was a disaster for them almost as bad as the Falaise pocket was in terms of casualties. Field Marshal Model, German Commander in Chief West, reporting to Hitler on August 29, when the last of his troops were crossing the Seine, the average strength of panzer divisions was "five to ten tanks each." Of the twenty-three divisions in Normandy, seven by then had been wiped out completely; and of the other sixteen, only enough to man four divisions got back over the Seine, "for the most part equipped with nothing more than small arms."

but any attempt to take command of the high hills – as the Royals do at one point – is made costly by guns firing from across the Seine. These could be silenced by 2nd Division guns, deployed since early morning on August 27 halfway between Bourgtheroulde and Elbeuf (4th Field near St. Ouen du Tilleuil), but firing across the Seine is banned. The reason: it might conflict with crossings by 3rd Division upstream. (When the leading Royals were approaching the forest via Elbeuf at 3:00 A.M., they met up with an American officer in a recce car, and later the marching troops were met by a company of Winnipeg Rifles under Capt. Cliff Chadderton.)

Still, the guns make things wretched for the Germans in the forest, with 4th Field alone firing seven thousand rounds during the two days and nights the Germans hold out. When there is no observed fire being called for by FOOs buried deep in the forest without any field of observation, either the major at Battalion or the colonel at Brigade lays on fire on likely spots. And each night the seventy-two field guns of the division fire a slow but long harassing-fire plan to make things miserable for the Germans moving through the forest to the riverbank.*

Just how miserable, the Canadian infantry and their supporting artillery carrier crews can now readily testify. All have come to dread the arrival of German shells and mortar bombs anywhere near them in the forest, for they detonate in the trees overhead with horrible, resounding airbursts that shower the forest floor with branches and steel shards that can maim and kill.

---

*   According to Gen. Blumentritt, Model's chief of staff, of the 2,300 tanks and self-propelled guns committed to Normandy "only 100 to 120 were brought back across the Seine." While they fought a courageous rearguard action and maintained some sixty ferries for varying periods between Elbeuf and the sea, many were merely rafts of cider barrels lashed together or logs cut from trees in the forest. And while they got men across, nearly all their guns, tanks, and half-tracks had to be left behind.

And while the combination of air attacks and shelling account for a great many German vehicles along the riverbank, reminiscent of the Falaise gap, and allow the enemy no peace as the infantry persists in trying to clear the forest, the German rearguards hold out until they decide no more men and equipment can cross the river. Their last effort is to threaten a counter-attack before fading away. Where to, no one quite knows or cares; the relief that the battle is over is universal.

The three armoured divisions of the British 30th Corps are now over the Seine at Vernon, twenty-five miles further upstream towards Paris, and about to drive to the Somme, and then on to Brussels and Antwerp, with the same dash as has been displayed by Patton's armour when unopposed. Canadian 3rd Division is firmly over the Seine and beginning to occupy Rouen abandoned by the Germans. And now beckoning is Dieppe, suggested as a suitable objective for 2nd Division by Montgomery.

Only three members of 4th Field carrier crews were casualties in the forest (including Gunner C. S. "Sid" Williams, a handsome young man of joyous temperament, who will lose a leg at the thigh). But the infantry has taken a bloody nose, which, after the severe casualties on the road to Falaise, none of the battalions of 2nd Division could afford – the Royals least of all.

By the night of August 29, when they march back to a concentration area where they can get a good night's rest after their exhausting experience of the previous few days, they have lost twelve officers and 137 men – thirty of them killed.

Not since the Dieppe Raid has the fighting strength of the Royals been so low. With the loss of so many of their experienced officers, including three company commanders and all their second-in-command captains, the battalion is in serious condition. The senior officers hold a meeting to decide whether four skeleton companies should be maintained and reinforced, or one strong company formed of what is left until reinforcements become available to build up new companies. It is decided to retain the four-company structure, although none can muster a full platoon. Major Ralph Young, the acting commanding officer, later explains the reasoning behind the decision: "In the end it is up to me. I have to decide if we are to cut the battalion down to one or two companies. If we do this, I believe we'll be withdrawn from the line and never go back in again – we'll be written off. So we retain four companies, though we have only eighteen men in one of them and none have the personnel to form a platoon."*

The Royals are now twelve officers and 280 other ranks short of their fighting establishment, and these shortages are mostly in the rifle companies. Officers, who only weeks ago were untested lieutenants, now command companies. And there is a serious shortage of NCOs. After the Dieppe disaster, the battalion had nearly two years to rebuild a unit. Now it must be rebuilt on the march, between attacks. And the Royals have much in common with other Canadian battalions that have been closing on the Seine.†

---

* Author interview.

† Of 20,178 Canadian casualties in Normandy (5,401 fatal), including 1,603 officers (461 fatal), suffered by the three Canadian divisions and the armoured brigade, between June 6 and August 31, the two infantry divisions (2nd and 3rd) accounted for 78 per cent: 7,869 dead, wounded, or missing per division, the highest casualty rate in all fifteen divisions in 21st Army Group. Of the 7,869 casualties per division, 5,980 or 76 per cent were infantry. The magnitude of this reduction in the fighting power of each division can only be fully understood when it is recognized that the 5,980 infantry casualties per division occurred among a fighting establishment of only 4,590 per division. And among Canadian officers, the casualty rate was even worse: 1,603 (461 fatal), the two infantry divisions averaging 625 officer casualties per division, 475 of them among the fighting establishment of only 270 infantry officers per division (30 × 9 battalions), producing a casualty rate in only two and a half months of 176 per cent. (Casualty records, National Archives of Canada, RG24 Vol. 18,502, File 133.009 (D1); and tables in *Memoirs of Montgomery of Alamein* (Cleveland: World Publishing, 1958), pp. 268-69.)

67

NOW THEY'LL NEVER HAVE
THEIR HONEYMOON

※

IT IS LATE AT NIGHT WHEN LEN HARVEY SEEKS YOU OUT IN A large, cavelike storage bunker the Germans had dug into the side of a hill, protected from the weather by a piece of tarpaulin hanging as a blackout curtain across its mouth, to tell you Jack Cameron is dead.

Knowing the news will hit you as hard as it hit him, Len shoves a partially consumed crock of cognac into your hands. And for a long, long time you and he hold a kind of a wake for your old buddy of 26th Battery. He says Jack was killed three days ago, on August 26, while fooing with the Essex Scottish as they were moving up to start clearing the Forêt de la Londe. A mortar bomb set fire to the gas tank of a vehicle under which he'd sought shelter.

The image of it rocks you rotten. Big, smiling Jack was the first officer of 4th Field you met on arrival at the Regiment back in 1942. And all that fall and throughout the winter of 1943, when you weren't out on training schemes, you, he, and Harvey shared an unheated bedroom on the ground floor of a house used as the 26th Battery officers' mess, halfway between Barnham Junction and the Labour in Vain pub at the next crossroads.

Obviously all your secret reservations about never allowing yourself to become emotionally connected with any comrade, because his death might be too hard to take, never worked in his case – couldn't possibly work with such a loveable guy, always smiling, always glad to see you, ever the patient, tolerant, helpful friend.

Every day, without fail, he wrote to his wife, with whom he shared only one day of married life before leaving Canada three years ago. And like you and every other married man over here, he'd promised himself a glorious honeymoon of infinite length, when the war was over.

Your heart aches for that poor girl in Canada, who'll continue to get his letters long after she's received a telegram from Defence Headquarters – until the letters stop forever.

Each time you learn of the death of a fellow officer, sadness and regret sweep through you, and if you knew him well, there is a great sense of loss. But you know you must not dwell on it, that in fact it is unhealthy to dwell on it, so you put it out of your mind as soon as you can. And if you were to be totally honest, you would have to confess that this is not really difficult, for each time it happens, you are profoundly thankful it wasn't you. There are no such thoughts, however, on hearing the news of Jack.

It is more like the death of a family member – most probably because you are with Len, who shares so many memories involving the three of you. And it is Len, using the strange vernacular of the day, who best expresses what you are both feeling: "Son of a bitch! Of all the guys who should never have bought it. . . . This one really hurts."

To Sammy Grange, "It was a terrible blow. Within a month of taking over Fox Troop from me, he was dead. I found this very hard. Of all the fellows in the Regiment, I think he was the one I was most fond of. He was just a prince of a fellow – thoroughly nice."

And one of the finest tributes an officer could ever hope to earn will appear in Sgt. Hunt's diary: "The news has a depressing effect on all of us. Few men hold so even-handedly the respect and affection that were his. An officer and a gentleman in the best Canadian sense of the words, Capt. Cameron is a very real loss to the battery."

As you are going to sleep, you find yourself recalling a November 11 back in the early thirties that fell on a Sunday, allowing school-children to attend the ceremony at the cenotaph. Watching the veterans march by, you hadn't been favourably impressed by their appearance. They looked not at all like the warriors you imagined – many of them looked truly seedy and down at heel. Of course most of the poor devils were unemployed. Tonight you solemnly vow that if you get back to Canada, you will never miss a Remembrance Day ceremony as long as you live.

Back at the guns in the morning, you find life "laughing onward." Elder's pals are still ragging him about the fix he was in a couple of days ago, just north of Brionne, when the battery command post "Y" vehicle, on an advance party, ran over a mine. The vehicle's big, heavy spare tire pitched up and came down over his shoulders, pinning his arms and immobilizing him in the back of the car while everybody else piled out in a rush to get away, expecting the punctured gas tank to catch fire and the whole thing to go up in flames. (Fortunately it didn't.)

Obviously Elder thinks it all very unfunny, remembering hearing his pals talking from a safe distance, as he waited for someone to come back and release him:

"We sure were lucky! Seems only Elder has bought it."

68

A LESSON IN CHARITY

———————————— ❋ ————————————

IT IS AUGUST 31, AND THE SUN IS ABOUT TO SET ON A REALLY remarkable day. You've just planted your gun markers to show where the guns will drop their platforms when they arrive, and have given the acks on the advance party permission to go over to a distant farmhouse to capture some Germans who, according to the farmer who visited Bombardier Morty Hughes on Baker Troop position, "want to give themselves up."

Now you look around for a place to relax. There isn't much choice. Between your gun flags and Baker Troop's is a huge, perfectly round crater, about thirty feet across and fifteen feet deep, excavated by a wayward buzz bomb that failed to make it even to the English Channel let alone its ultimate target of the London docks. You try sitting on the edge of the crater with your feet hanging down, contemplating the twisted remnants of its ram-jet engine rusting in the bottom of the conical hole. But there is nothing to lean against, and you want to catch forty winks before the guns arrive, so you move away to sit with your back against one of the stooks of grain that dot this very large stubble field.

As you lean back into the rustling dry sheaves, the dust you stir up has a homely, earthy, granary smell that is so comforting in its association with more peaceful days in other quiet fields glowing yellow from the dazzling rays of a setting sun. Even before the little scouting party of acks has disappeared up the lane leading to the farmhouse hidden in a clump of trees some five hundred yards away, you are dozing off.

You hope you were right in approving their enterprise, and that they took seriously your parting admonition to be careful and not get themselves shot up.

There's been a strange quality about this whole day, starting with the unusual early-morning stillness that lay over the whole front as the guns were being limbered up back on the south bank of the Seine at St. Ouen de Telleuil. This was in deep contrast to the previous three days of incessant, reverberating roars in the Forêt de la Londe aroused either by the enemy's mortars and guns or those of 2nd Division.

It seemed evident that the last of the enemy crossed the river during the night, when shortly after dawn recce parties were called and the order came to limber up and prepare to move to a new position across the Seine from Elbeuf, southeast of Rouen. But no sooner were the guns and limbers hooked up to the quads, ready to move off, than a target came down.

Quads wheeled the guns around back into the field, trails were dropped, and for the first time since coming to France, they were brought into action and put on line by the old "crash action" method, allowing them to respond quickly with "fire for effect." In fact the guns engaged two targets, called for by a FOO in rapid succession, each involving a respectable scale of forty-five rounds per gun, said to be required to break up a counter-attack. But it was clearly only a skirmish with a pocket of Germans still attempting to make it to the river, for no sooner had the Regiment fired off the second target, than orders came to cease fire and limber up.

By 6:30 A.M. all batteries were out on the road, moving briskly along in regimental convoy, rolling over the crest of a high hill so openly and boldly it felt as though you might take off into the blue morning sky, with the beautiful, sunlit valley of the Seine spread out below, its shining silver waters snaking and winding away to the left in search of the sea.

This was all in great contrast to the furtive tactics required of carrier crews with the infantry, tormented day and night by air-bursts among the trees of Forêt de la Londe, and the cautious, pinched-up, frequently stalled movements of the guns since Falaise – to be associated forever by the gunners with the names Friardel, Orbec, Livarot, and Elbeuf. There was abroad this morning almost a holiday atmosphere, which persisted, and may even have been enhanced, when the pace was reduced to a crawl by a congestion of trucks, armoured cars, and tanks waiting their turn to drive over the chuckling planks of the gently rocking and dipping pontoon bridge that stretched its impressive length across the great, shim-mering river.

And the feeling that it was a holiday commemorating some notable event became reality when, after a brief stop at a gun posi-tion southeast of Rouen, the Regiment rolled into the city to as tumultuous a welcome as ever was extended to a crowned head in those ancient streets. Totally unexpected, the enthusiastic expres-sions of gratitude, so warm and genuine, struck all ranks with shocking force. Suddenly there were thousands of cheering, flag-waving men, women, and children lining the streets, many of them crowding dangerously close to rotating wheels and clanking tracks as they handed up fruit and wine and flowers – such masses of beautiful blooms, the dusty old vehicles took on the appearance of colourful floats, and the regimental convoy, so tired and battle-shabby only moments before, was transformed into a victory parade.

Only for a fleeting moment did a dark echo of the detestable years of German occupation mar the glorious passage through Rouen. Having noted during one of the abbreviated halts several glum-looking women along the route, standing in doorways with towels draped around their heads like turbans, you inquired of a male bystander who had greeted you in perfect English why so many women had chosen to wash their hair this morning. He explained the towels were covering not wet heads, but bald heads, shaved bare by members of the French Resistance in punishment for having consorted too intimately with the hated enemy during the occupation. Why had they chosen to appear in public, wearing their badge of dishonour in full view of the liberating troops? He couldn't say, but perhaps they were ordered by the FFI to thus display their shame. Anyway, you were glad when the convoy moved on out onto the highway to Dieppe, and you could no longer see the sad eyes of those embarrassed women.

For hours after, at a gun position ten miles north of Rouen, in farming country untouched by war – so peaceful and quiet after that clamorous reception in Rouen – you could feel everyone glowing with satisfaction and pride, in themselves, the Regiment, and the army of which they are part. For weeks, everybody has been aware that the guns are a decisive factor in the taking of ground and holding it against enemy counter-attacks – often the most decisive factor, for, unlike air support, the guns are always available regardless of weather or cloud conditions in daylight or in darkness. And all ranks – from the CO down to the lowliest of the ORs – know that the gunners have done everything that could ever have been expected of them, and, on occasion, more than ever should have been expected of ordinary mortals. They don't need to have anyone tell them this. But still, it took the Rouen experience to place things in proper perspective, to bring significant meaning to that symbol of the Allied invasion: the crusader's sword and shield.

Those joyous crowds – sometimes applauding and sometimes cheering deliriously – showering symbols of their thankfulness on the Regiment as it passed along the streets within sight of the great Cathedral and other noble buildings (pock-marked by Allied fighter-planes strafing German headquarters during the occupation), could not fail to leave a remarkable impression on all who passed that way today. Witnessing the joy and gratitude of a people released from bondage, all were reminded of the primary purpose of the invasion – something easily forgotten during the sordid, strenuous weeks in the bridgehead before the break-out, when personal survival was the chief objective for days on end.

And now this evening, as you enjoy the pleasant feeling that you and your comrades have justified your manhood and those long years of training in England, you allow yourself to consider the intoxicating possibility that the end of the war may be near. Paris has fallen – the German garrison surrendering without serious fighting. Surely this means that German resistance is collapsing everywhere. Even if Hitler is able to persuade his generals to keep it going, postponing his own fate for a few weeks, the worst of the fighting must surely be over.

Suddenly, from the direction of the farmhouse, you hear the rattle of a machine gun. You jump up and make for the lane leading up to it, believing the worst has happened, that the acks have been led into an ambush. Almost completely untrained in infantry tactics, they can get themselves badly messed up. You hope and pray they'll pull back . . . But as you enter the tree-lined lane, you see marching towards you a platoon of soldiers in grey uniforms with their hands behind their heads. As you step to one side to let them pass down the lane, you count forty-five before you come across one grinning gunner with a Sten bringing up the rear.

"What was the shooting about?"

"Oh, one of the young guys fired by mistake. He'd never seen live Germans before up close, so when this mob started coming out of the orchard and the house, he got a little excited and fired off a burst."

"Did he hit any of them?"

"One of them in the neck. He's lying dead on the road up there."

When you reach the farmhouse and the dead German soldier lying in the dust of the roadway, you find that a bottle of cognac has been found in one of the several wagons in the large orchard to the right of the house and it is being passed around. Everybody is overly excited and ready to laugh at anything, as though trying to shake off the useless killing of a man trying to give himself up.

Gunner F. M. Westaway, a Baker Troop batman – normally not part of an advance party, but who must have volunteered to come along, ostensibly to help dig the command post, but in fact to get a chance to poke through derelict houses for booze or other loot – makes what he thinks is a hilarious gesture when he lights your cigarette with a flaming hundred-franc bill, and hands you a packet of fifty more crisp, brand-new banknotes, with the expansive remark: "Here, have five thousand on me, sir!"

In the dust not far from the German's body is Westaway's source: a black leather bag, somewhat like a doctor's bag, its top spread open.

Examining it closely, you see it's jammed with packets of freshly printed notes. There must be hundreds of thousands of francs in there! How unfortunate they are worthless. (Before you left England they told you that all money in circulation on the continent would be worthless until new money was printed to replace what the Germans had debased. And to overcome this handicap you were issued specially printed Allied script to be used in place of regular money.) At that moment, Lieut. E. A. McCarey, a Signals Corps officer attached to 4RCA, arrives in his Jeep with a message that the guns will not be up until morning, but that the advance party is to remain here for the night. Spotting the black bag with the money, he bends down, snaps the lid closed, and throws it into the back of his Jeep. When you inquire what he hopes to do with it, he says, "Oh, the boys at the guns might like some as souvenirs."*

---

* Weeks later Gunner John Elder made the discovery that French banknotes were perfectly good when his bank in London accepted for deposit a tissue-paper-looking thousand-franc note that the younger Gunner Walkden had given him as a joke on his birthday. Then Lieut. McCarey revealed he had deposited the entire contents of that black bag in his bank account in London.

For a moment you wonder about his sudden altruism. But just then someone finds another bottle of booze in a wagon under the hay the Germans had mounded up in each to hide its contents and the "gold rush" is on. Everybody chooses a different wagon and starts feeling under its thick mattress of hay among ammunition, rifles, and other equipment; obviously this was a quarter stores that got cut off from the retreat by the rapid advance of 4th Brigade.

Choosing a wagon, you lean over its low tailgate, raise the hay, and stick your head and shoulders under it. In a clutter of webbing, water-bottles, and other equipment, you find a bottle of cognac. Placing this on a narrow ledge outside the tailgate, you dive under the hay again. But you find no more, and when you come out from under the dusty rustling mass, you discover your original find has vanished.

Swearing that if you find another bottle, you will sit down and consume it on the spot, you go to another wagon. After some searching you locate a long-necked, bulbous bottle that turns out to be a full litre of Benedictine. True to your oath, you climb up onto the hay and start sipping away at the strong liqueur. Not having had anything to eat since noon, you find the sweet liquid delicious. And this being the first time you've been without responsibility for a gun position or an OP since coming to France, the sense of relaxation is marvellous – and gets progressively more so with each passing hour.

When the sun goes down, a great orange harvest moon rises over the orchard, inspiring you to start singing "In the Evening by the Moonlight," beating time on the side of the wagon with the now-empty bottle. This seems to act as a beacon for a shadowy figure coming through the orchard. In due course he looms up beside the wagon to ask a most improbable question of the "officer and gentleman" reclining there: "Sir, you officers all carry shots of morphine, don't you?"

That each officer before leaving England was indeed issued two shots of morphine, to be carried in holes drilled in a little block of wood buttoned in the watch-pocket, on the right leg of your battledress, doesn't make the question any less astonishing. The voice, recognizable as that of the wandering batman, Westaway, continues:

"You know that German we all thought was dead? Well, he's still alive. The French people have got him up on a bed upstairs in the house, and he needs a shot of morphine real bad, sir."

The response of said Christian officer and gentleman is immediate, precise, and stern: this morphine is for Canadians, and you have only two precious shots.

Westaway refuses to be put off.

"But won't you just come and look at him, sir? He's in awful bad shape!"

Giving in to his plea, you get down off the wagon with some difficulty, for a litre of Benedictine on an empty stomach does wonders to relax legs, not to mention your cross-level bubble, and you weave your way through the orchard, managing not to miss a single low branch of an endless lineup of trees conspiring to block your path to the house.

In the gloom of the front hall, you are confronted by a most formidable staircase leading to the second floor, so awfully steep and long – almost disappearing into the darkness above – that for a moment you pause at the bottom step to gather your determination. What little light there is in the entrance hall is spilling from the parlour on the right, from candles on a table in the centre of the room, around which people with solemn faces are sitting, stiffly erect, on chairs. No one is talking. The atmosphere is clearly that of a death watch; the candles, the woman with bowed head holding her hands in an attitude of prayer, and the eyes of the man when he looks at you, all seem to say, A man is dying upstairs.

As you struggle up the stairs, largely on your hands and knees, you marvel at the attitude of these people. This morning that bugger up there in his grey uniform and jackboots was a hated enemy. Now they really seem to care what happens to him.

Westaway is waiting at the head of the stairs and leads you into the first bedroom on the right, lit by another candle, which sits wavering on the bureau against the wall at the foot of the bed. On top of the bed covers, fully clothed, just as the family had picked him up from the dust of their laneway, lies the German. He is on his back, unmoving, his eyes closed. Still alive, he breathes noisily through a gaping, blood-encrusted hole in his neck, just below his chin on the left side. But for how much longer, you wonder, for his face is the colour of gun-metal.

In spite of everything, there is something about the way he lies there that reminds you of your brother, and with this thought a wave of compassion sweeps through you; a man who could be your brother is dying alone among strangers, without medical aid. Suddenly you realize you are no longer struggling to function in a fuddling haze. Something in the shock of seeing a dying man, looking like your brother, has sobered you up – if not entirely, at least enough so that you now remember the drill for administering morphine laid on by the MO.

He is lying more on the left side of the bed, and as you move around there, you realize you'll need a knife or something sharp to slit his tunic sleeve so you can find a muscle in his arm in which to stick the needle. Westaway doesn't have a penknife either, but, seemingly now quite familiar with the contents of the room, he readily comes up with a pair of manicure scissors from the dresser. As you cut a wide slit in the man's sleeve, you review the procedure that sounded simple enough when the MO described it in England when they were issuing the stuff.

You remove the adhesive tape from the wood block and pull out one of the little vials. It resembles a miniature toothpaste tube with a disposable hypodermic needle attached. A wire pin, resting loosely in the top of the needle, underneath a tiny protective glass sheath, has only to be depressed to break a seal and make the needle operative. After discarding the pin, the needle is ready to be stuck into the arm or rear end of the wounded, but you must make sure that it goes only into a muscle – never a vein. After you've squeezed the collapsible tube to eject the morphine, you will have to mark his forehead with a black "M," so that those giving him treatment later will know that he's had a shot.

With his left upper arm bare, and one of the little needles ready for action, you grab hold of his arm and jab the needle hard into the muscle. You hope it's in far enough. But when you squeeze the soft little tube, the contents run down his arm and drip down onto the bedspread. You've blown your first attempt.

You're astonished at how resistant flesh can be to a needle – especially this very blunt needle. You have only one more chance. As you depress the pin to break the seal, remove it and discard it, and get the little tube firmly in your fingers, you find your hand is shaking. This man may not survive even with the morphine, but without it, he surely will die. You simply have to get it deep in the flesh this time.

Taking a deep breath, you jam the needle into his arm with all your strength. This time you know it's in far enough, for the stubby little needle is in up to its neck. Slowly you squeeze the tube, and with satisfaction note this time you don't lose a single drop. You remove the needle and rub the arm as you've seen nurses do.

In a matter of seconds, the German's colour begins to improve, and soon he opens his eyes. And although he makes no attempt to move even his lips, he calls out one word in a thick, but understandable accent: "*Dok-tor.*" He repeats it over and over, "*Dok-tor . . . Doktor,*" while his eyes follow you and beseech you to help him.

You send Westaway off to get a message back to Regiment to send up a stretcher-bearing Jeep to transport the German back to the MO. And then you try to reassure him that he's going to be all right, that you're going to get him back to a doctor as fast as you can. But he doesn't seem to understand, and continues to call "*Dok-tor, Dok-tor*," with only a slight decrease in frequency as you pass the time waiting for the stretcher, trying to find something to mark "M" on his forehead.

A few days later, when you get a chance to talk to the MO, you ask him if he thinks the German you sent back, with a red "M" inscribed in lipstick on his forehead and a big hole in his neck, survived his trip back to a field surgical hospital. The MO is quite certain he did. Obviously no artery had been severed, and all bleeding had ceased long before he'd seen him. He believes that all he needed was a few pints of blood and that hole in his neck sewn up and he'd be okay.

You marvel at the sequence of events and mixture of motives that went into saving that man's life. Westaway, clearly, was poking around where he shouldn't or he never would have come across that German in that upstairs bedroom. What he was after, you don't want to know, but clearly it was connected in some way with self-interest, for he's not one to expend any more energy than is absolutely necessary on anything not of direct material benefit. For instance, he always chooses to eat his own meal first before delivering one to his officer. This has the obvious advantage of messing up only one set of mess tins and eating utensils. He cleans the mess tins of travelling dust meticulously before eating his own meal out of them, and so feels it necessary only to bang out the remnants of his meal and refill them for delivery to his officer. While the shared knife, fork, and spoon, swilled off in the remnants of his tea, are dried off in a most memorable fashion as he goes, sawing them under an armpit of his battledress right up until the moment he presents them to his officer with a flourish worthy of a waiter at the Savoy, cheerfully and solicitously announcing, "Your dinner, sir! Better eat it while it's hot."

On the other side of the coin, however, is the indisputable fact that a man was pulled back from the grave and given another chance to live out a normal life after the war, solely through the initiative of Westaway, who may not be quite "thou true and faithful servant," but who truly believes that, enemy or not, "a man's a man for a' that," and persuaded an "officer and gentleman," very much against his inclination, to follow his leadership in common decency and humanity.

69

THE MOST SIGNIFICANT
CANADIAN PARADE OF THE WAR

———————— ❊ ————————

ON THE FORTY-MILE RUN UP TO THE COAST FROM THE JOYOUS reception in Rouen, 2nd Division units cross the path of only a couple of small pockets of Germans (at Tôtes and Longueville). By dark on August 31, 8th Recce armoured cars are just short of Dieppe, and, at ten-thirty next morning, they enter the town, meeting no opposition. The Germans have gone.

They left in great haste, it seems, when they heard Canadians with dark-blue patches on their shoulders were headed this way. This is according to the owner of the Château d'Ambrumesnil, close to where 4th Field is directed to park the guns and vehicles for rest and maintenance. About eight miles as the crow flies southwest of Dieppe, the château was used by the Germans as an officers' mess of the Dieppe garrison near Offranville.

Fortunately the abandonment of the port was discovered by some Royal Marines who landed last night, and the RAF bombing raid that was scheduled to precede a ground attack by 2nd Division was called off in time. Marines, standing outside a café with glasses of beer in their hands, are among the first to welcome a 4th Field FOO with the troops arriving on the outskirts of town.

Anticipating a delirious welcome from the people of Dieppe for each and every man, and fearful things may get completely out of hand, Divisional Commander Foulkes decides the bulk of the division should bivouac outside town until a formal parade can be arranged after the troops have had a chance to rest for a couple of days and spruce up.

This is eminently sensible, as for many this is their first chance since arriving in France to peel off all their filthy, flea-infested clothing and bathe – this being the first time the guns of 2nd Division have been out of action and at rest since July 9, fifty-three days ago.

When you remove your two pairs of socks, worn one over the other, they stand up like rubber boots. And when you pull off your woollen undershirt, the appearance of your back causes a sensation among onlookers, causing one to ask, "What the hell happened to you?"

For weeks you've been scratching, particularly around your wrists and ankles and back – sometimes ferociously scrubbing your back up and down against a post or tree – but until they produce two polished-steel hand-mirrors and allow you a view, you have no conception of the vigour of your attack: a mass of dried and blackened blood covers your back from top to bottom. What caused that ferocious itching? A heat rash, you think.

Sgt. Dunsmore, who happens to be passing as you advance this possibility, lets out a yelping chortle: "Heat rash, my ass – you're just lousey, sir! Let me have your battledress blouse."

Protesting that you have checked the seams on more than one occasion without finding any cooties, since you first started itching back at Ifs after sleeping on a cot in an abandoned German dugout, and the next day on a bare mattress left by the Germans in a barn near Verrières, you nevertheless give him your blouse and follow his advice to "watch closely and be quick when I spread open a seam." And there, wiggling to get out of sight, is a yellow sand-flea – and another, and another, and another.

After some kind soul soaps and washes your back, the burning itch is intolerable. The MO finds it difficult to believe that such massive irritation could have been caused by fleas, and asks, "Has anything been bothering you?"

Turned speechless by the question, you can only listen as he goes on to say, "If this calamine lotion doesn't clear it up in a couple of days, I'll have to evacuate you."

To which you reply, "With the war about to end? Like hell you will."

It is to get your mind off the damned itch that you and Bob Grout head up the road that evening for a village café in search of some drinkable cognac, and end up visiting the Château d'Ambrumesnil on the advice of the publican, who has nothing but the rawest of raw Calvados in his little café.

Even when you are still some distance down the lane from the noble building, the "squire," as he will later refer to himself jokingly, calls out from the front door in perfect English, "Come on in, fellows, and have a cup of coffee."

It turns out he is a Dutchman by birth who in the twenties learned English in North Africa from an associate travelling-salesman for Wills Tobacco. He was in Canada seeing the Dionne quintuplets the day war broke out, and he refers to the unreliable German flying bombs that have crashed all over the landscape around here as "Tin Lizzies" after Model-T Fords. He's kept a scrapbook of both German propaganda and clippings from Allied publications he somehow managed to get his hands on. He tells how he inwardly wept and raged when the German officers held a boisterous party here in his house to celebrate the destruction of the Canadian raid on Dieppe. That night, taking pride in their athletic prowess, as always, on their way down to dinner they vaulted, one after another, over the banister, their hobnailed boots crashing on his fine parquet flooring. (He points to the desecrated hall floor.)

After dinner one of them, an Olympic champion discus or javelin thrower (he isn't sure which), "to amuse the peasants," pulled the pins on grenades and fired them high in the sky to explode like fireworks.

This spring they'd become very nervous, certain the invasion was coming, and he taunted them that Germany was losing the war and that the Canadians would soon come to settle an old score. While they pooh-poohed this, claiming Hitler's secret weapons would wipe London off the face of the globe and end the war, they gradually lost faith when they saw more V-1s crash in France than took off over the Channel. There were countless false alarms, when they all rushed off on bicycles, returning after a while looking sheepish. But yesterday, when they learned Canadians with dark-blue patches on their shoulders were on their way up from Rouen, they took off. And this time they didn't return.

They would always be a mystery to him. They treated him and his wife with the utmost courtesy, even apologizing for causing her some mental anguish when corporals brutally disciplined their own soldiers in full view of her kitchen window, promising that henceforth when soldiers were required to fall on their faces on the ground while standing rigidly at attention, it would be out of sight of her window.

After lunch the next day (September 3), as you watch the first of some fifteen thousand men – all of them astonishingly well turned-out considering what their uniforms have been through – go swinging six abreast down the long steep hill into town, to turn right into a street covered with flowers cascading down from above, you wonder how many of them are having to flex their shoulders to get the cloth of an undershirt massaging an itch, as now and then you must, to the obvious amusement of the men in the troop behind you.

But when the moment comes for the artillery regiments to move off down the road into Dieppe, you forget the itch and are swept up in the significance of this great march – as much a march to honour those who were lost at Dieppe as a victory parade.

"The most impressive and meaningful Canadian parade of the war," is how Canadian war correspondent Ross Munro sees it.

Munro, who broke the first eyewitness account of the Dieppe Raid to the world in 1942, appropriately was in one of the first 8th Recce cars entering Dieppe two days ago. And one day, in his book *Gauntlet to Overlord*, he will describe his "pilgrimage" to Blue Beach at Puys, just east of Dieppe, where in 1942, in a ship just off shore, he'd watched the Royals and a troop of 4th Field gunners spill out of their landing craft and charge up the beach for the sea wall in the face of murderous fire from the cliffs.

> I went through the lonely, gray-brown town, and down the gulch towards the beach. The mines on the road had not been lifted and I had to pick my way cautiously. When I reached the beach I wished I had not come alone. It was like walking in a tomb. I shuddered to look at the beach, at the 12-foot stone wall across its top, where so many of the Royal Regiment were cut down before my very eyes. I shuddered as I looked at the quaint houses still there on the cliff top from which fire had poured into our boats. Here one of the finest regiments in the Canadian Army had fought and died. . . .*

As you march into town, the reception is incredible. Though nine infantry battalions have already passed the reviewing stand before the gunners come up, blooms are still showering down from the outstretched arms of women at windows high above the street. And the densely packed crowds of men, women, and children lining both sides of the street are still cheering earnestly without pause, in a steady, uninterrupted way you never have heard before anywhere.

The surging, wailing gale of human voices, which reaches you at least a mile before you get down into town, and which never for a second lets up until the tail of the parade has moved through town

---

* Ross Munro, *Gauntlet to Overlord* (Edmonton: Hurtig, 1945), pp. 208–209.

and up the road for Puys, is so intense it is disorienting – drowning out the Essex Scottish pipers leading 4th Brigade and the brass band beside the reviewing stand, where Army Commander General Crerar is taking the salute, flanked (most appropriately you think) by two 4th Field 25-pounders.

When at last you're broken off near a cliff edge to stare down at the beaches where men came ashore in 1942, you can hardly believe your eyes. Down there rusting in the gravel of a narrow stretch of beach is a Churchill tank, its puny, pea-shooter, two-pounder gun pointing at the base of the cliff. Where on earth was it supposed to go?

And farther east along the coast at Puys, walking down the narrow defile to where Capt. George Browne, Capt. Tommy Archibald, Lieut. Tait "Moose" Saunders, and the 20 Other Ranks from 4th Field plunged ashore and the Royals were cut down by the dozen on the gravel as they headed for the high sea-wall covered with a tangle of barbed-wire coils, you wonder how any of them managed to get through here and reach the fields and bush at the top that day.* They would all have been under observation every step of the way from the fortified house at the left of the defile with a field of fire covering the entire beach and the full length of the narrow, steepsided valley through which they had to go in daylight. That George Browne, Col. D. A. Catto, and nineteen others made it to the top, cleared two houses, and held on until 4:30 P.M., is a miracle.

The gloomy silence of the dead houses along the cliff top, the

---

* Sgt. J. W. Dudley, Lance-Bombardier F. M. Lalonde, and Gunner Donald McClean of 4th Field were killed, and the others were captured. Capt. Browne escaped twice – once from the Germans and then from the Vichy French – got back to England with valuable intelligence, and returned to France on D-Day, with 3rd Division. Out of the 528 Royals on the raid, 487 were casualties – 227 died.

rusting derelict landing craft in the restless shallows on the beach, the endless coils of barbed wire, the ragged, faded cloth strips in the camouflage netting, fluttering forlornly at a deserted gun emplacement, and the threatening ACHTUNG MINEN sign with its skull-and-crossbones warning trespassers of the danger of anti-personnel mines, all combine to induce a state of melancholia, and no one wants to linger here.

There's a ceremony in a cemetery above Dieppe where the Canadian bodies were collected by the townspeople and buried under neat wooden crosses of their devising. All would wish to attend, but the cemetery is so confined that only a select number from each unit are allowed to attend, with priority being given to those very few who are returning to Dieppe for the second time.

All next day Dieppe is out-of-bounds to officers so that they will not be around to inhibit the enjoyment of the troops (from 2:00 to 11:30 P.M.) as the people of Dieppe take them to their hearts, entertaining them as lavishly as possible. That this is lavish indeed, at least in terms of liquid refreshment, 4th Field drivers can testify. At the request of the mayor, attending a 4th Field officers' reception held in a house near Offranville after the parade, the Regiment supplies several trucks to transport wine from distant points. And according to the drivers, Dieppe is not likely to run dry for some time to come. There is also the rumour that champagne will flow like water tomorrow night at the mayor's reception and dance for the officers, to be attended by the belles of the town.

However, the officers of 4th Field will never know whether the rumour is true, for just as they are about to pull out for the reception, there is a conference phone call for battery commanders, warning them to have all personnel packed up and standing by, ready to move on short notice. And though the Regiment doesn't move off until 4:15 A.M., towards another concentration south of Montreuil, no one gets to attend the officers' reception though it will be talked about for years after by the infantry officers who attended.

It seems the party provided them with a wonderful chance to get some things off their chests with brigade commanders and up. Mostly they'll recall taking turns asking Gen. Foulkes why he exposed five of his badly under-strength battalions to 577 needless casualties in the attempt to clear the Forêt de la Londe when it could have been bypassed and the Germans left to rot in it until ready to give up.

The disappointment among 4th Field officers at having to miss this great "bash" does not, however, run very deep – for two reasons. First, many are still recovering from a regional "pub crawl" last night – especially from the effects of a heavy intake of Benedictine at a certain café beyond a trout stream named Scie. To reach the café you used an obscure ford that you and Bob Grout had discovered the second night here when confronted with the fact that all bridges had been destroyed by the fleeing Germans. At this café (where a child displayed a hat badge acquired from a Royal Regiment of Canada soldier two years ago), the sweet liquor was a welcome alternative to the raw, throat-rasping, unaged Calvados served in every other village café for miles around. The result, however, was giant hangovers – not to mention the bruises and lacerations suffered by the occupants of a Jeep that failed to locate the right turning to the ford on the way home and twice drove off the end of a bridge that wasn't there. These painful injuries are most visible on the visages of Bill Murdoch, the driver of the wayward Jeep, and one of his passengers, "Stevie" Stevenson (now noticeably short a couple of teeth), who was dozing in the back when the intrepid Murdoch, not once, but twice, managed, within a few hundred yards, to drive off non-existent spans.

The second, and perhaps more meaningful reason for the lack of resentment at missing the mayor's party, stems from the fact that everyone is convinced the war is about to end, and it would be preferable to be among the spearheads converging on Berlin than languishing here at Dieppe. And British tanks (according to the

BBC) are rumbling through Belgium three hundred miles north of here on their way to *Der Vaterland*.

That the war will continue for another eight months, and that for much of the time you will be engaged in bloody battles in the most horrendous conditions of mud and water since Passchendaele in World War One, is of course beyond imagination. Even the most pessimistic soul could never conceive of a course of events that will see eleven thousand more Canadian casualties as the Canadian Army clears the Scheldt Estuary to open the port of Antwerp and next spring clears the lower Rhineland. If anyone were to suggest that five months hence your guns will participate in the biggest barrage and attendant bombardment of the entire war, involving 2,645 guns in support of a 400,000-strong Canadian Army pushing through the Siegfried Line, and that the fire-power of 3,411 guns for the Rhine-crossing next March will exceed the fire-power for the Normandy landings, you would write him off as a lunatic.

APPENDIX A

ONE OF FOUR ALLIED ARMIES IN NORMANDY

Supreme Commander Allied Expeditionary Force
General Eisenhower

Commander-in-Chief of Ground Forces
Field Marshal Montgomery

21ST BRIT ARMY GROUP	12TH USA ARMY GROUP

2ND BRIT ARMY	1ST CANADIAN ARMY	1ST USA ARMY	3RD USA ARMY
Lt-Gen Dempsey	Lt-Gen Crerar	Lt-Gen Hodges	Lt-Gen Patton

2ND CANADIAN CORPS
Lt-Gen Simonds

2nd Cdn Infantry Division

4th Brigade
The Royal Regiment of Canada
The Royal Hamilton Light Infantry
The Essex Scottish Regiment

5th Brigade
The Black Watch (Royal Highland
  Regiment of Canada)
Le Régiment de Maisonneuve
The Calgary Highlanders

6th Brigade
Les Fusiliers Mont-Royal
The Queen's Own Cameron Highlanders of Canada
The South Saskatchewan Regiment

Divisional Troops

8th Reconnaissance Regiment
  (14th Canadian Hussars)
2nd Cdn Divisional Engineers
2nd Cdn Divisional Signals

4th Field, 5th Field, 6th Field,
  2nd Anti-Tank and 3rd Light
  Anti-Aircraft Regiments RCA
The Toronto Scottish Regiment
  (Machine Gun)

3rd Cdn Infantry Division

7th Brigade
The Royal Winnipeg Rifles
The Regina Rifle Regiment
The Canadian Scottish Regiment

8th Brigade
The Queen's Own Rifles of Canada
Le Régiment de la Chaudière
The North Shore (New Brunswick) Regiment

9th Brigade
The Highland Light Infantry of Canada
The Stormont, Dundas and Glengarry Highlanders
The North Nova Scotia Highlanders

Divisional Troops

7th Reconnaissance Regiment (17th Duke of York's Royal Cdn Hussars)
3rd Cdn Divisional Engineers
3rd Cdn Divisional Signals

12th Field, 13th Field, 14th Field, 3rd Anti-Tank, 4th Light Anti-Aircraft Regiments RCA
The Cameron Highlanders of Ottawa (Machine Gun)

4th Cdn Armoured Division

4th Armoured Brigade
21st Armoured Regiment (Governor General's Foot Guards)
22nd Armoured Regiment (Canadian Grenadier Guards)
28th Armoured Regiment (British Columbia Regiment)
Lake Superior Regiment (Motorized)

10th Infantry Brigade
The Lincoln and Welland Regiment
The Algonquin Regiment
The Argyll and Sutherland Highlanders of Canada

Divisional Troops

29th Reconnaissance Regiment (The South Alberta Regiment)
4th Armoured Divisional Engineers
4th Armoured Divisional Signals

15th and 23rd Field Regiments RCA
5th Anti-Tank Regiment
8th Light Anti-Aircraft Regiment

1st Polish Armoured Division

10th Polish Armoured Brigade
1st Polish Armoured Regiment
2nd Polish Armoured Regiment
24th Polish Armoured (Lancer)
  Regiment
10th Polish Motor Battalion

3rd Polish Infantry Brigade
1st Polish (Highland) Battalion
8th Polish Battalion
9th Polish Battalion

Divisional Troops

10th Polish Mounted Rifle Regiment
1st Polish Divisional Engineers
1st Polish Divisional Signals

1st and 2nd Polish Field Regiments
1st Polish Anti-Tank Regiment
1st Polish Anti-Aircraft Regiment

2nd Canadian Armoured Brigade
(independant brigade from D-Day landings)

6th Armoured Regiment (The 1st Hussars)
10th Armoured Regiment (The Fort Garry Horse)
27th Armoured Regiment (The Sherbrooke Fusiliers)

1st Canadian Parachute Battalion
(of 6th Brit Airborne Division)

Other Army and Corps Troops

2nd Cdn Army Group Royal Artillery
  (3rd, 4th and 7th Medium Regiments)
2nd Cdn Heavy Anti-Aircraft Regiment
19th Cdn Field Regiment
6th Anti-Tank Regiment RCA
6th Light Anti-Aircraft Regiment RCA
2nd Survey Regiment RCA
1st Armoured Personnel Carrier Regiment
25th Cdn Armoured Delivery Regiment
  (The Elgin Regiment)
1st Royal Cdn Army Group
  Engineers

2nd Corps Engineers
1st, 2nd, and 3rd Battalions,
  Royal Canadian Engineers
1st Cdn Army HQ Signals
2nd Corps Signals
Army HQ Defence Battalion
  (Royal Montreal Regiment)
18th Armoured Car Regiment
  (12th Manitoba Dragoons)
Number 1 Cdn Railway
  Operating Group

In addition to the units listed above, are the Royal Cdn Army Service Corps, the Royal Cdn Ordnance Corps, and the Royal Cdn Medical Corps, providing crucial services without which the army could not function. A large number of Ordnance personnel (detached sections of the Royal Electrical and Mechanical Engineers), and of the Medical Corps (one medical officer and one dental officer per regiment), serve at the fighting-unit level.

The war establishment of a Canadian or British armoured division is about 18,800 men, of which 2,500 are in three infantry battalions of its one infantry brigade. An infantry division calls for 19,300, of which 7,500 serve in three infantry brigades (of three battalions each), and 3,400 in five artillery regiments: three field regiments, an anti-tank regiment and a light anti-aircraft regiment.

APPENDIX B

RECORD RATES OF SHELL CONSUMPTION

RCASC DUMPS OF 25-POUNDER AMMUNITION
OVER 7-DAY PERIOD ENDING JULY 27, 1944

	At 2nd Div Guns (72 guns)	At 4th Field (24 guns)	RPG
July 20 (0030 hrs–0900 hrs)	25,200	8,400	350
(1645 hrs–2100 hrs)	33,400	11,334	464
(2100 hrs–2300 hrs)	2,400	2,400	100
21 (early afternoon)		8,400 ★	350
22 (0240 hrs–1230 hrs)	12,000	4,000	167
(1230 hrs–1830 hrs)	12,000	4,000	167
22–23 (2000 hrs–0730 hrs)	46,800	15,600	650
23 (0730 hrs–1200 hrs)	25,200	8,400	350
26 (2000 hrs–0600 hrs)	36,000	12,000	500
	193,000	74,534	
Total rounds per gun:	2,680	3,105	
Rounds per gun per day:	383	444	

★ An emergency dump by 4RCA trucks and ammunition numbers who brought up unexpended rounds from previous gun position and from an RCASC dump beyond Carpiquet, when the guns threatened to run out of ammunition.

ROUNDS FIRED PER GUN PER DAY BY 4TH FIELD

(As recorded in gun log D Sub, Easy Troop, 26 Battery, which can be taken as representative of all guns of 4RCA, since all targets during the period were Mike or higher, involving all guns in the Regiment)

24 hours ending 2030 hours July 19	518
20	505
21	384
22	230
23	30
24	80
25	390
Total fired per gun during 7-day period:	2,137
Average fired per gun per day:	305

APPENDIX C

A COMPARISON OF TANKS AND
THEIR PERFORMANCE

Tank	Armour		Armament	Muzzle Velocity	Penetration
	Front	*Side*		*in feet per second*	*at 30 degrees*
Churchill VII	152 mm		6-pounder	2,700	63 mm
Tiger MK I	100 mm	80 mm	88-mm KwK 36 (barrel 16.2 ft)	2,484	102 mm
Tiger MK II	150 mm	100 mm	88-mm KwK 43 (barrel 21.5 ft)	3,186	164 mm
Panther	100 mm	45 mm	75-mm KwK 42 (barrel 17.2 ft)	3,070	110 mm
Firefly	75 mm	51 mm	17-pounder (plain shot) (Sabot shot)	2,900 3,950	113 mm 231 mm
Sherman	75 mm	51 mm	75-mm	1,950	68 mm

Data in the above table for the two 88-mm guns, provided by the Militargeschichtliches Forschungsamt, are recorded in *Taschenbuch der Panzer 1943–1954* by von Senger and Etterlin, Munich, 1954. Slightly lower muzzle-velocities (2,463 and 3,156) are recorded by Fritz Hahn in *Waffen und Geheimwaffen des deutschen Heeres, 1933–45*. Data on 17-pounder provided by the Imperial War Museum.

INDEX

108496

The guns of Normandy

DATE DUE

FEB 28 1996 *4351*	
MAR 07 1996 *5662*	
MAR 29 1996 *4524*	
APR 23 1996 *4796*	
MAY 18 1996 *5753*	
JUN 14 1996 *4624*	
JUL 23 1996 *4537*	
AUG 08 1996 *EMB*	
NOV 29 1996 *6444*	
DEC 31 1997 *5707*	

BRODART, CO.   Cat. No. 23-221-003

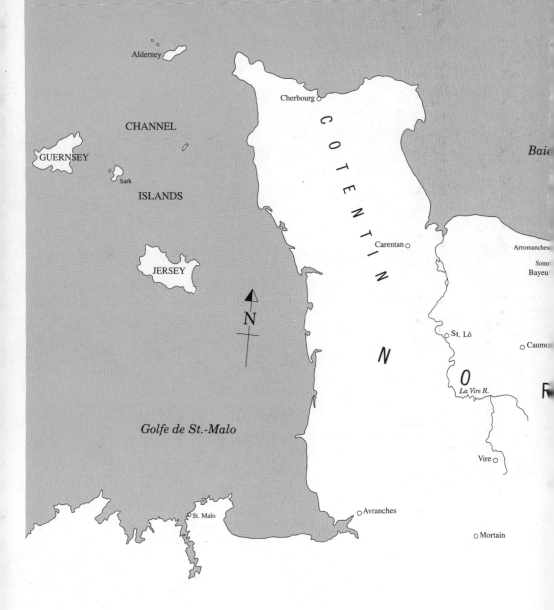

ENGLISH

Alderney

CHANNEL

GUERNSEY

Sark

ISLANDS

JERSEY

Cherbourg

C O T E N T I N

Carentan

Baie

Arromanches

Somr
Bayeu

St. Lô

Caumo

N

O

La Vire R.

R

N

Golfe de St.-Malo

Vire

St. Malo

Avranches

Mortain